THE ARAB CHRISTIAN

Also by Kenneth Cragg

The Christ and the Faiths
Readings in the Qur'an
Muhammad and the Christian
The Call of the Minaret

KENNETH CRAGG

The Arab Christian

A History in the Middle East

Westminster/John Knox Press
Louisville, Kentucky

THE ARAB CHRISTIAN

Book design by The HK Scriptorium, Inc.

First edition

Published by Westminster/John Knox Press
Louisville, Kentucky

PRINTED IN THE UNITED STATES OF AMERICA

9 8 7 6 5 4 3 2

Library of Congress Cataloging-in-Publication Data

Cragg, Kenneth.
The Arab Christian : a history in the Middle East / Kenneth Cragg.
—1st ed.
p. cm.
Includes bibliographical references and index.
ISBN 0-664-21945-4

1. Christians—Arab countries—History. 2. Arabs—Religion.
3. Arab countries—Church history. I. Title.
BR1067.A7C74 1991
275.6′0089′927—dc20 91-15206

"... winnowed with so rough a wind."

To the Memory of
Fā'iz Ṣāyigh (1922–1980),
Philosopher and Diplomat;
Tawfīq Ṣāyigh (1923–1971),
Teacher and Poet.

Sons of Christian Ministry, Brothers in Adversity,
Sufferers with Palestine

Contents

PREFACE ix

CHAPTER

1 Arab and Christian: Strands of Identity 13
2 In Arabia Before Islam 31
3 Arabicization and *Dār al-Islām* 52
4 Christian and Muslim in the Early Centuries 71
5 The European Factor 95
6 The Ottoman Centuries 114
7 Modern Arabs and the Intentions of Arabism 141
8 Perspectives of Egypt 170
9 The Tragedy of Lebanon 204
10 Arab Christianity and Israel 233
11 The Arab Christian Soul in Poetry, Art, and Liturgy 257
12 A Future with Islam? 279

SELECT BIBLIOGRAPHY 305

GENERAL INDEX 317

INDEX OF SCRIPTURE 336

Preface

WHEN NOUNS SERVE as adjectives they may undergo some inconvenience—in the strict sense of that which does not seem "to come well" with them. So it is here with "Arab Christian." One would more readily expect "the Arab Muslim," if looking for what "Arab" is likely to describe.

There lies the whole point. In proposing "the Arab Christian," this book has to do with an identity the elements of which are often thought to be dissociated. Arabism is so deeply involved in being Muslim, for reasons inherent in Islamic history, that it is thought to belong exclusively to that faith and culture. Yet "Christian" was a descriptive of Arabs centuries before Islam, and there has been a Christian Arabism, an Arab Christianity, throughout the Muslim centuries since Muḥammad's day. The Muslim dominance of Arabness, however, from the beginning brought a tension and a tribulation into that Arab Christian existence under which it has labored and survived. The story of that labor and survival is the subject of this book. The adjectives are used in the singular in order to focus squarely on the strains of one identity. The book is not a statistical survey of "Arab Christians," abstracted from the living vicissitudes of coexistence with Islam as if their situation was in any way analogous to that of English Quakers or American Methodists. On the contrary, it has to do with a self-definition and a self-fulfillment in which the religious dimension, from the seventh Christian century, could only be fulfilled out of an ethnic, or "national," dimension that was sharply and subtly aligned with an alternative religion endowing itself with prerogative rights over that ethnicity by virtue of its Arab Prophet and its Arabic Qur'ān. Arab Christianity has lived ever since in the varying incidence of that situation, shaped by the flux of circumstance, in the tribal, political, regional, and economic occasions and mutations of culture and society across the Arab world. The constant theme for the church and the churches has throughout been the stresses of destiny and vocation in coexistence with Islam—stresses in which issues of faith and worship have perpetually tangled with questions of land and people, of place and belonging.

The early chapters explore the definition of "Arab" and the incidence of Christianity within the Arab world prior to the advent of Islam. These chapters assess the meaning of Islamic conquest as interpreted by those who underwent it and study the theory and the pattern of *dhimmī*, or tolerated minority, status given by the Islamic conquest to Jews and Christians. These groups were allowed to covenant for exercise of their ritual acts of faith and their laws of personal status, in exchange for a total political subjection and communal inferiorization under Islamic authority. The exigencies of conquest, however, left room for a significant role for Christian minorities in the century-long arabicization of language and culture throughout the Damascus caliphate of the Umayyads. Christians played a vital part in the growing sophistication of the Muslim mind in philosophy, theology, the arts, and architecture, during which Islam's enlarging cultural diversity itself affected, without undoing, the original Arab character of Islam, complicating in turn its bearing on Christian Arabs.

With its Red Sea/Meccan origins, Islam in expansion showed an instinctive fascination for the Mediterranean, the struggle for which between its southeastern and northwestern shores became a constant feature of its history. The presence in varying forms of "the European factor" in the history of the Near East bore upon Arab Christianity in vexing and sometimes tragic ways. Europe, as a competitively "Christian" continent in trade, crusade, pilgrimage, and diplomacy penetrated, disrupted, and disconcerted the eastern Christian scene through the long middle and modern centuries, engaging for good and ill with the complex local factors—creedal, communal, and regional.

Against a long background of that history, the narrative passes into the issues of Arab nationalism stemming from the steady decline of the Ottoman caliphate and the intensifying pressures of modern change and European politics. By the late nineteenth century, Arab Christianity, playing a significant part in newly minted Arabism, found itself exchanging the *dhimmī* status for the open destiny of participatory nationalism, which offered both risks and occasions absent from the old order. A study of the Arab Christian options of continuing Ottomanism and nation-state Arabism involves deep dilemmas both of faith and psyche. The nationality principle set Christian fortunes more vitally and less predictably on the mercies of a still-dominant Islam than had the contracted subservience of *dhimmī* status. Arab Christianity moved out of regulated inferiority into the unpredictability of the successor states that followed Ottoman demise and the trauma of the First World War.

There are three areas of this history that obviously call for particular study, namely, Egypt, Lebanon, and the entail of Israeli Zionism. Coptic Christianity with its participation in Egyptianism centuries before the coming of Islam to the Nile Valley has lived in perpetual debate about its place in the expression of Egyptianism and in the Islamic shape of the heritage of the pharaohs. The anguish of Lebanon through the seventies and eighties of this century concerns the very definition of the Lebanese identity, torn between pan-Arabism and Maronite determination to interpret "Lebanon" on its own Christian terms drawn from an old Phoenician romanticism and bedeviled by French political intrigue in the enlargement of Grand Liban, at the expense of Syria, in the early twenties. The separatist instinct in some forms of Lebanese consciousness, precariously held in check by calculations of prudence and commerce, degenerated into potential, then actual, anarchy under stress of the Zionist factor in inter-Arab relations.

What Israeli Zionism has meant, and means, for Arab Christianity is rarely understood in its full implications by Western reading of the Middle East, characterized as that reading is by the long ambivalence of Zionist intentions and by religious predilections that either ignore or override the ethics of politics. Arab Christianity and Christian Palestinianism in particular suffer what all other Christianities in the West, in Africa, and in far Asia can escape, namely, the ambiguity between biblical loyalty to Hebrew scriptures as part of Christian heritage and the actualities of contemporary Israel with its enmity to Palestinianism *per se.* How does one relate the "benediction" of "the Lord God of Israel" according to old Zechariah heralding the promise of his son, John Baptist, to the "malediction," as it is to Palestinian land and people, of "the Israel of God" today?

Some reference to Palestinian poetry and to Arab Christian spirituality in liturgy and art may serve to illustrate that paradox between spiritual ancestry and present deprivation ensuing from the Zionist politicization of all things Judaic. A final chapter aims to consider the agenda—and the enigma—of a future with Islam. There is a constant question mark over that study; yet the question mark can be removed in the realization that there is, in fact, no future except with Islam. What is "not yet" must ever turn on the Islamic mood and mode, for Islam is everywhere the senior partner. When the Qur'ān in the final Surah—in a quite unusual turn of phrase—describes *Allāh* as "the God of the people" (or, as some would translate, "of the masses") it is Muslim people who are meant. Yet it is significant that when Arab nationalism affirmed itself decisively early this century it was against a sacred Islamic institution, namely, the Ottoman caliphate, that it did so. In that decision Christian Arabs played a crucial part and, so doing, significantly qualified any concept of an Arabism in which they had no place or of an Islam in which Arabism had no say.

Whatever misgivings that Christian Arab role in nationalism may have registered or the sequel has renewed, decision it was, and it placed Christian Arab fortunes squarely in the will of the dominant Islam. For that long-standing Christian situation in the Middle East there are implications in the new circumstance of minority status of Muslims in Europe. Into these it is not our purpose to enter in these pages, except to note that vulnerability is often a crucial test of religions.

This may explain why the title is "The Arab Christian" rather than "The Christian Arab." It is theologically the more correct. The ethnic is always meant to be adjectival to Christianity, and that order is followed in the first chapter. But the heart of what we are studying lies in the fact that faith cannot here have the advantage of nationality. The Islam of Arabism forbids. We need to stay where the problem lies. Arabness and Christianity, to be sure, have to interrogate each other, but there can be no doubt which calls the questions. "Middle East" in the title is meant to exclude North Africa, Nubia, and the Persian sphere where for the most part Syriac-speaking Christianity had its thrust and fulfillment. Effort is made to conform to standard transliteration, except in names of places and persons where more familiar usage is appropriate. The separate bibliographies with each chapter may help the reader locate further reading in a field that makes such large claims on comprehensiveness—and comprehension.

"Winnowed with so rough a wind," from Shakespeare's *Henry IV*, had first suggested itself as a subtitle. But, if less poetic, "A History" will be more serviceable in ensuring that the title, *The Arab Christian*, will tell of mutuality, thus capturing the entire concern of these pages. The winnowing has become more drastic with the Gulf crisis, the war, and its unresolved aftermath. A variety of factors are leading to the steady attrition of the Arab Christian communities in the region. There is therefore an urgency about perception of them in the West lest the aura of "the Holy Land" should lead us to think of a spiritual museum rather than of living, dying people in the throes of a deep struggle for survival and fulfillment.

Qur'ān citations are from my *Readings in the Qur'ān* (New York: Harper & Row, 1988).

My warm thanks to the editorial staff at Westminster/John Knox for their care and diligence.

CHAPTER

1

Arab and Christian: Strands of Identity

I

"A FIRST DIFFICULTY of the Arab Movement," wrote T. E. Lawrence in *The Seven Pillars of Wisdom,* "was to say who the Arabs were."[1] Observers have occasion to wonder, comparably, who the Christians were, and are, in the bewildering diversity of churches and communities in the Middle East. When the two identities are joined, the tasks of perception are livelier still. There are aspects of being Arab that almost necessitate its equation with Islam. That fact has been the burden of Arab Christianity since the seventh Christian century. Yet Christian faith had a long history within Arabia in the six centuries before Islam emerged to dominate the ethnic and cultural determinants of Arab existence—though not entirely to annex them. The total monopoly of its original territory, which Islam was able to enforce within the peninsula of Arabia proper, has never obtained in the rest of the East.

It was from "the island of the Arabs" (*Jazīrat al-'Arab*), between the Red Sea and the Persian/Arabian Gulf, between the Hadramaut in the south and the northern territories east of the Dead Sea, that many scholars derive the entire population of the Near East. Arab demographers in particular consider Arabia the fount of a "gulf-stream of desert wanderers" who, "on the well-roads of the wilderness," peopled the lands beyond.[2] This spilling out of "the desert into the sown" in periodic eruptions, of which the Islamic expansion after the death of Muḥammad was the most memorable example, is believed to warrant the claim that the denominator "Arab" belongs in some sense to the whole Semitic peoples throughout the area of Near Asia.

Population movements and relationships are rarely as tidy in analysis as theorists suppose, but the pride of Arabness cherishes the associations of the theory in both directions. The Lebanese historian Philip Hitti sees Babylonians, Assyrians, Hittites, Amorites, and the Hebrew tribes as having been, one and "all, nursed within Arabia,"[3] whereas the Palestinian Ismā'il al-Fārūqī considers Arabism to have been "the fount and source of all the cultures in the whole region."[4] Conversely, Muslim tradition finds a direct lineage between the origins of Islam and the patriarchal generations of humanity. It traces some twenty-one or two generations from 'Adnān, the reputed ancestor of the North Arabians, to Muḥammad, 'Adnān being reckoned nine generations from Ishmael and ten from Abraham. The Prophet, by like tradition, was thirty-two generations from Qaḥṭān, (the Joktan of Gen. 10:26), who was five generations from Noah. The figures represent much too short a time even by patriarchal measures. But the traditions enshrine the sense—important to Muslims, as Arabs— of sharing the progeny of the inhabitants whose lands the Islamic conquest overran but did so in the long wake of earlier excursions of tribes whose descendants Islam at length enfolded in its inclusive sponsorship of what was already ethnically its own.

This reading of Arabness must be allowed its romanticism, whatever the actualities at any point in the historic past, for there are truths of conviction as well as truths of fact. The latter suggest many questions and caveats. Speculation needs to reckon with the issue of northern and southern "Arabians," those of the sands and oases of the Najd and the nomads, and those of "Arabia Felix," the Yemen and 'Asīr, blessed with abundant rainfall and fertile hills.

Moreover, there is the possibility that, whatever the size and frequency of Arabia's human excursions into the world outside, there were also movements in the reverse direction, whether from Mesopotamia, Ethiopia, or Egypt. Climatic changes may have played their part here. Was there, for example, as some have argued, a pluvial period in the area of modern Kuwait, when the River Pison, the first of the rivers around Eden in Genesis 2:11 and the only one not readily identifiable, flowed in Wādī al-Rūma?

However we choose to resolve the questions of demography as to ethnic Arabness across the Near East, it is clear that Sumerians, Akkadians, Egyptians, Phoenicians, Hebrews, and others possessed their own languages and cultures. It seems fair to assume that the ethnic factor had become very attenuated through the centuries and that what Islam brought was not, primarily, an accession of Arab blood but rapid arabicization via language. It was Arabness through Arabic that within a century or so became the vital factor in the making of identity. This process is the subject of chapter 3. Be residual ethnic Arabness what it may, the Arabic factor in the thrust of an Islam uniquely in Arab custody in the seventh and eighth centuries was decisive. When the Arab Muslim recited his Qur'ān he believed he encountered his own kin there in the patriarchs and prophets of old time. All were his. The pride of those many generations flowed in his blood whether inside or outside the peninsula, famed as the birthland of them all.

II

But what of the denominator "Christian" in the story of this equation of Arabness with Islam both in the retrospect of a far past and within the near actuality of conquest? Chapter 2 concerns Christianity prior to the advent of Islam, within Arabia proper, but that Arabian Christianity cannot be understood except in relation to the Christianity of western Asia and North Africa. The central christological concerns that characterized that eastern "Christendom"—from which Arab Christianity could be in no way exempt—were to prove a crucial factor in encounter with the new faith. For it was, in part, by reaction against those concerns, read as misguided or perverse, that Islam had been conceived and launched. It is tempting to wonder how Arab Christianity might have fared in the evolving situation of the seventh and following centuries if it had been less tied by what we may call "the Greek connection" in its faith and forms.

The great citadels of that connection, the patriarchates of Constantinople, Alexandria, Antioch, Jerusalem, and Edessa, were one in the orthodoxy of the creed known to history as Nicene. They were unanimous in their faith about the unity of God, the saviorhood of Jesus, the one sacrament of baptism, the one Eucharist. They cherished the prophets, apostles, and martyrs of the common centuries and still met in ecumenical councils. Indeed, it was precisely the strength of their unity that explained the stress of their divisions. For these, implicit before, emerged beyond Nicea in the fourth century to sunder Greeks from Copts, Diophysites from Monophysites, to all of whom—on their own showing—we must accord the title "Orthodox." This happened when minds and passions, divided over the right formulation of the natures—divine and human—in the one Christ, both God and man.

The clause, from Nicea, "of one substance with the Father" was not in question. But how was the person of Christ to be understood in the categories of divine and human nature? Did the divine nature wholly supersede the human? Or could they be held to coexist without the diminution or compromise of either? The decision of the Council of Chalcedon in 451 sought, in subtle phrasing, to say the latter, but its terms became the theme of further contention and estrangement the tedious course of which had been running intermittently for two centuries when Islam arrived to scorn away the subtleties in its own insistent, nonchristological theism.

Some measure of what was at stake belongs to chapter 4. Might Arab Christianity, both in the pre- and post-Islamic centuries, have fared more hopefully had the Greek factor in its story been less intellectually fastidious about formulas, more tuned to Arab sympathies and cast of mind? As it was, the complexities prevailed. The principal sides in the Christ issue were the Chalcedonians; otherwise Melchites (or "emperor's men") and the Monophysites, insisting on the one divine nature against the two natures of Chalcedon. The Nestorians, with their further refinement of the formulas, gravitated eastward from their center in Edessa and belong only peripherally to our area of concern.

The doctrinal issues were compounded, if not directly championed, by local political and ethnic factors. Regional loyalties and passions, as well as historical resentments, embittered, if they did not occasion, christological strife. Arab Christianity through all the centuries can be understood only in its stressful human context.

The Muslims' Qur'ān had sharply identified a divided mind as the habit of Christianity. The minority status that Islam imposed on Christianity after the conquest confirmed it further. Christians–and Jews–became *dhimmīs* (*Ahl al-Dhimmah*) with rights of ritual religion and personal legal status under a covenant of complete political submission. This pattern, sometimes known later as "the *millet* system," falls for study in chapter 3, in the context of the aftermath of conquest. Two broad interrelated features at once emerged. They are central to the whole subsequent story of Arab Christianity. The one is the travail for Christianity inherent in the very nature of Islam; the other is what, thanks to the mediating Mediterranean, we had better call the European equation. The inland sea inexorably bound the Christianity of the East with that of the West. Constantinople as the seat of eastern empire was known to Islam as Al-Rūm, Rome, city alike of the Bosphorus and the Tiber. The European connection has throughout history been the abettor of the problems of Arab Christianity vis-à-vis Islam and of the prejudices or estimates of those Christians by Muslims. Some review of these two determinants of history will be the best introduction not only to the early centuries after 632, when Muḥammad died, but also to the Ottoman era and the complexities of the modern day. For they are elements in the drama of a continuous history.

Their significance derives from the fact that Islam, emerging from and belonging with Arabia despite the land nexus with West Asia, had not shared the Greco-Roman heritage by which historic Christianity had interpreted the Semitic tradition of its Hebraic origin. Muslims represented a Semitic ethos sharply antithetical to dimensions of interpretation grounded in the faith of the Incarnation. Muslim conquest as far as Anatolia and Morocco took Islam into a culture and faith of which its definitive origins were quite intolerant. The Christology of Christians stood in sharp contrast to the ardent positivism of Islamic credenda. "There is no god but God: Muḥammad is the apostle of God"—no truck here with the Chalcedonian formulation of doctrine about the God-Man, no mind for the mystery implicit in the engagement—whether via Jesus or via the Qur'ān—of eternity with time.

It is true that through arabicization of its empire Islam underwent a counterprocess of hellenization. Muslim philosophers came to participate in western preoccupations of thought adjusted to Islamic issues. But the founding quality of Islam remained inviolate. The dynamism of the original faith did not readily allow the niceties of thought or the habits of debate familiar to others. It was ill at ease with the subtlety of any theistic belief. "They knew only truth and untruth, belief and unbelief, without our hesitating retinue of finer shades . . . a dogmatic people despising doubt, our modern crown of thorns," wrote T. E. Lawrence.[5] And "the crown of thorns" itself, so central to Christian imagery through the doctrine of Christ and the sacrament of the Eucharist, was altogether to be abjured as conceivably a truth for theology.

The high disdain Muslims had for the faith they invaded has been a permanent circumstance attending Arab Christianity. It derived not only from the sanction of conquest and the contrast between victors and victims. It stemmed also from the assurance of a superior theism, superior and final because rooted—as Muslims saw it—in an invincible simplicity, a faith that could be told in fifteen syllables.[6] It was a "rough wind" that blew out of Arabia, a triumphalism to inferiorize and ghettoize the surviving heirs of Chalcedon and their Monophysite cousins. Despite whatever racial bonds of Arabness remained and despite the common Semitic heritage in Abraham, the two faiths were ill-suited for mutuality.

To be sure, Muslims came to realize the paradoxes present in their own Qur'ān as an eternal revelation housed in the vicissitudes of earthly biography. Unfamiliar as they were with Augustine's *Confessions* and sure that *The City of God* need in no case be two realms since Islamic polity could embrace one sovereignty, they nevertheless came to appreciate the dilemma of divine providence and human responsibility. They had to register the same issue in the prophetic vocation of Muḥammad himself, but these mental obligations of intelligent faith remained for the most part external to the practice of fidelity. Thus they did not help a sensitivity to what Arab Christianity—albeit gropingly—had in trust in its apparently tedious

Christology. The concerns dividing Christians in their possession of Christ found short shrift from Muslim attitudes. That fact in turn served to deepen the introversion of Christian communities under *dhimmī* status and occupation. The partisanship into which Christian controversies about Jesus and the unity of God had fallen, their political overtones and the complexities involved, precluded their effective translation into Islamic comprehension. Relations between the faiths were, therefore, liable to sterility or impasse. Sectarian temper engendered a doggedness engrossed in mere survival.

Chapter 4 studies the encounter of Christian with Muslim in the early centuries. What of the European connection, which, thanks to the Mediterranean, was woven into the Christian situation, for good and ill? Whether via Constantinople or the western Rome, the European factor conditioned Arab Christian communities of every generation. The Muslim conquerors rapidly responded to the fascination of the Mediterranean. Within eight decades of Muḥammad's death they became masters of the whole eastern and southern shores and of the Iberian peninsula. Naval confrontation, islands Cyprus and Sicily, the rivalries of Ottomans and Venetians, corsairs in the Aegean, the Adriatic, and the Tyrrhenian, armadas battling at Lepanto—all these were the themes and scenes of the maritime meeting of Islam and Europe. The missionary voyages of Paul and the posthumous seafaring of Muḥammad might be seen to symbolize the encounter joined between the New Testament and the Qur'ān and, therein, between the faith that linked the Middle East with Europe and the faith binding the Middle East with Mecca. Arab Christianity lay athwart the two.

III

At stake was the very nature of Christianity as Hebraic in its messianic quality and Greco-Roman in its christological expression. Islam brought an imperious theism, reasserting a Semitic faith that had been not only subtilized but betrayed—as Islam saw it—by Christian theology. That theology Islam assessed as blighted by the malign influence of Greek culture over the status of the prophet Jesus. Not that Arab Christianity saw it that way. The communities that differed so forcefully about Chalcedon, in the very context of doing so, were one about "God in Christ." Islam, however, believed that Christians had "de-Semiticized" Jesus, distorting him into the Incarnate Word who had to be restored to the authentic tradition of prophethood alone. Contrarywise, Christians held that the doctrine of God in Christ, despite subtle refinements in its definition on which they differed, had properly and truly developed in the creedal form they gave it. Indeed this, for them, had crucially verified Semitic theism.

The imponderables of history are many, and conjecture around them for the most part futile. But it is intriguing to wonder about a west Asia cradling Christianity without the long legacy of Alexander of Macedon. The Qur'ān itself is only obliquely concerned with that strange figure *Dhū al-Qarnain* (Surah 18.83f.), supposedly the great Macedonian from whom stems the Greek ethos in the eastern world. That conquest ultimately ensured the hellenization of the Christian faith in its historic expression in the Near East. Original and definitive Islam escaped that Greekness. The Aramaic and Aramean sources of Christianity in the immediate world of the apostles of Jesus came to be clothed and propagated in an idiom and vocabulary owed to Greek thought both in the questions aroused and in the answers those questions received. The New Testament clearly evidences both the Hebraic, Semitic nature of the faith and the Greek shape of its self-definition. The latter was taken further in deepening Greek categories of thought and word in the period of the church fathers beyond the New Testament.

Anticipating the review of Muslim–Christian encounter during the early centuries, it is well here to raise the query latent in the story, namely, whether Arab Christianity would have been less alien and more articulate under Muslim conditions if it had been less dominated by Greek idiom and Greek associations. There was a preponderance of Greek ethos even within the Monophysite Christian communities, among Copts and others, who differed in controversy with the Greek Orthodox or Melchites. Speculation and polemic were as familiar to them as to the emperor's men. To that extent even their different racial quality had been grecized. They shared in the Greek will for debate, its instinct for the role of the intelligible which originated in the long influence of Plato, Plotinus, and Parmenides. The Christian mind-set followed Greece in giving reason free rein in the perception of mystery.

Hence the intricacies of Christology as *all* parties pursued them. The pursuit became a besetting preoccupation with minutiae. With these came the danger of turning faith into enigma via the impasse and mutual alienation that characterized the inter-Christian situation in the centuries after Chalcedon. Thus Arab Christianity was at a great disadvantage in its faith relations with Islam by this factor in its history. The terms of its Christology ill served it. The fact of "God in Christ" would always be anathema to the people of the Qur'ān. But how it might be commended to Muslims nevertheless was under the heavy disability of the Greek assumptions in its formulation.

The point at issue was that in the commendation of the faith about Christ, the "Word made flesh," both the Chalcedonian and the Monophysite language was dominated by concepts of "being," "substance," and "nature." Aside from how readily these could be translated into Arabic, their focus was abstract and conceptual. The Monophysites, laudably wanting to preserve the divine from compromise—a very Islamic desire—incurred an unhappy unreality about the Jesus they confessed as God and man. His human reality was made suspect. The Chalcedonian formulation could be held in part responsible for this because of its own intricate complexity, straining the possibilities of language and making loyalty hinge on near enigma. Yet neither party had the mind to enquire what the impasse between them indicated about the propriety—not to say the abandonment—of the terms that led to it.

They lacked that capacity because of their Greek captivity. The lack was crucial for their relation with the Arabness of Islam. Had there been, either at Chalcedon or in rejection of it, a Christology of action rather than of "substance" and "nature," Christians in either allegiance would have been better able to converse with Muslims about faith in the incarnate Lord. Insofar as there was significant, rather than merely terminological, distinction between Greek "Orthodox" and Copts over the two natures of Christ, it was the issue of the real humanity of Jesus. The Monophysites put it at risk more than the Chalcedonians, though the latter only retained it by careful reservations. How a Christology of action would have better served the issues present in meeting with Islam will become clear in chapter 4. In the strongly Semitic cast of Islam, both as to divine sovereignty and the belief that "prophethood is all," the humanity of Jesus was all there was. On any Islamic score the Greek shape of the confession of a divinely human and a humanly divine Christ was least qualified to mediate its meaning into Muslim prepossessions. Islam, in any event, was minded to dismiss and deny the Incarnation as a travesty of the divine. Perhaps on Islamic grounds that verdict is irreversible. Yet how, on Christian ground, there is no travesty of the divine but a veritable divine self-expression was not cogently evident in the pattern either of Chalcedonian or Monophysite theology. Arab Christianity in both camps suffered acute difficulty in its ethnic participation with Arabia, and so with Islam, thanks to this mental participation with Greece and the Latin fathers. By the time of the rise of Islam, the christological controversies were three centuries or more old and, though at times quiescent, were deeply ingrained. To Muslims, taught by observations on them in the Qur'ān, those controversies were all so much futility and confusion, a confusion that served only to attest the folly of those who indulged them and the final authority of the Islam that silenced them.

Another disability of the European connection, explored in chapter 5, was the dominance of Greek personnel, hierarchy, and influence throughout the Arab areas of Melchite Christianity. Only in the late twentieth century is authority in the Greek Orthodox Church in the ancient patriarchates on "Arab" soil beginning to give way to local leadership. The patterns and the problems of Greek–Arab relationships within eastern Christianity will concern us later.

In sum, if we bring together the two determinants of Arab Christianity thus reviewed–namely, the Islam that conditioned it from the seventh century and the form that it had received and interiorized from the Greek mind–we discern a harsh, exacting destiny. We realize how antithetical its traditions were to the genius of Islam and that genius to them. The sustained loyalty of both major wings of Arab Christendom to its doctrinal inheritance from the Fathers had Muslims asking, with no less sustained insistence, how "Arab" they had ever really been. So far, in the Muslim view, does Islam dominate and determine the criteria of what is Arab. One revealing way to take this point, as chapters 7, 8, and 9 will indicate, is to study the separate significance of Egypt and of Lebanon because of their distinctive Christian elements and observe the tensions there within Arab nationalism in modern times. But the roots everywhere go far back into the very shaping of Christianity, a shaping that Islam repudiated not only as demeaning God and distorting Jesus but also–so Islamic assurance implied–betraying Arabness, an Arabness only authentic in the confession of Islam. To be Arab *and* Christian has been to live with that situation. It was easier to meet it where, for example, the River Nile or the mountainous terrain of Lebanon made strands of identity capable of tempering either the equation of Arabness or the fact of Islam, by dint of the particularities of place, memory, and inheritance.

The point is often made that the Arabness of Islam is offset by the fact of Islamic universal dispersion enclosing a great variety of languages and cultures. The populational center of gravity of Islam is well south and east of Karachi. Arab Muslims, in number, architectural achievement, and cultural diversity, are far outmatched by non-Arab Muslims from the Caspian to the China seas. This, however, does not diminish the Arab factor among Arab-born Muslims. These participate emotionally and politically in the awareness of a pan-Islam, but, in doing so, still retain that sense of their Islamic "primacy" stemming from the Arabness of Muḥammad and the Arabic of the Qur'ān. Those twin elements in the heritage of Islam will always be uniquely theirs, with a corresponding otherness for Arab Christians in default of such possession.

There is an illuminating comparison for historians in the differing sequel to Arab conquest in Persia from that among Greek-, Syriac-, and Coptic-speaking Christians in the first two centuries of Islam. While Zoroastrianism succumbed almost completely, perhaps for economic reasons, Arab Christianity in part survived. But it is noteworthy that the Persian language effectively resisted arabicization. Persia was more able to sustain its cultural heritage, territorially housed, than were Egypt and the Greek- or Syriac-speaking lands under Islam. But Persia contrived this by adopting, in Shi'ism, a persianized form of Islam. Although Persia's physical subjugation to Arab arms was even more total than that of west Asia, its identity was strenuously secured. Shī'ah Islam may be read as a Persian response to Islamic conquest in the form of an adaptation involving features congenial to the Persian soul and attained in the Shī'ah doctrine of the Imām. The process, to be sure, was gradual, and Sunnī Islam initially proved strong in Persia. But by the time of the Safavids in the sixteenth century, Shi'ism had become supreme. Arab Christianity, unlike Zoroastrianism, persisted. Its greater resilience, however buffeted, contrived no amalgam with Islam. Its identity, greatly attenuated in numbers and confidence, remained intact. But, by the same token, its languages retreated into purely liturgical survival before the tide of Arabic and, in the case of Syriac, became almost extinct. Yet, ironically, it was these retreating languages of Greek and Syriac which, in the great centuries of translation, became the instruments of the new sophistication of Islam.

There was, in the Persian case, no counterpart to the role a continuing Byzantium played in the life of the Melchite church, loyal to Constantinople and Chalcedon in the conquered Christian lands and, indirectly, in the life of the Monophysites. The Nestorian churches in their centers in eastern Syria and Iraq looked more and more to the further east. Much Arab Christianity, tributary to an Islamic power still vigorously at war with Byzantium, was cut off from participation in councils and debates, but its emotional bearings were still with the fluctuating fortunes of emperor and patriarch in Constantinople and with the varying, troubled relations of these with Rome in the West before and after the rise of Charlemagne and the Great Schism in the ninth and eleventh centuries. While the Monophysite churches conceded more readily the finality of Islam, thanks to their earlier tensions with Byzantium, there was even in their case a residual bond with the wider Christendom simply by the common factor of an Islam antithetical to each and all in their Christianity. The Coptic and Syriac Monophysites had long memories, symbolized in Alexandria and Antioch, as great early patriarchates not entirely forfeited by their submission to Islam and their distance of soul as well as circumstance from Byzantium and the West.

IV

Whatever the problematics for the Arab Christian East of the Greek association, those of the Latin West were, for the most part, blatant and malign. They had to do not with the subtleties and strife of theology but with arrogance and intrusion. The western, Latin Rome saw the Christian East in terms of juridical dominance and ecclesiastical power. Outremer (the current name for the Crusading Kingdom, or "Beyond-the-Sea"), once the crusaders established it, defined their point of view. The Crusades became an enduring symbol of malignity as well as heroism, of open imperialism and private piety. Fired by an ardor for Palestine as "the holy land," the Crusades ended centuries later in a forlorn defense of eastern Europe against the inroads of a Turkish power their story had done much to engender. They wrought much havoc along their path, culminating in the sack of Constantinople in the iniquity of the Fourth Crusade. They left noble piles of architecture on the eastern landscape but seared the eastern soul. They gave Arab Muslims through every succeeding century a warrant of memory to hold against Christian Arabs as, by association, liable to pseudo-Arabness or worse.

What the crusaders did to the eastern psyche, Muslim and Christian, long outlived their tenure of the Latin kingdom of Jerusalem and the Latin patriarchate in Constantinople. The image of them is one that no century since has been able to exorcise. When the Crusades finally exhausted themselves against the dominant Turks and Constantinople fell in 1453, Christians in the arc from the Bosphorus to Egypt came slowly into the orbit of western commercial and economic penetration. Local Christians in major centers such as Izmir, Alexandria, and Aleppo, taking advantage of *dhimmī* status and/or protected rights of trading functions, forged associations with European merchants, developing lucrative commerce across the Mediterranean. By dint of the "capitulations," or chartered rights, that the Ottoman state allowed, Christians, thanks to faith, language, or initiative, were preferred as local agents, dragomans, or interpreters under these prescripts. It falls to chapter 6 to study this aspect of the Christian story from the late sixteenth century on. It prefaced many of the tensions implicit in the definition of Arabness—and its proper associations—when the nineteenth century brought the yet more insistent political penetration of Europe into the life of the eastern churches.

Both commercial and political aspects of "Europe-in-the-Orient" provoked the emergence of so-called Uniate churches from within all the major forms of eastern Christianity. Eastern Christians, or rather their ecclesiastics, were subtly recruited into latinized allegiance by the benefits, or the blandishments, of the Roman church, the agents of the papacy, and

Jesuit or other missionaries. The Maronite church in Lebanon is the salient example, and its story will concern us in some detail in chapter 9. Originally Monophysite and sharply local, it passed into obedience to Rome by stages and owed much of its resilience and its partial autonomy to the Maronite College established in Rome in 1584. Nowhere has the tension of separatism within Arabism been more intense and tragic than in Lebanon, with its distinctive geographical and historical identity. It is a separatism sharply, though not exclusively, drawn by the Maronite association with Europe.

Elsewhere also the attractions of Latin church power and the ecclesiastical finesse of the papacy induced secessions from Orthodox, Monophysite, and Chaldean Christianity to form Greek Catholic, Coptic Catholic, Chaldean Catholic, and Armenian Catholic churches in communion with the Pope. The story of the gradual surrender of patriarchs and clergy to the persuasions and advantages of western Rome makes a fascinating study. Despite the length of old loyalties, there was economic advantage as well as intellectual prestige in the new allegiance. And there was always the factor of Islam, suggesting, if not always justifying, the urge to security which participation with European nations in their rising reputation could be assumed to undergird. Ironically, that very implication, insofar as it delivered Christian sentiment over to alien sponsors, served to sharpen the suspicions that fed the insecurity. Psychic fears all too often deepen through their own remedies. Muslims were not reassured to find *dhimmīs* seeking religious shelter under foreign wing, when all the religious shelter they properly required was juridically provided by the Islamic statehood to which they were contractually bound. The secessions also weakened and embittered the old allegiance. The churches, by and large, despite obvious enrichments in some areas, were not advantaged by still further pluralizing their identity.

By the mid-nineteenth century non-Roman western churches, in their turn, brought separate churches into being from within eastern Christendom. They did not do so, in the main, by deliberate intent but as the consequence of an evangelism that alarmed old traditions and, when it was heeded, created pastoral needs which, it was held, could only be met in separate *ecclesiae*.

This ecclesial fragmentation coincided with increasing inroads from western Europe into the politics, economy, and culture of the Ottoman caliphate and of those parts of it which enjoyed varying degrees of provincial independence. After the arousal that accompanied Napoleon's invasion of Egypt (in the interests of his Anglo-French quarrel as well as of his eastward romanticism), the western scramble for influence, and competition to wield it, quickened in the apparent, or actual, deterioration of Ottoman imperial competence in the nineteenth century.

The complexities, for Arab Christianity, of nineteenth century experience concerns chapter 7 as a prelude to the more local study of their incidence in Egypt and Lebanon. Central to that story was the issue between Ottomanism as the right and genuine form of Arab loyalty and Arab independence as the authentic Arab destiny. Christians were caught acutely within this dilemma and its painful resolution in the first decades of the twentieth century. They were, in a sense, passengers within it, despite their lively participation, because it hinged on an interpretation of Islam. Yet there was no way in which they could be exempted from its resolution.

V

The Ottoman Empire, for all its unwieldy structure and, during the nineteenth century, the provincial separatisms to which it was prone, was nevertheless a thoroughly Islamic entity, juridically heir to the Prophet himself via the caliphate and maintaining in its own form the *dhimmī* status of its Christian minorities. However far its oppressive moods and patterns might provoke Arabism to independence from it, such Arabness was duly bound by Islam to firm allegiance. The caliphal obedience apart, there were times when the Ottoman power appealed to Islamic universalism, notably during the Tanzīmāt reforms of the 1860s and under the Young Turks, at the outset, in the first decade of the twentieth century. Down to 1918, there was a strong Arab sentiment for Ottoman "federalism" and a readiness to contain and fulfill Arabism within the Ottoman structure.

The counter policy aroused by seasons of Ottoman tyranny and by mutual distrust cherished the Arab *waṭan,* or *patria,* against the imperial *Ummah,* the "fatherland" against the one Islamic "community." Arab nationalism necessarily implied an end to *dhimmī* status inasmuch as *all* Arabs within independent statehood(s) would share identity and citizenship. Contrariwise, continuing in the Turkish-led *Ummah* meant perpetuation of the inferior status in the *dhimmī* tradition. It is not, therefore, surprising to find Christians–Syrians in particular–taking up nationalist aspirations, despite the fact that nationhood(s) dominated by Arab Muslims must constitute an unknown risk.

The stirrings of Arab nationalism *and* the persistence of a will for Ottomanism belong to the two decades before and the two after the turn of the century. Arab Ottomanism resisted nascent nationalism during those forty or so years, partly in search of an Islamic universality that might discipline particularism and partly thanks to a loose provincialism that the Ottoman system afforded, when it was not minded to deny it. We have to study Christian Arabs in ambivalence about their Arabism in the diversity of their Christianity as this situation shaped it.

The issue was finally resolved in the closing stages of the First World War. Ottomanism as an Arab option died with the demise of the caliphate at the hands of the Turks themselves—a demise that the Arab Revolt had helped to engineer. National Arabism came to full tide in the aftermath of the 1914–18 war, only to be sharply abridged by continuing European interests and designs. Christian Arabs played a significant part in the renaissance of Arabic, in the enterprise of ideas, and in the cost of martyrdom, during the last excesses of Ottoman tyranny during the war years.

There was uneasy ambiguity in the national citizenship the new states held in prospect. How would it compare in practice with the old subservient "security" of *dhimmī* status, given the unpredictability of Muslim majorities? For majorities, except in Lebanon, they would continue to be. In numbers the old inferiorization would persist and—predictably—in mood as well. It would do so in new and untried form, however ardent the Christian participation. The choice in the process itself had been a vexatious one: its outworking would be no less so. Christian elements would still be under the suspicion of being the pawns or dupes of western powers set to pursue their own ends in the new map of the Arab East. Christian insistence to the contrary, even when sincere, could be read by Muslims as only concealing their unreliability. How, conversely, would the stresses of emerging statehoods affect Muslim Arab pledges of common interests and mutual loyalty? The occasions for nervous friction and reciprocal distrust lay both in the inheritance of the old order and the experience of the new.

In Lebanon after a quarter century of uneasy promise, the issues plunged all parties into desperate crisis around the very survival of nationhood itself. Where prospects—perhaps deceptively—had been the brightest, the reality turned into the direst tragedy. Of Egypt and the Muslim–Copt relation perhaps brevity may say that the constituents of Egyptianism have been in negotiation with Islamic destiny around the theme of Arabism ever since the seventh century.

These tangled concerns of chapters 8 and 9 tangle further, and painfully, with the saga of Zionism and the State of Israel. In vision and resolve the achievement of Zionism may be said to be a resounding fact of the twentieth century, a drama of splendid tenacity and verve. But it is, by the same token, a fact of unrelieved anxiety and distress to the Arab mind at large and Arab Palestinianism in particular. Because of it, the Arab psyche has undergone a prolonged and bitter experience of being vulnerable—a condition of things with which the Islamic mind finds itself instinctively at odds. It may be said that history holds many examples in which Islam has related to adversity, but the trauma in which Israel has involved it is different. Israel's presence, as Arabs know it, is not simply another colonialism. For Zionism understands itself as reclaiming its "mother country." It is not therefore a colonialism ever minded to retreat.

Moreover, the Arab tragedy is compounded by their own political miscalculation and military defeat. Within their Arabism, Palestinians have learned the pitfalls and betrayals of brotherhood and the costly embarrassment of friends. Arabism as a whole has contrived its own frustrations and, so doing, found itself worsted not only in the outward scene but in the inward sense. Extenuations can be sought and found in the external world, but there is no satisfying exoneration. Yet the lack of one in no way relieves the retrospect of a century since the Arab world, under Ottoman, British, or "independent" auspices, first confronted the intentions of Zionism. It only sharpens the sense of having been brought into suffering and tragedy alike by injustice and by failure.

This experience, for Palestinians most of all, has entailed a slow and stressful cycle of tribulation—the state of refugee dispersion, twice suffered and still continuing; the effort to persuade the international community that nationhood, not charity, was their quest and claim; the ultimate realization that these would demand more than inflexible doggedness; the late acceptance of nonviolence as the price and condition of political hope; and the knowledge that such acceptance must constitute a slow and testing risk with no assurance of success. All this—and more—is in the experience of being vulnerable, which the Palestinian has to suffer, interpret, and resolve.

It falls to chapter 10 to study the role of Arab Christianity in general, and of Palestinian Christianity in particular, in this situation. We must beware of presuming that Arab Christianity can be isolated from the response of Muslim Arabs if we look for factors distinctive to the Christian mind. For, minority status apart, the entire destiny is and can only be common to them all. Yet biblical loyalties in the Christian field and many other factors that must be explored place a peculiar burden on the Christian conscience in regard to Zionism and Israel.

The whole enterprise of these turns on concepts of covenant and chosenness, of prophecy and return, which concern Christian theology and the interpretation of its scriptures. Though the Qur'ān records the mandating of "the holy land" to the Jews (Surah 5.21), Islam can readily deal with the mystique of Zion by dint of the sharply anti-Jewish passages in its scripture and by simple confrontation. The Christian posture has to be much more anxiety of spirit and travail of mind. It has to beware of responding to invocation of divine warrant on the part of Jewry by the stridency of *Allāhu akbar* ("Greater is God") as a countering search for celestial support. The feasible interpretations of biblical meanings have to be reached in loyalty both to the ethics of justice and equality before God and to the reverent concern of the New Testament for these and for a due indebtedness to the Judaic within a universal Christ.

But the sense of such vocation and the will to it are hard to sustain in the immediate context of desolation, anxiety, and enmity. Israel only heightens the burden for Arab Christians by its avid, sometimes cynical, welcome to an American "Christian Zionism" approving every policy and by its solicitude for Christian minority affairs only so long as they remain innocuous and docile. Local Christians are caught in a degree of museumization. They suffer attrition by exile and emigration. They are aware of tourists who come in great volume from the West to savor holy places but who are, for the most part, blithely disinterested in the people who indwell them. The pain of that indifference is not eased insofar as the same tourism is subtly manipulated to make the case for the entire legitimacy of the statehood that regulates it.

There is one central and inescapable theme in that legitimacy, namely, how the reality of Israel is denominated—and dominated—by the Holocaust. Its bitter helplessness and utter desolation can never be undone: they can only be taken up into the total will to hold them ever in the memory and steel that memory in the full assertion of the will to be and to defy all that would impede or question it. Palestinians, Christian and Muslim alike, are caught in that questioning by a legitimacy of their own—of land tenancy, of justice, and of human will to be where they belong. So they come to be—through no direct association of their own story—the implicit gainsayers of the Holocaust. They become guilty, by implication, of resisting the irresistible logic of the Holocaust, a logic that must implacably demand capitulation to its case. The Holocaust thus becomes, in Israeli thinking, a warrant of innocence—or, if not innocence, exoneration—for all that action in its sequel must pursue both to respond to the past and to ensure the future.

That ineluctable situation entails on the Palestinian people a strange vicarious destiny impossible either to escape or to sustain. Life and history, to be sure, contain many such occasions in which wrongs in one quarter fall as sufferings in another, but few so grievous or so harsh. The Holocaust, which so tragically underlies and undergirds Israel's rightfulness in its own eyes, was a German, not a Palestinian, enormity. The Nazi myth of Aryan chosenness and destiny could not tolerate the divine status of the Jews. The assertion of pure Germanness, in Hitler's terms, demanded the elimination of what patently and insistently denied those terms as a reading either of the German or the human. What denied them was alike Jewish, Christian, and "liberal." But the encounter was essentially Germanic and did not involve the Arab world, until some elements there–following the example of some Zionists during the First World War–saw political mileage for their cause in the anti-allied quarter.[7] But it is the Arab world that is uniquely the sphere of the cost of Israel and, therefore, where the burden of Israel, as that by which Jewishness outlives the Holocaust, exacts its price in the homes and persons and fate of others. By what lights, then, when survivors create victims, when the former retrieve by statehood and the latter seek reprieve from what that statehood does to them, may the vicarious suffering be resolved? How do the new victims in their tragedy relate to the old victims in their recovered power? Where are the springs of reconciliation? How do they and the parties emerge from the welter of accusation and vindication, of charge and countercharge, of the will to innocence and the fact of guilt?

These tangled questions, beyond the exploration of the history in chapter 10, take us, through the spiritual dimensions in chapter 11, into the conditioning theme of Arab Christian engagement with Muslim Arabs. There is a distinctive Christian theology of things vicarious in life and history which Islam, broadly, does not share. But there can be no unilateral Christian response, present or future, that does not seek and find a measure of mind and spirit concurrent with Islam. The task of chapter 12, finally, must therefore be a testing climax of the whole study.

In the bitterness of confrontation Zionism has entered into the strands of identity by which Arabs in general and Palestinians in particular experience themselves in this century. For it identifies Gazans and Nablusis, Haifans and Jerusalemites, the folk of Bethlehem, Ramallah, and Tulkarim, with Poles, Armenians, Kurds, and Amerindians as people whose pride in themselves rides painfully with adversity and whose self-definition turns harshly on the deeds of others.

Notes

1. T. E. Lawrence, *The Seven Pillars of Wisdom* (Garden City, N.Y.: Doubleday, Doran & Co., 1935), p. 31.

2. Ibid., pp. 34–35.

3. Philip K. Hitti, *A History of the Arabs,* 10th ed. (New York: St. Martin's Press, 1970), p. 3. "As the probable cradle of the Semitic family the Arabian peninsula nursed those people who later emigrated into the Fertile Crescent and subsequently became the Babylonians, Assyrians, Phoenicians, and the Hebrews of history."

4. Ismā'il al-Fārūqī, *On Arabism: 'Urūbah and Religion* (Amsterdam, 1962), pp. 1–9; see also his *The Cultural Atlas of Islam,* jointly with Lois L. al-Fārūqī (New York, 1986), pp. 7–18.

5. Lawrence, *Seven Pillars,* p. 36.

6. Namely, those of the Shahadah or confession of faith: *lā ilāha illa-Allāh: Muhammadūn rasūl-Allāh.*

7. It was Chaim Weizmann who steered Zionist policy into "the British option" before and during the First World War and received his recompense in the Balfour Declaration of 1917–the cornerstone of Jewish success in the postwar period. But in his words there were Zionists, like Menachem Ussishkin, who "believed . . . in the inevitability of a German victory" and looked upon Weizmann as "a crank and an Anglo-maniac." See Chaim Weizmann, *Trial and Error* (New York: Harper & Bros., 1949), pp. 210–211.

CHAPTER

2

In Arabia Before Islam

I

THE CRUX OF Arab Christianity might be linguistically expressed; it is bound over to a language that is bound over to Islam. By contrast, New Testament faith is committed to the feasibility of its scriptures in any and every language of humanity. It has no necessarily sacred speech. Christian origins had their strong Hebraic and Aramaic quality. Greek and Latin became the major vehicles of their development and creedal definition. In the centuries before Islam, when the faith was mediated into Arabic by these or other inheriting languages, Arabic, in its several modes and dialects, had no more than a receptor status in the expression and the possession of Christianity. It could claim no more than to participate in the incidental manner of more influential languages within the equal availability of languages which Pentecost had symbolized.

But Arabic's destiny was to become the uniquely sacred language of a new faith disallowing universal viability of its scripture in whatever tongues men used. The new faith sacralized the Arabic language as the unique and indispensable medium of its sense of revelation. When Islam expanded in conquest over the whole territory in which the Hebrew, Aramaic, Greek, Latin, and other tongues had enshrined a multitongued Christianity, and when arabicization ensued throughout the area, Arabic-speaking Christians were caught in a strange paradox, which has attended them ever since. The paradox passes from language to identity, from the medium of faith and culture to the psyche and the soul. The language that gives them identity has its supreme identity elsewhere. By virtue of the Qur'ān and its role in Islam, they are ambiguously Arab in not being religiously possessed of that in which, via the sanctity of language as Islam holds it, Arabness is consummated. The fact that they are not possessed of it by their own will for another faith only compounds their situation.

Islam, to be sure, has currency far beyond the Arab milieu. Muḥammad's first people are far outnumbered by other Muslims across the world. Nevertheless, the Arabic nature of the Islamic scripture and its being exclusively Arabic in the divine economy make that language a religious preserve which no other faith can comparably own—and certainly not a faith committed to the equal feasibility of any language to the housing of its meaning and its worship. Yet Arabic *does* own and speak that other (Christian) faith. It does so, disconcertingly for Muslims, as one among others—and not one that was a major factor at the outset. Arabic in Arabic-speaking Christianity thus carries, in Muslim eyes, the reproach of being in the strict sense vernacular, that is, a slave (*verna*) speech, recruited for what it did not initially possess and, unlike the Arabic of Islam, never divinely consecrated.

This unilateral relation of Arabic and the Qur'ān is peculiarly the burden of Arab Christianity. It is further compounded by the fact that, unlike the New Testament, the Qur'ān stands independently of the Hebrew Bible. It did not associate its own prophethood with the great prophets of the Jewish tradition. Though it incorporated the patriarchs, it did so on its own terms. Its finality made it the repository of all else without necessary reference to them, since it crowned them all. This self-sufficiency of the Qur'ān, and its corollary in respect of Arabic as essentially identified by it, questions the warrant of Arabs to be Christian and of Christianity to be Arabic.

That sense of things, of course, postdates six earlier centuries in which Arabic and Christian belonged together. It is a commentary on those centuries that Islam in the seventh could align both Arab and Arabic so emphatically with itself. To enquire into how it so transpired is our study here. The matter of the Arabic Bible will come more readily in chapter 12.

II

Was there, perhaps, something in Christian faith at odds with what essentially characterizes Arabs? As noted in the previous chapter there were certainly impediments in the strongly Hellenic form in which through all the pre-Islamic centuries it was enshrined. The point will recur in chapter 4. Christian faith, to be sure, is at odds with all cultures in terms of the radical regeneration to which it invites them. Moreover, its will for its own genuinely plural existence in that "whosoever will may come" may offend the *amour propre* of cultures thus denied any exclusive pride. It was not in the nature of Arab consciousness to take readily to this aspect of Christian significance.

But does the issue not go further in the Arab context, if we look down the six centuries of Arab Christianity before Islam in an enquiring retrospect? Participants in history do not have the benefit of hindsight, as historians do. But it may illuminate a forward study to ask why those centuries ended in Islam. What is the sense of that ending as a clue to all that preceded it? What might the fact that Islam captured and fulfilled the Arab spirit indicate about the antecedent story?

Was the emphasis on divine compassion and costly forgiveness as the heart of the Christian Gospel seen not to accord well with the Arab sense of *murū'ah,* or "standing up for rights"? This Arab "virtue" of "virility" (to borrow terms of Latin origin in a similar sense) belonged squarely with tradition and figured prominently in the *Jihād* of Islam. Total renunciation of the old Semitic right of retaliation was no part of Arabian social conduct. On the contrary, family and clan loyalty and the pattern of the feud, with their claim on male prowess, were basic assumptions of life. Islam related to them by fulfilling the will to sacrifice and the valor of combat in a larger cause. So much is clear from the Qur'ān and its reproach of reluctant combatants. Was Christianity in that context disadvantaged by its very quality, its message of the suffering Christ and the God of hope? Or did that message never penetrate?

It would be wise to beware of assuming that the seventh century is the key by which to understand the ones preceding it. Yet the bond it forged between Arabness and Islam must be some index to them, given how congenial the bond proved and how enduring. There was a further factor it reveals respecting the earlier occasions of Christianity, namely, the subtlety of Christian doctrine. The Qur'ān moves within an Arab characteristic of mind for which concrete imagery was preferable to abstract ideas. It explicitly reproves the Christians for the disputatious issues of belief which divided them and which it took as evidence of their futility. When the Qur'ān took their beliefs to task it mistook what they were or itself adopted what they disallowed.[1] But this is proof of how elusive to Arab minds the themes central to Christianity were seen to be. Was the faith out of Jerusalem as ill-suited to the instincts of Arab mentality as it was to the norms of Arab society?

To these actual, or conjectural, handicaps alike of the content, the practice, and the language form of Christian faith we must add one other, perhaps more decisive factor. It has to do with the Arab search for identity, for an Arab self-assertion–assuming that we can reliably argue from the logic of what Islam finally afforded. The term "nationalism" would clearly be an anachronism applied to Arabs and Arabism in those centuries. But something akin to it is evident both in the Qur'ān and in the career of Muḥammad. It seems clear that Christianity was held not to satisfy this Arab quest for something to possess them of themselves. Islam availed to do so, against the Christian option—and, indeed, the Jewish option, if the latter was ever an option at all. There are several scenarios about the Jewish factors in the rise of Islam.[2] Common to them all is the simple fact that Judaism and Jewishness were too exclusive to "fulfill" the Arabs. The case with Christianity was different. Judaism repelled by the privacy of a distinctive covenant, Christianity by the terms belonging to its openness. However, both monotheisms had within them a theme capable of finding a satisfyingly Arab version, namely, the sacred-book factor in their identities and, with it, the necessity of prophethood as a means to scriptures. The phrase in the Qur'ān *ahl al-Kitāb*, "the people of the Book," is eloquent enough as the decisive feature common to the two monotheisms. Why not such a dignity for the Arabs? But how so, without an Arab prophet? The precedent of becoming "scriptured" could only be realized in Arabness by an Arab. There was a need to be independent of the precedent in the very form of fulfilling it.[3]

It is legitimate to recognize this conscious yearning and to appreciate its entire satisfaction in and by the Qur'ān. Arabness and scripture came together in the identity and vocation of Muḥammad. Surah 7.157–158 describes him as "the messenger, the prophet, the unlettered."[4] The third descriptive characterizes him as belonging by birth to a people as yet without their scripture. That understanding of the term *ummī* in the two verses chimes with the repeated Quranic emphasis on its being "an Arabic Qur'ān," which might equally be translated "an Arab Qur'ān."[5]

It is this Arabness inherent in the very nature of the Qur'ān and of Islamic origins that conditioned Arab Christianity from the time in the third decade of the seventh century when Arabia acquired the new faith and the new faith understood and offered itself as what the older faiths had always been meant to be, in their descent from Abraham, when not distorted. How decisive that acquiring proved to be for Arabia was demonstrated in the abrupt exclusion of Christianity from the territory of *Jazīrat al-'Arab*, the sacred soil where not even subject, or *dhimmī*, status was to be permitted.

III

What then of the narrative of Christianity in the territory before that expulsion, engaging there with a destiny of final demise? New Testament readers recall the mention of "Arabs" in the Acts of the Apostles as present at the very genesis of the church (Acts 2:11). Which Arabs they were—from the border regions of the Idumeans or the Nabateans, or other adjacent tribes—is the question, hard to resolve, noted in the previous chapter. Paul in Galatians records his sojourn in "Arabia" (Gal. 1:17) and later in the same letter refers to this, or another, "Arabia" as containing Sinai (4:25). While it is true that Sinai was within the Roman province of Arabia, some interpreters of the two passages have visualized Paul meditating on the gospel of grace upon the very slopes of the mount of Moses and the law. But it is likelier that the place of his sojourn was close to Damascus, where its celebrated rivers petered out into the desert sands.[6] Imagination may very rightly play with the association of "the apostle to the Gentiles" with the birthland of "the prophet of the Arabs."[7] But it must be doubtful how far Paul's journey actually took him into the Arabian peninsula proper.

Even so, minds accustomed to that modern usage must reckon with a terminology that stretches the naming into areas of wide interplay between "the desert and the sown," the heartlands and the margins. The peninsula as a geographical expression was never identical with political or tribal elements. Study of Christian Arabia has to concern five main aspects: the shifting political allegiances in the northwest and the northeast; the lands known as Arabia Felix in the southwest; the scattered evidences of Christianity in the coastal lands to the east and, possibly, other coasts also, in which trading fairs moved and with them itinerant Christians in loosely organized bishoprics; and finally the influence of Ethiopia across the Red Sea to the west, the strength of which was reflected not only in Arabia Felix but in the early stages of Islam itself.

The Roman province of Arabia was a geopolitical entity for more than five centuries–if one keeps in mind the double meaning of the one word *Al-Rūm,* denoting both the Latin capital to the west and the Byzantine capital to the north. Its southern borders lay, often fluctuating, across the northern lands of Najd between the Gulf of ʻAqabah and the region between Basrah and Kuwait. Here, through the centuries before and after the birth of Christianity, the empires, Greek and Parthian, Roman and Persian, busying themselves with rivalry in the area of "the sown" in the whole Fertile Crescent, were content with clients in varying circumstances occupying the fringes of the desert. After the suppression of the Nabateans in the reign of Diocletian (ruled 284–305; d. 313) the emerging clan, later known as the Banū Ghassān, became tributaries as guardians of the edges of imperial power. Similarly to the east, the Lakhmid, or Tanūkh, federation of tribes filled a comparable role, from the third Christian century, around and south of the border town or camp of Ḥīrā, on the lower Euphrates.

The locality of these groupings of tribes brought them into steady contact with Aramean Christianity in its populous and influential spheres to the north, notably Edessa, Jerusalem, Palmyra, and Damascus, with which they were associated through the trade routes that crossed their territory and linked them via Gaza with the life of Egypt. Their buffer role in the political sense was in measure complemented by the place they filled in mediating the life of that riper Christendom, its patterns and controversies, into the remoter paganism on their further side. The actual history is often obscure and there is much that sources, both chronicle and archaeology, leave conjectural.[8]

They do not allow us to follow the scattering "Arabians" of Acts 2:11 when they departed from Jerusalem. Luke's narrative assumes a sharply western partiality in its account of the original Christian diaspora, with the story of "desert" beyond Gaza in Acts 8:26–40 as almost a marginal allusion, where the Ethiopian—for all his high rank—goes anonymously on his way without sequel and Philip his mentor is safely back on the Mediterranean shore. The story is symptomatic of the geographical bias of the only canonical church historian we have. There are no epistles surviving to Arabia. Tradition has to do duty for hard information about the spread of the faith in the areas that had these client Christian rulers from the third century.

It is well to recall here the cosmopolitan nature of the Galilee region and its significance, in distinction from Jerusalem, as a likely source of the diffusion of the Christian faith among Idumeans and others present there in gospel time and still more numerous in the areas east and south across the Jordan. *Galīl ha-Goīm,* "Galilee of the (pagan) nations," was how Jews described it. Julius Africanus, near the end of the second century, wrote of Christians in those regions descended from "the cousins of the Lord," by whom he seems to have meant "Galileans."[9] Aramaic was the language of this stream of faith, which found its most vigorous expression beyond the Roman province of Arabia in the region of Edessa. Its steady gravitation northward and eastward was partly induced by the vicissitudes through which it passed at the hands of Greek-shaped Christianity and, much later, at the hands of Muslim invaders. Its increasing orientation into Persia and into Asia beyond took it further away from Arabian contacts. Its repute and influence from northern Iraq continued to be significant in Ghassānid and Lakhmid territories, and its language—Aramaic/Syriac—supplied many words to the vocabulary of Arabic theology, some of which found their way into the Qur'ān itself.[10] But as it became identified in the fifth century with the (alleged) heresy of Nestorius it was further distanced from the Jacobite/Melchite, Monophysite/Diophysite issues that contended within the Roman province of Arabia.

The bearing of those differing Christologies on the themes of theology and on Muslim relationships after Islam emerged will occupy chapter 4. Lacking the missionary zeal which the Persian-based Nestorians showed in their Asian dispersion, the Christianity of the northern borders fell prey to the strains of border cliency, with the empires themselves at odds and doctrines politicized. Pagan sympathies, especially in the Lakhmid sphere, were always near to hand, with changing moods of acquiescence and belligerence. *Ferax haeresis,* "a fertile ground of heresies," was how the centers of prestige described the frontier tribes. Was the charge laid against a native restlessness? Or was it rather that a people haphazardly evangelized became victim to esoteric cults or to the sheer diversity of the factors linking them to prior Christendom? Should we surmise that Qumran as well as Bostra, *Al-'Uzzā* as well as Antioch, shared in their uncertain nurture?[11] They belonged territorially with Job, but only as strangers to his quest.[12]

We might find a symbol of this situation in the three visits paid to "Arabia" by the great Origen of Alexandria and Caesarea (185–254). He came, by invitation–though only as far as Bostra–in the second and the fourth decades of the third century. The bishop there, Beryllus, was suspected of unhappy speculation about the preexistent Christ and the nature of the human soul. But it would seem that the visitation was more in the context of the intellectualism that the Greek spirit had willed upon the church than a genuine encounter with the Arab spirit.

That factor, however, was not the only element with which would-be mentors of the Arabs such as Origen had to contend. The regions east of the Dead Sea and beyond proved a fruitful field for movements of Semitic-style prophetism, which complicated the questions and patterns of Christian faith. One of the most fascinating was that of Elkasai, an Arab leader whose story and following, in the second century, had features closely akin to what Islam became five centuries later. It is idle to speculate whether the Elkasaites should be considered a partial semiticizing of early Christianity.[13] They spread also in the West and into the Greek language, but, in anticipating central aspects of the career of Muḥammad, they may at least signify the restlessness that characterized Arab possession of Christian faith in its Greek-formed Christology.

Elkasai, a figure of evident charisma and personal force, was delivered of oracles and messages for which he claimed direct mediation, as a book from heaven via the angels in original Aramaic. All was in the name of "the most high God" and with the warning refrain "I am witness over you in the day of the great judgment," a sentence close to the feel of the Qur'ān. The collection of revelations in "the book" exercised a total command over its disciples. Believers turned to Jerusalem in prayer, practiced circumcision, observed the Sabbath, and used bread and salt in an exclusive table fellowship or sacrament.

Baptism was the central rite of this prophetism, combining Judeo-Christian precedents in a ritual of washing, candidates being fully clothed, using the water of rivers or springs. The remission of sins was crucial to their identity. There was a certain Gnostic element in their view of "Christ" as a celestial being present in the actual Jesus but frequently born into chosen personalities in the mystery of prophetism. The spread of Elkasaitism in the West suggests that its appeal had wider human fascination. Even so, it may credibly be read as a commentary on the vagaries and tensions besetting the diffusion of what, broadly, we see as "orthodox" eastern Christianity in the territory of Roman Arabia and still more so in the ultimate Arabia beyond it. Some would question whether it was ever truly orthodox, or, more properly, whether the idiosyncrasies of cultures—not least of Arab culture—admit of orthodoxy at all.

IV

The Christianity of the southwestern corner of the Arabian peninsula was the fruit of factors different on several counts from those obtaining to the north on the fringes of the empires. While the strife of the empires had repercussions in the far south, geographical location and the proximity of Ethiopia determined the southern scene. Najran and the Yemen, Qataban and Sheba, the lands of the Ḥimyarites, together comprised Arabia Felix, mountainous and fertile and sited on the sailing route to India. Arabia Felix was happy also in its engineers, whose works of irrigation such as the dam at Ma'rib sustained for centuries a notable agriculture and a proud culture.

It would seem that trading to India served the origins of Christianity in this part of Arabia. Tradition concerning the apostle Bartholomew and "India" relates to its shores. According to the historian Eusebius, he was followed by Pantaenus in the third quarter of the second century, a leader born in Sicily who later moved to Alexandria. There were also links with Axum and the nascent church in Ethiopia. But, Najran apart, it would seem to have been an implanted faith cherished more by traders and travelers than by the local population, affecting the latter more as an impulse to monotheism than as a conscious Christianity.

Explicit Christianity is in surer evidence in Najran, where Syrian missionaries, or wanderers, brought a Nestorian, or Monophysite, faith. The picture is somewhat clearer for the two centuries preceding Islam, in which later Muslim chroniclers were interested because of the bearing of events on the content of the Qur'ān. It is mainly a story of persecutions and martyrs of a faith jeopardized by association with mentors or exploiters pursuing their own ends. The spice trade route in the west via the Red Sea and its littoral had become increasingly important by the sixth century and stimulated rivalry between the (Monophysite) Ethiopians and Byzantium. Early in that century a Ḥimyarite, Yūsuf As'ar, known as Dhū Nuwās, seized power and, in the interests of local assertion, converted to

Judaism—as being both anti-Axum and anti-Christian whether of Diophysite or Monophysite vintage. He used it to subdue the Christians. Those who resisted forced conversion to Judaism he massacred, destroying churches and devastating villages. The reference in Surah 85.4–8, to "the trench," or "irrigated valley" (*al-ukhdūd*), is to one incident in this Judaic persecution. Dhū Nuwās sought with little success to enlist Arab tribes to the east of Najran, while the Christians sent pleas for aid to Mundhir of Ḥīrā. Meanwhile Axum prepared to turn the tables on Dhū Nuwās, who was himself defeated in 525.

The episode is significant in that Christian belief, extensive and at risk, is documented by tragedy and owes both its danger and its rescue to external factors. The Ethiopians installed their own garrisons but left indigenous leaders in charge of the churches. Both Byzantium and Egypt were interested in the fortunes of the survivors. Some years later a local ruler, known to history as Abrahah, rebelled against Axum and for three decades sustained his power, in Najran and parts of Ḥimyar. His was the ill-fated venture against Mecca which Muslim historians coordinate with the birth of Muḥammad in A.D. 570—a date probably beyond the life and reign of Abrahah. The expedition against Mecca, repulsed with loss, as Surah 105 ("The Elephant") has it,[14] is said to have been in reprisal for desecration allegedly committed by Meccans on Abrahah's great cathedral in Sanaʿ. The narrative from Muslim sources is some measure of the reach of Christian power in the southwest and also of the likelihood of conflict with the rising fortunes of (still) pagan Mecca under the commercially vigorous Quraish.

In all that is obscure concerning the Christianity of Arabia Felix the aspect that emerges is the seeming incapacity of the faith to root itself authentically within Arab consciousness. There is evidence that the monotheism it affirmed found responsive hearing in local paganism and at least some accommodation in cults of tribal and nature deities, stimulating the yearning after unity which many scholars associate with the *ḥunafāʾ*.[15] There was also a certain welcome for, and fascination in, prophetism and the cult of sacred writings. It may well be that the phenomenon of Muḥammad, at least in initial stages, was not so exceptional as is usually thought.[16] Yet somehow these elements in the context of Christian faith failed to encompass in the Arabic sphere and in the Arab soul the Christology that, in Christian terms, monotheism necessitated and where prophethood found consummation.

It seemingly failed to do so because that vital sense of "God in Christ"—of the Incarnation and the cross—did not translate into Arab acceptance since it came in partly alien form and was harnessed to external interests which sought to impose themselves politically on a subject, or a hostage, people.

Arabia Felix was *infelix* in its vicissitudes vis-à-vis Ethiopia, Byzantium, and Persia, in its abortive venture with Judaism as a ploy for independence, and in its final encounter with nascent Islam as a faith and power ready to enjoin for it, and upon it, an Arab monotheism disencumbered of the features that made Judaism inapt and Christianity uncongenial. Islam had its own formula for an *Arabia felix* and its own definition of "felicity."

V

A comparable diagnosis is appropriate for the Christianity pertaining to the third region, namely, the gulf coasts of eastern Arabia. The whole area south of the Lakhmid territory as far as Oman and including Bahrain, the islands, and the peninsula of Qatar, was largely Nestorian in its character with numerous bishoprics relating to Ḥīrā and Edessa. The Nestorians had a notable evangelizing zeal, and the coastal areas they frequented offered access deep into the hinterland via the trade routes. The diffusion of their faith was served also by the trade fairs held down those eastern shores and also elsewhere southward and westward.[17]

Data on this eastern Christianity become clearer the closer we come to the antecedents of Islam in which the later Muslim historians were interested. In the fourth and fifth centuries there are records of episcopal relations with the Catholicos and the Synod of the Nestorians. It was in this area, among the Ḥanīfah tribal group, that the prophet known as Maslamah, or Musaylamah,[18] preached and was able for a time to sustain his claims in rivalry to Muḥammad, whom in some measure he resembled. The strength of his following, despite the force and prestige that original Islam was able to bring against his local followers, suggests that he too appealed to an Arab/tribal sentiment with which Nestorian Christianity did not well tally. Was he arabicizing Christian elements, in that he invoked the single God, *Al-Raḥmān* ("the merciful"), commended asceticism and temperance, and used a rhyming prose akin to the *saj'* of the Qur'ān? If so, he would constitute further evidence of our conjecture that the several bearers of Christian faith and worship–Byzantine, Monophysite, Axumite, or Nestorian–each so far failed to marry itself strongly with the Arab psyche.[19]

It may be argued that the different situation in Ethiopian Christianity illustrates the point. For there, on the African side of the Red Sea, the diffusion of Christian faith and worship achieved what proved to be a lasting fusion with the ethnoculture. In their geographical proximity and natural similarity Arabia Felix and Ethiopia shared many of the same features and were closely linked in trade and travel. As earlier noted, Ethiopia played a significant part in the spread of Christianity across the straits. Both were involved in the political ambitions and conflicts of Persia and Byzantium, and both were affected by important Judaic influences entering into their struggle for identity.

In the second quarter of the fourth century, after earlier gaining control of parts of southwest Arabia, Axum made Christianity the state religion and through the Syrian Frumentius (b. c. 320 in Tyre and consecrated bishop by Athanasius) had links with Alexandria. Late in the next century, however, monks of Monophysite persuasion from Syria brought to Ethiopia the boon of translation of the Gospels into Ge'ez , a language that was closely related to the old southern Arabian Arabic. It proved to be the major factor in the indigenization of Christian faith in Ethiopia. The firm association with Syrian Monophysites enabled the church in Ethiopia to distance itself from the claims of Byzantium and thereby to assert its native autonomy. It was also able to integrate Judaic elements into its identity, through traditions of Solomon and the Queen of Sheba.[20] That option could well have existed also for Arabia Felix, rather than the reverse situation by which, thanks to Dhū Nuwās, Christian indigenization with Judaic undertones was ruled out. Had Ḥimyarite Arabic, through scripture translation, developed the vital role and the liturgical function that Ge'ez attained in Ethiopia, Christian Arab history in the southern corner of the peninsula might well have been transformed. That surmise, however, needs to be tempered by the fact that, in their mutual relations politically, Ethiopia intermittently ruled in Arabia Felix whereas Arabia Felix could only rebel or defer. A more ready capacity to dominate is no impediment to a sense of identity. When Abrahah, for example, sought to spread his wings, it was pagans rather than fellow Monophysites who were his quarry.

VI

This territorial summary of Christianity in Arabia—north, east, and south—before Islam needs to be filled out with some notice of features common to each locale. The most significant was the life and influence of monks and hermits, both solitary anchorites and those associated in cenobitic devotion in monasteries. The habit of siting these in desert places, for better withdrawal from the pursuits of the world, made them both ready of access and foci of fascination to nomads or seminomads around them. Several factors came together in the emergence of monasticism. Among Aramaic-speaking Christians there was an emphasis on the example of the human Jesus, who spoke a variant of their tongue and whose "imitation" Aramean Christianity keenly prized. In the Sinai region and the Nabatean country there was the mutual stimulus of Coptic asceticism as fathered by Antony and Pachomius in the late third century in the Nitrian desert. Aspects of Gnostic teaching, with its Neoplatonic antecedents in the Greek world, as well as Jewish or Persian doctrines of an enmity between flesh and spirit, also played their part in the will to mortification and contemplation. The bizarre forms that at times accompanied its expression only kindled the wonder of observers. The celebrated Arab Simeon Stylites, on his "pillar" (or pyramidal structure?) at Antioch, drew many admiring crowds seeking the *barakah,* or benediction, of his holy precinct or healing in his shadow.

Hilarion (291–371) was another eminent example of the way in which ascetic pietism became, even unwittingly, an instrument of evangelical propagation of faith. Converted from paganism in Alexandria, he lived solitarily in his native region south of Gaza for some two decades, where at length his repute made a solitary life impossible. He decided to abandon it for active preaching among the tribes who sought him out, retiring again to solitude and travels afield in his final years. His disciples formed Aramaic- or Arabic-speaking clusters of monks in wide dispersion in the Negev and toward the frontiers of Roman Arabia.[21] There was a fascination for ascetics in mountains traditionally associated with Moses. Among them was Jabal Sirbāl in southwestern Sinai. Others established themselves around Madyān, the area between ʻAqabah and the Hijāz. All these were vulnerable to marauding tribes, for whom they were easy prey. Astride the trade routes northward from Mecca, they played their part in the antecedents of Islam and the travel education of Muḥammad. There is an eloquent allusion in Surah 24 to

> houses He [God] has willed to be established, in which His Name is remembered and where, glorifying Him morning and evening, are men whom neither trading nor merchandising diverts from the remembrance of God nor from the performance of the prayer-rite. . . .[22]

Through the merchants—here contrasted with the monks—the repute of the latter passed into the currency of tribal and oasis life as a powerful witness to the theme of the Oneness of God symbolized in a life of undiverted worship. By the same token, the very strength of monasticism raises the question of pastoral nurture—not to say theological expression—outside these units of contemplation.

Yet, if those outside the cells and monasteries were more likely to be bemused than instructed by them, the Christian elements in the population were certainly hierarchically governed. Documents and chronicles give ample evidence of bishops and their bishoprics, of jurisdictions carefully guarded and at times competitively possessed. Arabian hearers at Pentecost have their counterpart in Arabian bishops at the vital Council of Nicea. Origen is rewarded for his ministries to Bostra by the loyalty of Arab ecclesiastics in his own conflicts. Bishops "of the Saracens" or "of the Encampments" are recorded as present at Chalcedon, though those terms are applied to districts east of Jordan and in Ghassānid country. Tenures were always caught up in the tensions and conflicts of local pride and of doctrinal allegiance. Episcopacy was both the agent and the symbol of ecclesiastical identity and is, therefore, always prominent in the annals. Appointments, depositions, reinstatements, were index to the fortunes of doctrinal formulas as well as the vicissitudes of personal life. Antioch and Alexandria dominated as patriarchates, but Cyril, bishop of Jerusalem from 349 to 386, used his long reign to develop place aura as a plea for patriarchal status, which came only in 451.

The episcopate of Rabbula in Edessa from 412 to 435 affords a useful example of the office as a focus of the wider issues. It coincided with a transfer to Persian control of the eastward part of his territory. As a west-Syrian, Rabbula was concerned to ensure continuity with Antioch but was faced with incipient schism aroused by the Nestorian issue and abetted by the change from Byzantine to Persian rule. Vacillating at first over the decision of the Council of Ephesus in 431 to condemn Nestorius, he resolved later to uphold it. This set him against the eastward trend of his church, its urge to prefer a vindicated Nestorius and a Persian orientation away from Syrian Antioch. In 424 at a Synod at Markabta a separate church appointed a "Patriarch of all the East," a Nestorian entity. Rabbula had to acquiesce in events he could not obviate or reverse. He had, in effect, presided over the breakaway of a Nestorian church from Byzantium, which became final some years later, and the removal of the theological academy from Edessa to Nisibis—itself a powerful symbol of the pains and distresses of jurisdiction. One long-range result of the schism was to deprive the Arab world, in broad terms, of the quality of vital energy Nestorian Christians were to demonstrate in their ventures into farther Asia. The enfeeblement of Edessa on the western edge, as it came to be, of Nestorian territory spiritually impoverished the Arab churches in Mesopotamia and eastern Arabia, where it had formerly been a lively factor.

In the earliest traditions of episcopacy from the New Testament, "bishops" and "elders" had been crucial in the unity and authenticating of faith, as well as in the commendation and reception of Christians on the move in Mediterranean travels. When doctrine diversified in contention and sees acquired roles in controversy, bishops became managers, or pawns, of local, linguistic, tribal, or other interests. Authority designed for unity became the ground of disunity, with successive councils the ostensible organ of the one and often the occasion of the other. In that context, bishops from *Jazīrat al-ʿArab* were liable to be more pawns than managers, their presence noteworthy as that which might not have been assumed, like the attendance of British bishops at Nicea.

Another feature of Christian Arabia in the pre-Islamic centuries was the tribal factor. Though the Aramean and Arab strands mingled in the lands of the Fertile Crescent, the native Arab quality predominated in the peninsula proper. Allegiance, even after the coming of Islam, was strongly tribal in character. Cliency to the Byzantines in the northwest or to Axum in the south served to make it so. Elsewhere also to be *mutanaṣṣirūn,* "christianized," was a register of standing or traditional posture, coinciding with varying degrees of explicit or proximate faith as customs dictated. The Banū 'Uthra in the region between the Dead Sea and Tabūk, the Banū 'Ijl of Yamāmah in central Arabia, the Banū Ṣāliḥ east of the Jordan, and the Banū-l-Ḥārith, victims of Dhū Nuwās in Najran, are conspicuous names recurring in the history. Conversion at various dates in succeeding centuries—elusive to history in respect of means and ways—conferred on the tribes involved a kind of stake in honor or repute, which then ensured a continuity. Christian doctrine, to be sure, never gave to such stake in identity the "private" dimension characteristic of judaized Arab tribes in the peninsula. These had ethnic bonds, even if tenuous, and mostly knew themselves as a diaspora from beyond their present habitat. In that sense "judaized" and "christianized" were contrasted. Nevertheless what might be called *naḥniyyah,* or "we-ness"—instinctively strong in the Arab tribal order of things—was allied with the faith element recruited to its feel and force. Evidence from language and other sources suggests that, in the amalgam of tribe and tenet, of being who they were and holding what they did, the latter was the junior partner.

VII

However uncertain aspects of the history remain, a widespread and persisting Christianity *did* belong in *Jazīrat al-'Arab.* There *was* an achievement of Arab and Christian, of this people and that faith. There has been a tendency among some scholars to think disparagingly of it. Thus, for example, Ignáz Goldziher, writing in 1889, invites his readers to

> consider how superficially Christianity influenced the few Arab circles into which it had penetrated and how alien it was to the main body of the Arab people, despite the support it found in some districts of Arabia.

"Few" is a wrong word, as we have seen, and "support," in this context an odd one. But, sure of his view, he continues:

> We must be convinced of the antagonism of the Arabs to the ideas which it [Christianity] taught. It never imposed itself on the Arabs and they had no

> opportunity to fight against its doctrines, sword in hand. The rejection of a viewpoint diametrically opposed to their own found its expression only in the struggle of the Arabs against Muhammad's teachings.[23]

This verdict makes a strange double inverting of factors. "To impose sword in hand" was never the Christian genius.[24] The seventh-century victory of Islam, by Goldziher's logic, would seem to rest on the view that Muḥammad's doctrine collided so violently with Arab mentality that it prevailed only by giving Arabs an equally violent urge to fight against it.[25] If faiths prosper only by arousing a physical belligerence against themselves which they can then subdue and enlist into militant belief, Christianity certainly failed to achieve this stratagem in Arabia. On the contrary, it was always laboring in the Arabian context under the constraints we have studied of its extra-Arab sources of transmission, its instinct not to be privatized in any culture, and those aspects of the Arab scene and society that proved intractable or compromising of its character.

But exist it did and survive, attenuated to be sure, yet enduring despite—and in some senses within—Islam itself. It was, indeed, lost to Arabia. There, however, the very language that came to be dominated by Islam through the Qur'ān owed its first classical shape to the Christian factor. It was probably Christian missionaries in Arabia who invented the Arabic script itself.[26] According to *Kitāb al-Aghānī*, Zayd ibn Ḥamad and his son 'Adī, Christians of Ḥīrā, were among the very first to write Arabic. There were vital Christian, and Jewish, factors in the very availability of Arabic vocabulary for the articulation of Islam. Scores of Aramaic loanwords found their way into Arabic, many of them into the preaching of Muḥammad. The word *Allāh* itself, presumably a conflation of *al-ilāh,* was already current, denoting the supreme, if not exclusive, "god." It was the sole worship of *Allāh,* not His existence *per se,* that Islam proclaimed. Muḥammad's own father, dying before his son's birth, had the name "servant of *Allāh.*" '*Abd* ("servant") reached Islam from Semitic sources: what Islam did was to restrict its Arabic use to "servant" of God alone. Similarly the word *Rabb* ("Lord") became exclusively a descriptive of God, no longer to be used of human superiors, who were now to be *sayyids* only.

Such bearings of faith on language had Christian sources, and, via Aramaic, a great cluster of Greek and Latin words came to be crucial to the Quranic education of Arab Muslims. *Qalam* ("pen"; cf. Greek *kalamos*) figures prominently as a cherished instrument of knowledge in the inaugural Surah (96.4) and supplies the significant title of Surah 68. The key word *Al-Ṣirāt* (Surah 1.6 and elsewhere some forty-five times) belongs with Aramaic, while the Latin *castra* yields *qaṣr* ("castle"). The Christian *qaryāna,* a "lection" or "reading" in liturgy, has obvious connection with the name of *Al-Qur'ān* itself with the cognate verb *qara'*, to "read" or "rehearse aloud" what is already set down.[27]

It is not only in the incidence of vocabulary that the vigor of Christian expression survives in Islam. Some of the ruling themes of the Qur'ān are of kindred Christian vintage, though, sadly, their relevance has been obscured by the long prejudice that has attended modern Christian reckoning with the Islamic scripture. That adverse reckoning no doubt belongs with the sharply contra-Christian stance of the Qur'ān in respect of Christian understanding of the person of Jesus and the actuality of the cross within "the counsel of God." But these and other fields of antipathy should not have been allowed to induce an ignoring or a disowning of the vital emphases of the Qur'ān that have to do with the creating intention of God, the entrusted creaturehood of human beings within creation, and the sacramental sense of the natural order which follows from them. These are not only central to the common theme of the unity of God; they are crucial to the role of prophethood in the guidance of responsible humanity in due positive, earth-consecrating "submission" to the divine ends. There is no point in prophethood if humanity is not liable to reverence, gratitude, and fidelity to trust under God in its tenancy of place and time. These basic truths of Quranic theology are in part in debt to Christian Arabness as their antecedent context.

It is here that we are wise to locate the main test, the most feasible proof, of Christian Arabness, namely, in its legacy to Islam. "Legacy" is the proper word in the other sense also that it happened, as far as *Jazīrat al-'Arab* was concerned, in a demise within that territory. Our study may best conclude by reflection on aspects of this situation.

VIII

Some note of Christian Arabic poetry prior to Islam is appropriate here. The language was only slowly moving from an oral to a scripted speech in the two centuries preceding Islam. Muḥammad's utterance was spoken before it was inscribed and, in the Qur'ān, the celestial words—though believed indited on "the preserved tablet" (Surah 85.22)—were always vocal. Such is the insistent sense of the initial command: *Iqra'* (Surah 96.1). This has nothing to do with perusal in silence: it is a word to be heard. Its destiny is, literally, to "sound its sense."

Christianity among Arabs shared the sequence of utterance and text in its own idiom. Whether to date written Arabic scriptures earlier than the fifth or sixth century is uncertain.[28] Liturgy in worship can hardly be only verbal, even if the *Targums* from the Aramaic, Syriac, or Greek long remained so. We do not know when or how soon there was a written

Arabic of the contents of Christian liturgy and its lections from the New Testament. But, alongside whatever oral currency such Christian Arabic attained in the churches, monasteries, and episcopates, there was a wealth of poetry—the medium vital to nonliterate society and especially dear to the Arab heart.

Louis Cheikho believed he had traced ample evidence of Christianity's diffusion in poetry among Arab tribes,[29] but later studies cast doubt on his enthusiastic, oversanguine presentation, prompted perhaps by his instinct from within a Christian minority community to overplay his hand. One recent critic finds only a few authentic cases from the twenty or so that Cheikho adduced.[30] The location of these is important, as they belong with areas to the north of Arabia proper. Outside ostensibly Christian poets there are oblique allusions to Christian monks, festivals, manners, hermitages, and sacred words. But in such a context, sophisticated awareness—still less articulate currency—of Christian doctrines is hardly to be expected. This is not to say that emotions of yearning for relief from life's weary sorrows, for forgiveness instead of revenge, for solace from the ravages of war, for hope in some final compassion are not present in pagan poesy and that Christians in native Aramaic or Syriac may not have been among their sources.

Why, within Arabia, should the positive presence of Christianity have left its "legacy" only in demise? Some of the factors we suggested at the outset in seeing those six centuries through the lens of Islam. Perhaps the answer lies in the absence within the peninsula of an initiative like that of the Syrian monks who gave the Gospels in Ge'ez to Ethiopia. Had the Gospels or the *Diatessaron* of Tatian (d. 172) been available and disseminated in Arabic, the Christianity using it would surely have been less proximate and more authentic. The earliest surviving manuscript of the *Diatessaron* was the work of Abū-l-Faraj ibn ʿAbdallāh al-Ṭayyib, who died in 1043. Its Arabic abounds in Syriac idioms, and it is clearly a product of the age of arabicization that ensued after Muslim expansion. Is that fact significant? Did Islam coincide with the nascent availability of written Arabic and itself enormously foster the process? Does the clue to the first six centuries of Christian Arabness lie simply in the fact that they lacked the possibility of textual religion in Arabic? Or was it that Islam had the vital asset in textualizing an Arabic religion by virtue of its oracular view of revelation in that language and the instrumentality in its own Arab Muḥammad? If so, again, was Arab Christianity the casualty in its own setting of its condition of belonging to all peoples, heir to a scripture that was not native, and subsisting when fully textual faith was not yet feasible in the givens of time and place? If these questions are rightly posed, then Arab Christianity was superseded in the Arabian peninsula by the obverse working of those very factors underwriting the advent of Islam, namely, a text orally possessed and literally inscribed, on both counts giving native Arabic its vocation and the Arab identity its fulfillment.

It follows that the subsequent story of Christian Arabness elsewhere beyond *Jazīrat al-ʿArab* had to be sought and found in constant, painful, yet persistent survival within the *modus vivendi* Islam controlled. But neither that eventuality nor the way it transpired nor the sequel it regulated is reason to depreciate the early chequered centuries of "Arab and Christian" or, on their account, to despair of the sequel. To that we must now turn, with the realism proper to the Arab dominance of Islam.

Notes

1. When the Qur'ān says that "God has not adopted a son" (Surah 17.111), it uses the verb *ittakhadha* ("adopted"), expressing what was in fact heresy to Christians. It no doubt intends to rebut the Christian doctrine of Incarnation but uses the verb that contrasts directly with that faith. It uses the same verb in 19.35, 92; 25.2; and 39.4. When in Surah 4.157 it refers to a "resemblance" of Jesus being crucified, the verb used is *shubbiha lahum* ("it was made to appear so to them"), which is equivalent to the Greek used by Docetism, a heresy for which the physical event of crucifixion was pure charade. See the full discussion in my *Jesus and the Muslim: An Exploration* (Winchester, Mass.: Allen & Unwin, 1985), pp. 169–172. The immediate point, however, in context here is simply that there were problems of comprehension of Christian faith for those concerned with its rejection.

2. The old orthodoxy among scholars, it might be said, was discussed in C. C. Torrey, *The Jewish Foundation of Islam* (New York: Bloch Publishing Co., 1933), in counter to Richard Bell, *The Origin of Islam in Its Christian Environment* (London: Cass, 1926). Muḥammad preached "the religion of Abraham," a renewed Semitic monotheism; he anticipated Jewish acknowledgment within Arabia, was bitterly disappointed, and turned sharply denunciatory. That understanding, congruent with the Qur'ān, is overturned by the thesis of Patricia Crone and M. A. Cook, *Hagarism, the Making of the Islamic World* (Cambridge, 1977), whose oddly intricate conclusions are far from convincing. They set aside Islam's own view of its "making," and opt for contemporary non-Muslim sources purporting to demonstrate that Muḥammad proclaimed a Hagarite-Jewish messianism, fulfilled by ʿUmar in the repossession of Jerusalem, and then seen to shed its Jewish connection by transforming Muḥammad into a contra-Jewish prophet of monotheism via Abraham and Hagar.

3. To think, in this way, into the source of Muḥammad's sense of vocation in no way detracts from Muslim understanding of its divine mandate. It is simply to see how that mandate came to him in the *Iqra'* ("Recite!") of Surah 96.1. See a fuller study in my *The Event of the Qur'ān: Islam in Its Scripture* (London: George Allen & Unwin, 1971), pp. 54–72.

4. The word *al-ummī* in these verses is best understood as denoting not a total incapacity to read or write but "one from a people without a scripture." When the word *ummīyyūn* (pl.) is used in the Qur'ān it is almost without exception in contrast to Jews, that is, to "scripturized people." If the translation "Gentile" is used it makes that point but without the element that here makes the contrast with Jews, namely, not "having a Book."

5. The Qur'ān is described as emphatically "an Arabic Qur'ān" in 12.2; 20.113; 41.3; 42.7; and 43.3. Its being Arabic is required as a message to Arabs. This emphasis, however, does not contradict its being a universal message to all. On the desire for an Arab prophet, someone "more theirs than Moses or Jesus," see Fazlur Rahman, "Pre-Foundations of the Muslim Community in Mecca," *Studia Islamica* 43 (1976), 5–24. In Surah 35.42 the irony is that having pledged to hear "one of their own," the Meccans resisted him (Muḥammad) when he came; 26.198 makes it clear that a non-Arab would not be acceptable.

6. For the romantic "Sinai" view, see J. B. Lightfoot, *St. Paul's Epistle to the Galatians* (London, 1890), pp.87–90. "He was attracted thither by a spirit akin to that which formerly had driven Elijah to the same region. Standing on the threshold of the new covenant, he was anxious to look upon the birthplace of the old."

7. One such venture is in my *Jesus and the Muslim,* pp. 210–233, "Paul and the Qur'ān."

8. Henri Charles remarks: "Through the course of these pages do not fear to multiply the question marks" (*Le Christianisme des Arabes Nomades sur les Limes et dans le Desert Syro-Mesopotamian aux alentours de l'Hegira* [Paris, 1936]). He refers to historians who cite each other or are silent about what does not interest them.

9. One location seems to have been Pella, east of the Jordan. See Philip Carrington, *The Early Christian Church,* vol. 1, The First Christian Century (New York: Cambridge University Press, 1957): "They might have developed a Jewish-Christian patriarchate similar to the rabbinic patriarchate at Jamnia. The reverence for the royal family of David and Jesus continued among them into the 3rd century, when the *desposunoi,* as they were called, were interrogated by Julius Africanus on the subject of the pedigree of Jesus" (p. 251).

10. See below; also A. Jeffery, *Foreign Vocabulary of the Qur'ān* (London: Luzac & Co., 1938) and n. 27 below.

11. Whether remnants of the Qumran sect survived in Arabia till the seventh century is discussed by Chaim Rabin, *Qumran Studies* (New York: Oxford University Press, 1957), chap. 8, pp. 112–130. According to J. S. Trimingham, the Lakhmid rulers "remained almost to the last ditch devotees of the goddess *Al-'Uzzā* . . . even after practically all the people of their federation had become Christian" (*Christianity among the Arabs in Pre-Islamic Times* [New York: Longman, 1979], p. 157).

12. Assuming that Job and his tribe of 'Uz belonged east and south of the Dead Sea. Perhaps to say "strangers" here is harsh, inasmuch as the pre-Islamic poets, Zuhair and Labīd, for example, gave notable expression to human pathos and wistfulness for solace in adversity.

13. On the plea that Christology as classical Christianity knew it is a totally

unwarranted distortion of "the actual Jesus," Muslim thought, early and late, has taken up what it sees as a "re-semiticization" of Jesus whereby he is rescued from the Christian aberration and restored to true Hebraic perspective as "a messenger to the Jews." Elkasai, however, would only partially fit such a role in that, while stressing prophethood, he held Gnostic ideas about its incidence in Jesus and elsewhere.

14. Abrahah's army included an array of elephants and was miraculously routed either by plague, or hailstorm, or other catastrophe, according to the exegesis of Surah 105. Abrahah's death is put by some records as occurring in 560, which would make the synchronizing of the defeat with Muḥammad's birth simply symbolic as an event with a great augury for Mecca.

15. The plural of *ḥanīf,* a term used of Abraham in the Qur'ān and probably signifying a concern for the oneness of God in a way that set *ḥunafā'* "apart" (the root meaning in Syriac?) from pagans.

16. Rival or concurrent claims to prophethood are recorded during the time of Muḥammad and during the *riddah,* or "reneging," which followed his death and which the energy of Abū Bakr effectively cut off (see n. 18). Further, the *saj'* style of the Qur'ān might plausibly be imitated—otherwise why the challenge in the Qur'ān to emulate it successfully (Surahs 2.23; 10.38).

17. See I. Krenkow, "The Annual Fairs of the Pagan Arabs," *Islamic Culture* 21 (1947) 111–113; and Sozomen *Ecclesiastical History* in J. P. Migne, *Patrologia graeca* 67:941–946.

18. Musaylamah is a diminutive of his name, used in scorn and contempt. He taught the unity of *Al-Raḥmān,* resembled in utterance the diction of the Qur'ān, and abjured militancy in the cause of his doctrines. The supremacy of Muḥammad demanded that he be execrated in Islam.

19. Trimingham examines in an epilogue what he takes to be the failure of Christianity in the Arab milieu, its Syriac quality merely "touching the surface" of Arabian life. He sees the real subject of his book as "Christianity among the Arameans" (*Christianity among the Arabs*).

20. "Sheba" is Saba of the Sabeans in southwest Arabia. It was Ethiopia that "borrowed" the queen to afford a legendary association with Solomon, in royal tradition.

21. A late-fourth-century account of the travels of Egeria gives an impression of the vigor of monastic life in the provinces (*Egeria's Travels,* ed. and trans. John Wilkinson [London: SPCK, 1971], esp. pp. 101–103, 118; see also the editor's comment, pp. 23–26).

22. Surah 24.36–37 with its celebration of "the light" in the simile of the sanctuary lamp and its sustaining oil must refer to a sanctuary within the monastery. The quotation here omits the conclusion about "bringing the *Zakāt,* or alms." This phrase might be translated more generally as "charitable works," unless it is the intention of the passage to bring the whole into the context of the Islamic way, in line with a possible rendering of the previous phrase "doing the *Ṣalāt,*" here translated "the prayer-rite." *Ṣalāt* is a word of Aramaic vintage that had a Christian connotation before it became the term for the Muslim rite.

23. Ignáz Goldziher, *Muslim Studies,* ed. S. M. Stern, trans. C. R. Barber and S. M. Stern (Chicago: Aldine Publishing Co., 1968), 1:21.

24. Christian tribal leaders could be redoubtable in arms in respect, for example, of frontier patrols for Byzantium, but not in faith-imposing belligerence. The long-reigning Ḥārith ibn Jabala (528–569) of the Ghassānids achieved a high standing in frontier politics and as a forceful arbiter in local tensions both tribal and religious. But a faith so characterized by monasticism had no genius for belligerent propagation. Existing Christians and their jurisdictional order did have their power politics.

25. Goldziher, in stressing the ways in which Muḥammad's mission collided with the vested interests of the Meccans, fails to reckon with the fact that they readily abandoned their pagan deity trusts when, in capitulation to Muḥammad, it was evident that those deities had not served them well. In other words the deities were disproved in battle, rather than persuasion—or, rather, in the "persuasion"—of belligerence. Why, men reasoned, should they be loyal to gods or goddesses who had not been loyal to them? To claim, therefore, that Muḥammad's faith succeeded by arousing a belligerence against it in physical terms—as his opening of hostilities did—is to turn the properly religious issue on its head. Or perhaps in that context the issue could not be "properly religious."

26. See *Encyclopedia of Islam,* ed. B. Lewis et al. (London: Luzac & Co., 1958–59) 1:564, s.v. "Arabiyya." See also Nadia Abbott, *Rise of the North Arabic Script and its Kur'ānic Development* (Chicago: University of Chicago Press, 1939), discussing the role of Christian poets of Ḥirā and other evidences of Christian Arabism, such as the Greek/Syriac/Arabic Christian inscriptions at Zabad and Harran. See also the comments on the Christian Arab role in the sixth-century story of the Arabic language by Reynold Alleyne Nicholson, *Literary History of the Arabs,* 2nd ed. (New York: Macmillan, 1930), pp. xxii, 137–138.

27. See Jeffery, *Foreign Vocabulary.* Words quite central to Quranic and Muslim vocabulary are arabicized from Semitic sources, e.g., *Sūrah* ("a piece of scripture"), *Al-Raḥmān* ("the Lord of mercy"), *'abd* ("worshiper"), *sabbiḥ* and *tasbiḥ* ("the ascription of praise" [to God]), *rabb* ("lord"). Islam gave its own feel and significance to these terms, restricting *Rabb,* for example, to *Allāh* alone and disallowing to *'abd* any but Godward "serving." This fact should set at rest the mind of Muslims over the dogma (for such it can only be) that the Qur'ān contains no non-Arabic vocabulary. See also Al-Jawālikī, *Al-Mu'arrab min al-Kalām al-'Ajamī* (Arabicized from Foreign Words) (Cairo, 1361 A.H.).

28. A. Baumstark believed that he had traced Christian Arabic script as early as the sixth century (*Islamica* [1931], pp. 562–575; see also 1929/30, pp. 356–359).

29. Louis Cheikho, *Le Christianisme et la Littérature Chrétienne en Arabie* (Beirut, 1919). His work showed great erudition and assembled a mass of epigraphic material as well as evidences from poetry. Other scholars, such as Henri Lammens, R. Aigrain, and F. Nau, have offered contrasted assessments of the diffusion and quality of Christian evidences from Mesopotamia to Hadramaut.

30. See the evaluation of Cheikho in Camille Hechaime, *Louis Cheikho et Son Livre* (*Le Christianisme etc.*) (Beirut, 1967). He insists on the need to beware of inferring the general from the local, of arguing from Ḥīrā for Yamāmah, or from instances to verdicts.

CHAPTER

3

Arabicization and Dār al-Islām

I

EARLY IN THE YEAR A.D. 637 the patriarch Sophronius surrendered Jerusalem to the caliph ʿUmar. Less than two years later, Sophronius died—Christian chroniclers said—of a broken heart. A little over half a century later the Umayyad caliph ʿAbd al-Malik erected the first, and perhaps forever the most beautiful, of Islamic shrines, the Dome of the Rock, on the site of Solomon's Temple on the holy mount. It was a supreme monument of arabicization, a moment of climax in the unfolding of history.

It is well to begin with a building rather than with battles, though the architects found their occasion through the desperate trial of arms at the river Yarmuk, which, despite resistance to a year-long siege, had sealed the fate of the Holy City. The significance of the Dome of the Rock, in the immediate as well as the long context, brings together many of the elements of the story we have in review. It heralded the new era of Islam in its most eloquent language but nevertheless recruited the skills and crafts of Christian artisans, some of them drawn from Constantinople itself, to enable and adorn the construction. Thus it stood as abiding evidence of an interpenetration of cultures and faiths. The arabicization of the vast areas of eastern Christianity conquered by the Muslim armies was also a deep hellenization of Islamic culture. Thanks to the finality of the conquest—once its finality was emotionally conceded—the political sway and the psychological victory of Islam were never in question. Dominance was achieved and symbolized in the supremacy of Arabic as the language of the centuries to come. Yet the lore and the wisdom that Arabic came to house and the sophistication the faith it carried was soon to acquire derived in large measure from the peoples Islam subdued. Nor should we imagine that

Islam broke unindebted and unbeholden on the Greco-Roman world. Reciprocal factors had been at work in the Arabian peninsula for generations. The devastating suddenness of the conquest, rather than outlandishness in its origins, accounted for its impact. Rome and Persia had been factors in parts of Arabia for a long time, and Jews and Christians had contributed to the shaping of Muḥammad's Islam.

But why had ʻAbd al-Malik wanted to build his exquisite edifice? The reasons are complex. The insurrection of Ibn al-Zubayr in the Hijāz had wrested Mecca, for the time being, from the Umayyads, and it is conjectured, probably falsely, that ʻAbd al-Malik was planning to mark Jerusalem as an alternative place of official pilgrimage. In any event, it already had unique status as the first *Qiblah* ("direction of prayer") of Islam and the focal city of Christianity, while from the Rock of Abraham, beloved patriarch of Islam, Muḥammad himself had "ascended" through the heavens following "the Night Journey" from Mecca. Was ʻAbd al-Malik also signaling some undefined association with Jewry by retrieving the site of the Temple from Christian neglect? Did not some Christian writers allege (or imply) that Muḥammad himself had learned, from Jews, of promised conquests sealed by temple-shrines and—from the book of Daniel—of empires in their sequence?[1] If these thoughts had been latent in Muḥammad's own mission and if they were relevant to Umayyad achievement, how better to proclaim the fact than to build so impressive an Islamic masterpiece in the superlative city of the Christians?

There was a more practical impulse also. Fifty years on from the rugged simplicity of ʻUmar[2] it was important that caliphs should not be outdone by the elegant style traditional to Orthodox emperors. Had not the first Umayyad, Mu ʻāwiyah, told his followers when reproached about his regal way, "Damascus is full of Greeks . . . no one would believe in my power if I did not behave, and look, like an emperor"?[3] One of the readiest ways of being imperial was to build magnificently. The Dome of the Rock was an index to such approximation by conquerors to the conquered taking place in all the spheres to which architecture belonged—art, prestige, identity, faith, and perpetuity.

Perhaps the prime purpose of the Dome of the Rock lay in serving notice on Christianity that a supersession was under way. Its splendor would certainly outshine the Church of the Resurrection hard by. The choice of Jerusalem for its site could hardly be misread nor the import of its quality. The calligraphy, moreover, from the Qur'ān had largely to do with passages incriminating Christology and the doctrine of the Trinity and underlining the role of Jesus as prophet and as an exemplary "Muslim."[4] The scribes and ceramicists of Christendom were thus employed to join the issues between caliph and patriarch, between the heirs of Muḥammad and the legacies of Chalcedon. The Dome of the Rock was in this way the sign and the herald of *Dār al-Islām,* the realm of displaced creed and of replaced power *and* the shape of their interaction.

"The State is an exhalation of the Spirit of God incarnate on earth," says the central character in *Respected Sir,* a novel by the Egyptian author Najīb Maḥfūẓ.[5] That verdict is written large in the origins of Islam within Arabian society. By sanction of its expansive conquests, Islam was and has remained the most political of religions. The founding pattern of its will for statehood in the *Hijrah* shaped the destiny it brought into the tally of its conquests. It was implicit in the whole ethos of Islam that, at best, the status of all other religions should be reduced to that of private communal affairs of ritual and customary law, while Islam exercised unilaterally total political control. Muslims showed no awareness of the paradox here by which other faiths were denied precisely that inclusiveness of all realms of life required by the very nature of religion. The privilege of such completeness, however, was understood to be unique to Islam as the corollary of its historical finality.

II

It is customary in the West to perceive the Muslim conquest of the East as success from the grave for the Prophet and an outflow of exuberant vigor from Arabia under the fervor of the new faith. The picture needs a greater realism. It is true that Muḥammad's people believed him poised at death to take over humanity, but his immediate successor as ruler, Abū Bakr, and the resolute men such as 'Umar and Abū 'Ubaidah who ensured his succession had first to overcome internal Arab revolt in the crisis that followed Muḥammad's demise. Some of the Arab tribes who had islamized held their engagements to be terminated by his death. They insisted that their adherence had been only contractual—a merely politic Islam—and that Muḥammad's death ended their allegiance. This *riddah,* or reversion from Islam, had to be subdued within Arabia by Abū Bakr before turning the military prowess of Muslims outward into the lands of Byzantium and the Persian Sassanids.

It is important to distinguish between "Arab" as "of Arabia" and "Arab" in the wider sense it was to acquire in the world beyond, through the Arabic language. For the former, that is, Arabia, only acceptance of Islam was allowable—or death. The *jizyah,* or poll tax, exacted elsewhere from non-Arabs who submitted, was not to be taken from natives of the peninsula. It was mandatory from others surrendering to Islam from communities having "revealed scriptures." These were initially thought of as non-Arabs, irrespective of their racial identity. Their option was either conversion or the poll tax. The differentiation persisted for some two centuries between Muslims of such origin and those who belonged territorially to Arabia proper. The latter carried the distinction of belonging with Muḥammad by race and by country. Veneration for him and his family implied God's choice of Arabs also as His people. It was a distinction not readily transferable to converts despite their Islam—an Islam at one remove or more from its territorial setting.[6] This factor needs to be remembered throughout the history of Islamic universalism, despite the several locations—Damascus, Baghdad, Cairo, and Istanbul—of the caliphate itself.

III

Medina, city of the Prophet's tomb, was the springboard of initial raids into the border areas to the northwest and northeast of Arabia, ruled by the Christian Ghassānids and Lakhmids. These were of a desultory kind. Once the *riddah* was defeated, Abū Bakr and ʿUmar, with commanders of great panache and skill, commissioned campaigns in two-pronged advance, surprising themselves by their immediate success. Damascus and the main towns of Syria surrendered even before the decisive battle on the river Yarmuk between the forces of Emperor Heraclius and the Muslim army in August 636, when—it is said, twelve thousand Ghassānid Arabs went over to the Muslim ranks, being mercenaries with little love for Byzantium. Jerusalem held out for a year and then surrendered, as did Antioch, the great Christian metropolis.

Eastward the story was equally dramatic. After capturing Ḥīrā, the Arabs fought the emperor Yazdagird at Qādisiyyah in 637, a battle of devastating consequences for his empire. After mastering the whole of Iraq, the Muslims united with their western counterparts. In 639 the general Amr ibn al-ʿĀṣ reached the Egyptian border and proceeded to take Babylon, the major center in the Cairo region. Alexandria, which had possibility of naval succor from Byzantium and was the stronghold of the "Greek" Orthodox in Egypt, loyal to the emperor in contrast to the disaffected Monophysite Copts, surrendered on terms that allowed the garrison to return to Constantinople. Efforts from the sea to retake it proved abortive.

On land, armed advance westward continued through the next half century reaching Tangier by the year 711, and thence into Spain. Elsewhere the tide flowed more slowly than in the first swift decade. Byzantium never recovered its Arab provinces, nor did the Persian Sassanids. But each prolonged its resistance in the heartlands of Anatolia and central Persia. The latter, apart from the missionary spread of Arab Nestorian

Christians, belongs outside our field of reference. In respect to West Asia it is important to remember that during the early decades of Muslim contact with Christians in the wake of victory armed struggle was continuing in Anatolia. Though the Byzantine capital was menaced and jeopardized from west and south and east, it survived within itself until 1453 and conquest by the Ottoman Turks. (The capital's tragedy in the time of the Fourth Crusade will concern us in chapter 5.) The long survival of the city, at least as a symbol and a focus of yearning for the Melchite Christians who were variously sundered from it under Islam, remained a significant factor in the Arab Christian story, both of hope and of frustration. There were ways in which it both enabled and impeded Muslim–Christian encounter.

To assess the lot of Arab Christians in the vast extent of the former provinces of Byzantium and Persia enclosed in this vast and sudden conquest it is necessary to keep in mind that, despite numerous conversions to Islam, Christians remained the majority population well into the ninth century. The emigrant Arabs from the peninsula were relatively few in number but strong and prestigious enough to hold the upper hand in society and the economy. They had, of necessity, to rely heavily on existing structures of administration and law. It was not, for example, until the time of the building of the Dome of the Rock that the caliph inaugurated his own coinage, terminating the Christian symbolism of the Byzantine coins used until 691.[7] Greek continued as the language of state registers in Syria and western Iraq until the same date.[8] In Egypt, Copts remained in central roles in the fiscal system for many centuries. The intellectual and cultural worth of the Byzantine tradition could not be metamorphosed into Islam with the suddenness of physical conquest nor without Muslims assimilating large elements in return. Fields such as medicine and architecture enjoyed little or no mention in the Qur'ān, nor did erudite theology. Here the Muslims were pupils rather than masters.

In studying the interplay of identities and its effect on Christian Arab destiny, we need to understand the legal order governing the situation. The Islamic tolerance of Jews and Christians (and certain other tolerable communities) was in theory and practice a strictly contractual relationship. Theoretically life was forfeit for non-Muslims but could be reprieved by an agreement to submit politically. At any point the contract to protect could be suspended if, in the judgment of Muslim power, its conditions had been broken. In practice the minorities—*dhimmīs* in this state of *Al-Dhimmah*—had reasonable security. The sword of Damocles remained but need not ever fall. The implementation of the theory, which continued through to the later Ottoman years, varied from time to time and place to place and was subject to the vagaries of officialdom at local level. In concept and largely in practice, however, it allowed Christians of any persuasion, as monotheists and "scriptured people," to maintain their own worship, teach their own offspring, and administer their own laws of personal status through their own communal hierarchy. In return for "protection," *dhimmīs* paid the *jizyah,* or poll tax, and were exempt, as non-Muslims, from the *Zakāt,* or alms, due only from Muslims. Thus separation was institutionalized in a form that effectively made the minorities inferior as noncitizens. Their submission in these terms was the legal basis for the suspension of *Jihād,* the obligation to subdue non-Islam by force incumbent on *Dār al-Islām* as such.

IV

The Byzantine Empire, for its part, had strenuously demanded and imposed a unity of state and creed and its non-Orthodox subjects (as it deemed them) had suffered accordingly from pressure and persecution, to the extent that Islam, especially in Egypt, was almost welcomed. What was different about Islamic *Jihād* and *dhimmī* status, as all Christians were to discover, lay in the experience of physical conquest and in the radical differentiation between Muslim and non-Muslim, which reduced the latter to political nonentity unless practical considerations in local incidence mitigated their situation. Councils at Ephesus or Caesarea or elsewhere in Byzantine days might quarrel and then oppress, differ, and be defied, but at least they met and access was open. The Islamic conquest effectively orphaned the churches within its range and by the *dhimmī* system both perpetuated their divisions (until the Ottoman consolidation of *Al-Dhimmah*) and consigned them to a limbo of irrelevance—as far as Islam was officially concerned.[9] Centuries of ghetto-style existence were to follow despite the paradoxes of opportunity within the system, which Christian individuals could retrieve within Islamic hellenization.

This introversion, and the Muslim assumption that it should be such, found expression in an array of regulations which, varied as they were in application down the years and from local factors, nevertheless supposed and served diminishment. Among them were the prohibition against the building of new churches or the repair of existing ones; the obligation of Christians and Jews to wear distinctive dress, to avoid using cherished Arabic words or exchange greetings with Muslims, to dismount in Muslim presence from their donkeys, to have their dwellings lower than those of Muslims, to refrain from bell ringing and public use of crosses, and the prohibition against possessing arms.[10] The conditionality of the suspension of *Jihād* hung over minorities and even when non-Muslims, for practical reasons, were able to exercise public functions as accountants or custodians, the fact that by status they were vulnerable made them more dependent and pliable. Occasions for venality were legion, though happily tempered by the possibilities of sheer human decency of which Muslims were no less capable than others. Strictly, according to exegesis of Surahs 3.28 and 5.57, Muslims should not allow authority over themselves to a non-Muslim. Nor were non-Muslims allowed to give evidence against a Muslim. Burial grounds had to be clearly segregated and distinguished.

There is no doubt that through all its vicissitudes, lenient or insistent, the Islamic status of *Al-Dhimmah* translated the "anti-others" animus enshrined in the Qur'ān itself into day-to-day expression and with it the inherent dominance of Islam. The *kharāj*, or tax for the right to cultivate land, hinged on the theory that all ownership belonged to Islam. *Jihād* was believed to be the recovery by Islam of what by right belonged to it as the true and final religion but which had been alienated from it by the unbelief or perversity embodied in the minorities whose survival—but no more—it allowed. *Dhimmīs* were on the receiving end of the Islamic concept of the world—a concept translated into conquest and by conquest confirmed. The two were the fusion of a destiny.

Inevitably the destiny had to accommodate to facts—facts of history, society, and culture, not to say population, which were only partially amenable either to the logic of concept or of conquest. There had to be partnerships and interaction. Even the most strenuous will to apartheid has to admit the paradox that it unites. Relations persist even in avoidance, and Islam was far from being an avoider. There was the urge to convert and recruit,[11] and there was the pride of Arabism, a pride that for its own approbation willed to assimilate. The new faith and its first ethnic identity here combined.

The form of their common action was the making of "clients" (*mawālī;* sg. *mawlā*)—recruits, that is—to Islam, who became such by association with an Arab tribe sponsoring their conversion. Thus began the initially novel idea of a non-Arab Muslim. There was attraction in the very success of Islam, not to say also prudence in the new allegiance. Given the evolving philosophy of Islamic dominion we have reviewed—in a perspective only slowly available to contemporaries—there were potent reasons, as there had been within Arabia while Muḥammad lived, for joining the elite, as far as their Arabism allowed, and forsaking the liabilities of the old faith in the new context. Now, however, there was to be no *riddah.* Islam, in intent and in fact, had become a faith that none was free, or likely, to leave, and a faith, by the same token, that many were liable to adopt, "free" to do so by the *mawlā* route of escape from *dhimmī* life.

There were warnings in the Qur'ān to Muslims minded to deter accession into Islam which were needed no less in the world of wider conquest. There was ambivalence in the *dhimmī* system. By disadvantaging non-Muslims it gave an incentive to becoming Muslim. If that involved the recruited in the obligation of *Zakāt,* or Muslim almsgiving, it relieved them of the non-Muslim *jizyah.* Just as new converts in Medinan days acquired a share in booty, so ex-*dhimmī* Muslims entailed a wider call on Muslim benefits, which the self-interest of old-timers might resent.[12] The presence of this kind of calculus has to be kept in mind in making historical assessments of the impact of the empowered faith upon the powerless.

In the first century and beyond, it was the ethnic, more than the fiscal, situation that determined the relations of the founding Arabs of Islam with the non-Arab population—Christian, Aramean, Copt, Berber, Syrian, and other. Those of them who islamized, through cliency or otherwise, in the century of the Umayyads with Damascus as their capital did so through a variety of factors, economic, social, and fiscal, operating through a mixture of human motivations.

V

However, prior to the lapse of the long century of arabicization, one should be wary of speaking of any "preaching of Islam," in the sense of any faith commendation that was articulate and considered. Intellectual Christian assessment of Islam was hardly feasible under the constraints of conquest and the pain of understanding that event providentially. Social and political inferiority apart, the secrets of Islam were locked in the untranslatable Qur'ān. Ignorance of Arabic and the linguistic custody in which Islam was set made it difficult even for alert non-Muslims to reckon with the new religion. Doubtless Islam could be heard in its tersest terms—those of the Shahādah: "There is no god but God; Muḥammad the apostle of God." That was the battle cry of the armies and, after them, of the rulers. Its very simplicity was no doubt impressive, short-circuiting the complexities of Christian formulas of faith. But its sharp brevity, however effective, could also be profoundly unsatisfying to careful minds and gentle spirits. Muslim faithful themselves were in due time to discover how in need of exploration brevity could be. But Christian convictions were not often the beneficiary of such discovery.

The impact of an invading faith upon a subjugated society is necessarily a matter of the generations. The first generation looks ruefully to a past, fending off the sense of change, the demise of a given order. It is oppressed by alienation from a heritage, as exiles where they had been lately natives. The second or perhaps third generation looks tentatively to a future, reckons more realistically with the actual situation as time admits of its due measure, and begins to reconcile, as weariness, prudence, or calculation take over. The process of adjustment in temper, language learning, and psychic reconciliation proceeds slowly and unsurely. It was certainly so in the century or more after the abrupt insertion of Islamic power and rule into the towns and tribes, the minds and emotions, of the Christian populations. The option to persist was certainly theirs. "The sword of Islam" was more subtle than the "death-or-deliver" formula reportedly required within the sacred territory of *Jazīrat al-'Arab.* The victorious empire set terms of survival for minorities in monotheism, if these in turn would accept containment within the duress of *dhimmī* status in permanent fee to Islamic authority and Muslim mercies.

A historical picture of how this *Dār al-Islām* actually proceeded in the articulate commendation of its faith to *dhimmīs* is hard to come by. The initial problem of its accessibility to non-Arabs was not easily resolved. A reluctance to share it persisted in some quarters as part of the pride of true Arabness, given also the sanctity of the Arabic language in which the faith was housed and through the recitation of which it was alone confessed. Nor did the imperial facts of life admit readily of careful or solicitous interpretation of faith meanings on the part of their assured possessors to the sadly, if not willfully, misguided who had distorted God's truth by their perception of Jesus.

Many in the wake of subjugation reasoned that the evident power of the newcomers was proof of their truth, or they followed the example of earlier associates of Islam as the pattern developed. Some Christians read in Muslim success a judgment from God against them and so a summons to repentance and a worthier Christian allegiance. But others read it as evidence of divine approval of Islam and therefore a warrant for conversion to it. To see the hand of God in one's conquerors was a logic for identifying with them. The sharp antithesis between the true and the false, which characterized the Muslim worldview from the Qur'ān on, exacted a kind of doggedness from those who resisted its verdicts when it did not bring about a will to accede to them. Muslim marriage with captive Christian women was a factor in Christian attrition, since their offspring necessarily became Muslim and there was no option in the other direction. Monasticism, furthermore, is not well equipped to compete with a society approving plural marriage, with respect to population.

It would seem that zeal for the conversion of non-Muslims was most marked in the reign of 'Umar II (717–720), brief as his rule was. But dependable detail about the actual shape of Muslim "mission" in the sense of persuasion, teaching, and *da'wah* ("call to belief") is hard to ascertain. The themes of Muslim–Christian controversy among the erudite and articulate will come in chapter 4. It would be rash, however, to suppose that the sophistication, for example, of John of Damascus, was available to ordinary Christians or even to many of the clergy. Illiteracy, in any language, precluded conscious reckoning with Islamic dogmas, as competence in Arabic only slowly became available and not then to common folk. Quranic Arabic terms—and the reading of the Qur'ān—were prohibited from Christian usage by the instinct to preserve their sanctity and to keep the faiths apart in their familiar forms of word and worship.

VI

Given the steady interpenetration and the economic factors in the acquisition of booty and land which had sustained the armies, it was inevitable that the language they cherished should share their dominance in due time. The process of the popularization of Arabic paralleled, at a slower tempo, many of the tensions present in the enlargement of Islam from its Arab pre-possessions. The Shahādah, with its juncture of "God" "the One" and Muḥammad "the messenger of God," made Arabic, as the revelatory language of both, instinctively inviolate and supposedly self-sufficient, free of admixture from outside. Yet the actuality of conquest followed by the necessity of administration brought the sacred language into common currency for purposes of state and society within the first several decades of the Umayyad period. The arabicization of learning came only in the first century of the 'Abbāsids after A.D. 750 by means of the great translators of the caliphs of Baghdad.

In the course of its adoption, Arabic absorbed both vocabulary and usages from Syriac, Aramaic, and Greek. It had to suffer being written in Greek script, as in the earliest Christian Arabic texts in that form by the eighth century. A Judeo-Arabic writing dates from the ninth century. The process was more rapid where adopting languages possessed comparable grammars and word forms. Terms were taken from them into Arabic initially and most readily by officialdom and administrators, more slowly by poets and scholars, slowest of all by theologians. Borrowing was most feasible where it did not tangle with the dogma that the entire vocabulary of the Qur'ān was native Arabic. That dogma was sustained despite the clear incidence of non-Arabic terminology in the Muslim scripture, an incidence resulting from the several factors attending on Islam's genesis.[13] But it contributed to a will for its immunization intellectually and a reluctance practically to accede to interlinguistic usages.

These, however, proceeded apace. There were numerous borrowings into Arabic from the prosaic realms of coinage and weights and measures.[14] *Qaysariyyah* meant the town center, and *dinār* stemmed from *denarius* among the marketeers who traded in *riṭl* (*litra*) and *qanṭār* (*kantari*). Greeks, Syrians, and Copts, consorting in various capacities with "native" Arabs, negotiated language equivalence with them in the spheres of their contact. Their proficiency in doing so was a condition of their recruitment. It was they who often presided over necessary artifacts of society or government, such as the near monopoly Copts enjoyed in the manufacture of papyrus or the skills of iconography when Muslims sought to embellish at least their domestic palaces with painting and imagery, as in the celebrated Umayyad halls in the Jericho region. Language usage followed the practitioners. Poetry, similarly, felt the impetus of the Arab love of it. Nabatean rhymers sought to impress their mentors in the Arabic idiom, while Arab ones learned Nabatean to match their skills with those "to the manner born"–for example, Al-Tirimmah, who died in 723. Loanwords moved in both directions and were adopted into currency. In many cases, the writers and officials were using the language of their Christian mothers. Intermarriage has always been a chief abettor of interculture–if it has not been prohibited as a principal menace. Islam prohibited it to Muslim women and Christian men, and Arabic was the beneficiary.

The great age of the translation of the Greek classics via Syriac had necessarily to wait until a degree of arabicization had taken place at lower levels. When it came, it paved the way for a wider hospitality of mind by which *Dār al-Islām* braced itself to reckon with the heritage its origins had largely ignored. That process assisted the theological encounter we reach in chapter 4, opening into obligations of mind that quickened spiritual relationships between Muslims and Christians, even though their vocabularies–in doctrinal fields and certainly in their liturgies–remained studiously apart.

VII

The story of the arabicization of the Greek inheritance is a fascinating study. How was Islamic assurance of self-sufficient finality to accommodate Socrates and Plato? Was their quality to be comprehended within the uncouthness of *Al-Jāhiliyyah,* the abysmal "ignorance" outside Islam? Could apartness be sustained either in practice or in dogma? Had not Plato, in any event, journeyed to Egypt in quest of Pythagoras? Was not Alexander himself a hero in the Qur'ān, where the Seven Sleepers of Ephesus also had honorable mention?[15] Perhaps the sharp religious authority of Islam, in trust with the ultimate revelation housed in the inimitable Arabic,[16] could coexist with the accumulated wisdom of the seers and philosophers of the Mediterranean sphere into which the heirs of Mecca had so vigorously penetrated. It was, indeed, not a question of "perhaps": the destiny was ineluctable. While it posed problems for the psyche, there were those who, at least in retrospect, could claim that there had been no problem at all but only a due fulfillment of Islam's own inner logic.

Yet, however retrospect might theorize, the process demanded circumspection and negotiation with the loyalties within. For that reason so much of the work of Christian translators on whom Muslims had, perforce, to rely was done under the protection of official patronage. The 'Abbāsid caliph Al-Ma'mūn (reigned 813–833), a notable sponsor of translation, is said to have seen in a dream a benign figure, bald-headed and of handsome complexion, seated in a chair. The caliph found himself addressing Aristotle with a deference unusual in caliphs. It seems to have been a dream of consequence, for Al-Ma'mūn drew warrant from it to foster Greek translations and sent to Byzantium to secure permission to send his emissaries to locate manuscripts in libraries. Such overtures to Constantinople had been out of question, if not also of intention, in Umayyad days when intermittent warfare still persisted in Anatolia and reservations about non-Muslim culture were paramount.

The pattern of patronage had some initiation late in the seventh century but came into full vigor in the ninth, though the Christian auspices of the new learning in alchemy, medicine, astronomy, philosophy, and the rest were not always open knowledge. Muslim rulers, provincial and local, took the translators into employment to work painstakingly on a mediation of Greek learning into Islamic society. The motives were both practical and visionary. It is not clear how far controversies in dogma, both inside and outside Islam, required such education, either to counter "heresy" or to set issues in the wider arena of logic and philosophy. Misgivings about dallying with wisdom drawn from *dhimmīs* or pagans in antiquity might be countered by limiting concern to scientific and medical areas, where such considerations could be discounted. Or, more widely, the embarrassments could be overcome by the plea that pagans in antiquity could be forgiven their non-Islam, since they had sadly antedated Islam and were therefore not to blame and not to be repudiated with respect to their useful wisdom. Such logics, for the boldest, might be reinforced by the Qur'ān's own witness that there was no people to whom an apostle was not sent (Surah 16.36), so perhaps the philosophers and sophists were the "prophets" of the Greeks. For the staunchest, however, the puzzle–if not the scandal–remained as to why heirs of the Quranic revelation should occupy themselves with "the foolishness of the Greeks" and Romans. Yet they could be absolved in partnership with Syrian Christians on the ground that translations were on behalf of Islam, quickening its ability to affirm itself against non-Islam. Then *Dār al-Islām* was not betrayed but fulfilled.

How dependent Islamic interests were on Syriac-speaking Jews and Christians as mediators of Greek wisdom is evident from the fact that great figures, such as Al-Kindī (d. c. 870), Al-Fārābī (d. 950) and Al-Sijistānī (d. 985), knew neither Greek nor Syriac. In the main, the Christian Syriac translators knew only that language and the Arabic they had acquired, though some were competent in Greek also. It was appreciated that recourse should be had where possible to Greek originals behind the Syriac versions. Persian was a further source of material.

The translators, operating in what was a second language to them, faced formidable difficulties, Arabic being less amenable than their native Syriac to the Greek syntax. They were happiest in the disciplines of their own schools, as these had come to shape the Greek lore of antiquity into the stock-in-trade of Byzantine Hellenism. In that sense paraphrases of or commentaries on Plato, Aristotle, and others often did duty for the masters themselves. Among the greatest of the translators was Ḥunain al-Isḥāq of Ḥīrā (808–873), followed by his son, Isḥāq ibn Ḥunain (d. 910). The caliph Al-Ma'mūn gathered his sponsored scholars into his Baghdad Academy, where *Bait al-Ḥikmah* ("the House of Wisdom") became a brilliant center of scholarly enterprise and cultural exchange.

Symbolized in that working library of scribes, grammarians, and scientists, arabicization via *Dār al-Islām* proved a radical transformation within its "household of faith." Islamic faith and order underwent a profound hellenization thanks to Syriac/Greek mediation of what we might romantically call "Alexander's heritage."[17] It was a rich legacy *to* Islam,[18] and it deeply affected Arabic Christianity (as by parallel process it became such), tempering *dhimmī* status with the element of mutuality, if not of partnership. The degree of this varied with time and place. Not all caliphs had dreams of Aristotle, and the innate superiority of Islam's sense of identity remained in control. But traffic with the rationality of the Greeks, their care about the credentials of knowledge, their competence in philosophy despite the "paganism" of their religion, at least set for Qur'ān scholars the issue of reason and revelation and how divine disclosure in a sacred tongue through an unerring Prophet could belong with a fount of wisdom for which that same language waited by favor of tolerated, but still misguided, followers of another faith.

It has often been observed that, Al-Kindī apart, few of the most celebrated Islamic men of learning, in all the fields of geography, medicine, optics, chemistry, mathematics, and the rest, including polymaths like Ibn Sīnā (980–1037), were Arabs by race. It would be unwise to invoke ethnic factors in explanation. If the one race gave the language, others used it to enshrine an Islamic civilization that achieved what lay beyond the originating peninsula and beyond the range of Islam's original content in the Qur'ān. Aflāṭūn, as Plato came to be known in Arabic speech, suffered a metamorphosis in name (since Arabic lacked the *p* consonant). Islam, in the currency of its own arabicization of Near Asia and North Africa, found its essential self effectively reexpressed by what it gave and received in expansion. Three centuries of history gave a fulfillment to its genius as transforming as the three decades of its caliphal story had been to those it first conquered. One signal token of that transformation might be read in the career of the great Al-Bīrūnī (973–1048), a commanding intellectual leader. In his study of Indian society, he was able, as a Muslim, to appreciate and assess the "idolatry" of Hindu religion with a dispassion far from the stridency of the Qur'ān on the theme of "pagans," the Quraish, and others in Muḥammad's mission.[19]

Yet, remarkable as were the implications of such capacious objectivity in revising the Islamic temper, it can rightly be claimed that there were dimensions in the Qur'ān well able to warrant and sustain the scientific mind. That conviction does not turn on the kind of pseudo-scientism to which some twentieth-century apologists have been prone.[20] Nor does it depend on facile reconciliations between reason and revelation that do not take the measure of the issues entailed. It does stem from the reiterated appeal of the Qur'ān for reverent attentiveness to what it calls "the signs of God." This is the crucial "perhaps" of the divine appeal there to humankind. What happens in the phenomenal realm, in the day-to-day order of human experience is meant to be the field of careful, reflective, and vigilant attention on the human part. The immediate point is undoubtedly religious, the perception of events in the natural order as sacraments of the mercy of God, as intimations which the casual dismiss or ignore but which the attentive observe, note, and weigh with gratitude. But that religious posture is equally an index to the scientific temper, the instinct to register, analyze, assess, and interpret. The whole scientific edifice is erected on submission to nature, to phenomena that, in fact, become such only by virtue of such active human cognizance. The fact that, in the Qur'ān, the same signs which properly evoke the thanksgiving of the worshiper belong with the curiosity and "dominion" of the scientist is eloquent of the Qur'ān's relevance to all that arabicization meant in that intercourse of cultures over which *Dār al-Islām* via Arabic presided.[21] Those *āyāt,* or "signs," of the Prophet's preaching in the Qur'ān were warrant enough for finding in scientific pursuits the experience of the sacred. The empirical and the spiritual belonged together, with the sense of wonder permeating both. It cannot be claimed that Muslim–Christian controversy, awaiting us in chapter 4, readily perceived or transacted this community in their scriptures. Polemics have an instinct to ignore such unities.

One final feature of *Dār al-Islām* in the interplay of its arabicizing of domains and the hellenizing of its mind concerns its own internal problems of theology and faith. Rationality–busy in the several sciences, widening perspectives and alerting intelligence–could not be excluded from the issues of belief, unless deliberately so on the part of those who sensed it sufficiently to take fright and seek cover from it. That reaction, unhappily, occurred, but not without interesting ventures elsewhere in coping with the perplexities of Islamic dogma. These, though not often in a constructive or irenic way, became also the material of Christian interest. Indeed, they emerged into Muslim awareness, in part from Christian influence as well as from the stimulus of the sciences. They engaged what perhaps we may call the mental introspection of *Dār al-Islām.*

VIII

Despite the unrelieved dominance of Muslim over Christian in the political and social sphere, both faiths were subject in some measure to the interior history of the other. This could be both for puzzlement and evocative comparison. The sheer categories of dogma had to give way, at least in part, to the commonality of experience. One dimension of this was the fact of moral declension in the quality of Muslim life and rule. In the early eighth century the caliphate produced less than godly, or seemly, rulers and gave sorry evidence in its courts of behavior reprehensible by the pristine purities of Muḥammad and his immediate successors. The issue of the durability of the impetus of revelation began to emerge into Muslim ken and, with it, the deeper theme of the precariousness in this human world of truth itself as supposedly given in divine perpetuity for human conformity. Even if its dogmatic form in the inviolable document of the Qur'ān and the *Sharī'ah,* or sacred law, could be intact, what of its evidently hazardous fortunes in the active world of imperfect obedience or actual defiance?

It was in this way that the times of arabicization became involved in the issue of faith and works, of the equation—or nonequation—of the divine will and the human will and, with these, the ultimate problem of how divine ends belonged within human means. There was also the question of how time coincided with the eternal in the fabric of the Qur'ān itself as the final divine scripture nevertheless housed in the incidents and occasions of Muḥammad's person, place, and people in the seventh century.

The Muslim intellectual response to these questions belongs with chapter 4, where we encounter the valiant, if at times evasive, effort of the Muslim mind through two centuries to resolve them. Christians were not well placed, in temper or circumstance, to participate in these solutions. What is important here is that the implications were to a degree shared by both faiths. Arabicization in that sense constituted an experience of convergence even though both mood and dogma qualified its recognition as such. What are the verbal and the spiritual tests of identity? How are these related when they conflict? What are the maximal and minimal criteria of religion in life? Who decides? What if Islam discovers in its history those things for which it had originally charged the Quraish? What if Umayyads succumbed to those blandishments of power and prestige that emulated the Greeks? Was their very "conversion" problematic? How viable, indeed, was pure faith in the given world? That question, it might be said, was the more significant in that the Umayyads whose regimes provoked it were descended from those who, in the first years of Muḥammad as prophet, had been inveterate enemies of the new faith.[22] How were the right and proper continuities of that faith to be understood and ensured in the course of longer time and wider place?

Much of what is implicit here belongs with us still in the twentieth century, as chapter 12 must allow. How these issues were resolved by the *Khawārij,* or "puritan radicals," the *Murjites,* or "deferrers in good hope," and the *Qadarites,* or "will-disposers," must be postponed. Their involvement in a degree of interior responsibility for the interpretation and custody of Islam itself was the direct consequence of arabicization. In expanding territorially and in establishing its own language dominion, Islam engaged itself with implications of its own meaning that were quite unknown in its Arabian origins. In its account of the story of Joseph, the Qur'ān (Surah 12.21) has the comment that God is (literally) "mastering what He has in hand" (*ghālibun 'alā amrihi*), at the point where Joseph is drawn up from the well and sold into Egyptian servitude. God's always "prevailing in His purpose" was the confidence of Muslim intellects in the contrasted circumstances of their faith's prosperity. But what should such prevailing purposes mean and require of them when arabicization had possessed them of so wide a world? Some of the most acute controversies over the Qur'ān occurred at the court of the 'Abbāsid Al-Ma'mūn, the caliph who most vigorously patronized the Syriac translators.

That these internal issues for Muslims were sharply divisive between them and even productive of persecution of Muslims by Muslims served to cut across the ruling distinction between Muslim and Christian. In some quarters it induced the kind of retaliatory dogmatism that drowned its interrogatives in assertions. Such reactions only increased antagonism toward non-Muslims, but in other quarters interior questioning excited external relationships or at least blunted instinctive enmities. This is not to say that Christians were either minded or equipped for the kind of participation that might have recognized how comparable the stakes were. Controversy, for the most part, was too partisan, but as Arabic came to be a shared territory, even of partisan controversy itself, there was occasion for the bringing together—though in self-defense—of the concerns and contrasts that obtained between Christians and Muslims.

Arabicization was concurrent also with the emergence within Islam of the duality of its Sunnī and Shī'ah forms. That traumatic and abiding division related to the several issues just noted. It had to do with the very continuity of revelation within community, its safeguards and evidences. It also belonged with a quarrel about the content of experience as the early politics of Islam had presented it. It bore strongly on the theme of suffering and frustration and the mystery of providence. Esoteric patterns of Quranic interpretation were one way of responding to the pressures of rationality. The central doctrine of *Tawḥīd* itself—the "unity" of God as an affirmation ("God is One")—could be claimed to denote the unitive state of gnosis in which the otherness of the One to the individual "me" was overcome in undifferentiated reality. This was the goal of the ultimate forms of Islamic Sufism that belonged to later centuries. But the factors destined to eventuate it were implicit in the access of Islam to the wider world which arabicization ensured. The essayist Francis Bacon made play with the old adage of "Muḥammad going to the mountain" when, exceptionally, "the mountain would not come to Muḥammad."[23] There was that, it could be said, in arabicization by which the two comings were simultaneous.

These developments belong with the history of Islam. But they also belong squarely with the destiny of Arab Christianity. *Dār al-Islām* was powerfully reductionist in matters of status, power, prestige, and circumstance, but strongly challenging in its assimilation of learning, thought, art, and culture. In the experience both of attrition and attraction, what of Christian engagements with it in the first mutual centuries?

Notes

1. See S. P. Brock, "Syriac Views of Emergent Islam," in *Studies on the First Century of Islamic Society*, ed. G. H. A. Juynboll (Carbondale, Ill.: Southern Illinois University Press, 1982), pp. 9–21. Two empires had yielded in part to the Arab invasion. What, then, was the import of this new arrival in "empire"? The question was a natural one. John of Phenak in the 690s cites Zech. 3:2; Deut. 32:30; and Gen. 16:12 as proof texts of a "divine calling of the Arabs." It is noteworthy that Christians in the aftermath of conquest tended to write and speak of Muḥammad as "the first of Arab kings," rather than as "apostle of God." Clearly the political was paramount in their thinking, though Muḥammad is sometimes referred to as "a guide."

2. His ascetic simplicity was a marked feature of the first chronicles, though some of the anti-Umayyad description of the excesses of later caliphs and their "worldliness" have to be queried for the distortion of partisanship.

3. Olaf Graber, *Islamic Art and Byzantium* (Dumbarton Oaks, 1964), p. 88.

4. It is interesting to note that the Dome houses the earliest surviving and datable citations from the Qur'ān. See Solomon Dob Fritz Goitein, *Studies in Islamic History and Institutions* (Leiden: E. J. Brill, 1966), pp. 135–148 ("The Sanctity of Jerusalem and Palestine in Early Islam").

5. Trans. Rashid al-Irany (London, 1986), p. 143. Though a sentiment in a work of fiction, it echoes the ethos of Islam. Elsewhere the central character, a government servant, observes: "the State . . . God's temple on earth and our standing both in this world and the next is determined by the extent to which we exert ourselves for its sake." The Muslim centuries agree.

6. The issues attending the emergence of Islam from Arab identity persisted throughout the Umayyad century and beyond. The distinction of Arabs from non-Arabs was explicit in measures to prevent change of status. (It was a dissident group, the *Khawārij,* ardent "separatists" from Umayyad claims, who first championed an openness of Islam to all.) Abū Yūsuf (d. 798), in his *Kitāb al-Kharāj* (The Book of the Kharāj Tax), explains how the Christian Banū Taghlīb (trueborn Arabs) were treated by ʿUmar as non-Arabs and allowed to pay the poll tax, whereas Arabs proper had only the option of conversion to Islam or death. See the translation of this work by E. Fagnan (Paris, 1923), pp. 95–100. Strictly they, as "Arab," had no right to be *dhimmīs.*

7. New coinage, like the building of the Dome, was part of his need to be and seem imperial. The two coincided in date. He was emulating the Byzantines—and not only emulating. The great Ibn Khaldūn in the fourteenth century confirms this; see *Muqaddimah,* trans. Franz Rosenthal (New York: Pantheon Books, 1958), 2:55 (on coinage), 2:258f., 265 (on ʿAbd al-Malik's building of the *Ḥaram al-Sharīf* "as grandly as God wanted him to do it"). Ibn Khaldūn says much less than one might expect about the inspiration and achievement of this edifice.

8. Ibid., 2:22.

9. Three of the four eastern patriarchates—Antioch, Alexandria, and Jerusalem—were severed from the rest of Christendom. An Antiochian Christian in the eleventh century wrote that no certain succession of the patriarch (or pope) of Rome was known in his city after the death of Pope Agatho in A.D. 681. There was, however, intermittent contact with Constantinople despite continuing conflict between Byzantium and the Umayyads. See R. W. Southern, *Western Society and the Church in the Middle Ages* (New York: Penguin Books, 1970), p. 53.

10. Mālik Ibn Anas said, "When bells are sounded the anger of *Al-Raḥmān* is aroused. Whereupon angels descend to the four corners of the earth and sing: 'Say: "He is One,"' until the anger of the Lord is appeased" (*Sharḥ al-Sharūt al-ʿUmriyyah,* ed. S. Salih [Damascus, 1961], p. 61). The sound of the word *islām* had to be raised as the only true invocation "to throw into obscurity the call of the infidel. These He has humiliated and rendered loathsome."

11. See T. W. Arnold, *The Preaching of Islam* (Chicago: Kazi Publications, n.d.). This work, subtitled *A History of the Propagation of the Muslim Faith,* was a laudable effort to correct the distorted image of an Islam "spread by the sword." But by the same token it does not reckon adequately with the factors uncongenial to its case, and some of its reasoning is of the "must-have-been" category. See below.

12. There is the basic principle in Surah 4.85: "Whoever commits himself on behalf of what is good finds himself sharing in it." New converts were not to be deterred or regretted because their accession would diminish the share of earlier Muslims in Islam's benefits.

13. See A. Jeffery, *Foreign Vocabulary of the Qur'ān* (Baroda, 1938); see also Al-Jawālikī, *Al-Mu'arrab min al-Kalām al-'Ajamī* (Arabicized from Foreign Words) (Cairo, 1361 A.H.).

14. One listing gives around 190 words of Greek-Byzantine origin domesticated into Arabic from many fields. An intriguing puzzle surrounds the Arabic *qalam* ("pen"), so important in the Qur'ān, and the Greek *kalamos* ("pen"). If there is borrowing here, then in which direction?

15. Alexander figures as *Dhū al-Qarnain,* "the two-horned one" in Surah 18.83–102. The story of the Seven Sleepers of Ephesus is in Surah 18.9–26. Surah 30 is named for Luqmān, the wise man who teaches his son and is often identified with the Aesop of the fables whose lore is found in several ancient cultures.

16. The concept of the *I'jāz,* or "matchlessness" of the Qur'ān's language has long held sway in Islam, leading to the dogma of its "untranslatability." This in turn affects the Islamic view of other scriptures and the wisdom offered in non-Arabic sources. The term *'ajamī* ("foreign" or "Persian") (see n. 13 above) has something of the aura of the Greek *barbaros,* i.e., uncouth, barbarous, sounding like a monstrous *bar, bar, bar,* to Greek ears. Access to knowledge via translation into Arabic could be uncongenial, if not repugnant, to Arab minds.

17. But we need not approve the reputed verdict of the German orientalist Carl Becker: "Without Alexander no Muḥammad." The Greek factor in Islam belongs only to times after the conquests, in any sense with which *Dhū al-Qarnain* can be remotely credited.

18. Rather than "the Legacy *of* Islam" (Islam not being in demise), as in the title of two admirable presentations; see *The Legacy of Islam,* ed. T. W. Arnold and Alfred Guillaume (Oxford: Oxford University Press, 1931), and new edition, ed. C. E. Bosworth (Oxford: Oxford University Press, 1970).

19. See chapter 4, n. 24.

20. See, e.g., the repudiation of pseudo-scientific Qur'ān exegesis by Muḥammad Kāmil Ḥusain, *Mutanawwi'āt* (Cairo, 1960), 2:29–37.

21. See my *The Mind of the Qur'ān* (London: George Allen & Unwin, 1973), pp. 146–162.

22. The first Umayyad caliph, Mu'āwiyah was the son of Abū Safyān, who only acceded to Islam after Muḥammad's victory over Mecca and in year 2 after the *Hijrah* had emerged as the principal adversary among the leading Meccans. Though his son later distinguished himself in the Muslim campaigns in Palestine and Syria, anti-Umayyad sentiment could always recall these antecedents.

23. Francis Bacon, *Essays,* No. 12, "Of Boldness."

CHAPTER

4

Christian and Muslim in the Early Centuries

I

THE POLITICAL ISLAMICIZATION of eastern Christians reviewed in the preceding chapter, with the century-long arabicization of language and culture, set the context in which the two faiths encountered each other. *Dhimmī* status, as we have seen, required that the churches become private to themselves, subject to steady decrease in numbers, and confined to their own kind. In that status were several factors making either for a polemical or a ghetto frame of mind, inhibited from any lively will to communicate and interpret. The contractual basis of security under Islam disallowed more than internal survival. Churches, people, and communities were to be, at best, no more than they had always been. No new structures was less serious than no new recruits. The marks of a circumscribed entity worn on the person reached into the soul within. The future belonged only with Islam, as did the final revelation.

The legal and spiritual inferiorization, however, was only gradually effected. The Christian identity, whether Orthodox (Greek and Monophysite), Coptic, Nestorian, or other, had too long a history and too rooted a tenure of minds, to yield precipitately to the new situation. Those Christians who, like Copts in Egypt, had anticipated the Muslim arrival with some eagerness welcomed the yet untried. In the early decades of the conquest the sense of irreversible finality, familiar to historians, did not immediately obtain for contemporaries. Intermittent warfare continued in Anatolia and at sea before the Umayyad and Byzantine frontiers were gradually aligned. Even when they were, Muslim armies were still in expanding flow in east and west. Though decisively established by the crushing battles of the first decade, the new empire was still exploring its success. Administrative measures only slowly overtook the rapid changes ensuing on sudden conquest.

The whole process of absorption into Islamic sovereignty involved for Islam the new dimensions of thought that were noted in the conclusion of chapter 3. Christian factors, as we have seen, played a vital part in that process. Even in the early Umayyad court, Christian personnel had leading roles. Mu'āwiyah himself, the first Umayyad, had a Christian wife, Maysum, and a Christian court poet, Al-Akhtal. A Christian physician presided over his health. Under the 'Abbāsids and their translators and academicians, the interpenetration of arts, crafts, and sciences prospered with the march of arabicization. Conversion into Islam, or the necessary employment of Christian skills by Muslim rulers, ensured that the mutual insulation implicit in the *dhimmī* system was mitigated at least in learned circles. What all this meant religiously for the two faiths is the subject of this chapter—if what is religious can be isolated—as *Dār al-Islām* widened its mind and became aware of new liabilities in respect of faith and dogma.

In a paradoxical way, the very self-sufficiency of Islam, magisterial as it was by dint of Qur'ān and conquest, made for self-confidence in acquisition. Its vetoes were always present to censor but not to exclude its adaptations. To see how the situation affected Arab Christianity it is first necessary to take stock of what the two faiths brought to their meeting.

II

It is clear that Muslims had their frame of reference fully in place. If we accept the traditional view of the finalizing of the Qur'ān in the first quarter century,[1] its supreme court of appeal was in control of its stance, with the steadily growing complementary authority of Tradition deriving from Muḥammad by criteria of authenticity developing with it.

By warrant of these, Muslims were equipped to teach Christians what thoughts about God were thinkable and what were not. The Nicene Creed and its subsequent elaborations with their divisive obscurities were in the latter category, once that creed got beyond the unity of God and the fact of creation. The divinity acknowledged in Jesus by Christians—assuming they knew what they meant—was unthinkable. God had made His word a Book from heaven. Books were all that prophets had, and they were only means to guidance and direction. God was only in a legislative relation to humanity; there was no imparting of the divine into the tragedy of the human condition.

It is well to review this harsh Quranic commentary on the whole quality of Christian faith before coming, in some detail, to the spirit and content of Christian encounter with it in the early centuries. Though the Qur'ān did have some favorable observations on Christians,[2] it had only reproach for the core of Christian faith and for Christian factions, which, as it saw them, arose from Christian confusion. Though it always entitled Jesus *Al-Masīḥ* ("the Messiah"), it called his followers *Al-Naṣārā,* from the place-name Nazareth.[3] Islam had no place for Christology. It dispensed with what it thought the subtleties behind Christian sectarianism. It had only impatience for what exercised the Christian mind in the defining councils of the fourth and fifth centuries.

Surah 112 insisted against the Nicene Creed that God is "unbegotten, unbegetting."[4] There was only God *and* His messengers. Patience was lacking to recognize or undertake the implication in that "and"—namely, divine relatedness to the human world—or to see how the connectedness of divine purposes with humanity, pursued in prophethood, might have a deeper dimension in personhood, without thereby impugning the divine unity. Clearly, both for Christianity and Islam, the being of God had everything to do with the being, the creating, the guiding, and perhaps the redeeming of humanity.

God's "begetting"—if we allow the creedal word—of "His Christ" was simply—in Christian reading—the ultimate and necessary, form of God's outgoing into human relationship, because He is the God He is, just as prophethood was an outgoing into the same realm of time and rule. God "begets" that in which He is fulfilled, as the poet in poetry, the musician in music. The source is in the medium; the medium enshrines the source.

It was this divine action from within the divine nature that the creeds meant by the phrase concerning Jesus "of one substance with the Father." "Father" expressed just this outgoing self-expression, to which "the Son" was reciprocal, namely, the very quality of God. Divine action in the world means a human actuality. Islam, in its terms, believes it so also, in holding that prophets are "sent."[5] Where Christians came into debate was how to understand and rightly express this divine-human action and actuality. They recruited the word "nature" and wrote of divine and human "nature(s)" in "one person," Jesus-Christ-Lord. After long and stubborn debate, in which personalities, politics, and place loyalties entered, the Council of Chalcedon in 451 decided on the two natures, believing that only so could they fully affirm either. But the council hedged the decision with clauses that reserved from explicit question the answer they gave. Philosophy often gives back questions as answers, and Muslim theologians were soon to do the same.[6] Chalcedon said that the two natures belonged in Christ "without confusion, without change, without division, and without separation." These clauses responded to certain perceived dangers. They meant that the divine and the human in Jesus must be affirmed appropriately to either. They rejected any separation into two persons and anything merely apparent or periodic about the union. Distinction of natures within the unity of the person was meant to preserve divine transcendence while also confessing a genuine divine presence in history.

It would have been well if the meaning had been left there. The formula of Chalcedon was too sanguine about mystery and too assertive with language. But, for many, uniformity of teaching was important. The Monophysites, however, as their name implied, resented the council's imposition of its mind and seriously contended for one nature, the divine, as immunizing the reality of God. There was something akin to Islam here, albeit concerning "incarnation," which Islam abhorred. Monophysites, given patience and a sense of the limits of verbal formulation, might have been willing to accept the provisos in the Chalcedonian phrasing. But they had an instinct comparable to that of Islam, in wanting to reserve the divine from the limitations—even the contamination, if they saw them so—of things human.

In that desire they inevitably compromised the humanity of Jesus and therefore the reality of his person. Always present in the Monophysite formula of "one nature—the divine"—was the docetic implication of an unreality, a mere "seeming," about Jesus as human, which would entail a strange division in the events of the Gospel, the divine and the human alternating in line with their content. Was Jesus' divinity in abeyance during the temptations? When he was journey-weary, would that be human? When he multiplied the loaves, was that divine? Or did Jesus, as the divine Logos, let human experience prevail over him in some artificial way, while the divine was quiescent? Was the ignorance implied in questioning the disciples only a pretense, the divine being omniscient? In such ways the narratives of the Gospels could be allocated to the one or the other aspect, making either way for a sort of charade. What could be the point of a Logos deliberately in abeyance while things thought incompatible with it ensued? Most of all, when the story reached the crucifixion, was it mandatory to assign that unthinkable dimension of suffering and shame away from the divine, so that if Jesus was divine it could only have been an "apparent" and not a real event?

Oddly, the Qur'ān itself was involved in this theme. Surah 4.158 affirmed that the crucifixion only "seemed so" to the crucifiers. The real Jesus was "not there." The Quranic motive here was to save true prophethood (in Jesus) from ignominy, since such a fate could not be allowed of divine messengers without impugning the rescuing power of the God who sent them.[7]

Monophysites were ready to risk this artificiality in the humanity of Jesus in the interests, as they saw it, of safeguarding the dignity of the divine. But this very fact disqualified them from commending the faith of the Incarnation intelligibly to Muslims when the conquest brought them together. To be sure, the complexities of Chalcedon were not conducive to ready comprehension by adherents of a faith so bound over as Islam was to assertive simplicity about God and transcendence. By its implicit Docetism (or the threat of it), Monophysite Christianity in Egypt and elsewhere seemed to admit the Quranic premise that somehow a human dimension was derogatory to the divine.

It would have been happier if the issue between Muslims and Christians about God and Jesus could have been moved away from the terminology central to Chalcedonian/Monophysite discussion and into the theme of self-giving, away from a theology of "substance" and "being" to a Christology of "action" and "grace." The theme of *kenōsis,* or self-expending (Phil. 2:1–11), found the reality of the divine in the event of the human without the sort of reservation derived from the un-Christian notion that to be transcendent is to be immune, that God is only properly thought to reign by being exempt in majesty, that the divine is inherently self-retaining, self-absorbed. If we change the category to "love," we at once realize that love is self-giving and, being self-given, is not thereby compromised or demeaned. On the contrary, it is fulfilled and justified. On that score, it would be right to think of love's self-spending or *kenōsis* as complete, not partial, in no way just "apparent" but total and entire, a self-giving in which the divine was fully present, thoroughly authentic, and yet, being so given, fully human—humanity being the context of its action. This is what the Christian faith meant by "the Father sent the Son," and by confessing "One, only begotten. . . ."

There is, therefore, no point or truth in allocating this or that in the Gospels to one or the other nature, nor reason to exclude either nature from an uncompromised and actual participation with the other. But, as heard by Muslims, the formulas of Christology neither presented a truly human Jesus nor effectively interpreted the divine one. Muslims were thereby debarred from glimpsing the central theme within the Christian doctrine of "God in Christ," namely, that a love which comes is the clue to the sovereignty which reigns. The Incarnation and within it the event of the crucifixion, the two poles of Christian faith and the two constraints of Christian worship, could not be intelligibly told to Muslims within the Christian formularies.

III

Would it be fair to think, as hinted in chapter 1, that this situation arose from the long disservice of the Greek mind to the eastern Christians? If Islam is any clue to the ways of the Arab mind—forthright, emotional, rhetorical, rather than analytical–then faith in the incarnate Christ might have been more congenially set forth had the Aramean and Arab world been in prior trust with the story by their own lights rather than those to which the Greek legacy came to bind them.

Arab Islam, by the very nature of its Arabian genesis, had an absolute concept of transcendence such as Christianity also demanded. Christianity was alike insistent on the unity of God against all idolatry. Prophethood too was a shared theme, which necessarily involves the relevance of personality and biography in its discharge. The message of prophets is translated also into the quality of their living and their reacting within the setting of their message and its world. Such living becomes in some measure an incarnation of its content. This might have offered a clue to what is central in the Gospels and vital for an Islamic Christology. For both Qur'ān and Tradition in Islam were replete with prophetic biography, God via the human.

However, the Qur'ān was silent about those Hebrew prophets–Hosea, Isaiah, and Jeremiah–in whom this interinvolvement of the divine word with the human travail reached into deep pathos and tragedy. Moreover, Islamic monotheism was more an urgent repudiation of polytheism than a reckoning with the evil of which monotheism itself is capable, and with "the sin of the world." Or it confined divine reckoning with sin to exhortation against it or retribution for it. It did not dwell in those areas of mind and spirit that constrained the Christian sense of God in Christ and of the divine Word, present and vulnerable within the human situation and there vindicated as love. Thus divine lordship remained virtually sealed against the Christian perceptions that Christology enshrined, the more so because, to Muslims, those perceptions seemed controversial among Christians themselves. This was only the penalty of their being misguided in the first place.

In this light it is no surprise when we come to the exchanges of Muslim with Christian in these centuries, to find a predictable estrangement within joined controversy. Where there are rival finalities of belief and dogma based on different scriptures, two responses are liable to emerge when philosophy comes into the reckoning. Either philosophy is given its head and–in a setting of required conformity–accommodates beliefs and lets issues rest, or dogmatists recruit and enlist reason in their own defense. In an encounter where scriptural revelation(s) are understood as final, reason affords no accepted tribunal by which to judge between them or to bring them into mutual negotiation. It is arbitrarily employed to corroborate what continues to be at odds. In default of a common engagement with reason, the sanctities of given belief separately invoke its warrant and sustain themselves, fortified by communal loyalty. The result is that the rival beliefs relate at best in mutual incomprehension, at worst in polemic.

This situation was borne out by the Christian habit of considering Islam a Christian heresy. The reciprocating habit of Muslims was to see Christianity as a heretical distortion corrected by Islam. The reeducating of heretics rarely serves a genuine perception of them.

IV

An early and celebrated pioneer of this pattern was John of Damascus (c. 660–749). A Greek-speaking Orthodox Arab Christian, he spent most of his life as an official in the Umayyad administration before withdrawing to the monastery of Mār Sābā in the Judean wilderness about the year 724, where his major works were written. His grandfather, Manṣūr ibn Sargūn, had formally surrendered Damascus to the Muslim general Khālid ibn Walīd in 635. The grandson John was in friendly relation as a youth with the caliph, Al-Yazīd, who succeeded Mu'āwiyah in 680. Thus he was well equipped to know Islam, and it becomes clear that his knowledge of the Qur'ān was discerning. Like so many of his successors he was minded to read it from the angle of controversy. But, located as he was in territory sundered from Byzantium at a time when active hostilities persisted, his rapport with Muslims is impressive. Detractors in Constantinople called him *sarrakenphron,* or "Saracen-minded."[8] But if he was "inclined to Islam" (as that word has been rendered) it was in somewhat combative terms, though his aim primarily was to alert and inform the Christian community. His main exposé of Islam comes as chapter 101 of his *De Haeresibus* in the third part of his *Fount of Knowledge.*[9] The discussion takes the form of a dialogue in which the responses of "the Muslim" are under the control of a Christian-based catechesis, echoing debates that had taken place, as tradition has it, in the caliph's presence.

Given the scriptural premises—Christian and Quranic—involved, appeal to Holy Writ predominates. The "sonship" of Christ is argued from prophecy. Alleged lack of prophecies about Muḥammad in the Bible is stressed as detrimental to Quranic claims. "The deceptive superstition of the Ishmaelites" (the opening phrase in *De Haeresibus,* ch. 101) strikes a note that becomes habitual later—the association of Islam with Ishmael, the son of Abraham debarred from the true line. Islam is dubbed "forerunner of the Antichrist," a term denoting a denier of Jesus' divinity.[10] John of Damascus conceded that Muḥammad had retrieved the Arab heirs of Ishmael from their idolatry in the time of the Quraish. Muḥammad was nevertheless a false prophet, forming his heresy from ill-assorted contact with Christians and Arians.

John's animus against Islam was tempered, however, by a sense of admiration for the Quranic emphasis on divine unity. He cites Surah 112, where he seems to appreciate that the denial of divine "begetting" and "being begotten" does not, properly understood, dispute the Christian doctrine of the Trinity, where "begetting" is not about paternity. He saw the kinship of the faiths also in the doctrine of creation, and correctly described the Quranic view of Jesus as repudiating sonship. But he queried Muḥammad's prophethood on the ground that it was "unwitnessed," either by contemporaries or previous scriptures. The appeal to Muḥammad's lack of any foretelling became a stock-in-trade of later Christian polemic. Equally standard were the Muslim reactions after John's time of discovering prophecies of Muḥammad and Islam by ingenious quarrying in biblical texts.[11] This feature exemplifies the capacity of all such apologetic to clutter itself with aggravating issues at the expense of what is authentically at stake. John came nearer to this in wondering whether Muslims, in accusing Christians of *Shirk*, or "associationism,"[12] in their doctrine of Christ, did not involve themselves in a reductionism of God in disallowing the unity of God and His Word and His Spirit.[13] For he saw that the unity of God may be denied as much by what is excluded from it as by what is unwarrantably included within it. Here John was close to a dilemma concerning the ontology of the Qur'ān itself, that is, its participation, as "God's speech," in the Godness of God. His perception at this point was remarkable, given the sharp epithets he had applied to Islam in general.

John countered Muslim criticism of Christians for the veneration of the cross with queries about Muslim veneration of the *ka'bah* at Mecca and the black stone in its wall. Behind this was the larger question of the actuality of the crucifixion. There was also crude discussion of how the divine in Jesus could be involved in human functions such as digestion, indicative of how remote from Muslim comprehension the meaning of the Incarnation was and how much Christians contributed to that remoteness. Chapter 101 of *De Haeresibus* concludes with sharp reproach or accusation of Muslim morality and the practice of concubinage and frequent divorce.

Another work of John of Damascus is the *Disputatio Saraceni et Christiani.*[14] It is in the form of a verbal debate in which many of the points already reviewed are repeated. In discussing divine decree and human responsibility it adumbrates the issues that developed within Islam between *Qadarites* and absolute predestinarians. It also reverts to the theme of the unity of God and the status of "the divine Word," whether understood as the Christ or the Book. Here one can detect in the Muslim party the rudiments of the inner controversy over the Qur'ān—whether eternal and uncreated or created. The *Disputatio* with *De Haeresibus* witnesses to the acumen of the author, to his awareness of Quranic themes and accents, and to the realization, at least in such erudite circles, of how intertwined were the theological problems of the two faiths. Yet that fact did not prevent an asperity of tone in John's presentation of Islam for his Christian constituency and his shaping of an intellectual disputation. But then Christians habitually addressed their own "heretics" in roundly hostile terms. We must conclude that something of the tradition familiar to John concerning Nestorians or Monophysites passed over to Ishmaelites and Hagarenes.[15] Islam in his day was a recent arrival and therefore liable to be fitted, however uneasily, into a known framework. It would be unwise to assume that his competence with the Qur'ān and his eye for what we might call "unifying controversy" was widely shared by his community at large.

V

Just before John of Damascus's withdrawal to write in Mār Sābā with the accumulated thoughts of his active career under the Umayyads, there reportedly occurred a correspondence between Caliph ʿUmar II, who reigned from 717 to 720, and Leo III in Constantinople, whose reign lasted from 717 to 741. It was Caliph ʿUmar who chided one of his officers, when he complained about the cost to the exchequer because conversions to Islam reduced the number of *dhimmīs* paying *jizyah,* with the rebuke that Muḥammad came as a prophet, not as a tax gatherer. The letters between caliph and emperor seem to have sprung from the former's zeal for his faith but may also have coincided with diplomatic contacts.

Leo, who came from Maʿrash in northern Syria, knew Arabic as well as Greek. ʿUmar asked why the emperor's "so imaginative religion" claimed to know more about Jesus than Jesus himself,[16] why he disregarded Jesus' foretelling of Muḥammad,[17] why he posited "three gods," and why his faith was fragmented into seventy-two sects. How, in incarnation, could "God be in the entrails of a woman"? ʿUmar accused Christians of corrupting their scriptures—a charge recurrent throughout the centuries. Leo's responses were at times truculent. He showed little of the alertness evident in John of Damascus. He told the caliph: "It is truly difficult to refute even the most palpable lie when the adversary dreams only of persisting in it."[18] He would not demean himself by exposing Christian doctrine to such heretics, whom he took to task both for citing Christian scriptures and for alleging them corrupt. He explained that Jesus, as God, had no need of prayer but nevertheless prayed to teach his followers how to pray. As for the enwombing of the divine, does it not "befit the everliving to have a living temple"? Do not the mechanics of pregnancy belong with God's creation and what happens in the bowels serve for the conservation of life?[19] As for the Holy Trinity, there are three "persons" in the divine unity just as there are rays of the one sun. These exchanges were typical of much that was to come.

Theodore Abū Qurrā (750–825), a Syrian who was Orthodox bishop of Harran and widely traveled in the East from Edessa to Egypt, was a disciple of John of Damascus and reproduced some of his arguments but with more asperity, in homilies and papers in Syriac and Arabic. He wrote—it would seem for prudential reasons—in Greek when expressing opinions derogatory to Islam and Muḥammad concerning both moral and revelatory issues. True prophethood, he insisted, is marked by clear prediction of it, by miracle, and by moral excellence—all of which Muḥammad lacked. On every count, and by assured logic and doctrinal consistency, the Christian faith is true, final, and authentic. Abū Qurrā enlisted reason to confirm what (biblical) revelation alone discloses. He invoked it to play the opposite role with respect to Islam. His work served to arabicize Christian theology and so to stimulate theological awareness among Muslims at a time when the great age of the translators was beginning. Even so, it was his view that Muḥammad was "demon-possessed."[20]

The curious fascination, in Muslim questioning of Christians such as John and Abū Qurrā, over the physical aspects of incarnation continued through many centuries. Thus we find in Al-Jāḥiẓ (776–869) perplexity as to how "learned people say that a man . . . who ate, drank, urinated, excreted, suffered hunger and thirst, dressed and undressed . . . and who later, as they assume, was crucified and killed, is Lord and Creator and providential God eternal. . . ."[21] Was this the concreteness of the Arab mind pitting itself against the universals of Greek thinking and insisting on particulars in its reading of "and was made man"? Which party in that confrontation was reading theism more wisely?

VI

A significant conflict within Arab and Greek Christianity in the eighth and ninth centuries was the iconoclastic controversy. The attempt of the emperor Leo III (717–741) and his successor, Constantine V (Copronymos) (741–775), to suppress the veneration and use of icons stemmed in part from the impact of Islam on Christian thought.

Though the emperors had popular support, the initiative to ban the use of images was an imperial urge. The caliph Yazīd II (720–724) sharply attacked the Christian practice of image veneration, and this may have inspired Leo. In general, Islam had left Christians to their own devices in this regard, seeing it as just another aspect of their waywardness, though the symbol of the cross was detested and often prohibited at least in public. Aside from the Islamic factor, there were the age-old prohibitions of

Exodus 20:4–5 against "graven images" and the precedent of earlier Christianity in avoiding pictorial representation and using only symbols. Whatever the several motives, Leo's Edict of 726 and the decision of the Council of 754 forbade the making and veneration of images and set them under ban. The council, however, at which there were no delegates from Muslim-controlled areas, banned the looting and burning in which some ardent iconoclasts had engaged.

The imperial policy was, of course, confined to its own regions, but it aroused intense controversy on both sides of the frontier with Islam. John of Damascus, despite his being dubbed "Saracen-minded," joined in it strenuously. The argument raised deep issues in which Islam itself was involved. Its love of Quranic calligraphy, which it sought from time to time to impose on Christian churches,[22] recruited eye to art in the interests of the faith. Icons did the same. The anti-iconoclasts in all churches insisted that icons were a teaching method for the illiterate. Did not touching icons or relics—did not kissing sacred objects—bring their prototypes or saints into the intimate ken of the faithful as a means of grace? Were not even imperial portraits a symbol of sovereignty and loyalty?

Practical arguments apart, the issue deepened into the whole meaning of Christology and the spiritual significance of matter. If the Word could be made flesh, with all the physicality involved, might not precious things, gold, silver, and the skill of artists, enshrine meaning? In an intriguing way the debate cut across both Chalcedonian and Monophysite positions in Christology. Iconophiles in either allegiance could argue that it was illogical to believe in the Incarnation and forbid imagery. A theology of the two natures, as with John of Damascus, could claim that icons looked back to the veritable humanity of Jesus "in the memory of His flesh," where "God had become visible for us by participation in flesh and blood."[23] Thus icons were not "image-ing" the invisible God. Germanus, patriarch in the time of Leo, insisted likewise that iconography served to exalt the humility of God the Word. Iconoclasts, however, were closer to the Monophysites in distinguishing the human—in the "one-nature" doctrine—from the reality of the divine and so disfavoring imagery. If icons had any significance, did they not "confuse the two natures"? The reservations of Monophysites about Christology in its Chalcedonian form could be extended to all use of the pictorial, as circumscribing what was uncircumscribable. Yet Chalcedon also had claimed not to be "confusing the natures." Passionate and concrete as the issue over icons was, it could not escape the subtler questions of worship, art, and theology, which had beset the christological themes.

There were periods of persecution against iconophiles under Constantine V, but later the controversy died down. What had been an expression of caesaropapism was, correspondingly, reversed under Constantine VI and his mother, Irene. A council at Nicea in 787 restored the veneration of images. Though there was a brief resurgence of iconoclasm in the ninth century, the peak of the controversy had passed. The distinction that emerged from the encounter, namely, between "worship" and "veneration," had a healing quality, though it seems rarely to have been appreciated within Islam.[24] John of Damascus, for example, had insisted that "image" and "prototype" were quite distinct. Worship was to God alone; devotion was addressed to Him alone. The same action concerning the icon or the saint was "veneration"; it was "adoration" when addressed to God. This helped to dispose of the argument, favored by Muslims, that the use of icons was a pagan proceeding. Christians had resorted to it historically only when their monotheism had brought paganism to an end.[25] Matter had an essential sanctity, which the sacramental principle acknowledged. The iconostasis screening the sanctuary in worship expressed to the "exterior" the meaning of the "interior." A refusal to concede the distinction between image and prototype–to which a consistent iconoclasm would lead–could hardly be held permanently compatible with doctrines of creation and Incarnation. In that sense Monophysites and Nestorians alike, in their own cultural idiom, were true "venerators." Properly disciplined, there was no reason why, as some iconoclasts alleged, iconography should displace or compromise the Eucharist as the true "image-ing" of Christ, nor jeopardize the inner, ethical "image" of the Lord in the life of the believer.

As a searching theme within Arab Christianity the iconoclastic controversy troubled the waters of all the churches, but inasmuch as its official measures of edict, councils, and revocation were within Byzantium, it is conjectural how far it affected Muslim observers or critics within *Dār al-Islām.* Subtle and elusive as some of the arguments undoubtedly seemed to those in Islam who took any cognizance of them, they nevertheless related to long-standing themes neither religion could elude. Inscribed medallions in mosques and calligraphy, handmaid at once of faith and of the arts, required the same distinction between the visual as servant and the cult of the visual. To disavow the Christian conviction about incarnation was not to escape the hallowing of matter, shape, and color, in the expression of the soul. But was the underlying paradox of the issue within iconoclasm ever joined in those terms in those times?

VII

There were other paradoxes for Muslims and Christians from the ninth century on in the sharp contrasts of their theologies. It would be wrong to attribute the internal ferment in Muslim thought about dogma solely to the Christian factor, for the questions were implicit in the nature of belief itself. But it would be false to assume that Christianity did not stimulate them. One paradox had to do with the mutual bearings of the divine and the human will in the incidence of events. Given the confident ultimacy of a victorious Islam, the worst attitude was unbelief, evil Muslims denying their Islam. There were political grounds for some of the compromises among the Umayyads in their century, but these went beyond the charges of the Shīʿah about usurpation or of the *Khawārij* about false pretenses to govern. In the eyes of the purists, there were moral crimes of un-Islamic living and hypocritical faith. Since the will of God was identified with a true Islam, how could it be that perverse human wills frustrated it, seeing that ignorance was no longer their condition? Could human will override, impede, and defy the will of God? It was inconceivable that God could be indifferent to unbelief, having sent the final revelation and charged humanity to "obey God and obey the apostle." Why then did unbelief occur? Did Islam have to concede something like the Christian answers here, namely, a certain divine vulnerability to humanity and a more long-suffering patience over human obduracy?

There were those who sought to defer the problem, rather than entertain notions so uncongenial. These were the *Murjites* ("deferrers in hope"), as opposed to those who turned to a sharp predestinarian stance. Why need the issue be adjudged in the immediate present? Behind judgment there lurked a more sinister problem. If the adequacy of Muslim belief and performance was to be assessed and, indeed, measured (as criticism implied), then who was to do the measuring? Who was competent to adjudicate on the Islam of others? Would not the self-appointed set up a tyranny of the only right, the only pure? What, then, of the peace and sanity of Islam? There was wisdom in leaving it to God. Doing so need not mean that compromise was never brought to book or moral apostasy left to its devices.

Practicalities apart, the problem rankled. Minds could not rest. Reason demanded solution. God's implacable sovereignty must be affirmed. Life was a forwarding of deeds to the last judgment: there could hardly be easy tolerance about them now.

There emerged with the famous Abū-l-Ḥasan al-Ashʿarī (873–935) a subtle solution: "God willed . . . in the will of the doer." This seemed to reconcile divine will and human responsibility. God remained the sovereign arbiter of all events, but the human doers remained responsible and culpable. Those who might be tempted to ask whether the doer could help doing what God willed or how the divine willing related to the conscious processes of reason and desire were advised that these were tedious and inappropriate questions, not to be pursued. Abū Ḥamīd al-Ghazālī (1054–1111) did develop a very careful and discerning psychology of temptation.[26] In general, however, Islam remained loyal to the absolute transcendence explicit in its origins and was generally inhospitable to those different dimensions of the divine-human relationship central to Christian theology, because of the Incarnation and the cross. There is no doubt that the pressure of the problem, if not the genius of the reply, belonged with Christian influence.

Faith and works, belief and unbelief, divine purpose and human freedom–these were not the only perplexities with common quality and divergent resolution in the two faiths. Islam by the ninth century had become alert to an issue that had been implicit from the beginning and in many ways was closely akin to Christian thought. It related to the Qur'ān and the fusion there of the eternal and the temporal. Articulate Muslims came to realize that they were involved, via the Qur'ān, in something of the same concern that Christians had in their Christology. To dismiss the latter out of hand was not to escape the paradox at its heart.

Revelation, whether in the *person* of Christ or the *text* of the Qur'ān, is an engagement of the eternal with the temporal. The Qur'ān, for Muslims, was "the very speech of God"–a conviction explicit in the doctrine of the *I'jāz,* or "matchlessness," of its Arabic and the total illiteracy of its instrument, Muḥammad. The Book in time, on earth, was one with the Book preserved eternally in heaven. As such, it must be "uncreated," as the term went. The speech of God could not have been acquired at any point by God, since had it been, He would earlier have, unthinkably, lacked it. One could only avoid that error by believing the Qur'ān to be as eternal as God Himself.

Yet manifestly the Qur'ān came to be in the seventh century within the *Sīrah,* or "course of life," of Muḥammad. It had wide relevance for immediate events, which, indeed, it incorporated into its appeal and its sequences.[27] In what way, then, could the exchanges with the Quraish, the battles, the household incidents, the commentary on people, be eternally existing? Did not exegesis itself turn on "the occasions of revelation" (*asbāb al-nuzūl*), seeing incidents as necessary clues to meaning?[28] Must the Qur'ān not be "created" as some Mu'tazilites insisted? Under the caliph Al-Mutawakkil, they enforced that belief by persecuting those who believed to the contrary.

It is evident that Islam was incurring concerning the Book of God issues Christians confronted concerning the Son of God, though with the vital difference involved in that contrast. Though Christian thinking, latent through conversion or contact in the Islamic milieu, contributed to awareness of the dilemma, there is little evidence that the similarity illuminated the polemic between them. As with the solution of Al-Ash'arī over divine and human willing, so here. The problem was contained, not explained, in the answer. The dogma of the Qur'ān's uncreatedness prevailed and was held to be resolved in the concept of *Tanzīl* itself. In the "sending down" of the Book, in *Tanzīl,* what remained eternal in origin was found to comprise events in the temporal. How it could be so was locked within the mystery itself. Arabic proved to be the divine language, the given counterpart of the heavenly words. What transpired in Mecca and Medina within the *Sīrah* was the making temporal of the eternal. Much sharp polemic might have been precluded if it had been realized that in disowning Christology, Muslims had in no way eluded its implications. Rather they had incurred them in their scripture. They would have been wiser had they perceived the common situation and applied themselves to the contrast in Book and Person.

VIII

A different sphere of Islamic development in which Christian factors played an undoubted part was the rise of Islamic mysticism or Sufism. There were certainly sources inherent in the example of Muḥammad, the Quranic concepts of *iṭmi'nān* ("tranquillity") and *dhikr* ("mindfulness"),[29] and ideas of esoteric knowledge to inspire a Muslim mysticism. Yet Christian precedents are also evident. When the issue earlier considered in the predestinarian debate emerged in the eighth century, there was a third reaction to "delinquent" Islam beyond that of political repudiation of the ruler's right to allegiance and beyond the hopeful acquiescence of the *Murjites.* It was expressed in an unworldliness and a piety that disowned renegades by ascetic "imitation" of the Prophet while remaining politically quiescent. As Sufism it certainly had its initial impulses in the will to *zuhd,* or abstention, by an inner Islamic *Jihād* against the self as acquisitive and restless.

One of the clearest examples of the Christian element present in Sufism, before the mystics acquired the highly subtle theosophy exemplified by Ibn 'Arabī (1165–1240), was Ḥārith al-Muḥāsibī (781–857). Self-examination (*al-muḥāsibah*)[30] was central to his teaching, and his writings cite many quotations from the Gospels, notably their warnings against prayer, fasting, and almsgiving paraded for the praise of spectators. He knew the parable of the wheat and the tares and the parable of the sower and offered his guidance in the mastery of temptation and the discipline of the self. He spent his years between Basrah and Baghdad in one of the richest areas of Christian tradition and drew on the distinction between *'aql,* or "reason," and *ma'rifah,* or "soul-knowledge," familiar in Christian spirituality, where love, pursued in contemplation, rather than abstract intellection, was the crux of theology. While the controversialists around him were busy with the uncreated or created Qur'ān, Al-Muḥāsibī was preoccupied with the inner "heresy" of the lustful soul. The patterns of ascetic Sufism that he inculcated and exemplified are a significant pointer to the interplay of Muslim and Christian in the early centuries.[31]

Al-Muḥāsibī may properly be seen as a precursor of Al-Ghazālī (1058–1111), a monumental figure in medieval Islam in whom a profound psychology of religion was achieved from within a biography of high intellectualism and mystical conversion. The eminence and long repute of Al-Ghazālī served to sustain a reconciliation of theology with spirituality by rescuing the former from an arid scholasticism and intellectual doubt and endowing the latter with an authentic expression in system and discipline. In Al-Ghazālī we return to controversy with Christianity, but in a form consonant with the range and quality of his experience. This did not exempt him from the minutiae of debate nor save him from asperities and prejudice. But it did confer an authority in the field that makes him properly the focus of interest in the concerns of this chapter.

His works are numerous, and some are attributed in whole or in part to disciples and interpreters. *Al-Rudd al-Jamīl* (Admirable Rebuttal), the main work against Christianity, may be included in this category. It has been regarded by some as emanating from encounters with Christians in Alexandria during Al-Ghazālī's wanderings in search of religious truth.[32] It demonstrates a capacity for abstruse argument and a confident bent in theology, as well as a ready textual familiarity with the Gospels and Epistles of the New Testament. Unlike other controversialists, it draws on these as valid Christian documents against which it does not range the familiar charge of *taḥrīf*, or "corruption."

Discussion, however, is partially distorted by a habit for which Al-Ghazālī can hardly be blamed since he learned it from Christians, namely, that of distinguishing in the Gospels between things done by Jesus humanly and things done divinely. This approach, which we have noted earlier in Christology, runs counter to the whole meaning of the Incarnation. It assumes—very Islamically—that the human is in abeyance where the divine is at work and that the divine is absent in the manifestly human, whereas the Incarnation means, precisely, their mutuality.

Here, we may conclude, Al-Ghazālī was little helped by his Christian discussants. Quoting freely and discerningly from the Gospels, he insists accordingly that what is human is factual and has to do with Jesus' teaching and ministry, while what is erroneously taken by Christian credulity to be divine can and must be fully understood as metaphorical. Thus, sayings such as "I and my Father are one" and "he who has seen me has seen the

Father" in no way require the divinization of Jesus that Christians have read in them. They simply state a way of understanding how, in the actions of the human Jesus, the ways of God may be perceived; in this quality of theirs they are evidence of an identity of will between Jesus and God. *Al-Rudd al-Jamīl* even cites a parallel from Muslim tradition about "servants who draw near to God and whom God loves": "When I love him [such a servant] I, says God, am his ear by which he hears, the sight by which he sees, his tongue by which he speaks and his hand by which he grips."[33]

Such identity of will between Jesus and the Father is, indeed, a formulation very close to the meaning of the Incarnation within the orthodox christological terms. Had Al-Ghazālī been situated in a context more adequately articulate he might have considered why reduction to the metaphorical could not suffice—and, indeed, could not suffice for a reason arguably Islamic. In Christian orthodoxy we would have no right to affirm an identity of will between Jesus and his Father not grounded in an identity of being. Metaphors must not be allowed to conceal *shirk.*[34]

"He who has seen me has seen the Father" cannot be reduced to metaphor, but the sense in which it is more than metaphor is necessarily within the constraints of the Incarnation, where there is a divine condescension so to be known and a human capacity to implement it.[35]

There is an exciting perceptiveness in *Al-Rudd al-Jamīl* here, since "will as an index to nature" is so much part of Christology. But the author was hindered from deepening it by the Islamic insistence on *al-mukhālafah,* the absolute distinction between the divine and the human. That ruling premise in Al-Ghazālī's whole logic excluded acceptance of the Christian meaning. Indeed, it predisposed him against the comprehension of it. Nevertheless, had he not been thus inhibited from thinking of the divine in deliberate and loving self-expenditure on behalf of humanity, the idea of Jesus as metaphor for God could have availed him as a proper clue.

In all metaphor, there is a readiness of either dimension for the other, an interpenetration whereby, for the purpose of meaning, difference possesses identity. As George Eliot observed, "it is astonishing what a different result one gets by changing the metaphor."[36] But if the result is to be truth, then metaphors may not be arbitrarily applied. They must be congruent and either element—*qua* metaphor—congenial to the other. It is just such fittedness of the divine to the human, in the context of grace and creation, which Christology has always affirmed and which Al-Ghazālī, and Islam in general, believe *a priori* to be uncongenial, because of the necessary exaltedness of God and the *'abd,* or "servant," status of humans. Christology likewise holds those two givens of belief but sees in the servanthood of Jesus Christ the action of divine majesty.

Without perceiving—still less conceding—that understanding, Al-Ghazālī reinforces his case in *Al-Rudd al-Jamīl* by questioning the exclusiveness in which Christians are involved in their Christology. Why only Jesus, if we are reading what the Gospels say about him in the sense of the Muslim tradition earlier quoted? Are there not innumerable souls in whom "God's was the ear by which they heard"? The point is well taken. Al-Ghazālī cites the passage in John 10:34, which quotes Psalm 82:6: "I said 'You are gods,'" and where the meaning is at once followed by a statement of mortal, human status, so that there is no question of real divinity.[37] Such being gods in mere metaphor, or being God's as instruments, is obviously plural and multiple in prophets, seers, and sages. As Al-Ghazālī sees him, Jesus rightly has this status but no more.

The surest way to appreciate Al-Ghazālī's critique of the Gospels and the limits of his vision is to engage with this crucial point. He cannot be met by sheer assertion. For his concern is honest, and Islam is wholly with it. Given his readiness to take the New Testament as a starting point, it is fair to ask how it came to be what it is as a document. Did the writers think themselves excessive divinizers or deifiers in recording as they did? Monotheists all, were they nevertheless deceived by their own ardor so that they needed saving from themselves? We should beware of putting the New Testament to rights without first reckoning with how and why it came to be the thing it is.

But, that apart, the significance the writers ascribed to Jesus as "the Word made flesh" is best commended as an invitation. Counterrebuttal, however admirable, only rebuts rebuttal. The invitation is to consider the entire event of Jesus—teaching, healing, serving, and suffering—as disclosing the nature of God within the actuality of our world as it was expressed in response to the event. The cross as the climax brings together what is most central to the human story and what is most apposite in God, namely, our wrongness and God's sovereignty.

Though necessarily housed and articulated in dogma, invitation it remains. Elsewhere in the *Iḥyā'* Al-Ghazālī showed himself eminently alert to human sinfulness, perversity, and guilt. There was much also in his autobiography, *Al-Munqidh min al-Ḍalāl*,[38] which sounded the same depths of yearning and grace that the Gospels explore. If the invitation is taken on its own proper terms of gratitude and freedom, it can be known in experience as inclusive of all that we need of God and of all that God means for us. It becomes to us, in faith, the drama of the divine in the theme of the human and—on both counts—the finally worshipable reality.

It is only in the sense of this inclusiveness of meaning that we can rightly perceive the exclusiveness of God in Christ, which so offended Al-Ghazālī. There is an Islamic case here, for if we have rightly recognized God's own self-disclosure, it must belong with His unity. It will deserve to be the criterion by which we identify and so exclude from worship what is *not* God's. It will not be diversified, contradicted, or superseded elsewhere. In what Christology affirms, to say that "God is One" and that "the Word is made flesh" is to hold two statements consistent with each other. The Oneness belongs with the revelation, if, in the language of John 1:1, "God was the Word."[39]

Given the divine self-consistency that the doctrine of the unity of God affirms, and given its definitive, once-for-all, decisive expression, that expression becomes endlessly imitable in those who "love because He first loved us." Such reproduction of the principle of the cross, of God in Christ, on the part of faith in its meaning is precisely the logic of such faith. "*Therefore,* present yourselves a living sacrifice," Paul had written to the Christians in Rome. Without allowing the divine paradigm, Al-Ghazālī treated with great and detailed care in *Iḥyā' 'Ulūm al-Dīn* the vocation of right selfhood, its snares and attainments, along the Sufi "way" of discipline and desire. Here, with a far more advanced system than Al-Muḥāsibī, he was closer to the core of the New Testament than when he was concerned in *Al-Rudd al-Jamīl* with its refutation. Perhaps that is an appropriate comment on the disability attending controversy and polemic, a state of affairs that attended so much of the history in the centuries after the rise of Islam. The genius of Al-Ghazālī only makes it more tragic. Reproach attaches to both faiths. Thanks to its origins in intense disowning of plural worships and pagan idolatries, Islam was insistently set against what seemed to put in question divine sovereignty. The Christianity with which it cohabited so long gave its theology a temper of mind and an ambition of dogma ill-tuned to a vocation within Islam. There was, we might say, a conflict of jealousies: for the Oneness of God in the zeal of the Shahādah—negating, affirming, enjoining—and the Oneness of God in "the mystery of Christ"—discerned, commended, and received. As their mutual and contrasted history shows, "One" is the most contentious and profound of metaphors.

Notes

1. There are modern scholars who question the finalizing of the Qur'ān from the recension of Zaid in the reign of the third caliph, 'Uthmān (644–656). John Burton argues strongly against the 'Uthmān text and sees the whole as Muḥammad's text (*The Collection of the Qur'ān* [New York: Cambridge University Press, 1977]), but John Wansbrough argues that the Qur'ān's composition is the product of prolonged controversy post-'Uthmān (*Quranic Studies: Sources and Methods of*

Scriptural Interpretations [New York: Oxford University Press, 1977]). Likewise P. Crone and M. Cook, *Hagarism, the Making of the Islamic World* (Cambridge, 1977).

2. There are fourteen references in all, mostly adverse. But Surah 5.82 says that "the nearest in love to the believers are those who say: 'We are Christians.'"

3. *Al-Naṣārā* has also been linked with *Al-Anṣār* ("the helpers"), a title given to the disciples of Jesus in 3.52 and also applied to those Muslims in Medina who "aided" the emigrants from Mecca in the *Hijrah.* The fact that the literal Arabic *Al-Masīḥiyyūn* is not used for "Christians" may underline the basic Islamic disallowance of what determined historic Christianity, which, in the Islamic view, had gone beyond legitimate discipleship to Jesus as prophet and teacher.

4. Properly read, the repudiation of "begetting" in this famous Surah of divine unity does not negate what Christian faith intends by the creedal term. The phrase is in apposition to the preceding *Huwa Allāhu-l-Ṣamad,* "the God who has all resources in Himself" and who, therefore, is "unbegetting, unbegotten, none is like to Him." The faith of the Incarnation does not mean that God either derives or relinquishes His being.

5. The root RSL ("to send") yields *Al-Rasūl,* the title of Muḥammad, and the plural *rusul,* precisely the significance of sending that belongs in New Testament language about Jesus. On the common theme of "sentness" in both prophethood and Incarnation, see "Islam and Incarnation," in *Truth and Dialogue,* ed. John Hick (London, 1974), pp. 126–139.

6. As, for example, in the celebrated issue of human free will and divine determining, which the great Al-Ash'arī (873–935) resolved by positing that "God willed in the will of the doer," thus reconciling divine disposing with human accountability. The question that is implicit in the answer—Could the doer help willing it?—returns the mind to the original question, which is given back as the answer. See further pp. 83–84.

7. The term used in 4.158, *shubbiha,* exactly corresponds to the Greek *dokeō,* from which Docetism took its name. The idea of "apparentness" about Jesus' death is the same, the sources of the idea quite different. The one may be an echo of the other.

8. Nowhere in John are "Muslims" so named. The terms "Ishmaelites" and "Hagarenes" (see n. 15) are used, perhaps because these biblically linked titles served to underline the notion of heresy. Apart from John's readiness for Muslim relations, it is an odd description to call him "Saracen-minded." In the iconoclastic controversy (see below), when iconoclasts were accused of siding with Islam in that respect, John himself was strongly for icons and their veneration.

9. J. P. Migne, *Patrologiae cursus completus: Series graeca,* 161 vols. (Paris: J. P. Migne, 1857–66), 94:764–773. There is an English translation taken from the Latin by J. W. Voornis in *The Muslim World* 24 (1934), 391–398. For an English version from the Greek text, see Daniel Sahas, *John of Damascus on Islam* (Leiden, 1972), where textual and other matters are discussed.

10. For this same phrase Bishop Peter of Maiuma, near Gaza, was executed in 743, the very year in which John was writing.

11. One example is the passage in Isa. 21:5–7, where the prophet has a vision of

a chariot of camels. Another is Deut. 18:18, which tells of a prophet, like to Moses, "from among their brethren," a phrase taken to echo the meaning of *ummī* in the Qur'ān. The references in Deut. 33:2 to Sinai, Seir, and Paran have been held to indicate a prophet from Arabia. But the most conspicuous is the application of the Paraclete passages in John (14:16 and 15:26) to Muḥammad. See Kenneth Cragg, *Jesus and the Muslim* (London, 1985), pp. 262f.

12. The root verb indicates "that which participates in, or with" and is used repeatedly in the Qur'ān to denote the habit of idolaters in "associating" pseudo-deities with the sole sovereignty of God. The Christian doctrines of Christ and the Holy Spirit are held by Muslims to do the same. However, "associate" is a problematic term. While denoting and denouncing the deification of nonentities, i.e., fictitious beings, idols, it excludes or confuses that divine association with the world implicit in creation and explicit in the sending of prophets. As creator and sender of the prophets, as lawgiver, God "associates" with humanity in vital relatedness. To believe so in no way involves *shirk.* The Christian sense of the Incarnation is simply a larger, more surprising dimension of this same solicitude of God for the world. To forbid it to God would be to deny to God His own freedoms. It is this mutilation of divine reach that John had in mind with respect to Muslim denial of the very possibility (its actuality apart) of the Incarnation. See next note.

13. *Koptai* is the Greek word used; see Sahas, *John of Damascus,* p. 82.

14. Migne, *Patrologia graeca,* 94:1585–1596; Eng. trans. by J. W. Voorhis, *The Muslim World* 25 (1935), 266–273.

15. Muslims were regarded as descendants of Hagar, mother of Ishmael, the bias of illegitimacy being implied in such Christian usage. The name has been revived of late in an attempt to argue a Hagar-Messiah clue to the genesis of Islam by Patricia Crone and Michael Cook (*Hagarism*). Their thesis, however, makes an odd—in part self-contradictory—case for a radical rewriting of the origins of Islam. See also chapter 2, n. 2.

16. Supposedly referring to the several passages in which Jesus disclaims sonship, but also to Jesus' speaking from the cradle (Surah 19.30–33), vindicating his mother, Mary, from calumny concerning him. See also Surah 4.

17. The crucial passage is in Surah 61.6, where Jesus foretells the coming of a messenger "whose name is Aḥmad" (i.e., Muḥammad) or "whose name is praiseworthy." It has been widely claimed by Muslims as a point of reiterated polemic that this foretelling is present in the Gospel of John (14:16) in the form of the promised Paraclete. This Greek term, it is alleged, is a corruption by Christians of the Arabic name/term *Aḥmad.* The clause about "abiding for ever with you" means the finality of Muḥammad. Numerous issues are overlooked here in the Muslim claim, notably how Jesus' disciples could find this fulfillment six centuries after their death; how corruption could have occurred when the Greek text had been extant five centuries before the advent of Islam; how the entire meaning of the Holy Spirit could be assigned to a messenger. The issue belongs to the vacuous sort of controversy that serious interfaith meeting should be able and ready to ignore.

18. For a discussion of the Armenian version of the exchange, see Arthur Jeffery, *Harvard Theological Review* 37 (1944), 281–330, esp. 283.

19. Ibid., pp. 319–320.

20. On Abū Qurrā, see Adel Theodore Khoury, *Les Théologiens Byzantins et l'Islam* (Paris, 1969), pp. 83–105.

21. See Al-Jāḥiẓ, *Al-Radd ʻalā-l-Naṣāra* (c. A.D. 850), paras. 143–53 ("Refutation of the Christians"). See also *The Life and Works of Al-Jahiz,* ed. Charles Pellat, trans. D. M. Hawke (Berkeley, Calif.: University of California Press, 1969).

22. For example, Severus Ibn al-Muqaffa in Egypt records how the caliph ʻAbd al-Malik ordered Qur'ān-based declarations to be set on churches in Miṣr, notably Surah 112 and Quranic texts about Jesus; he also made attacks on Christian symbols.

23. Migne, *Patrologia graeca,* 94:1320b.

24. One noted exception was the Muslim Persian polymath and traveler Al-Bīrūnī (973–1048), whose account of Hinduism in his *Tārīkh al-Hind* indicated a lively awareness of the subtleties of Indian mythology and ritual worship. See *Albiruni's India,* trans. E. Sachau (London, 1888), vol. 1, ch. 11. He argued that representation was necessary to simple minds but warned of the danger that objects of worship could usurp the ineffable reality they were supposed to signify. One might compare the sensuous descriptions in the Qur'ān of the future state in heaven and hell as necessary to the tuition of minds incapable of grasping abstract meanings.

25. It was, for example, the pagan philosopher Celsus in the second century who had asked how Christians could condemn idolatry while "worshipping a god made flesh."

26. In the third part of his four-part *Iḥyā' ʻUlūm al-Dīn,* consisting of ten books dealing with *al-muḥlikāt,* "the things destructive of the spiritual life." The whole *Iḥyā',* on the revitalizing of all that pertains to religious life and knowledge, together with his numerous other writings gave Al-Ghazālī an ascendancy in Islam second only to that of Muḥammad himself.

27. It is not simply that events "occur" in the Qur'ān but that they entwine into its very content. Thus, for example, the encounter of Muḥammad with his hearers leads into exchanges in which they allege charges against him and he is given the response he is to make. Thus, like a refrain, recurs the pattern "They are saying .... Say thou...." Some of the events on which the text turns are highly consequential, such as the battle of Badr (Surah 8). Others are inconsequential, such as domestic tension in the Prophet's ménage (Surah 66).

28. The very periodicity of the Qur'ān indicates this point. The Book was not "sent down" as a whole in one piece, but, as 17.106 has it, *ʻalā mukthin,* "at intervals," so that content might participate in occasion and the two belong in one.

29. *Iṭmi'nān* ("soul-rest," "tranquillity") and the cognate verb figure in the Qur'ān as the blessed fruit of contemplation and reliance on God alone. *Dhikr* is a rich root of ideas comprising God's "reminder" to humans and their "mindfulness" of God, which Sufi techniques of recollection made into a high art. Sufism could also call on the central concept of *niyyah,* or "intention," which was vital to acts of ritual and devotion, all of which should have the deliberate focus of being sincerely meant.

30. His name has the same root, meaning "the accountant" of the self.

31. See Margaret Smith, *An Early Mystic of Baghdad: A Study of the Life and Teaching of Hārith b. Asad al-Muhāsibī, A.D. 781–A.D. 857* (London: SPCK, 1935), p. 83. He echoes expressions such as "Take no thought for the morrow" and shows an evident kinship with them.

32. *Al-Rudd al-Jamīl,* ed. R. Chidiac (Paris, 1939). The Arabic title continues ". . . the Fair Rebuttal of the Divinity of Jesus with what is Genuine of the Gospel." For a point turning on a Coptic term, said to be equivocal, see J. Windrow Sweetman, *Islam and Christian Theology: A Study of the Interpretations of Theological Ideas in the Two Religions,* 3 vols. (New York: Gordon Press, 1980), 1:297. Sweetman's analysis is useful for its exhaustive citation and discussion of Al-Ghazālī's quotations from the New Testament. For Al-Ghazālī's story, see W. Montgomery Watt's translation of *Al-Munqidh min al-Ḍalāl* (The Deliverer from Misguidedness) (London, 1953). He forsook his prestigious role as philosopher in Baghdad and wandered as a Sufi to find true *ma'rifah,* the inner knowledge of truth, with long sojourns in Damascus and Jerusalem.

33. See Sweetman, *Islam,* 1:268. The tradition is quoted also by Annemarie Schimmel, *And Muhammad is His Messenger: The Veneration of the Prophet in Islamic Society* (Chapel Hill, N.C.: University of North Carolina Press, 1985), pp. 223–224. It is called *Ḥadīth al-Nawāfil* (The Tradition of Supererogatory Piety). In applying this to Jesus in the sense of the Johannine and other passages in which Jesus tells of "oneness with the Father," Al-Ghazālī justifies the usage as "a sort of metaphor . . . good and acceptable and not disapproved." To urge that it can only be metaphor he cites Jesus in Matt. 26:39, distinguishing between wills by saying, "Not as I will but as Thou wilt," not realizing that this *is* a willed identity of wills in a situation of acute crisis and desolation.

34. *Shirk,* or "associationism," is the supreme sin of accounting divine what is not divine and according worship where it cannot belong. Metaphors by their very nature "associate" *a* with *b.* If, in usage, metaphor aligns the human and the divine in one entity or descriptive, it can only *not* be *shirk* if we believe that God positively overrides the *shirk* that would otherwise be involved. We must then understand the meaning in the way in which it can be true of God, given the fragility of all metaphor. The doctrine of the Incarnation takes care of both caveats.

35. "Implement" is a correct word here in that *plērōma,* or "fullness," actively understood is precisely how the New Testament understands how the divine "infills" the human in the person of Christ. See Col. 1:19; 2:9; Eph. 1:23; John 1:16. Fire "fulfills" fuel as fuel "fulfills" fire.

36. George Eliot, *The Mill on the Floss,* introduction by Antonia Byatt (New York: Penguin Books, 1980), book 2, ch. 1.

37. Psalm 82:6 has been a notorious verse in controversy, since it "names" mortals (see v. 7) as "gods," either in irony or as exercising power. Difficulties are compounded by Jesus' use of the verse according to John 10:34. Al-Ghazālī cites the passage in John to prove that this is purely metaphorical language. He understands Jesus to borrow a mere figure of speech of no theistic import and then to liken to it his own usage of "son of God." But this would refute the charge of blasphemy

in a very different way from the one John seems to intend. *A fortiori*—he seems to mean—Jesus is *not* blaspheming because "Son of God" is expressly true. Or is the import satirical, a point made in the manner of talmudic exegesis, an *argumentum ad hominem?* We cannot be sure. But the immediate relevance is to show the meticulous nature of Al-Ghazālī's handling of the Gospels.

38. See n. 32. The wistful quality of Al-Ghazālī's search, his lostness, his destitution of soul, might have been a surer starting point for his encounter with Christ and Christians. One can more readily come into Christology by starting with the self in its disquiet, its interrogation of life, its distress as to truth, than with the arguments of the schools. But argumentativeness was somehow implicit in Islam when confronted with others outside its finalities. Comparably, the Greek temper had made Christian doctrine metaphysically preoccupied and tediously technical. Such instincts were better suited to confrontation than to patient exploration. When it came, then, to Christianity, Al-Ghazālī, for all his acumen and depth of spirit, was primed for controversy.

39. The Greek is significant here. It is not *ho theos;* there is no definite article. The writer is *not* saying: "God was the Word," as if wholly equating subject and predicate. He is not exhausting what we mean by "God" in what we have in Jesus. The sense is restrictive in the same way that "the Son" is restrictive when we say "God the Son." "God is the Word" in the sense that "the author is the authorship," wholly but not identically. Al-Ghazālī, however, carefully noting the Greek, reads it as meaning "God in His own knowing" and so unrelated to the status of Jesus, which he further discusses in relation to the Qur'ān's designation of Jesus as "a word from Him [God])" and "His word." See Sweetman, *Islam,* 1:293–298.

CHAPTER

5

The European Factor

I

EUROPA IN GREEK mythology may have been a lovely Phoenician princess carried off to Crete by Zeus disguised as a white bull and destined to give her name to a whole continent. But any satisfaction Phoenicians may feel[1] about such share in the ancestry of Europe has to be grimly weighed against the tribulations suffered in the reverse direction. Our task in this chapter is to examine the impact of Europe on Arab Christianity, taking the Crusades between the eleventh and the fourteenth centuries as the prime symbol of that dimension but tracing other aspects that both preceded and followed them. The very terms "Near" and "Middle," current in European speech about the Levant, or the Orient, betray a mind-set as well as a convenient usage. They are correct only by reference to Europe, and it is by reference to Europe that so much in the history of those "easts" has been both experienced and told. "The American factor" has to be added–benevolently for the most part–in the nineteenth century, crucially in the twentieth.

Later chapters will have ample occasion to study this theme in its modern form. Our present concern is with the bearing of Europe on the East in the centuries that overlap with the times considered in the preceding chapters and the rise of the Ottoman power. We earlier noted the vital role of the Mediterranean in the mutual history of Muslims and Christians. The great inland sea mediated and monitored their tensions. Spain at the western end was ruled throughout the century of the Umayyads (ending 750) from their Syrian capital, Damascus. There was a Christian enclave in the northwest corner of the Iberian peninsula at Finisterre ("the earth's end") that survived the Islamic conquest. When Islam was dislodged from France and receded into Spain, western Christendom began to ponder and pursue attempted reclamation at the other end of the Mediterranean.

The abiding instincts of pilgrimage, setting "the road to Jerusalem in the heart," suggested the enticing but elusive ambition for a physical repossession of those holy haunts. For all the pathos in the endurance the ambition evoked, and the long tragedy entailed on generations of pilgrims, it mediated to the East only the perversity of its own pride. It was a strange requital of the debt it owed to the lands its sense of history coveted. In cherishing the sacrament of places, it cruelly betrayed the sacrament of communities. Its sequence of arousal, venture, conquest, possession, dislodgment, and retreat through more than two centuries left a permanent trauma in the soul of Arab Christianity.[2] In their inspiration and their legacy the Crusades have troubled all succeeding centuries with the suspicion and the fear, in whatever idiom, of their reproduction. Few preachers have had so far an earshot as Peter the Hermit of the First Crusade. The memory is strident still.

The instincts which the First and later Crusades brought to the climax of physical assault had long been maturing within the innate superiority of the Latin West. Even after the crusading impulse had consented to defeat,[3] Rome was still in the conceits of lofty self-assurance. When Muḥammad II, the Ottoman conqueror of Constantinople, had lately entered on that long-sought prize of his ancestors, Seljūqs and Ottomans, in 1453 Pope Pius II wrote to him with an intriguing proposal:

> Be baptized and no prince of the world will be your equal in glory and power. We will call you the Emperor of the Greeks and of the Orient and what you now possess by force and injury you will hold by right. All Christians will venerate you and make you the judge of their disputes. . . . The See of Rome will love you like any Christian king.[4]

So well had Pius measured the eclipse of Byzantium, so far had he misjudged the caliber of Muḥammad II. His crass overture was much in character.

We cannot here retrace in detail the vicissitudes of East–West relationships before the Great Schism of 1054. Our concern with Arab Christianity is involved, however, to the extent that its scattered churches, cut off as they often were from both Byzantium and Rome from the time of the Muslim conquest, nevertheless had stakes of both hope and fear in the course of those relations. The eastern patriarchates of Antioch, Alexandria, and Jerusalem, whether Orthodox in Greek or Monophysite terms, and the Nestorians thinly among them and strongly in Edessa and beyond, had only precarious physical links with the eastern Rome. The western Rome was remoter still.[5] Yet, given the partial occasions Byzantium enjoyed in the Mediterranean and the sustained intercourse of the two Romes,

Christians in *Dār al-Islām* had vital interests in what ensued outside the reach of their capacity to control. It needs to be remembered that western Rome was politically under Constantinople, actually or nominally, until the time of Charlemagne in the ninth century. In the century coinciding with the Umayyads, no fewer than five Syrians and three Greeks became popes in Rome, and many refugee monks fleeing from Islam found their way there. Theodore, archbishop of Canterbury from 668 to 690, was one of them—a Greek-speaking Tarsan. Yet, despite visits to Rome by the eastern emperor and of popes to Byzantium and common converse in councils, the papacy grew more wholly western with Gregory II (715–731)—a process accelerated by the accession of the Germans to the faith and to power. Charlemagne was crowned "King and Emperor" on the western Christmas Day, A.D. 800, in Rome and "the Holy Roman Empire" began.

That epochal event had many ultimate consequences in its train for eastern Christendom. Tensions with Byzantium deepened with the new arrogance of the papacy, conniver with and creature of the new imperium. Iconoclasm still rankled, and there was the latent, then sharply active, issue of the "procession of the Holy Spirit."[6] The Greek East despised an emperor who could neither read nor write. The forcible collapse of eight centuries of single, then disputed, always prestige-laden, authority, in such a form and sequel, vexed the eastern soul. There were new discordances of race and speech and culture to face, and animosities were sharpened by tedious issues about rites and ceremonies and dates, celibacy and jurisdiction. These became more chronic through a marked decline during the tenth century in ecclesiastical and political leadership in both East and West. But it was finally the intractable claims of papal pretension that culminated in the Great Schism of 1054.

The separation had profound consequences for Arab Christianity. The ancient patriarchates aligned with an enfeebled Byzantium and, with the non-Greek Orthodox around them, were promptly exposed to the ardors of western Christianity intent on their sacred territory with scant regard for or perception of their long tenure and travail. Those ardors were nourished by the venom that attends on rupture. Western preoccupations with Islam in Spain contributed to a belligerence eastward, now disencumbered of formal bonds with eastern Christians. The extreme west of Europe had suffered the incursion of eastern Arabs thrust far from their native realms by the dynamism of a militant faith. Long resentments and traumas gathered around that memory. The passions engendered by its brutal erasure in the ultimate expulsion of Islam from Spain were endemic long before and found sanction in something not unlike the Muslim concept of holy war. The Christian East was caught in the consequences of that confrontation pursued in its territory and either blind or hostile to its interests.

II

It is a tragic irony of history that Europe's response to Islam should have so far and so long distressed and distrained the Christianity that had first known Islamic invasion and had learned at cost how to subsist within it and to live without the perspectives of resistance and riddance by which the Latin church was guided. Was it the very fact of that eastern tolerance of Islam—albeit mandatory—that excited the western contrast of belligerence and retaliation? Eastern Christendom became to western eyes a provocation rather than an education, a subject of pity or scorn, not an index to truth. If there were Christians who had, at least in political terms, capitulated to Islam, was it not the more important that feasible repudiation and defeat of Islam should be pursued elsewhere both as example and as mitigation and then be carried eastward to rewrite a deplorable story? Given the new pride of the western Rome, the infusion of the Germanic strain and the passion of the Spanish scene, the East could not fail to become the victim of the West's impatient rejection of any *modus vivendi* with Islam. The original militancy of Muḥammad's people recoiled again in the lengthening centuries on its first, eastern victims in the form of western countercrusade. When the Crusades had exhausted themselves in final failure they lingered on through the growing menace of the Turks on Europe's own soil.

The temper of western Latin Christianity as adversarial to Islam had both symbol and incentive in the encounter within Spain and one of its legends in the cult of St. James, "brother of the Lord." Paradoxically, there was a certain imitation of Islam in the idea of knightly martyrdom and the sense of a destiny to prevail. Battle for the faith, graphically invoked in the Spanish context, kindled the ardor for reconquest where Islam was most of all entrenched. What had fired Asturia as local and defensive had to issue into an inclusive offensive by the arousal of Europe overall. Advocacy to that end was all too ready elsewhere to be implemented by orders of chivalry, born to fulfill the visions of monks and the strategies of popes. By these Islam had to be dispossessed of "holy ground." The Great Schism could, as it were, be corroborated in a great concert against Islam, for was not Muḥammad the ultimate schismatic in God's universe?

By such logic the vulnerability of eastern Christianity gave no pause to the assurance of the western church. That vulnerability had a survival logic of its own, a wisdom of sufferance that ran counter both to the mood and the authority of the Latin world. Despite commendable efforts from within the Greek church, both before and after the Great Schism, to participate in Latin Christian thought and life, the western soul was little minded to reciprocate.[7] On the contrary, it became set to pursue its central dispute of arms with Islam and, in that cause, to ignore the restraints of inter-Christian obligation. It would proceed at any price on what had become the papal view of Christendom in which western Rome could brook no Christian rival. For that view Islam could serve as total warrant. Arab, Greek, Syriac, and other eastern Christianity would pay a long and heavy price for such mind and mood in Europe.

The price was made the more exacting by the fact that the Arab dimension paying it had never enjoyed nor directly shared the comfort of the consciousness by which Byzantium sustained itself through good and ill in the encounter with the western Rome. That consciousness, even when it became myth and illusion, belonged with the Greek ethos to which, at best, Arab Christianity had access only by proxy. The trials of the ninth to the fifteenth centuries served only to intensify in the soul of Byzantium the pride of identity that its retrospect demanded and its tribulations fortified. Even when emperors such as Michael VIII sought western help and placated western interests at the Union of Lyons in 1274, his less realistic subjects deplored his policy and dubbed him "Latin-minded."[8] In their eyes he had betrayed the old self-image of the emperor as the elect of God, His regent on earth, and the terrestrial image of the divine Logos. Byzantines were the only true *Romaioi,* their empire the only legitimate realm of the sovereignty that derived from God.[9] No theory of *translatio* by which that sovereignty had been transferred elsewhere could be allowed. Constantinople held Europe to be *pars occidentalis* of its empire. Whatever the stresses of Seljūq pressure and the fluctuations of the frontiers of Byzantine territory in Asia Minor and the Balkans during the long cycle of the Crusades, the emotions of Byzantium remained insistently regal in the conviction of a divine mandate.

The great countertheorist in the West was Pope Innocent III, whose pontificate (1198–1216), chastened by the loss of Jerusalem and the failure of the Third Crusade to recover it, sealed antipathy to Byzantium by consolidating papal power and claim. Building on the ideas of Pope Gregory VII (1073–1085) and Bernard of Clairvaux, he saw primatial authority in Constantinople as indispensable and western arms a means to gain it. Was it not the papacy that had translated the empire from East to West in fulfillment of the apostolic primacy of the western Rome? Further, he claimed, the western emperors were properly assistant to papal ends and exercised their power only by papal leave. It was a theory that both curbed and bribed western actual or potential emperors in that they might aspire to a universal role, albeit subordinate, which Innocent's theory projected for them. Innocent himself might be formidable, but there might be later popes with less acumen and dominance.

Thus the fervor of the crusading instinct was channeled more expressly into hostility to Constantinople. This in turn served to arouse within the East an identity consciousness tending, despite "universal" theory, toward a sharp self-assertion that a later term would call "nationalist." Byzantines might still be the true *Romaioi,* but in holding it against the other Rome they felt themselves to be the more Hellenes. "Emperor of the Greeks" began to displace "Emperor of the Romans" in their imperial language. Given crusading fact and theory, could it be otherwise? They were forced on the defensive by a prolonged threat both to their security and to their self-image. The entire experience of the Crusades represented a violation of their sense of history.

Nor was the offense relieved by crusading animosity to Islam. Byzantium had reconciled itself to adversity under Islam by a confidence in its own economy under God. The actual power of Muslim and Turk had to be tactically conceded until providence restored what providence had mysteriously withdrawn. Western belligerence, manifestly prejudicial, was also vulgar and intrusive, offending the givenness of Byzantium under God and compounding adversity with trespass.

In the confrontation of ecclesiastical theory and spiritual prestige in which the Crusades were both fuel and fire, the local Christians–Arab, Syrian, Melchite, Jacobite, Nestorian–were hapless sufferers. They might be fascinated by the claims, the castles, and the conquests of the westerners, but time would prove that these had no lasting shield to afford them. Some, notably the Maronites, might be tempted to military cooperation with crusaders but thereby only prejudiced their standing and their future. The friendlier relations the non-Greek Orthodox enjoyed with the Latin hierarchs stemmed from the fact that they were considered not to have been involved in the Great Schism. Seeds were planted that ripened into "uniatism" in later centuries. For non-Greek races within the Greek allegiance the slow shift from a universal to a national awareness in the eastern empire could only mean strain and dismay. Greek bishops could withdraw to Constantinople or Cyprus for refuge and ease while local folk were left to the chances and afflictions of disruption, whether from Ayyūbids, Seljūqs, crusaders, or other mutual adversaries in their towns and villages. Survival was hard purchased in the two centuries before the cycle of crusading fervor spent itself, having inspired and devoured adventurers and devotees, dreamers and schemers from every corner of Europe and having burdened the relationships of Christendom with long and tragic legacies of enmity and suffering.

III

Of chief significance in the present context are the First, Fourth, and Sixth Crusades, the one leading to the capture of Jerusalem and the establishment of the crusading kingdom between 1099 and 1187, the next to the sack of Constantinople and the Latin regime there from 1204 to 1261, the last to the treaty tenure of most of the pilgrim towns in Palestine by the skill and contrivance of Emperor Frederick II of Hohenstaufen in 1229. The story of miscarriage, frustration, or ineffectiveness belonging to other Crusades adds to the record only those features we must examine here, reflecting the diversity of initiatives within Europe and the strife of ambitions and intentions within the East.

When Ṣalāḥ al-Dīn recovered Jerusalem from the Latins in 1187, his Qādī, Al-Fāḍil, paid a generous tribute to the physical legacy of the expelled crusaders.

> Islam received back a place which it had left almost uninhabited, but which the care of the unbelievers had transformed into a paradise garden. . . . Those accursed ones defended with lance and sword this city which they had rebuilt with columns and slabs of marble, where they had founded churches and palaces of the Templars and Hospitallers . . . houses as pleasant as their gardens which made them look like living trees. . . .[10]

They had indeed repaired—and in that sense avenged—the ravages in Jerusalem of the caliph Al-Ḥākim in 1010, the long memory of which had stirred in the Council of Clermont when Urban II (1088–1099) had called the church to undertake crusade.[11] There were more immediate incentives also. Advancing Seljūq Turks had defeated the Byzantine forces at Manzikert in 1071, and the resulting apprehensions had been confirmed by their capture of Jerusalem in 1076, which was followed by increasing menaces to the safety and even the hope of pilgrimage.

But had the victors of 1099, inaugurating what Al-Fāḍil generously admired, known what they had vowed? They had much blood to wash from their hoofs when they made massacre in the first mad ecstasy of their possession of the city. Thereafter pilgrimage must wed the aggressive mood required to secure it. The Holy Sepulchre was at its heart, and for its sake penances at home had been lifted, debts remitted, and pardons pledged. Achievement could be thus arrayed in innocence, but the sepulchre lay in a city and the city in a land, alike holy. Some pilgrims might see their journey as their vow fulfilled and so return—hazards allowing—whence they came. But what of the security of their successors? Establishment must follow to ensure them. There was land hunger to be satisfied and the opportunity to indulge the ways of power implicitly sacralized by godly ends. Bonds of knightly fealty imposed their patterns of devious ambition, both regulating and unleashing human frailty.

The vicissitudes of the Latin kingdom of Jerusalem through almost nine decades and of the shrinking coastal territories to their final demise at Acre in 1270 present an all-too-human story of bravery and intrigue, of staunch determination and sharp discord. Inevitably the crusading temper produced few contemplatives despite the large role of Bernard of Clairvaux and Cluniac houses in the initiation at Clermont. It was not until 1157 that the great Abbey of Belmont was founded southeast of Tripoli. Church building was, for the most part, a symbol of dominion, in which the original local Christianity could largely be ignored, except insofar as sectaries might be occasional allies in the necessary vigilance of crusading life in Outremer (the current name for the Crusading Kingdom, or "Beyond-the-Sea"), the very name expressing the priority of the European connection.

As Latins the crusaders brought, of course, their own hierarchy, displacing the jurisdictions of the Greeks and others by virtue of the primacy of Rome. Crusaders, whether knights, builders, landed gentry or artisans, susceptible to local contagions of culture and tradition—as many proved to be—found their assimilation in the Islamic rather than the eastern Christian. Heat and the climate, lethargy or weariness, and the appeal of the exotic inclined some to fraternize with Muslim habits if not with Muslim faith. A degree of mutual admiration obtained in the context of honor and the charm of bravery, with no will or effort to pursue those affinities further into the common or contrasted reaches of doctrine and theology. The kingdom of Jerusalem may have known a certain meeting of manners, hardly of minds or wills. It was only at longer remove and in disappointment at the forfeiture of Jerusalem that minds in the next centuries sought other than martial relations with Islam or were ready for humility in the presence of eastern Christianity.

Meanwhile church building told the western pride. The Templars took over the Al-Aqṣā Mosque. The Dome of the Rock was consecrated as "the House of the Lord" in 1142, with a gilded cross above the dome. A marble casing was built over the sacred rock for use as a choir and to the north of the Temple area a church was erected. The Holy Sepulchre itself was entrusted to the protection of the Hospitallers, and the church renewed and enlarged. But it was the castles rather than the churches that told both the prowess and the precariousness of the Latin kingdom. Huge hill fortresses were erected to control the routes and dominate the landscape. Control of the countryside was often uncertain, menaced by bands of marauding Turks or disputed between rival fief holders themselves. Interior rivalry was built into the very patterns of the life of Outremer. Though the major ports were held, immigration from the West ill sufficed defensive needs. The massive solidity of the fortresses was a necessary reassurance to their occupants needing more than towers and bastions to make it good.

All the leaders and their followers, saving Raymond of St. Gilles, had taken a feudal oath of fealty to the Byzantine emperor Alexius Comnenus in exchange for their facilitated passage across the Bosphorus in 1077, promising to restore to him all territories they might recover from the enemy. That had been, no doubt, on both sides a diplomacy of convenience, and the crusaders had subsequently relied on their own devices in making their forward way through Seljūq Anatolia. Compromise could sit lightly on them. For their real vows were to God and the pope, while pledges to schismatics such as Alexius had been merely politic. Yet that trivial factor in their story was a symptom of the ambiguity attending their existence. Ecclesiastical usurpation might be repaid by military reverse. If we read the history of the Latin kingdom backward it can be seen to be a drama of reprieve, of deferred climax pending the emergence of the great Ayyūbid, Ṣalāḥ al-Dīn, the Kurdish chieftain who, from his mastery of Egypt and Syria, outmatched and outfought the Latins and decisively defeated their kingdom at the Horns of Hattin in July 1187. Jerusalem surrendered three months later. The Dome of the Rock was rid of its choir and altar and its golden cross.

IV

It was out of the dismay and chagrin of this catastrophe that what history knows as the Fourth Crusade was generated. Pope Innocent III's ecclesiology could not brook so decisive a reversal of its logic, but now the acquisition of the eastern empire was seen as the prior necessity. His objective coincided with the commercial aspirations of the Venetians in particular and of western trading in general. That mercantile dimension of the European factor began to be central with the Fourth Crusade, but the traditional motif of pilgrimage and holy Palestine remained to underwrite and promote it. An unholy alliance of devices and devotion came into play. From an original intention for Egypt, base and flank of Ayyūbid power, the thirty-thousand strong flotilla was diverted to the Bosphorus. Venetians supplying the ships could dictate the terms. There followed in 1204 the sack of Constantinople, in which western violence proposed to resolve schism finally in its own favor and set in train thereby the recovery of Jerusalem.

Pope Innocent seems to have approved of the diversion, if he had not designed it. The violence, though deplored, was in pursuance of his theory of the papacy. It is true that sharp enmities existed and that anti-Latin feeling in the city had resulted in the arrest of Venetian merchants in 1171 and in a massacre of foreigners in Constantinople in 1182. These, it could be argued, had gravely jeopardized commercial interests as well as ecclesiastical ambitions. Latin control lasted only until 1261. The French, Flemish, Germans, Venetians, and others who had engineered it quarreled after their success. Emperor and patriarch fled; clergy and monks repudiated the Latin jurisdiction. Nicea, Brusa, and Trebizond became strongholds of Byzantine resistance. Dissensions and misfortunes befell the Latins, and anti-Venetian maneuvers on the part of Genoa contributed to the end of the Latin tenure. Venice was still able to purchase recognition of its commercial demands thereafter, but irreparable damage had been done to eastern Christendom. Venice was enfeebled in the face of enemies from farther east, and its territorial power was confined to the coastal fringes of Asia Minor, to Thrace, Macedonia, and some Aegean islands. The anti-Latin animus in eastern Orthodoxy intensified with sharpening religious fervor among the clery and the common folk, making more difficult the western relationships that realism demanded of the rulers. For Arab Christianity within the strife of Christendom and hapless exposure to Muslim vagaries, the Fourth Crusade meant nothing but confusion and disaster.

The interest of the Sixth Crusade is the measure it affords of how far papal imperialism had suborned the pilgrimage impulse. With the sanction of force available but by the art of personal diplomacy, its leader, Emperor Frederick II of Hohenstaufen (1194–1250), took advantage of a brief favorable moment in contemporary politics to achieve by negotiation the dearest hopes of pilgrim hearts. Yet in doing so—uniquely in crusading history—he incurred sustained hostility and excommunication from Pope Gregory IX for his pains. A Sicilian by birth, Frederick had become familiar with Islam in the island and set up a colony of Saracens in his employ in Lucera, Italy, with their own mosque and school. He was himself an able Arabist and established a personal rapport with Al-Malik al-Kāmil (1218–1238), nephew of Ṣalāḥ al-Dīn and sultan of Egypt. By treaty in 1229 Al-Kāmil granted Frederick Jerusalem (save for the Dome of the Rock), Bethlehem, Nazareth, and a strip to the coast, ensuring full pilgrim access. Delighting to pose as an oriental and relishing the highly personal nature of his success and the direct trust between rulers on which alone it rested, Frederick fell foul of western ecclesiastical norms and concepts. He was repudiated in Rome, and the Jerusalem patriarch forbade his pilgrims to enter the city. Frederick had offended in being friendly with Muslims and with Constantinople. He married his daughter to the Greek emperor John during John's exile in Nicea. Frederick's diplomacy, Rome complained, had abandoned even the pretense of a war for the faith.

Crusade was clearly about more than peaceful access to holy places. These could not be divorced from necessary belligerence as their *raison d'être*, or so it seemed.

Admittedly, the setup was precarious and short-lived. The Templars intrigued treacherously against it. Both Frederick and Al-Kāmil were accused by their respective faiths, the former for having conceded Muslim worship at the Rock, the latter for having bought off a crusade by generous concession. Each had thus betrayed the instincts of confrontation to which—unless checked by prescripts of chivalry, which obtained only in battle—both religions were prey. Historians might well ask who was imitating whom. Was Al-Kāmil emulating what one might think akin to Christian irenicism? Was the church Islamic in its requirement of necessary belligerence for which faith and devotion would be the pretext or the occasion? Or was the episode only a juncture in the story of two idiosyncratic adventurers who happened to fraternize congenially and successfully? It would be wise not to make too much of the one war-free, at first war-bent, crusade, save its dire revelation of the hypocrisy in all the rest. That lesson is clear when we turn to truly irenic efforts to relate to the Muslim East and their tenuous bearing on eastern Christianity, which otherwise the crusaders only afflicted and distressed.[12]

V

But before coming to Francis of Assisi and Ramon Lull and the dimension they exemplified of the European factor, it is useful to note how the central preoccupation of the papacy in the Crusades with power and jurisdiction developed when their lingering collapse, through the closing years of the kingdom at Acre, occupied Rome's canon lawyers with the question of lands and peoples they could no longer aim to control.

Pope Innocent IV (1243–1254), an able legist, was a notable theorist of Christian power, papal and imperial, in relation to territories beyond Rome's Christendom. There was no *de jure* surrender of the right to the Holy Land, no legal abandonment of the legitimacy of crusade. But Innocent was aware of the rising power of the Mongols east of the Levant and was exercised, as his successors were to be, about Christians actually or potentially outside Christian protection. Papal theory claimed that all Christians everywhere were the responsibility of the Vicar of Christ—a doctrine that implied there was little difference between Islam and Byzantium in respect of Christian subjects.

But the right of "infidel" rulers to rule had to be respected, where—in contrast later to Latin America—they could not feasibly be displaced. Innocent's theory required them to admit the activity of Christian mission and ensure that their *dominium* was not injurious to Christians in their midst, given the inability of Christian power to rescue them from that sovereignty. This pragmatic line raised the question of papal/imperial reciprocity vis-à-vis Muslim subjects in Christian territory. Might non-Christians argue the right to aggress against Christian powers on the ground that these should be deprived of sovereignty—the just war in reverse? Christian lodgment in Europe might then be disqualified and undone by adapting the argument on which the Christian right to regain the Holy Land was based. Were Christian rulers to settle for something like the Muslim *dhimmī* system, squaring *de facto* power with *de jure* care for minorities?

It is interesting that canon law theory as the Crusades petered on and out began to reach for some kind of natural human rights and the need for a prudential realism in the face of facts. The papacy was well aware that a theological or ethical disqualification of power-wielders could be turned by sectaries against established Christian rulers. Indeed, one of the intriguing factors after the Crusades is the way in which sectaries could appeal to Islam in their quest for liberation from what they saw as the tyranny or the corruption of the papacy. This was not merely the principle of a common enemy provoking friendship. It was the fruit of wider awareness and reflection, which in some quarters the saga of the Crusades induced, while the friar movements brought more penetrating contact with "infidel" lands and culture. It is fascinating that in the waning of the Crusades something like a readiness for *regio religio* emerged, whereby canon law linked rule and faith with concession of minority status under conditions. Rome's canonists had practical conclusions not unlike the *Dār al-Islām, Jihād,* and *Ahl al-Dhimmah* concepts of Islamic jurisprudence. The irony, however, was that eastern Christians in the Muslim sphere had suffered heavily in advance of them, while Christians in Byzantium's shifting borders, as alleged papal subjects anyway, lived outside their scope. Yet, for these last, papal power and papal mission had nothing but pressure to be Latins.[13] They would always be prey in western consciousness to the claims both of papal jurisdiction and the West's crusading fascination with Islam.

VI

It is significant that Francis of Assisi's celebrated encounter with the sultan Al-Malik al-Kāmil in July 1219 at Damietta took place in the context of the Fifth Crusade. Francis's disavowal of the sword in his obedience to the precept "I send you as sheep among wolves" (Matt. 10:16) had nevertheless a sense of the wolves analogy. Muslims were, indeed, to be loved as fellow humans, susceptible surely to the evidence of the poverty and humility which alone commended the suffering Christ. Yet that vision of the obedience of Christ was necessarily pursued by Francis in a loyal obedience to the Holy See, whose mandate was inseparable from his mission. That Holy See was entirely committed to the legitimacy of armed crusade and was currently realizing the relevance to it of new movements of preaching developed by both Franciscans and Dominicans. The radical tension implicit in that contradiction both ennobled and compromised Francis's encounter with the sultan and the scene at Damietta. The nobility lay in the effort to displace force with love and power with poverty. The compromise stood in the actual context of siege and belligerence from which Francis was only symbolically freed.

The sultan marveled at the strange configuration of faith that Francis embodied and sent him back through the lines with safe conduct, reportedly saying when Francis was out of earshot: "Pray for me that God may deign to show me the law and the faith that are most pleasing to Him." This was the sultan who had responded to the Fifth Crusade with the offer, later accepted by the Sixth Crusade, of a negotiated cession of territory to the western Christians. Evidently Francis, at perhaps a favorable political juncture, had touched a nerve at least of puzzlement, if not of human feeling. But it would take more than a lone gesture to surmount the power-structured order in which both faiths were held. The vexed question of the prophet Muḥammad and his status, which Christendom was impelled to disavow, cut across the love to humanity—Muslim humanity—which Francis was set to bring. For though the imitation of the love of Christ could not fail to be inclusive, faith concerning it could not brook its explicit disownment in Islam. Long generations since Francis—often lacking his single-hearted simplicity—have failed to reconcile that final issue.

But within that paradox, what of the eastern Christians in relation to the mission of Francis and that of others, notably the followers of Dominic, who in the thirteenth century developed a lively activity of preaching in the flow and ebb of military crusades? In part that vocal missionary activity was directed to the edification—and also the reproaching—of crusader settlers who had "gone native" or lapsed into negligence of faith. Local Christians it was designed to wean from their heresy or schism or both, while presenting to Muslims a Christian account free of those eastern features they thought liable to arouse Muslim distaste or scorn. Rarely were local Christians, of either eastern Orthodoxy, seen as partners. They, for their part, had little incentive to be, sensing in the western preachers a menace to their status quo with Muslims. In these ways the sermon-crusaders could hardly be differentiated from the fighting ones.

The inherent tension of the whole situation was dramatically present in the call Francis reportedly issued during his extended colloquy in the presence of the sultan, which, we must assume, took place by interpretation from French into Arabic. Francis's "love for the sultan's soul" was generously conceded, but he himself refused the invitation to rational discourse about the Triune Name and Savior Jesus that warranted his mission. For, Francis affirmed, reason and logic were not the feasible grounds of his Gospel. He further rejected the sultan's offer of lavish gifts to expend on Christian poor. How could the impasse of mingled courtesy and disparity be resolved? Francis made the Elijah-like offer of a *mubāhalah,* or *ordalie,* he and Muslim doctors submitting to a trial by fire in which God would intervene to vindicate the truth. When the offer was declined, safe conduct of Francis back to the Christian lines brought his whole gesture to an end in both its nobility of heart and its futility of will. Europe had contrived a legend for the Christian East but no more.

VII

In the waning century of the crusading fervor the career of Ramon Lull of Catalonia and Majorca (1232–1316) renewed the ideal of Francis and found the same hard frustration, ending after eighty-three years in the satisfaction of martyrdom. Physically, he scarcely belongs to the Arab East. The western Mediterranean and North Africa were his chosen sphere. After his Francis-style conversion in his early thirties, he made a pilgrimage, but it is not clear whether only within Spain or also to the eastern holy places. Around the year 1301 he traveled to Cyprus and into Armenia, drawn by what proved a false hope of impending liberation of the Holy Land through the agency of the advancing Tartars, who, it was thought, would christianize. On that occasion he seems to have encountered local Christians, whom he regarded as schismatics—Jacobites, Maronites, and Nestorians of doubtful lineage. That perception was in line with his loyal, if at times eccentric, Roman allegiance and his preoccupation with Islam to the exclusion of eastern Christian participation.

Even so, Lull's long and single-minded career has its place within the European factor in Arab Christianity. His passion for the West's mission in *Dār al-Islām,* despite its unreadiness for eastern partnership, made him an ardent pioneer of Arabic studies. In 1276 he founded the college at Miramar in Majorca to be a house of Arabic studies for the better fulfillment of mission. Papal blessing was vital to him, and he traveled to Rome to press on John XXI the hope of similar colleges to study all the languages of the world in the context of Christian vocation to evangelize. Miramar became the idyllic symbol and—as far as Lull's restless travels admitted—the nursery of his prolific writings in the expression of his mind and spirit.

Here a fascinating reverse influence is evident. Lull's long novel *Blanquerna* and wide-ranging expositions of philosophy and devotion, notably *The Book of the Lover and His Beloved* and *The Book of the Gentile and the Three Wise Men,* reflect an intimate knowledge of Islam, of Muslim rite and scripture. They also betray the influence of ideas common to mystical faith in both Christian and Muslim writers. He thus combined a deeply mystical distrust of the rationalism associated with Ibn Rushd (1126–1198) with a lively sense of the role of contemplation in the tradition of Islamic *dhikr,* or recollection of God. Here, as in Francis, was a different fulfillment of chivalry. The knight, dedicated to holiness of will in the quest of sacred ground within the risk of death, had become the scholar given to the care of love within the setting of discourse around creeds and rituals—discourse at once comparative, erudite, and missionary. The intention of victory, now in terms of persuasion and conversion, remained, but was no longer served by arms and violence. The Crusades in their nadir had given way to an apostolate that required, in Europe's universities, a vision of Arabic studies and a readiness for spiritual venture with Islam. In Ramon Lull one might imagine that Peter the Hermit had discovered Al-Ghazālī. It is unfortunate that in Lull's story there was no place for the native Christian users of the language he made so central to his marriage of mission, scholarship, and contemplation. Could the reason be that there was no Arab Christian counterpart of Al-Ghazālī significant for the Latin world? Or was it that Lull, the Catalan, and his western island academy, were too remote in sympathy and vision from the East, to which the martial crusaders had been so insistently drawn?[14]

Miramar faltered and failed, but its visionary founder gave an impetus to Arabic and Islamic studies in Europe that was destined to affect the Arab East profoundly, not least in mediating into Europe influences that in turn and at long range would condition their intellectual relationships. Lull had his most remarkable heir in Nicholas of Cusa (1401–1464), who, in the very year of the fall of Constantinople to the Turks, dreamed in a sermon of a congress of all peoples, summoned by angels, to meet in Jerusalem, where they would renounce mutual slaughter and learn by calm engagement with each other the shape of a true faith that would afford a wide diversity of rite and symbol. After the wise delegates had dispersed with such harmony of truth to their several lands for its realization there, they would return to a second conclave in the Holy City to set their seal upon it.

This dreamer was a cardinal who had earlier striven to achieve conciliation with the Hussites and to make the papacy more open to the mind of a Curia in which cardinals would serve as representatives of their nations. He was also actively involved in efforts to heal the breach with the other

Rome, sharing in a delegation there in 1437. His ecumenism reached ambitiously to Islam. His contemporary John of Segovia (1400–1458) had proposed conferences with Muslim *fuqahā'*, or lawyers, in hope of which he had made his own Latin translation of the Qur'ān, mending the errors of the Cluniacs. Nicholas of Cusa wrote his *Cribratio alchorani (Sifting of the Qur'ān)*,[15] in which he set Islam in the context of his overall philosophy of religious truth. He believed that Muslims, even without knowing it, possessed the main elements of *unica vera religio* and that Muḥammad had a role akin to that of the old Hebrew prophets, a veiled and simplified form of the truth which had its fullness in the God made man, the Christ. That conviction belonged with Nicholas's belief that faith was no more than "learned ignorance," inasmuch as the mind knew the necessity of the unknowable, truly seeing the darkness of the ineffable, in awareness of its limitations and of the mystery that they should remain such even when love was rightly and truly knowing. Nevertheless, what was enfolded in the reality of God was unfolded to the love in which the simplest could participate, all intellect aside.

It was this sense of truth that enabled Nicholas to sit lightly by forms of ritual and impelled his mind to seek unity beyond division. His thought of a theology that was at once affirmative and negative gave him some affinity, perhaps unconsciously, with Islamic mystics, in the way of contemplation. For him, the contemplative way was *through* Christ for the sake of the active way pursued *with* Christ. His *Cribratio alchorani* was published in 1461, three years before his death and eight after the entry of Muḥammad II into Constantinople. The era of the Crusades had at length brought forth a quality of mind they had tragically lacked. Yet untimely so, for the full tide of Ottoman power was set to rise in the next century and reverse the flow of aggression into the heart of central Europe and southward to enclose the shrines the West had so desperately coveted. It would be centuries before the European factor could attain a like sense of what was owed to the East in the logic of the will of Christ. Meanwhile, 1453 had left the western Rome without a rival. Muḥammad II's possession of Istanbul sealed the failure of four centuries to resolve the Great Schism. At no time had the Latins "earned the loyalty of their Christian Arab subjects in Palestine and Syria."[16]

Impregnating the crusading instinct was the commercial factor, since the resources of transport and victuals, ships and convoys, depended on the capacities of the great trading cities and harbors of the European shores—Venice, Genoa, Pisa, Marseilles, and the island of Sicily. When Latin territorial ambitions were thwarted and warfare receded, commerce persisted, setting a pattern of local agencies and depots that developed further in the Ottoman time. Commercial activity in some measure displaced the crusading ideal without significantly improving the mutual attitude of the cultures. Arab Christians might be usefully recruited, but they remained *pagani* and *barbari* to the pure Latins who despised all else. Trade furnished a milieu for the friars and preachers in which to propagate a pure faith, recover lapsed, de-latinized settlers whom they dubbed *pullani*, and disavow the local schismatics, whom they censured on every count of rite and doctrine for not being Latin.

While it is clear that there was in these centuries an interpenetration of culture on the human level, it was of a sort, for the most part, to repel the minds of those who might perhaps have deepened it. There were Franks—pilgrims, soldiers, and traders—who married with Christian Arab women and with Muslims also. But intermarriage, concubinage, and other deviations only fortified the will to rejection. When inter-Christian it still fell foul of Latin prejudice. Melchites were thought of as *Suriani*, and Jacobites, Maronites, and others as "oriental," a prejudice of race ousting an affinity of faith. When sexual bonds were made with Muslims, they served only to confirm the charge of libertinism and lasciviousness which Latins instinctively leveled against Muḥammad and the Qur'ān, as they perceived these to be. Latins who had "gone native" were no occasion for the ideal of Nicholas of Cusa. He had been careful to have angels summon only "sages" to his conclave in Jerusalem.

Even when it could no longer be physically achieved, the crusading temper still lived in the Frankish mind. The offspring of intermarriage symbolized a connivance with the enemies of Christ. Vows that could no longer be fulfilled stayed to haunt that situation. Even if personally attained they had a future tense in that their logic could never be superseded. There was about them an irreconcilable hostility both to Islam and to Arab Christians as long as Latins believed that they and they alone must hold the key—the key of power—to the fulfillment of vows.

The world, nevertheless, proceeds in defiance or neglect of what prejudice may cherish and demand. The ecclesiastical factor had to accommodate to the interests of merchants and the traffic implicit in the nature of the Mediterranean. It did so without conceding to those interests any supersession of its own priority. When the classical Greek heritage was mediated to Europe through the exodus of oriental *Suriani* scholars from Constantinople after 1453, the resulting Renaissance could still virtually ignore the Greek church while accepting antiquity. In due course the Mediterranean would cease to be the principal sea route of Europe. With the Ottoman sultans astride the land routes to Asia, the West took to the western ocean to circumvent them. Arab Christianity, still involved in European merchandising, was reprieved from the ecclesiastical domination that the western Rome from the tenth century to the fourteenth had tried repeatedly to impose. But it was rescue from an enormous failure.

Notes

1. Romantics in the Lebanon have long indulged in the Phoenician connection as a theme of pride and a clue to identity. Examples are numerous. Dr. Charles Malik, distinguished Lebanese Minister, diplomat, and academic (see chapter 9) alludes to the princess legend in "The Near East: The Search for Truth," *Foreign Affairs* 50, no. 2 (January 1952), 231. See also K. S. Salībī, *A House of Many Mansions: The History of Lebanon Reconsidered* (Berkeley, Calif.: University of California Press, 1989), pp. 167–181 ("Phoenicia Resurrected").

2. Examples are legion of the Arab, Muslim instinct to find "the Crusades" at every turn in the road of relationship with the West and/or Christian minority behavior. Thus, at random, Muḥammad Farīḍ in 1911 referred to the Egypt Congress as "a continuation of the Crusades." In 1910 Copts in Egypt held, under protest, a Coptic Congress to symbolize their identity. The national party and Muḥammad Farīḍ deplored this and repudiated also the Egypt Congress held to balance the Coptic one as British mischief-making (see chapter 8).

3. "Defeat," that is, with respect to the Ottoman Arab East. The old crusading complex with Islam passed into the defense of eastern Europe itself.

4. Pio II Lettera a Maometto II, ed. G. Toffanin (1953), pp. 113–114; cited in R. W. Southern, *Western Views of Islam in the Middle Ages* (Cambridge, Mass., 1962), pp. 99–100.

5. It is not necessary to see this isolation in terms as complete as in R. W. Southern, *Western Society and the Church in the Middle Ages* (New York: Penguin Books, 1970); he writes that the Muslim conquest resulted in the three eastern patriarchates being "in a limbo . . . lost to the consciousness of Christendom." The eleventh-century Christian of Antioch whom he quotes as saying that "no certain succession of the Patriarchs of Rome was known in Antioch after the death of Pope Agatho in 681" must have been himself a recluse. Antioch had itself been reabsorbed into the Byzantine rule by Nicephorus Phocas in 969 more than eight decades before the Great Schism.

6. The controversial clause "proceeding from the Father and the Son (*Filioque*)" by which the Christian West deviated from the East, for whom, as originally for the whole church, the clause ran ". . . through the Son." The issue was a subtle one, magnified by communal stresses. The East held by the words of John 15:26 and argued that there should be a distinction between the Father and the Son in the matter of the Holy Spirit's activity in the world.

7. While Byzantine power and Greek ecclesial life survived in the western Mediterranean, notably in southern Italy and Sicily, a number of Greek theologians sought to understand the thought and life of the Latin West. Aquinas was much admired later, and translations of Latin Christian writings were made into Greek.

See Southern, *Western Society,* p. 82: "The West never discovered the Byzantine Church as the Greeks discovered the Latin Church in the 14th century."

8. The term was *latinophron,* and it was malicious enough to deny him later a Christian burial.

9. Insofar as papal claims turned on the primacy of the western Rome and, therefore, of its bishop, the ancient duality between East and West represented a vital issue for the papacy. Medieval and modern western assumptions tend to ignore the abiding name and status of Byzantium as "Rome," the usage explicit in Greek, Arabic, and other eastern languages. When the word occurs in the Qur'ān as the title of Surah 30 it refers to the Greeks' capital.

10. Ibn Khallikan, *Extraits de la Vie du Sultan Salah al-Din,* trans. MacGuckin De Slane (Paris, 1842), pp. 421–422.

11. The word "crusade" emerges only later. "Pilgrimage"—albeit equipped with force and intending conquest and repossession of what was inherently Christian—was the primary term.

12. See Norman Daniel, *The Arabs and Mediaeval Europe,* 2nd ed. (New York: Longman, 1979), pp. 326–327: "That word *devastavit,* so often repeated in so many times and at so many places throughout the Middle Ages, either as a plaint by Europeans, or as a boast, is the key to the whole relationship . . . Xenophobia and hysteria were compounded at the inception of the Crusades."

13. See James Muldoon, *Popes, Lawyers and Infidels: The Church and the Non-Christian World, 1250–1550* (Philadelphia: University of Pennsylvania Press, 1979).

14. Edgar Allison Peers, *Ramon Lull: A Biography* (New York: Macmillan, 1929). This is still a most compendious source and interpretation. *The Book of the Lover* comes within the novel.

15. See Pauline M. Watt, *Nicolaus Cusanus: A 15th Century Vision of Man* (Leiden, 1982); and Henry Bett, *Nicholas of Cusa* (London: Methuen, 1932). His *Opera Omnia* were edited by E. Hoffmann and R. Klibansky (Leipzig, 1932). See also Nicholas Rescher, "Nicholas of Cusa on the Qur'ān," *The Muslim World* 55, no. 3 (July 1965), 195–202.

16. Daniel, *Arabs and Mediaeval Europe,* p. 115.

CHAPTER

6

The Ottoman Centuries

I

REGALED WITH "THE wine of perpetual felicity, it holdeth all the rest of the world in scorn," wrote a seventeenth-century English traveler of the Ottoman power.[1] There are aspects of the rise and expansion of the Ottoman Turks that resemble the original conquests of Islam in the seventh century: the same mingled awe and apprehension in the Christian populations, the same instinct to read their prowess as a divine scourge or judgment, the same discovery of irreversible contours of experience. But there were significant contrasts also. The hegemony of Islam, following a period of political fragmentation in the wake of the decay of the 'Abbāsid caliphate, passed for six centuries into non-Arab hands. In Europe, as instanced by the writings of Martin Luther and the English *Book of Common Prayer*, the word "Turk" became a synonym for "Muslim."[2] It remained so at least until the days of David Livingstone, who had occasion for it in his last journal.[3] But it could never be a synonym for Arab Muslims; rather, the passage of Islamic suzerainty to another race and language meant a profound psychological change. Ottoman power in Anatolia and eastward and southward across the Arab Muslim worlds was achieved against Muslims themselves, making havoc of the original concept of *Jihād*—a theme that figured largely in Ottoman expansion into Thrace, Greece, and eastern Europe. Arab Muslim attitudes to Ottoman rule throughout the six centuries ending with the First World War, in all their diversity, deeply affected the fortunes of eastern Christians.

The rationale of this chapter is to carry forward the European factor of chapter 5 and to take our main story on to the threshold of the nineteenth century and into the intentions of Arab nationalism in chapter 7. This means a necessary overlap between the three chapters, the last of the Ottoman centuries being more usefully studied under the rubric of the

Arab nationalism in which its developments were so much involved. On the one hand, the wide and sanguinary incursions of the Ottomans into eastern Europe and their successes in the naval sphere prolonged the crusading instinct in the Christian West long after its final failure in the possession of holy lands. On the other, the long and fitful demise of the Ottomans in the nineteenth century set the stage for the emergence of Arab renaissance—albeit against a Muslim sovereignty—so posing anew in modern terms the issue of the Arabism of Christians. Oddly, the two poles of the Ottoman story came together. Europe returned physically and politically to the Near East at the expense of the power which, in the fourteenth century, had cowed Europe's crusading pretensions into urgent self-defense on its own continent.

It was early in the fourteenth century that Osman (1280–1324), the first of the Ottoman Turks, established a small principality in northwest Anatolia in independence of the Mongol Ilkhān, who had conquered their Turkic predecessors the Seljūqs. From those modest beginnings, under Orhan (1324–1359) came the advance into Europe, the conquest of Thrace, and the capture of Adrianople, which as Edirne became the European Ottoman capital in 1361. Constantinople was thus virtually surrounded a whole century before its fall in 1453. Consolidation in other parts of the Balkans and in the rest of Asia Minor followed, despite the temporary setback of defeat at the hands of Tamerlane in battle at Ankara in 1462. Serbia, Bosnia, and central and southern Greece were occupied by Muḥammad II, "the Conqueror" (1444–1481) following his capture of Constantinople itself—an event that symbolically marked the final demise of eastern Christendom. The city of Constantine became the Istanbul of Islam. Muhammad assumed the title of *Kaysar-i-Rūm,* "Caesar of Rome," and set himself to capitalize on the possession of the city on which he had set his heart, by merging the Islamic concept of *Jihād* into a Muslim assumption of the dimensions of the old eastern Roman Empire.

As "Lord of the two lands and the two seas," namely, Asia Minor, the Balkans, the Aegean Sea, and the Black Sea, he drove farther into the Balkans, Hungary, and the Crimea, took the island of Rhodes and served notice on the western Rome by landing in southern Italy in 1479. It was his sixteenth-century successors, however, Salīm I (1512–1520) and Sulaymān the Magnificent (1520–1566), who extended Ottoman power into Arab territories south and east of their Anatolian heartland. The former defeated the Mamlūks in Syria and Egypt, hitherto their rivals in those areas but much enfeebled after the death of Qait Bey (1468–1495), their doughty champion. Here for the first time—with some exceptions in Anatolia—the Ottomans were engaged against Muslims. By liquidating the Mamlūk sultanate they added an emphatic Islamic dimension to the vast gains they had made at the expense of Christian Slavs, Greeks, and Thracians. They symbolized this new aura by carrying off to Istanbul the titular caliph of Islam, whom the Mamlūk sultans had held under their power in Cairo. Thus the ʿAbbāsid caliphate, brought ignominiously to Cairo after the sack of Baghdad in 1260 by the Mongols, passed into Turkish custody, and the Ottoman caliphate was inaugurated, devising devious genealogies to underwrite the "Arab" descent from the Prophet, understood as essential to the title. Just as Damascus had given way to Baghdad and Baghdad to Cairo, so in 1517 Cairo gave place to Istanbul. The authentication of Ottoman Islamicity was complete. It endured until 1924, when, withdrawing from imperial grandeur into Turanian nationalism in the aftermath of military defeat, Ottomanism ended in a "Turkey for the Turks." There has been no further caliphal city to take over from Istanbul.

The far-reaching implications of caliphal fortunes in both the sixteenth and the twentieth centuries steadily accompany the study of Christian Arab experience. To write large his Islamic stature Salīm's forces advanced down the Red Sea as far as Aden. Sulaymān, in turn, spread wide his martial wings, with three campaigns in the east, capturing Baghdad, Armenia, the Yemen, retaking Rhodes, then seizing Oran, Algiers, and Tripoli in the West and occupying Cyprus. He suffered defeat in Hungary at the battle of Mohacs in 1526 and abandoned his brief siege of Vienna. These reverses, while giving Europe respite, only fired his eastern ambitions. His successors, however, could not emulate his quality, and the peak of Ottoman splendor passed. Western Christian powers achieved a memorable victory at sea at Lepanto (1571), and a treaty with Spain in 1580 indicated a halt to Ottoman aspirations in the far West. By the early seventeenth century the quality both of Ottoman rulers and of Ottoman military prowess began to decline.

The apex of Ottoman military success broadly coincided with the end of the first millennium of Islam (c. A.D. 1592). That epochal event generated a heightened commitment to Sunnī Islam, in part as a measure of unity and in part in distinction from the Persian Empire to the east, which in the sixteenth century had acquired a new cohesion under the Safavids and their adoption of Shīʿah Islam as the faith of both rulers and ruled. The conquests from Syria to the Yemen and Iraq had given the Ottomans for the first time a majority Muslim population, whose ethnic Arabness the Turks were never either minded or able by colonization to dilute or reduce. But they certainly meant to dominate and enshrine Islam, to embody *Dār al-Islām* as a Turkish reality. Centuries later, there were to be acute strains about this dominance in its caliphal form, whether from Wahhābī-style rigorism within Arabia or from modern interpretations fueling Arab nationalism. Yet the caliphate in their custody had powerful fascination and appeal both for nineteenth-century "federalists" among Arabs espousing a Turkish-led pan-Islam, and for Muslims in the subcontinent of India never politically within it.

Those issues, however, lay far ahead at the time of the Ottoman apogee. As far as non-Muslim elements were concerned, the Ottomans inherited and reinforced the concept and application of the *dhimmī* system. But there was a difference in the manner of its enforcement between the European areas, where Greek, Slav, Bulgar, and other Christians were liable to be in league with European hostility and abettors of it, and Christians of the Arab East, who were remnants in a realm Islamic in fabric, form, and faith. To be sure, as European commercial—and later political—interests developed in the Arab areas, the Christian communities came under suspicion and duress because of their stake, whether for faith or for profit, in the European factor. In the Arab sphere Ottoman power gave an intriguing twist to the minority situation by classifying all non-Chalcedonian Christians as "Armenian," by virtue of the Monophysite character of the Armenian church. Thus the Syrian Jacobites and the Egyptian Copts found themselves curiously realigned within an Ottoman effort to consolidate the *dhimmī* elements.

The (Greek) Orthodox, for their part, found themselves reckoned within the patriarchate of Constantinople, which became their sole channel of communication with the Ottoman state. Prior to the Ottoman advance into Arab territories, Syria and beyond, these Orthodox in those regions had been cut off from Constantinople. Despite renewed access to it by virtue of overall Ottoman authority, the patriarchate of Antioch little relished having to deal with the state solely through the rival patriarch there. This unification of Ottoman dealings with their Arab *dhimmīs* was part of their policy and was pursued also in the Balkans. Some writers have seen it as an expression of Turkish Muslim contempt for Christians and their divisions.[4] Yet it was certainly administratively convenient and congruent with the whole philosophy of *dhimmī* status as a contractual situation whereby internal minority matters remained within the purview of their own pundits, on condition of a total political submission. There was about Ottoman handling of the *Dhimmah* more than a hint of impatience with the troublesome minutiae of Christian theology as reflected in schism and dispute.

Contemptuous, impatient, or merely operational, the pattern worked great hardship on all involved in it. It perpetuated a Greek dominance throughout Arab Christian Orthodoxy, which has persisted to the present. A regulation of Patriarch Germanos of Constantinople after Salīm's conquest of Syria barred all Syrian-born Christians from entering Orthodox monastic life, a measure that made them ineligible for higher ecclesiastical office and confined them to the status of parochial, or secular, clergy. Malign consequences have followed from this system for Arab Christian communities ever since.

Furthermore, the funneling of Christian (Greek) Orthodox minority matters in the Ottoman pattern through the single patriarchate at Istanbul, and others through the Armenians, served to intensify the factious temper it so evidently held in contempt. It made the tenure of the vital patriarchal throne a fertile focus of intrigue and insecurity. It enabled the Turkish state to play politics with minority issues, and it instigated around these an unhappy tradition of strife and conspiracy. Heavy bribes were extracted, or offered, for the "recognition" of patriarchs by the state and of other hierarchs aspiring to office. Between 1595 and 1695 there were no fewer than thirty-one patriarchs with an average tenure of little more than three years. Some lasted less than a few weeks. Of the thirty-one, many were deposed and reinstated, making a total of sixty-one changes in that century—an index to the degree of vacillation on the part of Ottoman officialdom, its susceptibility to bribery, and the readiness, whether depraved or merely politic, of ecclesiastics to play by the Ottoman rules. It was, all in all, a perverse system. In 1726, Callixtus III paid 5,600 pounds in gold for his appointment and died the following day of a heart attack brought on by the excitement. There were bribes to dethrone as well as to enthrone, and the poison of the system spread degradingly into lower levels of the churches. It is true that the next century, ending in 1795, had only thirty-one changes, but the damage persisted and was certainly aggravated by the Ottoman usage of the *dhimmī* order of things. As the case of Cyril Lucar (1572–1638) was to prove, with his seven intermittent tenures of the patriarchal throne, the system also militated against bold leadership by crippling authority and devaluing integrity of mind.

Aside from these factors in its implementation, the *dhimmī* system and its basic concept of rigid identity via community ministered to introversion and stagnation. The Islamic *Sharī'ah* left all relationships within the *Dhimmah*—that is, matters of religious law, personal status, family, marriage, inheritance, and the like—to the law and custom of the community through the local church officials. Centralization at the apex, under the Constantinople patriarch of the Greeks and the Armenian Catholicos (for Jacobites, Nestorians, and—when they emerged—Uniates, or Catholics), necessarily left local specifics to local bishops and others, as religious guardians enjoying the prestige afforded by family connection or social influence.

II

To penetrate to the actual daily experience of the common folk within the Christian communities requires an effort of imagination—of which historians must beware but for which, in the paucity of hard evidence, there is no substitute.[5] The overriding factor belongs with the Turkification of Islam and a different temper in the concepts of power. In their earliest days as conquerors in Anatolia in the time of their founder, Osman, the newly islamicized Turks had tended to hold somewhat loosely to religious identity and approve a degree of flexibility in which Christian elements might be accommodated into Islam, with the help of appeal to mysticism and the esoteric. The Bektashī order of Sufis, the most celebrated of Turkish mystics, exemplifies the fruit of this trend, though caution is needed in tracing Christian factors within its patterns of devotion and discipline.[6] When, however, the more rigorous equation between Turk and Sunnī Muslim developed, not only did the Sufis know tensions with authority but Christian groups underwent a harsher condition. Not that influential occasions for some in administration, commerce, and society did not exist but the very shape of these entailed increasing attrition on the communities at large.

Until the sixteenth-century Turkish conquests in Arab lands, Christians had been isolated from Constantinople. When the conquests reunited them territorially, it was with a Turkish East in which Damascus and Baghdad, Cairo, and, symbolically most important of all, Mecca and Medina, the sacred *Ḥaramain* of Islam,[7] were no longer politically Arab. The circumstances in which the last ʿAbbāsid caliph, Muḥammad Abū Jaʿfar al-Mutawakkil, had forfeited the caliphate to Salīm, to be imprisoned in Istanbul,[8] were humiliating in the extreme. In the very act of being assumed by the Ottomans, the Arab caliphate itself was humbled, despite the importance that later historians have ascribed to caliphal sequence.[9] Having been so long the prisoner of the despised Mamlūks whom the Turks had subdued, Caliph Al-Mutawakkil was hardly a figure to be proudly succeeded. The Ottomans had the prestige of victory and their own springs of pride. Arab Christians were merely incurring new ways of being vulnerable.

It was as "Sultan" and "Commander of the Faithful" that Salīm, Sulaymān, and their successors preferred to be known. The Ottoman state through two centuries after the capture of Arab lands was committed to military expansion and the dominance of war, sustained by taxation and dominated by the soldiery. The sultans operated as absolute rulers, divinely established and accountable only to God. Local lordlings of administrative and fiscal necessity could flourish, albeit precariously, within the system and even perpetuate themselves for generations, but many islamicized in doing so. Lesser folk lived always under the disdain that queried impatiently why they should be so stubborn as to refuse Islam. Christians who might be recruited as officials became creatures of the sultan, identifying their very personalities with his claim. The system of *Devsirme,* or army recruitment, steadily diminished the Christian communities. For it forcibly enlisted children from the Christian peasantry, turned them into Janissaries, and permanently withdrew them from Christian allegiance. Orphans also, bereft of Christian parents, were held to be Muslims.

These military measures, it is true, predominated in the European fields of Turkish conquest and were less frequent in the Arab lands. But, insofar as experience in the one realm penetrated to the other, Christians in the Arab area were apprehensively aware of the subjugation of Christian lands far beyond the Bosphorus. The dispiriting fate of the Balkans may not have affected so keenly the Monophysite Syrians and Copts, who for centuries had been either indifferent or hostile to "Romes," east and west. But it was a burden in the psyche for the (Greek) Orthodox or Melchites to reconcile with the Ottoman reality beyond their northern and western horizons, in the crown lands of old Byzantium. Proof of those yearnings may be read in the attraction in later centuries that such Orthodox Arabs found in "the Third Rome" of Russia and its czars.

Moreover, personnel—islamicized Christians by *Devsirme* or otherwise—from European areas were a familiar feature of Christian Arabdom throughout the Ottoman centuries. Pilgrims to Mecca, travelers in trade, skilled artisans passed through the towns and villages of the Copts, the Melchites, and the Nestorians, bringing incessant reminder of the force of Islam and the prudence of the option of access to it, or just the dismay of its wide incidence. The greatest of all Muslim architects, Sinān, repairer of Hagia Sophia in Istanbul, restorer of ʿAbd al-Malik's Dome of the Rock, and creator of numerous exquisite mosques, was of Greek or Albanian Christian origin, as doubtless were many of the skilled craftsmen he employed.[10] For such men of genius as he, religion, at least in dogmatic form, may have meant little. But, by the same token, his very eminence in the architectural service of his adopted (or not adopted) faith implied a lesson in the futility of being persistently Christian.

The advantages of Islam appealed in other and sinister ways. Conversion to it could afford a way of evading the consequences of crime or misdemeanor or of gaining the better of opponents in litigation by dint of differing rules about witness or by coming under the *Sharīʿah* instead of community laws. Ecclesiastics escaped retribution for nepotism, sexual offenses or criminal acts by opting to islamicize. Such patterns in higher places, when they obtained, could have devastating effects on the morale or the probity of day-to-day Christians. Defection, demoralizing in itself, is more unsettling in circumstances of such moral compromise. Human nature, rather than Islam as such, may be held accountable in this, but human nature takes its ends from the means it finds at hand. There were numerous factors through the Ottoman centuries to render the survival of Arab Christianity more remarkable than its attenuation.

The sense of insistent inferiority induced in the Christian and Jewish *millets* (communities), or *ṭawā'if,* as they came more frequently to be called in some Ottoman areas, came not only from such defections, nor only from the outward signs of subordination—intermittently enforced—of dress, domicile, manners, and social norms about riding and dismounting, greeting, giving way, and studying to be obsequious. It owed much also to the broad Ottoman style of state religion. The Islamic *Sharī'ah,* to be sure, did not have the status in practice that it had enjoyed among the Umayyads. For law now stemmed from the personal rule of the sultan: it was his *Qānūn* (corpus of law). It was the Ottomans who had annexed the caliphate, as was clear from the circumstances after the Mamlūks had been defeated, rather than the caliphate, with its institutional obligations to the *Sharī'ah,* that had recruited the Ottomans. The *'ulamā'*, or scholars, as the custodians of Islam were officially appointed and salaried by the Ottoman state within its own autocracy. Their function was to preserve Islam and to ensure the sound continuity of its religious doctrines and institutions. Their authority, exercised in local setting, could be relied on to sustain the *dhimmī* regulations or to limit any abeyance of them to matters in the state's interest. The practice, for example, of forcibly drafting children of the minorities into military training was at variance with the prescripts of *dhimmī* surrender, since the minorities were at peace and thus fulfilling their part of the contractual bond under which they were to be unmolested. The Sufi orders, conceivably the most potential source of neighborliness to minorities, were from time to time officially subsidized by the state, their spirituality duly aligned to state interests.

III

Reflection on these aspects of the situation of Arab Christianity during the Turkish hegemony of Islam brings us to a factor that was to prove a large occasion of suspicion and disquiet, namely, the readiness and opportunity of European powers to take Christians into protégé status, the protected of foreign "protectors." This feature of eastern Christianity will concern us crucially in later chapters having to do with many areas but with Lebanon most conspicuously and tragically of all.

Protection developed from the Ottoman practice of "capitulations." It was not until 1793 that the Ottoman sultan established a permanent embassy outside his domains. The outside world was *Dār al-ḥarb,* or "realm of war," in Islamic theory and not susceptible, as such, of diplomatic relations. But neither politics nor trade will stay for ideology. Ambassadors were named by and received from western European states in the mid-sixteenth century. Sulaymān the Magnificent made an alliance with Francis I of France in 1536 granting the French commercial privileges in his empire. The English queen Elizabeth I had sounded the sultan about a pact against Spain around the time of the Armada. French, English, and other traders from the Mediterranean were granted trading rights and privileges, which the great trading cities of the inland sea had been enjoying—or taking—long before. Was not Venice known in the West as "the vestibule of Islam"? The spread of Ottoman power in the Balkans and central Europe had made sea-bound western trade all the more vital for all parties. Materials of warfare were important to the Ottomans: Europeans sought the silks and spices, the oils of the east, while their wool fascinated the robe-makers and upholsterers of Ottoman elegance. The English Levant Company originated in 1581.

In its charter it referred significantly to possible "reliefs of many Christians that be or may happen to be in the thraldom of necessitie." It meant "the peace of Christendom" to be its concern as well as commercial benefits. It was only the latter that Ottoman policy had in mind, in the capitulations they granted. So named from the Latin *capitulum,* a "chapter," the documents granted to foreign merchants gave them exemption from certain criminal procedures and relief from customs dues, with right to recruit for commercial purposes the services of local agents, as dragomans or translators, and as facilitators of their enterprises. The recruitment of Christians for these roles stemmed from mutual advantage. Turks, in any event, tended to despise trade as unbefitting their dignity, or they disdained close association with foreigners from beyond Islam. Christians were more likely to know foreign tongues or be willing to acquire the knowledge and also to see, in the connections they could develop, some respite from their inferior status under Islam. Indeed, as the system grew, it could be said that it displaced the *dhimmī* status with foreign cliency or blunted its incidence in practice.

Diplomacy corroborated trade inasmuch as the capitulations involved the consular representatives of the states concerned, who either doubled as merchants themselves or negotiated for them. Local recruits to the system knew well how to improve its occasions, how to make themselves indispensable and build small empires of their own in its workings. The fact that the privileges had to be periodically renewed necessitated diplomatic action in which, for a variety of reasons, western states began to extend the idea of protection from trading clients alone to whole communities in the major ports and cities and beyond. In some cases local consuls and resident merchants were actually granted alien citizenship, which became in turn a pretext for intervention. It took Ottoman authority some long time to realize the menace implicit in capitulations, and especially in their being in the gift of foreign governments and open to abuse when they could be bought and sold. Steps were taken to bring local Muslims into the pattern and to curb the foreign liberties. The sultans began belatedly to reciprocate the claim to communal protection so that Muslims outside their domains could enjoy the shield of their influence. It was in part in that context that the theory of the caliphate assumed a practical pan-Islamic significance for the Ottoman sultan.

The attraction of foreign protection for the Christian minorities had a long and ambiguous sequel, which we must defer to chapter 7 in the context of nineteenth-century Arabism within the Ottoman order as European pressures and pretensions intensified. Insofar as it modified their *dhimmī* status it gave them new perspectives and horizons. Albeit uneasily, it linked their Christianity with wider dimensions. Some it tempted into emotional or psychic alienation from their own locale, making them, if no longer *dhimmīs,* resident aliens where yet necessarily they belonged. When Ottoman power declined in the nineteenth century, protection became at once more congenial but to the Ottomans, by the same token, more suspect and even treacherous. Long legacies of ambivalence, perplexity, and suspicion were bequeathed to Arab Christianity from this history, as well as rivalries within it. No cliency is without its costs, and no patronage without its vested interests. Both were such as to beset the course of Arabism once Ottomanism reached its term in the twentieth century.

Christians of all eastern communities came, in some measure, to share the western perception of Islam, as the corollary of their readiness to take external Christian aegis into alliance. There was pressure—and there was yielding—to extend the logic of protection to that of ecclesiastical affiliation. Churches that could be protégés could well be also "uniates"—as the term went—accepting the rule and discipline of the western Rome through the labors and the wiles of its French, Italian, or other emissaries. All the major groupings during the later Ottoman centuries experienced the schisms in which erstwhile protégés threw in their lot completely with Latin Catholicism, bringing Arab Christianity into yet greater division. Greek Catholic, Coptic Catholic, Syrian Catholic, Chaldean Catholic, Armenian Catholic "Uniates" all eventuated in the Ottoman period detaching from their parent churches and aligning with the papacy.

IV

The story of the Maronite church in Lebanon, the closest and the longest of the Uniates in communion with Rome, will come in chapter 9 as a major factor in the fragmentation and the conflict there. The Coptic Catholic church in Egypt will be involved in chapter 8, but the pattern there is comparable to that which obtained elsewhere in the several affiliations with Rome that transpired in the sixteenth, seventeenth, and eighteenth centuries. In every case the bitterness of division entailed hostile interpretations of history both in the immediate context of separation and in the retrospect to the further past. In every case the initiatives that resulted in the Uniates—those from Rome and those within the yet intact originals—were resisted by non-seceders who saw themselves as loyal faithful betrayed by their own people. Seceders, for their part, claimed that theirs was the true continuity. One of their (western) historians stated the notion bluntly: "The Uniates are the old line. . . . The Orthodox of Syria, who pretend to be the old Church, are a schism away from that Church, formed in the 18th century, when she returned to her original Catholic obedience."[11] That verdict begs a host of questions and, doing so, indicates how so much in the life of Arab Christianity was disserved, if not vitiated, by the wooing of Rome, despite the undoubted stimulus in education, resources, and outlook that the Latin connection brought.

Those "Orthodox of Syria," meaning the Arabic-speaking patriarchates of Antioch, Jerusalem, and Alexandria of orthodox (i.e., Chalcedonian) doctrine, commonly dubbed Melchites and set by the Ottomans within the purview of the patriarch in Istanbul, were the last of the eastern churches to undergo a Uniate secession, and the most significant.[12] It came in 1716 in the patriarchate of Cyril V of Antioch, who in that year made his submission to Pope Clement XI.

It has to be understood against the background of the prolonged aftermath of the Schism of 1054 and the abortive efforts made, for example, at the Reunion of Lyons in 1274 and the Union of Florence in 1439, to reverse it. Human tensions, ambition for office, and strains between cupidity and fidelity have to be kept in view. There were individual patriarchs, bishops, and clergy who schemed or conspired to fulfill their hopes by overtures to Rome in defiance of their own tradition. They could argue that the pope had not officially excommunicated the three patriarchates and that the Great Schism had really been a local difficulty concerning only Constantinople. Nonexcommunication, however, was no proof that, in the papal view, their continuing orthodoxy did not make them the real schismatics. The vigorous activities—and blandishments—of Latin missionaries, Jesuits and Franciscans, were steadily so insisting, as they preached among them and drew laity and clergy to their persuasion setting up strong pressures on patriarchs to follow suit.

Those pressures could be emphasized by the activities of Latin corsairs at sea raiding shipping and cargoes bound for ports or merchants that did not side with papal claims. This distraint was a significant factor in conducing to agitation for, if not capitulation to, the policy of submission. Inevitably the ecclesiastical issue was embroiled with the political. It could be alleged that the continuing Orthodox were scheming with the Ottoman sultan against "the chief Patriarch of all in the West"[13] and, indeed, against Christ. Latin missionaries and papal influences were necessarily matters of unease and suspicion to the Ottoman power. The whole *millet* system was at issue if the Christian elements within it could not be held to its long-standing contractual shape of "tolerance" for "allegiance."

The patriarchate of Cyril V, which lasted for nearly half a century (1672–1720), knew all these tensions. Patriarch of Antioch, some of his own bishops in Aleppo and Sidon had made formal submission to the pope as early as 1683, claiming the support of their people—thanks to economic factors as well as the case for their noninclusion in the schism, though it is puzzling why they needed to submit if they had never been in schism. Cyril's fellow patriarch in Alexandria had succumbed, and Cyril himself in his old age was "sore beset." Jesuit missionaries recognized his dissident bishops, hailing them as purifiers of Catholics deemed unwilling schismatics simply by a tradition of communion with Constantinople under whom the Ottomans had regimented them. Arab, or Syrian, prejudice against the Greeks facilitated their case. Had not Gennadius, Muhammad the Conqueror's quisling patriarch in 1454, been fanatical in his hatred of Latins? Should true Christians be pro-Turk and, against the Vicar of Christ, emulate such misguidedness?

The burden was too much for the aged Cyril. He vacillated and consulted the Maronites from his seat in Damascus. The papacy, advised and locally "timed" by the French Consul, invited, cajoled, and warned Cyril, his Orthodox loyalty slowly eroding, until finally he opted for submission to Rome, trusting diplomatic protection against the risks involved. The fear of Latin power against his tottering jurisdiction outweighed the fear of the Greeks in Constantinople. Almost simultaneously his counterpart in Alexandria, Samuel Kabasilas (c. 1721) followed suit, though later patriarchs remained Orthodox. Jerusalem, a far less important jurisdiction, records examples in both directions. Antioch, the most ancient of sees, was the greatest prize.

V

It followed inexorably that the resulting Uniate church of erstwhile Orthodox, now aligned with Rome, occasioned a schism in Orthodox ranks. Human passions and vested interests weighed both ways. Tensions have a way of perpetuating themselves within the situations their one-sided resolution makes. When Cyril VI (1724–1759) ratified Cyril V's decision, only ten of fifteen bishops in the see adhered to him. The others rallied to Sylvester, a non-Uniate patriarch. The succession of both, as a partisan affair, was disputed. The Uniates went off to Lebanon and a haven with the Maronites, and each claimed that theirs was the true loyalty. The Ottomans finally in 1743 recognized both Cyril and Sylvester within the *millet* system, bemused, no doubt, by Christian fractiousness but cannily aware of French and papal clout. Cyril received his *pallium* from Benedict XIV in 1744, and thus the Uniate known as Greek Catholic finally and divisively entered history. The very name was a contradiction in terms if "Catholic" was to be read only in the sense of Roman or Latin. Yet the adjective "Greek"—if the whole term was read in any other way—proved that there had been something authentic and distinctive that had not been and never could be synonymous with Rome.

Greek Catholicism proved a bittersweet experience. The Greek Uniates soon quarreled with the Maronites and freewheeling Latin missionaries paid scant respect to their jurisdiction. There were vexing problems of marital law, liturgy, and custom to trouble their future. The assets of papal allegiance were at the cost of far-reaching actual and potential debit factors in disunity and rivalry. The story can be seen in part as a delayed legacy of the crusading centuries with memories and impressions enamoring to some and embittering to most. Rome's role in the making of the Uniates bedeviled the Ottoman relationships of the continuing Orthodox. A gentle and compassionate Latin association could have eased the lot of eastern Orthodoxy if Rome had been ready to offer spiritual and intellectual resources without the lust for power and control and the pretensions of ecclesiastical sovereignty. But ecclesiasticism in its given perceptions of history and dogma had no such mind. Orthodoxy became the more in fee to Ottoman behests and the Greek–Arab tension within its parishes and monastic houses was sharpened with consequences persisting to the twentieth century.

The Greek Catholics, in turn, had perforce to maximize the European connection. It served them well in theological sustenance, organization, and sponsorship, but the benefits were at the price of forfeiting, to a degree, the community of the past, the local milieu, and the Arab dimension. The continuing Orthodox became ambivalent about Europe and had accordingly to become more realist about Islamic facts of life around them. Losing part of themselves to the Uniates they were more circumspect within the testing conditions of Ottoman power. We must defer to chapter 7 the consequences that ensued when that power declined and gave way to nation-state concepts and the new dilemmas of both Orthodox and Uniate.

Uniatism—if we may so speak—extended through all the churches. The emergence of a Coptic Catholicism was comparably engineered. A Nestorian Uniatism had been accomplished as early as 1553, when Pope Julius II recognized a Chaldean Catholic patriarch. The Syriac Uniates came in mid-seventeenth century, the Armenian at its end. The Armenian Catholics, however, did not receive recognition, in *millet* terms, from the Ottomans until 1830, and only then with French assistance, but their story has two points of relevance to Arab Christianity. The one is the fact that there was no particular tension involved in the language equation. The Armenian language could accommodate Latin translation without the kind of problematics attending the Greek–Arabic–Latin trinity involved in Greek Uniatism. Arabic-speaking Orthodoxy, unlike Armenian Gregorians, had to sustain ecclesiastical loyalty across a linguistic-ethnic tension. In the second place, however, there was an illuminating parallel. The Armenian Mekhitarist order of monks, inaugurated by Mekhitar of Sivas (1676–1749), with its widespread westernizing activities through cultural expression outside Ottoman domain, was more modestly imitated by monks of St. Saviour and of Shuwair, who developed their activities at the time of the secession to Rome and had a vital role in the consolidation of Greek Uniatism.

It is, of course, evident that the inroads of Latin Christianity into the East via capitulations and diplomatic influence from European states, played into the hands of Ottoman venality, to which reference was made earlier. The strife it engendered over recognition and legitimacy and the insubordination it encouraged within the hierarchies gave ample occasion for intrigue, the cultivation of favor, and the habit of accusation between ecclesiastics and of compromise vis-à-vis the ruling power. There was about Uniatism that which made all parties "schismatic" in the deeper sense of conducing to situations violating, in themselves, "mercy, righteousness, and the love of God." Merchant classes among the laity were much involved in the argument, with their vested interest in foreign facilities or at least in the lifting of constraints on trade. The entail of events on humbler folk was certainly unsettlement and dismay. The story deserves some eastern William Langland, with his biting satire and grim perception of the hypocrisy and mischief besetting the politics of the churches as Uniatism and disunity abetted them. For lack of him, imagination must suffice.[14]

He would certainly have remarked how far the things at stake were seen and transacted wholly in jurisdictional terms even though jurisdictions were also pawns in the equation. It is true that Latin scholarship greatly aided and stimulated the Uniate churches, but the issue of who was or would be "in schism" dominated all else and was resolved entirely in terms of papal claim and patriarchal tenure. Ecclesiastical status, not doctrinal meanings—except insofar as these were subsumed in the other—determined the stakes. The Ottoman state had adopted its *millet* regimen on the basis of communities of faith, administered by religious heads duly acknowledged by ruler and ruled. Uniatism reversed the situation, making communities of faith the creatures of a determining headship.

VI

Contrasted at many points with the story of Latin Uniatism was the entry of western reformed Christianity into the eastern scene. As it came later and had much to do with the genesis of Arab renewal (which concerns chapter 7), it will be useful to review its impact here. The influence it had on Arabism was due in part to the fact that its instincts, unlike those of the Latins, were not jurisdictional. In the context of the education, medicine, and philanthropy that accompanied its doctrinal concerns, intrusive and even disruptive as these were, came a lively independence of mind in people accustomed to hierarchical control. This enabled and stirred them to interrogate the totality of their heritage and their environment. The intellectual and spiritual effects could not fail of political consequences when events otherwise induced them. The careers of some notable Lebanese with whom we are involved in chapter 9 illustrate the ferment of mind that developed within Arab Christianity from the penetration of the criteria of faith, worship, and authority, obtaining within the reformed tradition.

This is not to claim that western Protestantism, in its activities in the Arab East, was innocent of political and commercial associations or that the Uniate connection, for its part, was wanting in vigorous mediating scholarship exciting to Arab Christians, but there was an implicit subordination complex in the primacy of the ecclesiastical power dimension. Uniates were beholden to Rome precisely in being Uniates. Hierarchical considerations were paramount also—and often inhibiting, as far as Arabs were concerned—in the (Greek) Orthodox tradition. The possibility of being authentically themselves, popes or patriarchs apart, came at least obliquely to Arab Christians by the logic of the reformed ethos with its doctrinal emphasis on personal faith, private conscience, and the concept of national church order. "Obliquely" is here a necessary word, inasmuch as those very postures of doctrine aroused an antagonism that took shape in jurisdictional controversy. When the reformed patterns of doctrine and usage attracted local following but were vehemently repudiated by existing hierarchies, pastoral nurture and structure had to be provided for the one against the anger of the other. Western reformed activities of philanthropy and preaching were thus involved, mostly against their will, in the establishment of churches. The bonds that were then formed had some of the aspects of Uniatism but with the vital difference made by the reformed tradition. We may surmise that, in long retrospect, that difference has also been significant in relations with Islam.

VII

Before coming to some review of this dimension in the life of Arab Christianity in the final Ottoman century and its implications for the themes of chapters 7, 9, and 11, it is fascinating to ponder, by way of preface, the career of Patriarch Cyril Lucar (1572–1638). Whether a Cretan, a student in Padua, Venice, and Geneva, warrants a place in the Arab Christian story may be questioned, but he merits inclusion if only as a symbol of issues ahead of his time and a sufferer for them. We need, however, to see the significance of Cyril Lucar, patriarch first in Alexandria and then in Constantinople, as reciprocal to the Reformers' effort in Europe to reckon with Islam and the Ottoman reality. We cannot stay here over western translations of the Qur'ān or, for example, Luther's estimate of Muḥammad.[15] But what–it was asked–did the fact of "the Turks" signify? Some radical reformers and others less radical theorized that they were a divine nemesis on, for example, the papacy, an instrument of divine wrath or, perhaps paradoxically of divine redemption, if Sulaymān could become a new Cyrus.[16]

We need not be surprised if Cyril Lucar had thoughts in the same direction and felt moved to take account of reformed Christian thinking in responding to his own more immediate and local experience of the Ottoman fact as it confronted his Christian responsibility as thinker and patriarch. Plainly, Christian existence under the Turkish yoke required more than inroads from Rome, which divided it. Lucar was concerned to counter the attempts by Jesuits and others to catholicize the Orthodox. It was natural that, given the experience of his traveling studies, he should look to Wittenberg and Geneva, alive with a similar concern. One of his predecessors in the patriarchate at Constantinople, Jeremias II, had corresponded with Melanchthon.

But Lucar's ardor outran his discretion. In his *Confessio Fidei* in 1628 he claimed the assent of his fellow patriarchs in Alexandria and Jerusalem, which was at least premature. Its contents dismayed the orthodox faithful and alarmed the Turks, by espousal of western Christian tenets of grace, justification, and the supremacy of scripture and the disavowal of images and the invocation of saints. Lucar was tragically caught in the dilemma of contriving to defend Orthodoxy against catholicizing by embracing European doctrinal measures kindled from within experience of Catholicism itself on its western ground. Eastern Orthodoxy had different resources and its own ethos. Their logic did not admit of such transplant. Cyril Lucar was deposed from his patriarchate at Constantinople four times between 1623 and 1634 and was strangled in 1638 on the orders of Sultan Murād. Only the intervention of Dutch and English embassies saved him from an earlier fate, and to them he owed his brief episodes of office once he had shown his hand. Synods at Jerusalem in 1638, 1642, and 1672 condemned his teachings, and the young ecclesiastics whom he sent to Oxford and Wittenberg proved disappointing in their subsequent careers. Cyril Lucar's tragedy has to be seen as an ill-fated effort to forestall what, later, Uniatism was to mean within Orthodoxy, in terms that his own heritage could not allow. Orthodoxy, in its wholeness, could not become "protestant" to secure itself from Rome, when the motives of Protestantism had no occasion within it—unless, as Lucar believed, incipient Uniatism or the threat of it supplied one.[17]

To say that the motives of Protestantism had no occasion within Arab Christianity of whatever Orthodoxy is to have in mind the collision with papal authority, in its Roman form, inseparable from those stirrings of private conscience that lay at the heart of the Lutheran experience. They sprang from the doctrine of justification by faith with its awareness of an immediacy between the soul and truth, between grace and the person. Authority in the East, however, had never been totalitarian in the Roman manner. Nor had its conciliar, ecumenical form focused so sharply the issues of sin and forgiveness, of faith and the private self. Its theology of the Incarnation and the divine indwelling in the human, where its heart lay, was less preoccupied with that form of rightness with God which burdened the monk Luther and dominated the resultant Reformation.

But, by the same token, the radical questioning of authority that the western Reformation entailed and required could have had deep relevance, within Orthodoxy, for the engagement of Arab Christianity with Islam. Cyril Lucar's efforts in theology were made from within, not against, ecclesiastical *officium*—a significant difference from the European scene. That fact, in the grim Ottoman context, made it easy to frustrate him. In other circumstances, and coming from below, the emancipation from fixity and the traditional could have meant exciting possibilities, relational and nonjurisdictional, in cohabitation with Islam. Among reformed sectaries in the West, often ignored by historians, there were intriguing ventures into the puzzle of competing faiths. In central Europe and the

Balkans sixteenth-century thinkers such as Jacob Palaeologus (c. 1530–1585), Simon Budny (1533–1590), and Adam Neuser (d. 1576) took their revolt against ecclesial rule into overtures of mind toward Islam, moved by the providential problem of its domain in Europe but also probing into its potentially mutual ground with Christianity. Neuser in fact became a Muslim after taking refuge in Turkey. Palaeologus, however, returned to Europe to pursue his vision of "an inter-faith church of spiritual Semites" in which he conceived of Jews, Gentile Christians, and Turks as "three branches of the people of God," insofar as they conformed to "the inner word." He saw the first as being such by race, the second by faith, and the third by their monotheism, their occupancy of Christian lands, and their acknowledgment of "the prophetic office of Christ."[18]

These were, indeed, radical ideas in the context of that time—ideas for which Palaeologus, as a discredited Dominican, paid with his life, suffering execution in Rome. Lucar's abortive initiatives, coming as they did from above rather than from below, had proved that neither Ottoman power nor the Orthodox mind could accommodate such ventures of thought. The Ottoman factor told powerfully against any suggestion of a common Semitic bond, while ideas emanating from the travail of reform and ferment within the western scene were out of context in the soul of eastern Orthodoxy. Only when Ottomanism had receded to give way to Arabism in its twentieth-century form could Arab Christianity see Islamic relations in such terms. Meanwhile, in the centuries between John Huss and Napoleon, radical reformers and sectaries from eastern Europe would take refuge with the Ottoman power.

VIII

Occupancy of Christian lands, which Palaeologus had thought would somehow qualify Muslims as within a dialogue of faith, continued through those same centuries to engage western Christian concern in a quite contrasted sense. The many travelogues that in the sixteenth, seventeenth, and eighteenth centuries enlightened western readers about the lands of the East tended to ignore people in deference to places. They often paid scant attention to the actual life of the churches while pursuing interests archaeological and scholarly concerning sanctuaries and ruins. This tendency to have its territory seen as a museum of history rather than an abode of living faith has persisted throughout the experience of Arab Christianity. The churches might be useful politically as protégés, their members commercially as trading agents, and their shrines romantically, but to penetrate their ethos or appreciate their liturgies was a less congenial impulse, if not entirely absent. Such was the price local Christians paid throughout the

Ottoman period for the way in which a western Christian sought out the holy geography in which they lived.

Their portrayal by Henry Maundrell in his *Journey from Aleppo to Jerusalem,* made in 1697, is representative both for its terse perception, within its own limits, and its later influence. He was briefly chaplain of the English Aleppo Company, where he had several notable predecessors who were pioneers in Arabic studies in their generation. The impression left by his rare references to the Christian world he met en route is one of decaying edifices and parlous clergy. Though he describes the Holy Week rituals in Jerusalem in detail he offers only one brief account of what he saw in worship. "Being informed that there were several Christian inhabitants in this place, we went to visit their church, which we found so poor and pitiful a structure that here Christianity seemed to be brought to its humblest state, and Christ to be laid again in a manger." He noted "a piece of plank supported by a post," which he took to be a reading desk. Just by was "a little hole commodiously broke through the wall to give light to the reader—a very mean habitation," all in all, "for the God of Heaven!" Other Christians he found south of Jubail "in a small grotto in a rock by the sea shore, open on the side toward the sea and having a rude pile of stones erected in it for an altar. . . . the curate of it told us (they) were not permitted to have any place of worship within the town." Maundrell's comment on the patriarch of Damascus (unidentified) has a caustic tone: "The place of his residence was mean, and his person (aged about forty) and converse promised not anything extraordinary. He told me there were more than one thousand two hundred souls of the Greek communion in that city." The chaplain's reader today is left wishing that he had perceived the local Christianity with the sort of diligent reckoning he applied to the walls of Jerusalem, whose circumference he paced out at 4,650 paces, which he took to be equivalent to 4,167 yards.[19] Nevertheless, his travel diary yields telling glimpses of churches in hardship and poverty, while leaving to silence those warmer features which his own state and stress of mind disposed him to neglect.[20]

Though the original charter of the Levant Company in 1599 had alluded to the possibility of aid to those who might be in need, the task of chaplains like Maundrell was to care for company personnel and local consuls, not to relate to eastern Christians. They held their services in consular chapels, where these existed. Many of them were able and perceptive men who interested themselves in oriental manuscripts and did much to promote Arabic studies in European universities.[21] The Ottoman conditions of their tenure precluded other ventures across frontiers even had they been minded to make them. Biblical associations were also among their motivations, as of other traveling residents like the Swede Frederick Hasselquist in the mid-eighteenth century, a disciple of the great botanist Linnaeus.[22] A somewhat later traveler was the redoubtable John Burckhardt, who roamed the Levant in the aftermath of Napoleon's invasion of the East—an event that dramatically stirred imaginations in both directions.[23] It was perhaps poetic fitness that Sydney Smith should have terminated Napoleon's oriental ambitions at the very place where the medieval Crusades had finally expired—the sea fortress of Acre.

It was via Malta that both English and American missionary initiatives began their slow and dogged espousal of the Ottoman East. It was there that the American Congregationalists established an Arabic Press (transferred to Beirut in 1834) and the Anglican pioneer, Joseph Wolff, began his flamboyant career through near Asia and beyond.[24] In 1841 came the launching of the Anglican bishopric in Jerusalem as a joint enterprise with the German Lutherans. The Ottomans yielded to Foreign Office persuasions in granting a firman for its establishment, while John Henry Newman found it an intolerable betrayal of church order.[25] Solomon Alexander, the first bishop and a former rabbi, survived only briefly, leaving the formative achievement to his successor, Samuel Gobat, a Swiss Lutheran who served from 1846 to 1879. He was a tireless traveler and a vigorous evangelist, and during his long episcopate the issues emerged that were equally experienced by the pioneers from the United States in Syria-Lebanon and among the Armenians, namely, the incompatibility between the reformed ethos and the existing church structure. Emphatically non-jurisdictional in their intention, their evangelism entailed jurisdiction upon them when local response led to the repudiation of the responsive by their own hierarchy.[26]

In the retrospect of a crowded century and more, it is easy to see how this tension was initially inevitable and ultimately surmountable, as both parties, eastern and western, became more perceptive of each other. Reformed Christian assumptions of the accessible Bible and personal conviction, of universal spiritual priesthood and the nature of Holy Orders, grossly infringed on the eastern understanding of ecclesiastical authority and lay discipleship. More immediate frictions multiplied when sharp contentions supervened in the local sphere, exacerbated by personal animosity. Samuel Gobat held himself obliged to set up a church-structure for the Arab folk—almost wholly from the (Greek) Orthodox population—when on his view the situation required it by virtue of their adoption of his form of faith. From the 1860s, beginning in Nazareth, came the creation of Anglican "parishes" and the ordaining of Arab clergy. The Anglicans, one may say, had church congregations in spite of themselves and yet also because of themselves. There was a similar emergence of Egyptian and Syrian-Lebanese evangelicalism via American mission and for the identical reasons.

As for the original churches, rejectionism on their part did not mean immunity. Loyalties sustained among the laity nevertheless changed slowly and perceptively in terms of new norms of conduct and sensitivity expected of the clergy, and of more enquiring possession of revered tradition. As the secular historians Braude and Lewis observe: "Missionary effort created an intellectual bridgehead in Ottoman territory."[27] Something of Cyril Lucar's aspirations, now no longer ahead of their time, began to register and more securely because from below. By a long and painful process the Evangelical Synod of Syria and the Lebanon, and the Palestinian Native Church Council—later to be more happily named the Arab Evangelical Episcopal Church—and the Coptic Evangelical Church in Egypt could find themselves compatible with the ancient churches, taking part with them in the Middle East Council of Churches and its more local, tentative predecessor councils.

But the progression was painful and chequered on many counts. There were uneasy relationships between foreign and local in the evolving story, perhaps most evidently in the Arab-British scene bequeathed to Gobat's second successor, Bishop Blyth, after the reconstitution of the bishopric in 1887.[28] No Arab bishop was appointed until 1958, and colonialism, politically current, inevitably had ecclesiastical corollaries. For all their will to autonomy, the local recruits to Protestant mission were beholden in various ways to its western sources, beneficiaries of its educational investments and conditioned by the vicissitudes of external politics. Throughout the Ottoman period their religious affiliation made for insecurity and prudence, both of which tended to strengthen the sense of ambivalence in their position. Was their participation in Arabness—given their separation from its normal Christian form—to align with continuing Ottomanism or to identify with an avowed quest for independence? The horns of this dilemma will concern us in chapter 7. The immediate point is that their western associations gave them stimulus and perspective, not shared by many in the older traditions, and did so precisely because they had already undertaken a vital reordering of their past in adopting a Christianity of a different idiom. It was an idiom that by its theology and its history had a vital relevance to the questions of loyalty, conscience, and conviction that attached to history and society in the whole. It is not, therefore, a matter of surprise that the influence of the reformed patterns of Christianity played a crucial part in the evolution of Arabism after Ottoman demise, whether directly through the actual membership or indirectly through those it inspired. For the institutions that accompanied and serviced that Christian presence had a range and impact far beyond the membership it was able to recruit.[29]

To appreciate the full implications of access to the reformed version of Christianity on the part of Arab Christians who acceded to it, it is necessary to grasp the antipathy that obtained between it and the Orthodox at large of both the Chalcedonian and non-Chalcedonian allegiance. Despite their initial—and good—intention not to proselytize, the nineteenth-century European and American missionaries, or many of them, became party to sharply critical, dismissive, or crudely hostile attitudes to the oriental churches as they perceived them. Thus, for example, Henry H. Jessup, doyen of the American Presbyterian Mission, roundly charged them with "corruption, idolatry and immorality."[30] What was vulgar and insensitive in such judgments, which only longer and happier perception has corrected, indicates the radical decision in which adherence involved the local recruits. There were doubtless unworthy motives at work among these and, as the Shidyāq family in Lebanon was to show,[31] there were psychological casualties and personal disasters involved among those for whom the tensions were too great. Yet in maturer minds and more stable personalities such as meet us in the renewal of Arabic and the initiatives of pen and press that served it, there was grateful proof of the positive gain derived paradoxically from the radical challenge of a temper to be deplored. The deep and often hidden quality of Orthodoxy could be trusted to survive and endure despite the harshness in what confronted it.

Disruptive both emotionally and ecclesiastically as the entry of the reformed tradition was in Arab Christianity during the last Ottoman century, it is important to appreciate its relevance to the inroads of secularity which coincided with it from other sources in the western relationship. Indeed, it is right to see within that western evangelicalism something of an act of reparation for the strains and confusions inherent in the wider dimensions of the traffic of the Mediterranean. From Napoleon on, the attraction of European technology and literature—not to say the provocations of its diplomacy—created a ferment of ideas and passions within the old traditions. How fascinating and religiously disorienting[32] these could be was exemplified in the character of Salāmah Mūsā, whom we encounter in chapter 8, a Copt with a pen and a style to give it expression. The issues his "education"[33] enshrined and his verve made articulate were everywhere latent. The very strength of Orthodox spirituality in all its forms lay precisely in its contemplative, apophatic response to the mystery of God in creation and Incarnation, which unfitted it to discern congenially the theological response demanded by the new humanism and the bewildering activism of western instincts. Had a western Christian presence, already chastened by Darwin, Marx, and Strauss, been wanting in the Arab Christian scene, it would have been the more ill-served in what modernity exacted within it.

This is not to say that all the western means and ends in mission were well calculated to interpret modernity aright nor to imagine that the necessary ministry within a Christian sympathy was well pursued. Much of it was preoccupied with the assertive dogmatism that seemed to be demanded by its encounter with Islam. Or it was minded to confine its sympathies to familiar forms of pastoral nurture and pious faith recruitment. Or, contrariwise, it was itself unnerved by scientific and secular perplexities and retreated into an ethicism no longer ready for a living theology. Matthew Arnold's lines "On Dover Beach" had claimed their truth for all "the naked shingles of the world." The Mediterranean would not be exempt.[34] But that intellectual challenge to the soul of Arab Christianity had at least served to give to the several ecclesiastical shapes of creed and power in which the centuries had sanctioned and divided it a common denominator and a common summons. The formulations of Christology and the hierarchies of authority found themselves required to interrogate what they had too long assumed. It was a demand that addressed them all, a circumstance that ignored while it also sharply tested what divided them. The religious preoccupations of David Strauss and George Eliot, of Ralph Waldo Emerson and Herman Melville, of Arthur Hugh Clough and Charles Darwin and their innumerable kindred minds in the western world took their way into the eastern world and merged with their human counterpart in eastern minds, translating themselves into the idiom of a reviving Arabic.

But this is to anticipate. The America from which those signals came was the America of Lincoln and emancipation and its aftermath. The Europe was the Europe of Bismarck and the *Drang nach Osten,* of Gladstone with his ardent moralism and eastern sympathies, of Disraeli purchasing Cyprus and outwitting French and Russians in the finesse of diplomacy. It was the age of a Europe busy with anticipation or anxiety concerning the survival—or the potential vacuum of demise—respecting the Ottoman Empire. At long last, the prostrate Turks in the 1920s opted for territorial nationhood and the relinquishment of empire. It is time to turn to those political events, the strains and tensions of the long ambiguity around them, and the trauma of their climax. The inward quests and questionings of the soul had bewildering and often harsh occasion in the complexities and contentions of politics. The Ottoman centuries were as fortuitous for Arab Christianity in their drastic conclusion as they had been through their long career.[35]

Notes

1. Richard Knolles, *The Generall Historie of the Turks to 1638,* 5th ed. (London, 1638), Intro., n.p.

2. As in the third of the three Collects for Good Friday. The word "Turk" came to be used in the late sixteenth century in England as a synonym for "target" in archery, and the phrase "to turn Turk" came from the same period. Europeans referred to Islam by the name of the people and power most intriguingly and–for eastern Europe most menacingly–within their ken as Muslim. "The Turk's Head" became a favored inn sign.

3. As the extract records on his tombstone in Westminster Abbey, Livingstone wrote in his last diary entry as he lay dying in central Africa: "All I can add in my solitude is 'May heaven's richest blessing come down on everyone, American, English *or* Turk, who will help to heal this open sore of the world.'" The date was 1873.

4. Steven Runciman, *The Orthodox Christians and the Secular State* (Oxford, 1971), p. 35: ". . . an almost affectionate contempt such as a good humoured bully feels towards his victims."

5. One example of the careful research required is Muhammad Adnan Bakhit's "The Christian Population of Damascus in the 16th Century," in *Christians and Jews in the Ottoman Empire: The Functioning of a Plural Society,* ed. B. Braude and B. Lewis (New York: Holmes & Meier, 1982), 2:18–66. It is the *Vilāyet* (district), not the city, of Damascus to which his statistics relate, which then included Tadmūr, Damascus, Safad, Lajjūn, Nablūs, Jerusalem, Gaza, 'Ajlūn, and Karak. His examination of registers, court cases, and so on leads him to conclude that the treatment of Christians "depended more on local considerations (e.g., political) than on any imperial canon. . . . Their numbers would not seem to have been large enough to cause them to be regarded as a significant threat. . . . Jerusalem stands out as an exceptional case" (p. 55).

6. See John Kingsley Birge, *The Bektashi Order of Dervishes* (Hartford, Conn.: Hartford Seminary Press, 1937). The founder was reputedly Bektash Veli (1248–1337), who migrated from Khurasan to Anatolia; the main development of the order dates from the fifteenth century. It later had close association with the Janissaries, and Bektashi pirs served as chaplains. The Bektashi order suffered diminution after these were disbanded in 1826. Some of its members used a commemorative meal in honor of Ḥusain of Karbalā', and they used initiatory rites and systems of penance in which confession was made and candles lit. They traditionally wore a cap, cloak, and girdle, the last carrying a seven-pointed stone. The tying of the girdle could be accompanied by a formula: "I tie up greediness and unbind generosity," continuing with six other evils: anger, avarice, ignorance, passion, hunger, and Satanism; unbinding: "meekness piety, fear and love of God, contentment, and divineness."

7. It is evident from the decision of the Umayyads to move out of Mecca and Medina, making Damascus their capital, that the government of Islam could not feasibly remain in the cities of its origin and of Muḥammad's *Sīrah,* or "life story." But the possession of them has always been a prime concern and a seal of prestige for all Islamic rule. The renown the Ottomans sensed in their acquisition of the *Ḥaramain,* "sacred Mecca and Medina the enlightened," was paralleled, for example, when Ibn Saud emulated them in 1924.

8. He was allowed to return later to Cairo, where he died in 1543.

9. It would seem that the importance given to the caliphal issue in narratives of

the history belongs more with later theory than with the circumstances of the time. Salīm himself seems to have laid little stress on the succession from the ʿAbbāsids, these being such pitiable hostages of the despised Mamlūks. Salīm did not use the title "Caliph" on his coins. Theory held it important in that the Ottomans were not of the Quraish, the only tribe duly qualified to inherit the office. Explicit resignation of it by the (Quraishī?) ʿAbbāsid could be held to legitimate Salīm and his successors in its possession by the will of Quraishī disposal. This was a nicety of which victorious Ottomans had little need. See T. W. Arnold, *The Caliphate* (Oxford, 1924).

10. Sinān ʿAbd al-Mannām (1489–1588), originally Joseph, was drafted into the employ of the Ottoman court and showed his first skills in military engineering. Later in a long career he adapted Byzantine church architecture into magnificent mosques of which he built some eighty, with a variety of palaces and tombs.

11. Adrian Fortescue, *The Uniate Eastern Churches* (New York, 1923), p. 185. Fortescue's is a very partisan account insisting that it was the continuing Orthodox who thereby became the schismatics simply, as he put it, by "maintaining communion with Constantinople" (p. 194). The asperity in his Latin partisanship may be sensed in his comment (see below) about Patriarch Sylvester, non-seceding successor to Cyril: he was "only one out of countless Orthodox bishops who have rested their claim to rule in the name of Christ on the approval of Mohammed [*sic*]" (p. 200), i.e., the Ottomans.

12. On the others, see below and chapters 8 and 9.

13. Fortescue, *Uniate Eastern Churches,* p. 190. The story of Cyril V's tribulation is well documented in Robert M. Haddad, "On the Melkite Passage to the Unia: The Case of Patriarch Cyril of al-Zaʿīm, 1672–1720," in *Christians and Jews,* ed. Braude and Lewis, 2:67–90.

14. William Langland was a fourteenth-century English poet whose *Vision of Piers Plowman* voiced a lively anticlericalism, grounded in deep practical piety and ardent to reform as well as castigate church and state as he perceived them in his wanderings in rural England and his savor of London. He writes:

"Then Covetousness came and cast about for means
Of overcoming conscience, and the cardinal virtues.
. . . . . .
His weapons were wiles for winning and hoarding:
With feigning and falsehood he fooled all the people . . .
chose prelates who to save their temporalities
. . . . . .
Made good faith flee the place.
He boldly overbore with many bright gold pieces
Much of the worth and wisdom of Westminster Hall . . .
Unseating Honesty with 'take this to amend your judgement.'"
(Passus XX, trans. Terence Tiller [London: BBC, 1981], p. 247).

15. The first Latin translation of the Qur'ān by Robert of Ketton dates from 1143. Four centuries later Theodorus Bibliander worked on a revised Latin version, but both ventures were flawed by error. Exact but with excessive Arabisms was the Latin translation by Louis Marracci in 1698. The first Arabic Qur'ān to be

printed in Europe dates from the end of the fifteenth century in Venice. Luther's German version was designed to expose the fallacies and heresies of Islam, though he was ready to allow the report that "there is no better government on earth than under the Turks . . . who have only the Qur'ān."

16. For such wildly ranging views of possible providences in the Ottoman sultans, see George Huntston Williams, *The Radical Reformation* (Philadelphia: Westminster Press, 1962), pp. 834f., especially John Hut, the Wittenberg Anabaptist bookseller.

17. On Cyril Lucar, see G. A. Hadziantonian, *Protestant Patriarch* (London, 1961); and Steven Runciman, *The Great Church in Captivity* (New York: Cambridge University Press, 1968). On his *Confessio* and its condemnation, see *Church History* (1943), 118–129; and J. N. W. B. Robertson, *Acts & Decrees of the Synod of Jerusalem* (1899), pp. 185–215. One of Lucar's young clerics was his "keeper of the Seals" sent to Oxford, who later became patriarch of Alexandria of indifferent merit. Lucar deserves gratitude as the donor, via Sir Thomas Roe, of the Codex Alexandrinus to Charles I in 1628.

18. Williams, *Radical Reformation,* p. 741. Palaeologus traveled between Prague, Chios, and other Greek islands and Rome. He distinguished between a Christian *fides narrationis* and an Islamic *fides promissionis* and stressed the common ancestry of Abraham.

19. Henry Maundrell, *A Journey from Aleppo to Jerusalem,* 3rd ed. (Oxford, 1714), passages cited from pp. 36–37, 9–10, 19–20, 175, and 147–148.

20. See the introduction by David Howell to the 1963 reprint edition of Beirut. Howell discusses personal circumstances that might have contributed to Maundrell's travelogue.

21. See Alfred C. Wood, *A History of the Levant Company* (New York: Oxford University Press, 1935); and J. B. Pearson, *Biographical Sketches of the Chaplains to the Levant Company, 1611–1706* (Cambridge, 1883).

22. Frederick Hasselquist, *Voyages and Travels in the Levant, in 1749–52,* trans. C. Linnaeus (London, 1766). He notes the enmity between Greek Orthodox and Greek Uniates and the latter's greater liberty in public processions, "as subjects of European powers" (p. 42). He also remarks laconically that "in a Greek Church the people cannot sleep, which often happens in churches of other persuasions, as these are obliged to stand up and be in constant motion by crossing and bowing." He adds that, consequently, they "are too much awake going out of church" (p. 44).

23. John Burckhardt, *Travels in Syria and the Holy Land* (London, 1822). He has interesting observations on the affluence of some monasteries (e.g., p. 169), and on the fewness and poverty of Christians in many villages, sometimes reduced to a single family. On Mount Tabor he found a single family of (Greek) Christians, refugees from the Hauran, hoping on its remoteness to avoid the *jizyah* tax, expecting to remain unnoticed ("for the time being they had succeeded" [p. 334]). At Karak he notes "ill-observant Christians who do not understand Greek" and Turks who request baptism as an insurance or preservative for their male children with priests concurring in a pious fraud by immersing only hands and feet, thus setting all priestly scruples at rest about the illegality of the deed. "Such is the

efficacy of this 'Baptism,'" Burckhardt continues, "that these baptised Turks have never been known to die otherwise than by old age" (pp. 386–387).

24. His energy was phenomenal from Gibraltar to Bukhara and was served by wide erudition. A contemporary likened him to a comet across the face of mission, in the 1820s. But it was left to a slow, fitful succession of more modest, solid practitioners of the Gospel to make good the trail he blazed.

25. The decision of the archbishop of Canterbury to seek an act of Parliament to establish the Jerusalem bishopric intensified Newman's misgivings about the legitimacy of the Church of England and its claim to be within apostolic order. He objected to the Lutheran connection, to the Jewish origins of the appointee, and most of all to what he saw as the uncanonical invasion of Orthodox territory and jurisdiction. In *Apologia Pro Vita Sua* (London, 1864) he wrote: "As to the project of a Jerusalem Bishopric, I never heard of any good or harm it has ever done, except what it has done for me.... It brought me on to the beginning of the end" (concluding words of part 5).

26. We have stressed here the contrast with Latin Uniatism in the reformed initiatives; readers may query why, in fact, a bishopric was established, when it could not be justified either on the (hitherto indispensable) ground of national territory, nor of Anglican faithful. The bishopric was, in fact, the only form under which foreign Christian presence could be had in Jerusalem, and state aegis was the only route by which authority for it could be secured from the Ottoman sultan. Effort was also made to seek the goodwill of the eastern churches and to reassure them. These scruples were more effectively fulfilled after 1887, but by then Gobat's evangelism had created congregations and revealed the dilemma. See *Religion in the Middle East,* ed. A. J. Arberry, 2 vols. (Ann Arbor, Mich.: Books on Demand, 1969), 1:570–595.

27. *Christians and Jews,* 2:28.

28. These are well researched in A. L. Tibawi's oddly titled *British Interests in Palestine, 1800–1901: A Study of Religious and Educational Enterprise* (London: Oxford University Press, 1961).

29. See chapter 9 below and, in particular, the saga of the American University of Beirut.

30. Henry H. Jessup, *Fifty-three Years in Syria,* 2 vols. (London, 1910).

31. See p. 226 below and chapter 9, n. 37.

32. "Disorienting" is apt in both senses. For what was disconcerting in itself was also dispossessing them of aspects of their local, mental habitat as "orientals."

33. The word he used, borrowing from Henry Adams as the title and theme of his autobiography. See chapter 8, n. 39.

34. The poem "On Dover Beach" became a symbol of the intellectual loss of faith during the nineteenth century in the West, with its metaphor of receding tides. Physically, of course, the Mediterranean was exempt, having no tidal flow, but the analogy carries.

35. I use "fortuitous" in the strict legal sense of "that which happens by a cause that cannot be resisted."

CHAPTER

7

Modern Arabs and the Intentions of Arabism

I

THERE HAS BEEN no historian for the decline and fall of the Ottoman Empire to emulate the achievement of Edward Gibbon in *The Decline and Fall of the Roman Empire.* The two empires had wide territories in common, and both went through a protracted demise that had resounding consequences for those caught in the throes of the vacuum that ensued, but there was little else the situations shared. Gibbon had seen as "a tedious tale of weakness" the weary centuries of Byzantium, which he deplored. Some historians might be minded to echo the sentiment about the Ottoman story of decay.

The verdicts of historians are often partisan—none more so than those of Gibbon's masterpiece, so redolent with his own persona. The telling portrays the teller: Rome's centuries are read through the lens of eighteenth-century London. Time's distance had not saved Gibbon's mind from the prejudice he cherished; rather, it had nurtured it. But time's proximity is no less liable to educate conflicting opinions about the meaning of events, the more so when their interpretation belongs with fates and fortunes in the living world.

Conflicting views on the drift of contemporary history certainly characterized the Arabs in their awareness, well before and after the turn of the twentieth century, of the problematic future of Ottoman power. Balkan provinces were forfeit. The French had acquired Algeria as early as 1832 and Tunis in 1881, the year in which the British began their prolonged mastery of Egypt. Italy invaded Ottoman Libya in 1911. Many Ottoman territories, thus vulnerable to European inroads, had long periods of local assertion against Istanbul in the varied forms its claims and capacities allowed. Back in the first half of the nineteenth century, it had taken French and British intervention to rescue the Sublime Porte from the successes of Muḥammad ʿAlī and his son Ibrāhīm Pasha of Egypt in Syria and Arabia. Earlier, in Arabia, the Wahhābī revolt had demonstrated how readily central authority could be interrupted and defied.

European states—Russia, France, Austria, and Britain—had long busied their chancellories with "the eastern question," and the debates and conspiracies between them inspired by the conjectures attending on "the sick man of Europe." There was the heritage of ancient Greece to be liberated from "the Turk," the lands and peoples of the sacred Christian faith to be shielded from his menace or incompetence. And he, with his unwieldy spread of provinces and peoples, had traveled far from the awesome days of Sulaymān the Magnificent, whose arms had humiliated all resistance from Hungary to Hadramaut.

Our present study, against this background, is the slowly emerging Arab reaction to the experience of Ottomanism

> . . . calculating the future,
> Trying to unweave, unwind, unravel
> And piece together the past and the future
> . . . . . .
> When time stops and time is never ending . . .

It was a gradual process involved emotionally and conceptually in the stimulus of European ideas and precedents and conditioned by the ambiguity of Ottoman policies. As it emerged, through the last quarter of the nineteenth century and the first of the twentieth, one root question persisted beneath all the tactical issues, local and immediate. How was Arabism to be conceived, defined, and achieved—if at all—when to be Arab was in some vital sense to belong with Islam and when the power against which Arabism must be affirmed was that of the Islamic caliphate to which all Muslims had a duty of loyalty and submission? Must not Arabism, unless defying Islam itself, be consistent only as the sort of peoplehood that the Ottoman Empire had long admitted in practice and also approved in theory? How could the equation between Arabism and Islam be sustained in any will to autonomy from or revolt against its due caliphal form? Was the alternative to Ottoman loyalty a retreat—or an advance—into some secular version of Islam? In the light of these radical questions, it is not surprising that, despite the stirrings of national ardor, an Arab Ottomanism persisted until 1918 and was not even finally abandoned when the caliphate itself was abolished in 1924.

The detail of this basic issue, which with some economy of narrative we must take up, entailed no less fundamental self-interrogation for Christian

Arabs. Were they to be parties to, even pioneers in, an Arabism nerved to repudiate sacred Muslim ties? If so, would the resulting Arab autonomies, plural as they must be on the assumption of nation-states, be a surer prescript for Christian security than the old *dhimmī* status of Ottoman tradition? Should Christians themselves be instigators, or abettors, of a course of action or ideal that involved Muslim Arabs in Islamic disloyalty? On what grounds and in what terms could Christians affirm their Arabness when Arabism itself presented a dilemma outside their religious frame of reference? We find Christians in fact in the vanguard of Arab ideology, opting hopefully for the principle of Arab separatism but thereby moving in ambivalence both about their European associations and the interests of separate states.

The Arabic language itself reflected this ambiguity of meanings and verdicts. There was the hallowed word *Al-Ummah*,[1] "the community" (of Islam understood), the sphere of the solidarity of the faith and the realm of the *Sharī'ah*, the divine law. The theme of the pan-Islamicists, it could not properly be applied to separate states or nations, sundering as these did the unity of *Dār al-Islām*. That unity, however, had come to be shared by Arabs, in a politically inferiorized role, with Turks to whose language their education, government, and culture were tied. In a paradoxical way, the very empire which housed *Al-Ummah* juridically provoked tension emotionally wherever a sense of Arabness demanded to prevail over Turkish or was discontent with its inferior station. Within *Al-Ummah*, of course, there was *'iqlīmiyyah*, localism, administrative and social, such as Ottoman rule readily allowed, indeed necessitated, in the looseness of its structures. *Waṭaniyyah* might roughly translate "nationalism" in the sense of "fatherland" and native soil. *Qaumiyyah* meant "nationalism" in terms of "peoplehood" and was the preferred word of the theorists of the nation-state. How localism, always potent in its immediacy, not least among rural and feudal societies, should yield to *qaumiyyah* and how both should relate to *Al-Ummah* were the burdens of debate and endeavor until the demise of the caliphate changed but did not resolve the perspectives by which to decide. The thread in our concern, through all the tangle of inter-Arab aspiration and controversy, has to be the mental and political predicament in which that tangle engaged a Christian Arabism or, rather, the Christian Arabisms. For "Arabisms" on every count of identity, history, emotion, retrospect, and anticipation they could not fail to be.

The special factors that obtain in Egypt and Lebanon with respect to the Muslim/Christian situation mean that those two countries, with their larger proportions of Christians, must be considered separately. It will be clear from the two succeeding chapters why the Coptic and the Maronite churches, respectively, take central place there. The present chapter needs to explore the Ottoman/Arab equation as it obtained throughout the Near East, but for reasons that will be evident Syria and Syrians, often living and writing elsewhere, have the major emphasis. Here, as later with Egypt and Lebanon, some focus on personal biography will be a useful means of illuminating what was at stake. Important as theories and theorists are, it is the human experience that we most need to measure and record. Greek Orthodox Christians are prominent in the story, in part because their church's hierarchy was monopolized by non-Arab clergy to the prolonged dismay of Arab subordinates.[2] Many of these Greek Christian mentors, however, shaped and promoted their ideas as journalists and activists within Egypt, to which large numbers of Syrians emigrated to take advantage of the greater liberty and security they could find there under British power and to escape the perils to which their ideas exposed them in Damascus, Aleppo, or Beirut.[3] Inevitably the Egyptian location of their non-Egyptian identity served to focus the issue we face in chapter 8 as to the inclusion or exclusion of the heirs of the Pharaohs and the Fathers in a nationalism of all the Arabs.

For obvious geographical and historical reasons Egypt and Lebanon posed more pointedly than the rest of the Arabic-speaking world the question of Arab definition. The will to Arabism within the modern Ottoman situation inspired those excursions into ancient ethnography that we noted in chapter 1. It also recruited history to show how religion need not divide Arab from Arab, seeing, for example, that the Christian Banū Taghlīb had joined Islam's first armies and how Christian Arabs had been preferentially treated in contrast to other *dhimmīs.*

But whether or not demography could agree that the entire Middle East region had been populated out of Arabia, or that "Arab" and "Semitic" were interchangeable, the undisputed factor was the Arabic speech and language. So it was that political Arabism found its kindling occasion in a literary revival. Long before any resolution of the politics of the Arab-Ottoman equation was possible there came a flowering of Arabic writing, translation, and journalism. This was one area in which Christian Arabs could fully participate and even contrive to lead.[4] Although it held political implications and dangers, much of it could be unimpeachable while giving stimulus to the art and the themes of Arab self-definition. Dictionaries and literary essays could propagate and yet be innocent of propaganda.[5]

There was paradox, however, in this literary renaissance. The will to rehabilitate and reform Arabic was prompted by the Ottoman requirement of Turkish as the language of state, authority, and education.[6] It is important to remember how many of the pioneers of Arab nationalism were Turkish educated and Turkish speaking. The Ottoman dimension had deep roots in their culture, whether Christian or Muslim. Yet so much of the inspiration and content in the renewal of Arabic derived from European sources—sources obviously suspect to Ottoman authority. Napoleon in Egypt had made western soldiering, cannons, and techniques intriguing to eastern rulers. But slowly the Mediterranean connection asserted itself also in letters, philosophy, and literature. Concepts of liberty, the nation, and the secular began to find their way into currency via the new Arabic and to arouse within the language itself a new shape to its function and ideal, away from the merely impressive to the truly expressive, fitting usage and vocabulary to current needs.[7]

II

While nineteenth-century Ottomans were not themselves impervious to these modernizing factors, they could not mistake their implications for Arab provincials pondering their loyalties. How would they affect a will to separatism, reinforced, as so much European influence was, by political, military, and diplomatic interventions? Ottoman power, as we have earlier seen, had accommodated European commerce and consuls, in the form of capitulations and extraterritorial privileges, in which their own minorities had profitably joined. Should there, could there, be something akin in cultural capitulations by which provincial strains could be accommodated? If so, how could a necessary infra-Ottoman cohesion be ensured and retained and how would the ethnic, religious, and local divisions within the provinces be controlled? The course of Arabism and its dilemmas for Christian Arabs turned, in part, on the response of the Ottomans to their own liabilities in the total situation as it both summoned and threatened them. For the hopes and fears, the vacillations and contradictions, attending on their policy contributed to the evolution of Arab opinion.

Early in the nineteenth century, as the Ottomans sensed their increasing problems, bureaucrats and military men sought to organize their empire the better to assert central control in the face of provincial assertiveness and to counter the latter by administrative and educational reforms. The Janissaries, who as in Algeria, Tunisia, and Libya had functioned under hereditary governors, were abolished and a new style of army was organized in the central regions. Attempts were made to mobilize local leadership in representative councils which fostered lay initiative in the *millets.* Changes in education also aimed to serve Ottomanization by reducing the role of the *'ulamā'*, while offsetting the influence of western missionary institutions, which authority suspected. European pressure was also countered in a partial secularization of law, as a means of bringing non-Muslims out from capitulation-style cover into a single Ottoman system.

These measures, known collectively as *Tanzīmāt* ("regulations") took shape in reforming edicts in 1839, 1856, and 1864 and in a new Commercial Code (1850), a new Penal Code (1858), and in the *Mejelle* (1870–1876), which sought to modify the Islamic *Sharī'ah* (except in personal status law) with a secular civil code. Despite their promise of a new version of Ottomanism that might have reduced its identification with Islam, there was an inherent ambiguity about these reforms. They reduced the role of the *'ulamā'* but did not suppress the capitulations, which European powers retained and non-Muslims found serviceable. *Dhimmī* status might still seem preferable to the uncertainties of an Ottomanism profferring—problematically—an equal, common citizenship under law for all. The latter might be welcome, but western powers were unwilling to forgo their protégés. That being so, these in turn saw their familiar *dhimmī* status a safer option than unproven changes.

Though the *Tanzīmāt* reforms foreshadowed the principles that later secularizers were to follow, they were impeded by the pressures from European interests. Furthermore, they incurred opposition from Muslims, on whose persuasion about them their effectiveness had to turn. In 1876, however, the impulses that had contrived them bureaucratically found political expression in the constitution of that year, to which Sultan 'Abd al-Ḥamīd II agreed as the price of his accession following the deposition in rapid succession of his two predecessors in the sultanate, 'Abd al-'Azīz and Murād V.

Thus began—in false hopefulness—the long regime of despotism, which was ended only by the coup of the Young Turks in 1908–1909. 'Abd al-Ḥamīd initially accepted a constitution that promised the provinces a share in parliamentary democracy at the center and aimed to obviate any incipient Arab separatism—still hardly articulate—by giving formal shape to an inclusive Ottomanism calculated to contain them. But the sultan quickly repudiated the constitution. There followed a long drift into tyranny and intrigue, fed by the ruler's personal character and his chronic suspicion of his subordinates. He had in mind, no doubt, the long tradition of soldier-adventurers, Mamlūks, rising to power on the strength of disloyal ambition, but the inordinate degree to which he carried his venom and jealousy, coupled with the political and military defeats he incurred, gave an image to Ottomanism that was to prove fatal to its survival in the decade after his demise. It was the long Hamidian regime that stirred an Arab political consciousness, gave it the sanction of personal suffering, and strained to near breaking the instinctive assumptions of Arab Muslims that to belong within Ottomanism was their proper loyalty.

Secret societies began to be formed in Beirut and Damascus in the 1880s in the wake of disillusion with the abrupt frustration of the constitution. They were the work of a tiny minority, at the outset, in which a few

Christians had their part, activists advocating vaguely separatist ideas and affirming that there was an Arab identity demanding to be vested in political autonomy. Western ideas of nationhood entered into the ferment of thought. Yet nascent nationalism, especially as conceived by the Muslim elements, meant a struggle also against the West. Indeed, there was a kind of triangular field of interaction: Ottomanism—fealty and foe; westernism—factor and foreigner; and Arabism—informing emotion and will but as yet without decisive policy. Each of these impinged on the reading of the other.

In the process by which the concept of an Arab nation displaced the age-old sense in which all were Ottomans, Christian Arabs faced the parallel question whether nation or caliphate was their safer option. "Citizens" or *dhimmīs* was an issue that perplexed their minds and puzzled their emotions. It has to be remembered that, in the unfolding of events, the Turkish dimension was reciprocal to the Arab in the disengagement of either—if such it was to be—from the unity of Ottomanism. For as Arab (not to say successful Balkan) secession emerged in theory, agitation, or fact, so a reacting Turkish consciousness discovered itself aiming either to retain the Ottoman whole on its own terms of Turkism (or Turanianism, as it came to be called) or to forgo the caliphal/imperial pride and affirm "Turkey for the Turks." The First World War settled the issue irreversibly, in the latter sense.

The tensions accompanying disengagement of Turk and Arab from Ottoman, and each from the other, became urgent in the period of the so-called Young Turks and the Committee of Union and Progress from 1908 to the entry of Turkey into the 1914–18 war. The deposition of Sultan ʿAbd al-Ḥamīd II brought the reinstatement of the Constitution of 1876 and the promise of inclusive democracy, which Arab feeling greeted with rapturous but brief delight. In some respects the scenario of 1876 was then repeated with the vital difference that the intervening decades had made Arab wills more conscious and their tasks more urgent. For Christian Arabs, they had also sharpened the Muslim–Christian dilemma within the stakes they faced.

In his sharp suppression of Arab separatism, goaded by restless vigilance and served by his secret police and network of spies, ʿAbd al-Ḥamīd had sought to bolster his rule by trying to recruit Islamic sentiment to his brand of Ottomanism,[8] by stressing the caliphate as its buttress and promoting mosque construction. The Hijāz railway facilitating the pilgrimage was a symbol of this policy. This strong accent on Islam and ideas of pan-Islam aggravated the question of the meaning of Ottomanism and so deepened the Muslim–Christian question within the Arabism responding to it.[9] When, finally, events and reverses overtook the regime, the Young Turks abandoned the prospect of an inclusive Ottomanism, which their accession to power had momentarily opened, but the issues, both political and religious, had been sharpened.

The reasons were not far to seek. A unitary Ottomanism, within which the Arabs sought reforms, quickly receded on two counts. Muslim dominance within it would ensure that it must point, as ʻAbd al-Ḥamīd had shown, toward a pan-Islamic goal and so disconcert the significant Christian elements in Arabism. Alternatively, the urge to identify Ottoman unilaterally with Turk and compel Arabs into acquiescence could precipitate dismemberment. Hence the attraction, for the Young Turks, of pan-Turkism, a unity of all the Turks, of whom there were many more outside the Ottoman domains than lived within them. Could not Turks emulate the pan-Slavism that had defeated them in the Balkans? That way they would be rid of restive Arabs, albeit fellow Muslims, if these were going to prove as incorrigible as the Slav, Bulgar, and other *Ghiaurs,* the Christians of Turkey-in-Europe.

Much suffering was to ensue before this exclusive Turkish version prevailed and Ottomanism learned the futility of enforcing Arab conformity and "pounding," as one British diplomat described it, "non-Turkish elements in a Turkish mortar."[10] In the Parliament of 1908–1909 some 72 Arabs were present out of a total membership of 260, 214 being Muslim and 42 Christian. Among the Arabs there were 35 members of the Lamarkaziyyah ("noncentralizing") Party, which had been organized among the Arabs to press for regional autonomy within the empire. Such limited separatism, however, only prompted the mind of the Young Turks and the Committee of Union and Progress toward the policy of Turkification, hardening as they did so the alienation of the Arabs. In effect—and despite the common factor of Islam—the Ottoman Empire was in process of relinquishing the imperial ideology that only Islam could provide. The Turks saw more readily than Arabs the secular implications such a forfeiture held for both.

III

One year before Turkey's entry into the First World War on the side of Germany, the first Arab Congress convened in Paris, with emigré Arabs present as well as still pro-Ottoman Arabs. The war was to end Arab Ottomanism once and for all. The congress, however, on its threshold, still debated a compatibility between Arab aspirations and an Ottoman whole but vowed that denial of these would make their "nationalism" decisive. The case for Muslim/Christian Arab unity and partnership was prominent in the congress with suitable arguments from historical retrospect and rhetoric.

The onset of war turned ideologues into martyrs and incipient nationalism into expectant reality. Turkey's decision to side with the Central Powers, fatal as it was for Ottomanism, was made in response to European politics, pan-Turkic designs on Russia, and awareness of Franco-British diplomatic intrigues in the Middle East. It made Arab separatism treasonable by throwing it into the arms of allies only too ready to serve their imperial ends by dint of Arab hopes. Events were to prove how readily hope and frustration weaved themselves into the same pattern.

The story of the Arab Revolt has often been told, with the romance of desert war and the bargains of diplomatic realism. The exigencies of war intensified Turkish oppression. The sultans of the war years in Istanbul were dominated by the triumvirate of Enver, Tala'at, and Jamāl. The last named in Syria, hard-pressed by allied blockade and driven, it would seem, by personal ambition coveting some Mamlūk-style independent fiefdom in Syria and beyond, aimed to crush or terrorize Arab sentiment in a ruthless campaign of repression. Meanwhile the 1915–1916 negotiations between the sharīf of Mecca, Ḥusain, and the British set in train the joint Arab-Allied advance that two years later dislodged the Turks from Arab lands and captured the emotive symbol of Damascus.

But that crowning triumph of Arab hope was soon to prove a bitter anticlimax. It is recorded that the French general Gouraud, arriving in Damascus in 1920 to implement the allied version of its future, went forthwith to the tomb of the great Ayyūbid Ṣalāḥ al-Dīn, who had ousted the crusaders, and exclaimed: "Nous revoilà, Saladin" ("Here we are again, Saladin"). The Mandatory system, which, under the League of Nations, filled the vacuum of Ottoman demise, was set to perpetuate western power for varying periods over the Arab provinces and to defer and embitter Arab anticipations of postwar nationhood. Western diplomacy had now other ends than those that had prompted its courting of Arab means. But the romanticism epitomized by T. E. Lawrence, the fact and the fiction, had sanctioned Arabism by both legend and betrayal. The two were subtly to interact in the tangle of the interwar years as legitimacy and frustration set the Arab scene. Faiṣal's brief "kingdom" in Damascus, crudely cut off by the French, symbolized aspiration only by denial, and the vision of a unitary Arabism, whether ever viable, was gone. Syrian, Iraqi, Jordanian, Lebanese, and Palestinian "nationalisms," however illogical in their dividedness, proved to be the logic of events in all the givens of mandated policy and Arab diversity. The peculiar circumstances of the last named—to be explored in chapter 10—were the sharpest and the most frustrating of all.

Yet frustrated realization is often the only meed that history affords. "Divide to rule" has long been an adage applied to imperial powers. Anglo-French rivalries determined the Mandate system after Versailles, and the

French manipulation of territories—for example, between Syria and Lebanon—had malign consequences, evident in the tragedy of the 1970s and 1980s.[11] The several Arab states, however, which emerged in the wake of the Ottoman Empire gave form in nationhood to regional identities long sanctioned within the loose patterns that empire had adopted. Fief holders, dominant families, ancient cities with their prides and commerce, and legacies of old geography and tradition were reflected, as well as Anglo-French will and wile, in the making of the Arab map of politics. Arabism had no capacity to abolish the sphinx and the pyramids, as one Arab publicist was at pains to observe.[12] But there were other features of necessary inclusion in the Arab identity, less massively distinctive, which nevertheless dictated the diversity in which Arabism has fulfilled, if not satisfied, itself since 1920.

One evidence of that necessity was the rapid demise of efforts in the 1920s to retrieve the caliphate as an Arab perquisite after its termination by the Turks. The right to an Arab caliphate had been urged by the influential author ʻAbd al-Raḥmān al-Kawākibī (1848–1902) in the hardening of Arab feeling against the Turks. Aligning Islam more squarely with the Arabs would, he argued, recover the pristine quality of the Prophet's "rightly guided" (Arab) successors.[13] But, by 1924, the Mecca which he had made central to his dream as *Umm al-Qurā* ("the mother of the villages") was in the hands of King Ibn Saud in *de facto* possession of the *Ḥaramain*.[14] That fact, along with other considerations, made abortive efforts elsewhere to concert agreement about any caliphal form of Arab self-fulfillment. Even had it proved feasible, it would in no way have resolved the issues operating in the solidifying of the separate nationalisms, distinguished as they were by the different pace at which their "independence" proceeded. Iraq's was formalized as early as 1932, when Faiṣal, bitterly ousted from Damascus, found a throne in Baghdad. Syria and Lebanon had to await the end of the Second World War, while the State of Jordan passed from emirate to kingdom within the policy of the assignment of the Zionists' purposes (against the ideas of the Revisionists among them) to the west of the river.

IV

The pan-Arabism that was desired or promoted within the sanction which time and tenure gave to the separate states had to contend with the finality they acquired. Abandonment of the caliphate meant that the guardianship of Islam, its symbolic unity no longer even theoretically ensured, passed to individual governments. The *Sharīʻah* remained its vital organ of identity but one exposed to a variety of political factors depending on the postures and policies of individual regimes and rulers. There were undoubtedly secular implications in the very notion of nationalism itself, especially in truncated form. The old formula of *Al-Dīn wa-l-Dawlah* had necessarily a different ring when *Al-Ummah* no longer existed or, worse still, when that term was purloined to denote merely the separate *waṭan.*[15]

If Arab Islam had thus to come to terms with its national destinies from the 1920s on, Christian Arabs, by the same token, had to reckon with their new condition as cocitizens, no longer contractually protected as subordinates—with all the vagaries that entailed—but in some sense partners in the jostling fortunes of statehood. It was in Syria that Christian Arabs were most strenuously involved in the conflicts of regional identity and Arab unity. Their dilemmas with Islam in that context pointed them strongly toward secular solutions of the perennial problems within and between faiths.

But the impulses for "greater Syria" had the effect of both sharpening and disconcerting the vaguer emotions of pan-Arabism. One critical factor in the equation has been the place within it of Palestinianism. Israeli thinking has always insisted on "arabizing" the issue of Palestinian nationalism in order not to concede a separate identity for Palestine. Israel will deal with Arab states *over* Palestine, not *with* Palestinians as, via the P.L.O. (Palestine Liberation Organization), they conceive themselves to be.[16] This underlies the current posture of stalling response to Palestinian policy since the decision of November 1988 in Tunis to "recognize" a still territorially indeterminate Israel. But throughout it has been the sheet anchor of Israeli attitudes, purporting to take Arabism at its own word as an inclusive thing and denying the right to a Palestinian "member" in the several statehoods Arabism presents.

The case, apart from admitting a "playing-for-time" stance to defer crucial decisions, is held to rest on the claim that no independent Arab state ever existed before the First World War. If all are newly come to their present genesis, the Palestinian claimant can be disqualified as a pseudo-imitation of Zionism and assigned to nonentity as a separate instance of an Arabism that its isolation is alleged to deny.

The ramifications of this Israeli dogma belong properly with chapter 10 below, but the fact of it has deeply affected Arabism in two ways. It has provoked it to prove itself in solidarity with "Palestinian brothers"—though to their great disservice. It has also searched and tested Arab identity by the obligations it has presented and the frustrations it has caused. Arab nationalism, in the decades since 1920, has related ambiguously to its deepest challenge, compelled to face in Zionism a most radical test, yet prone to betray itself by the resulting intrigues and suspicions of the Arab nations. The story is at once the despair of the ideologues and the undoing of the politicians. The menace and the disquiet emanating from Israel have been present throughout and, for painful reasons, have vexed Christian Arabs most of all.

Varying territorial and ideological mappings of Arabism have been drawn up. Sharīf Ḥusain of Mecca spelled out its physical extent in negotiation with the British in 1916, as did the Druze revivalist Amīr Shakīb al-Arslān.[17] The Arab League was set up in 1945, partly to counter the blandishments of western powers bent on postwar containment of the Soviet Union. The charismatic leadership of Jamāl ʿAbd al-Nāṣir and Egypt's role in the Suez crisis brought emotions to high pitch and gave birth to the ill-fated union of Egypt and Syria in 1957, to which Yemen was attached. Egypt's military intervention there proved both costly and futile, and the union came to an early demise in 1961. Its collapse demonstrated how intractable were the problems, and the aftermath deepened them. Periodic armed confrontations with Israel, in 1948–1949, 1956, 1967, and 1973, were similarly occasions of ardent Arab expectation and, except on the last date, devastating disappointment. President Sadat's "peace with Israel" in 1977 effectively detached Egypt from political Arabism for a whole decade, despite his intention, via "linkage with Palestine," to vindicate his policy as the truest Arabism. That hope, arguably inscribed in the Camp David agreement, foundered on the obduracy of Menachem Begin and his contrasted interpretation of what "linkage" should mean. Sinai, recovered in Egypt's "peace" with Israel, was in any event a negotiable territory in a way that, in Israeli eyes, *Eretz Yisrael* could never be.

Arabism, ostensibly cold-shouldering Egypt until 1988, in effect conceded the Egyptian legitimacy of Sadat's policy. It has proved unable to offer any better succor to the Palestinians by devices of its own. Palestinianism within Arabism has been continually ill-served, if not victimized, by the self-seeking and divided counsels of its Arab context. Its frustrations were overtaken by the trauma of Lebanon, cruelly exposed as they were by Israeli invasion. Lebanese disintegration stands as a tragic symbol of the bankruptcy of Arabism, its emotions drained and wearied and its illusions dramatized. Its separatisms have proved too chronic or too calculating to make politically effective its common speech, common heritage, and for the most part common religion. The wealth and political leverage accruing from oil and the potential of Arabism's vast human resources have not measured up to the acute problems of contemporary history, where political will and wisdom have faltered and failed. There has been no Ṣalāḥ al-Dīn for the twentieth century. That powerful unifier was a Kurd.

The long disarray of unitary Arabism was compounded by the protracted misery of the long Iran–Iraq War, a tragedy that aroused old Sunnī/Shīʿah tensions within an Arab–Iranian conflict, kindling apprehension and intrigue across inter-Arab politics. Syria in Lebanon has been consistent only in a wary opportunism, mindful of Israeli power, of Iraqi rivalry, and of its own inner strains. The long-standing regime of President Asad, in marked contrast to earlier violent and frequent changes in Damascus, has legitimate interests, closer than any other party save the Lebanese themselves, in what should–or can–eventuate in Lebanon. Shifts and tacks in policy, however, have contributed more to frustrate than to achieve it. Syria, as the familiar term the "Fertile Crescent" implies, has to be the keystone in the arch of the inner Arab world; a vital part of any viable Arabism, as some Syrian thinkers have clearly seen.

That arch, though, is harshly distorted not only by the pull of Arab wealth elsewhere but by the post–Gulf War ambitions and power of Iraq, whose annexation of Kuwait has brusquely derided the romance of Arab brotherhood. That violent action has also highlighted the long persisting problem of economic imbalance among the parts of the Arab world–an imbalance all the more difficult to correct because of the diverse structures within which it obtains–structures inherited from a very different past. The worldwide stakes are such that the issue cannot be left to inter-Arab resolution–even assuming it attainable. Hence the abrupt insertion of western power to ensure vital oil supplies and world economies, as well as in some way to vindicate standards of international behavior to which Arabism itself must presumably be committed. Yet that insertion arouses all the traditional fears and suspicions about imperial machination and Arab humiliation. It is also clear that the occupation of Kuwait by Iraq gravely prejudiced, if not destroyed, any Palestinian hopes that might otherwise have attended détente between the superpowers, with its implications for American attitudes to Israel.

Despite all these embarrassments–and paradoxically because of them–Arabism persists and cannot be denied. The Arab provinces of retreating Ottomanism in the first quarter of this century were denied by geography and history and by their very extent and diversity the kind of cohesion that enabled Turkey to survive and cohere. And they produced no Ataturk. Under western mandate, with the attending ambiguities, they did not undergo the kind of utter dereliction out of which Ataturk's rescue of Turkey was contrived.[18] It is fair also to ask whether the intentions of Arabism could have tolerated the radical secularism by which he prevailed. Arabism had to wrestle with an ongoing Islamic identity and with the centrifugal forces inseparable from its temperament and its traditions. It was the victim of its own legacies while never ceasing to cherish them as victorious assets.

V

It is time to turn in the century-long story to the experience of Christian Arabs, filling out its detail and taking its human measure biographically in the meaning of minority experience. So doing we will also be gathering material for chapter 12, since "the future with Islam" stems from the long past of being "with Islam."

To survey Christian response to the demands made on mind and spirit by the course of Arabism as now reviewed is to realize that it went often in parallel to thinking in Islam. Both faiths were forced by the nature of nationalism to take stock of the role of religion in nationhood. In praise of citizen unity Muslims found themselves expressing sentiments of mutual compatibility quite alien to the classical Islamic theory of the place of non-Muslims under its rule and within its society. Correspondingly, there were Christians ready to be sanguine about the supersession of that theory and its replacement by a philosophy of equal membership and of religion as "spiritual" and beyond politics. The Lamarkaziyyah Party at the time of the Young Turks took for its slogan the legend "Religion is for God: homeland is for all." 'Abd al-Raḥmān 'Azzām, of the Arab League, declared in a speech in Cairo in 1946:

> We Arabs have received from the renaissance of the 7th century a noble heritage to which we invite people to adhere today. . . . People are free to believe as they will. We invite them to adhere to ideals, principles and rules adopted by our forefathers which will serve well to realise international unity, perpetual peace and human brotherhood.[19]

His words were more a reflection of the need to transcend religious differences than a viable formula for doing so. The same might be said of 'Abd al-'Alayīlī's claim in *Dastūr al-'Arab al-Qawmī* ("The Constitution of Arab Nationalism"):

> Religions have become functionless except in the moral and ethical spheres. . . . Agreement is dictated by community of interests in the Arab homeland. What objection is there to our having one national creed and differing religions?[20]

There were Christians eagerly wishing to reciprocate such views, often out of a certain distaste for or despair of confessionalism,[21] and providing also a way out of vexing inter-Christian tensions. Constantine Zurayq, Orthodox (Greek) educator and historian, insisted that "in the present day the bond of nationalism is supreme over every other." It was "the duty of every Arab, regardless of his religious faith, to study Islam," seeing that Muḥammad was the supreme architect of Arab consciousness.[22]

Research, writing, and publication were important ways in which Christian Arabs contributed to the awareness and appreciation of the heritage that made their common identity. Given due circumspection, they were freer—as Christians—from the obligations that bound Muslims to Ottoman loyalty. At least they could profit from that difference by turning their energies to the groundwork of renewal in literature and what, later, African and other writers would call "conscientization." Newspapers multiplied and debated issues in lively controversy, while the infusion of new criteria as to faith, authority, interpretation, and belief brought new stimulus to self-understanding. It was possible to absorb ideas from the West via translations of seminal works while tracing the Arabic and eastern sources to which the West owed its wisdom. These aspects of "the Arab awakening" were diligently—if, in the view of some, overzealously—explored by George Antonius in a book of that name which was itself a factor in the stimulus it described.[23]

But behind the fascinating experience of self-repossession lay the ultimate questions: How to disengage nationalism from religion? How to reengage nationhood with religion? If not the assimilation of minorities, nor their autonomy, nor a secular statehood, nor a superstate, nor a fatal agnosticism, what then? Enthusiasts for the "nation" had to measure how deep was the assumption of the *millet.* As one Muslim writer put it, "My grandmother died without the Arab concept: hers was the Islamic concept."[24] Christians of any allegiance had still more urgency to cling to the old order under which religious, confessional sanction preserved their law, their communal life, and their folk identity. If statehood were to replace these havens with a conjectural citizenship, what of the shape, the feel, and the guarantees of survival?

Among the earliest twentieth-century theorists was Najīb ʿAzūrī (d. 1916), an official of the Ottoman administration in Jerusalem who moved to France and published *Le Reveil de la Nation Arabe* in 1905 and edited a short-lived review, *L'Independance Arabe,* organ of *Ligue de la Patrie Arabe,* which he founded. The aim was an Arab empire from the Mediterranean Sea to the Indian Ocean, excluding Egypt, with "a spiritual caliphate" replacing the Ottoman and based politically in Mecca. With Uniate Christian sympathies, he envisaged a single Arab Christianity bringing various rites into one, and genuinely Arabic in worship and control. Greek dominance of Orthodoxy he condemned. If he had anxieties about the viability of Christians within this imagined structure, he did not reveal them except to urge autonomy for Lebanon. He assumed the Muslim/Christian distinction to be absorbed in and abolished by true Arabism. His propaganda was inevitably conditioned by its European connection. He died in Cairo after participating in the Arab Congress in Paris in 1913.

A contemporary Christian thinker of different vintage was Shibli Shumayyil (1860–1917), a Syrian and a scientist, who had clashed with authority in the (then) Syrian Protestant College over the theory of evolution. He saw religions, especially in their *ʿulamāʾ* and clergy, as a blight on society, an incubus on the reform not merely of institutions but of ideas. He approved nationalism but only in a relative sense as offering liberation from Hamidian tyranny but needing to be transcended in a world consciousness appropriate to science and truly free persons. It was the British tenure in Egypt to which he owed the free propagation of such far-reaching ideas.

Another Syrian Christian emigré writing in Egypt was Faraḥ Anṭūn (1874–1922) of Orthodox (Greek) lineage, born in Tripoli. He was first friend, and then intellectual adversary, of the noted Muslim thinkers, Muḥammad ʿAbduh and Muḥammad Rashīd Riḍā. He advocated a secular solution to the political and spiritual problem of religious diversity. He decried the *millet* mentality and the obscurantism, both Christian and Muslim, which—he alleged—stemmed from it. But his readiness for European philosophy (Ernest Renan, Auguste Comte, and Jean Jacques Rousseau) did not endear him to Arab Uniate Christians, whom he saw as compromising their true identity. Orthodoxy's (Greek) subordination to Greek authority provoked an anticlericalism in his thought. True faith he saw as a "lay" discipleship on the Tolstoy model, rid of theological subtlety and clerical status mongering and alert to social needs.

Anṭūn crossed swords with Muslims, both rigorist and "liberal," in urging a comparable religious personalism on Islam also. He cited Ibn Rushd, the twelfth-century Muslim sage, to sustain his separation of rationality from religion and to scout ʿAbduh's case for including Islamic revelation within natural law. He also resisted ʿAbduh's claim that the marriage of Islam with power was legitimate. Vigorous and inconclusive as this debate was between a would-be secular Christian and a leading Islamic protagonist of an Islam mandatory on all society because it was rational, at least it penetrated into areas and issues that affected politicians also.

Anṭūn sided with the Ottomanists, believing that Christians needed Ottoman protection and should not risk disloyalty. He hoped that Ottoman power would become capable of a secularized future—as indeed it did, but only for Turks in imperial retreat. He decried ideas of an Arab caliphate on the lines mooted by Al-Kawākibī and believed in a "Syrianism" distinct from the Arabism that belonged, for him, only to the Arabian peninsula and Iraq. But these differing identities should be understood as nonpolitical within the Ottoman whole. That posture owed something to the psychic "inferiorizing" emigré Syrians felt residing in Egypt. "Christian and Muslim brothers should rally round the great Hamidian throne," as equals, even if "provincials." At least one Egyptian, Salāmah Mūsā (see chapter 8) became an ardent admirer of Anṭūn, describing *Al-Jāmiʿah*, the magazine he edited, as striking him "like a Sufi revelation." There were other Copts also who responded to his anticlericalism. Wrestling with the quandaries of Christians in the eastern world he was minded to see the essence of all religions as one and the same beneath their doctrinal and ritual forms, and to hold that conviction not only against the classic theory of *Dār al-Islām* but against all rational revisions of it that still argued or assumed some essential primacy (as 'Abduh did) for Islam *per se.* More pragmatic thinkers, in resolving Arab Christian dilemmas, might have conceded such revised Muslim claim (with the corollary of an Islamic state) as the prudent price of any Arab political unity at all. But it was Muslims themselves who by and large repudiated 'Abduh after his death in 1905.[25]

A more long-lived contemporary of Anṭūn was Khalīl Sakākīnī (1878–1953) whose diaries were published by his daughter in Jerusalem in 1955 under the title *Kadhā anā yā Dunyā* (Such, O World, was I). Again of Orthodox (Greek) allegiance, he shared the objective of deconfessionalism as the task of Christians, striving to emerge from centuries of *dhimmī* mentality within which the religious community was all. That tradition was "a badge of servitude," from which they should seek release in a private view of faith and a common trust on Muslim goodwill—assuming that Muslims too would hold their dogma as private personal belief. Religion should not be "the constitutive principle of society." Sakākīnī finally abandoned Greek Orthodoxy in his ardor for Arabism as such. This was due, however, less to his confidence in the Young Turks, who proved a broken reed, than to his dispute with the church hierarchy and his disquiet about the lowly, ignorant quality of the Arab clergy. He died in much disillusionment. For, like many in his time, his idea of confining religion to the personal sphere, failed to comprehend not only the role of dogma in Islam but Islam's inherent preoccupation with the power factor central to its history.[26]

That preoccupation may be indicated from numerous Muslim sources, of which it may be wise to take a recent example, affected no doubt by developments much later than the times of Shumayyil, Anṭūn, and Sakākīnī, but for that reason underlining how inveterate the attitude is. Yūsuf al-Qardāwī, writing in 1977, insisted that the only bond of political association is the fact of Islam. *Dhimmīs* are, and can only be, politically within *Dār al-Islām,* submission to which is the only sanction for Islamic duty toward them. A common secular nationalism is inconceivable, since Islam, both faith and law, is implemented not by individuals but by the state. It is improper for Muslims to be ruled by or share rule with other than Muslims—a doctrine sustained by the Qur'ān.[27]

Such deep-seated sentiments make clear how venturesome—or how sanguine—Christian advocacy of a common Arabism had to be, how dependent on precarious initiatives of change within Arab Islam, how bound up with Islam its misgivings. A few Christian writers were moved to be obsequious and make Islam's own case, conceding that all Arab "denominators"—Muḥammad, the Qur'ān, the Umayyads, history at large—were inherently Islamic, and that Christians must confess and feel them as such. Thinkers such as Adīb Isḥāq and Nadrah Muṭrān from the time of the Arab Revolt had accepted that Islam was essential to Arabism, seeing that Islam had "made" the Arabs who and how they were.

The European factor, seen as a compromiser of Christian Arabs, may go far to explain that stance. Did not the western powers of France, Russia, and England and figures such as Gladstone and Alexander II espouse Christian obligation to Christian minorities, whom they saw as victimized by Ottoman power? Was not such protection state action in support of religion? Muslim Arabs were liable to read all such intrusions as Christian application of the power-faith equation so dear to Islam. In that light Muslims found both a logic and a spur to assert unmistakably their own version of the principle. Caught between that menace and uncertain European graces, most Christian minds and communities—Maronites apart—had reason for the prudence of subservience to Islam, failing fluctuating hopes of its tolerance.

The Syrian Christian Constantine Zurayq, quoted earlier, was conspicuous among those who sought to resolve this quandary by accepting the realism of Arabism as necessarily Islamic but pleading for a nationalism neither opposing nor negating "true religion." It was only fanatics who wanted communal (i.e., religious) affiliation to override national harmony or who—in his different metaphor—"refuse to dissolve in the all-consuming crucible of the nation." In a speech on the Prophet's birthday, he urged that faith should be decommunalized and nationalism religiously consecrated, as being itself a spiritual movement. A sane Christian Arab acknowledgment of Muḥammad in those terms and on Arab grounds was entirely proper and desirable.[28] But could or should Muslim Arabs, correspondingly, comprehend their religion in those gentle terms? And what of numerous problems of law, society, and government? Could Islam be "just a religion" in that idealist sense, against the grain of its historic instincts and its traditional sanctions?

Occasionally a Christian writer was prepared to untie the ancient knot by proclaiming that Islam alone was the inclusive religion, the very formulation of the spirituality for which thinkers like Zurayq were pleading. Thus, for example, Khalīl Iskander Qubrūsī took the formula and identified it with Islam, saying that Christian Arabs should islamize so that there would only be "Muslim Arabs and Christian foreigners." An Orthodox (Greek) Palestinian, he published in 1931 his *Da'wat Naṣārā-l-'Arab ila-l-dukhūl fī-l-Islām* (The Summons to Arab Christians to enter Islam).

There was a sharp element of antiwesternism in his position, as well as resentment at Greek repression of Arab clergy. Primitive Christianity had long been corrupted by Europeans, who made it into an instrument for humiliating easterners. Islam was true Christianity without "a Frankish dress." Christian Arabs should, therefore, realize that Arabism, via the Arabic Qur'ān, was exclusively Muslim and islamize accordingly.[29] The easternness of Christian origins was totally obscured for him in the bitterness of his westward grievances. He made the demise of the patient the cure of the suffering in remedy by elimination.

VI

But Europe, alas, had more subtle influences than could be exorcised by common Arab refuge in an eastern Islam. What if such Arabism was to base itself on cultural factors alone, arguably corroborated by pure ethnicity? Would Islam then be itself relativized, subordinated along with any religion, to the supreme factor of race and *Volk?* Such was the view of a movement within Syrian thinking and action which developed into the formidable Ba'th, or "Resurrection," parties in Syria and Iraq and in which leaders, born in Christian families, had a striking part.

The factors were not far to seek. There was the abiding consciousness of "Syria," land of Damascus and Aleppo, seat of the Umayyads, burial home of Ṣalāḥ al-Dīn, and linchpin of the Fertile Crescent. Syria was resentful of territory around Alexandretta, ceded to the Turks in 1939, and, what is more, about the French creation of Grand Liban at Syria's expense in 1921. The forfeiture of areas it had then undergone gave it a vital urge to their recovery or, at least, a crucial interest in what happened there. On many counts, it is not surprising that the theme of "Greater Syria" should emerge, linking old Mesopotamia with the Mediterranean shore even as far as Sinai. Indeed, such a "Syria" might stand in for Arabism as a whole, excluding Egypt as the Nile's but adding Cyprus to be the star within the crescent and to recall its possession by the first Umayyads, who had ruled as far as Spain. In this sense one might speak of "Syrianism" as a surrogate for true Arabism, however Hashimites might feel, or the Saudis in the peninsula.

But ideas of Greater Syria were fed from sources deeper than territorial. There might well be dispute about the precise extent of Arabness, but what of its biological root? The modern Arab East, with its wartime (both World Wars) uncertainty about the rival ideologies of "allied" and "central" powers from the westward continent, and with the gathering example of ideological Zionism, could not escape the fascination of German and Italian theories of race and state.[30] Fascist thinking of such vintage had obvious attraction for aspirations and resentments seeking salvation. German and Italian unification the previous century had engendered invigorating, if also perverse, doctrines of racial identity and state sovereignty. For these, the nation-state became in itself the core of allegiance, the theme of destiny, if not of worship. Religion in that context was reduced to a function of racial consciousness, a mere concomitant of history, in no way controlling but merely subservient to the peoplehood it happened to characterize. Such a race-state demanded the "leader," the *Duce,* the *Führer,* as its symbol and executant.

It was an Orthodox (Greek) Christian from the hills of Lebanon who adopted these doctrines and centered them on his own person. Anṭūn Sa'ādah was born in 1904 and was executed for treachery in Lebanon in 1949. His father went, as many Syrians did, to Brazil during Anṭūn's boyhood, and Anṭūn only returned to Lebanon in 1929. In the meantime he had learned German and imbibed ideas akin to those of Nazism in the 1930s in Germany. Private teaching in Beirut afforded him occasion to promote them in the American University, where, under a cover-name, he formed the secret Syrian National-Socialist Party. When his cover broke, he spent a time in prison, where he continued to write. After his release, intermittent and erratic political activity followed within the tensions of Lebanon. Both pan-Arabism and Lebanese separatism were condemned in the name of a "Syrianism" of which Sa'ādah was the self-styled *Führer.*

Party membership was small but intense with the kind of discipline and personal surrender to the ideology demanded by its counterparts in Europe and urged by such writers, in the Algerian context, as Franz Fanon.[31] Society, not religious faith, was the finally real. Syria was paramount. Submission to its destiny was a kind of metaphysical *islām,* not susceptible of rational debate or personal disavowal. Every religion had to be subdued to state authority. Clerics and *'ulamā'* had no role in politics or jurisprudence. Differences between religions were of no significance. Private belief and conscience could be indulged only within the demands of state allegiance.

Despite its paramilitary activism, its accent on youthful ardor, and its defeudalizing of the economy, the National-Socialist Party had no mass appeal and is significant mainly for its extremism in attempted resolution of the religious problems of Arabism. Its viable aspects were left to the Ba'th Party, emerging in its wake, which shed the irrational notion of a mystic Syrian reality in the name of a wider concept of Arabism. Ba'th thinking also jettisoned the wilder themes of ethnicity while retaining the subordination of religion to nation-state allegiance. "Greater Syria" became a more pragmatic concept without losing drive, and even ruthlessness, in its pursuit.

Here too an Orthodox (Greek) Christian from Damascus, Michel 'Aflaq (1912–1989), was the leading mentor and initiator. He formed the first Ba'th group in the 1940s with Syrian students out of the Sorbonne. They were joined by other groups of national and socialist conviction, strong pan-Arabists committed to a philosophy about religions akin to that of Sa'ādah. Ironically, the Ba'th, pledged to an Arab unity from the twin rivers to the great sea, divided into bitterly opposed Syrian and Iraqi Ba'ths. Their relations tangled with 'Abd al-Nāṣir's Egypt-led version of pan-Arabism and old tensions between Damascus and Baghdad. They were involved in the numerous coups d'état that punctuated the politics of both countries prior to the advent to power of President Asad in 1970. For all its fervor for Arabism, the inspiration came strongly from European doctrines of the state and was associated, in its early days, with the German-oriented regime in Iraq.

Writing "To the Memory of the Arab Prophet," 'Aflaq declared:

> Christian Arabs will become aware, when nationalism fully awakes in them, that Islam is a national culture which they must assimilate until they understand and love it. Then they will be devoted to Islam as to the dearest aspect of their Arabism. If this aspiration has still to be achieved, the new generation of Christian Arabs is called to achieve it with audacity and disinterest, sacrificing pride and egotism. For there is no honor equal to that of belonging to it.[32]

Christian Arabs could still be denominated as such in this counsel, but could "disinterest" extend to the convictions and the liturgies that made them Christian? Yet confessional disinterest was precisely what 'Aflaq required of all religion. His quest for a Christian assimilation of Islam sprang simply from the fact that Islam was entrenched as the central cultural denominator of the Arab.

The stance was akin to that of Turkism in the Ataturk years, as worked out in the formative philosophy of Ziya Gökalp (1875–1924), the mentor of post-Ottoman Turkey, who tolerated Islam as the long-standing heritage of Turks, the cultural presence of which was—or must be made—compatible with secular statehood. Thus, Article 15 of the Constitution of the Arab Ba'th made no mention of Islam in affirming: "The national tie is the only tie that may exist in the Arab state." Islam was part of the genius of Arabism, not a divine revelation of overriding warrant. Muḥammad had responded to contemporary Arab needs. Islam's origins were an epitome of the Arab soul. Belief in God meant belief in justice organized in national-socialism. Every Arab should be a present-day Muḥammad in the sense of perpetuating that chosen Arab destiny he had attained. The mission of Islam was and is to shape an Arab humanism. In that mission it was not religion that utilized the state but the state that utilized religion.

Michel ʻAflaq wrote with verve and ardor, with an emotion that did not pause to wonder what might survive of religion if its absolutes of revelation and tradition were assumed by and into statehood. Politics had, in effect, become religion. Nationalism was love, the cult of a great family. Love needs no argument but itself—its passion and its goal. Marriage became the person's obligation to the nation. Teaching and education were the sole preserve of the state. Experienced nationhood dissolved all discords born of definitions, dogmas, and confessional disease, but there was need for *niḍāl,* or heroic struggle, to bring these things to pass, this higher patriotism and its *risālah khālidah,* "its eternal mission-message."[33]

Reflection on Baʻth thinking, its Christian sponsors, and its passionate intensity, opens many questions. Was it born primarily of despair at fractious and incorrigible sectarianism? Was it, indeed, prescient about the tragic fate awaiting Lebanon? Was it responding to the stimulus—and the menace—of Zionism? Israel, it thought, had been created by western imperialism precisely to prevent Arab unity. It was imperialism that fostered and fed on Arab minorities, enticing them with vain notions of separatist survival. These blandishments had to be decisively resisted, and the only way to do so effectively was to unify the nation-state in a total theory and a triumphant emotion. Was ʻAflaq invoking a mystical concept of eternal peoplehood and sacred mission, as if to counter Jewish election with an Arab vocation or to translate the Christian dimension of "people of God" into Bergsonian ideals of an Arab *élan vital?*

What, his critics might ask, of other nationhoods? What of their role within a unitary Islam—Kurds, Persians, Sudanis, Pakistanis, and the rest? Since Arabism was already an enfolding of diversity, from Phoenicians to Berbers, it need not be read as chauvinistic. Its true humanness could serve to sanctify other humanisms. Classes, not nations, engendered strife, and these would be transcended in the "resurrection" and the Baʻth. Misgivings would be met in an entire trust in Arabness.

But what of the means to the end? ʻAflaq held that while the movement was a minority it must claim to be the minority on behalf of the whole as representing that whole before it was ready to be entrusted with its true destiny. Thus coups d'etat and revolution were proper to it. That necessity would pass once the whole was sound. It might be said that, so reasoning, the Baʻth was close to the logic of original Islam after the *Hijrah.* But it was also a logic opposing minorities could plead. The fate of the Baʻth, sundered by rivalry and frustrated after numerous vicissitudes, is perhaps the most apt commentary on its thwarted idealism. It left the basic problem of the thrust—and the recalcitrance—of religions unresolved. In August 1971 ʻAflaq was condemned to death in Damascus *in absentia.*[34]

It is clear in retrospect that religions are not as tractable as 'Aflaq's vision required. Islam does not submit to have a merely cultural, spiritual role. The Syrian Constitution of 1973, for example, affirms that Islam is "the religion of the President of the Republic" and that "Muslim law is the principal source of law." However, it balances those concessions to religious tradition by refraining from saying that Islam is the state religion. All regimes have been obliged to defer in some sense to their zealots, and the dominant status of Islam is obviously appropriate. But it argues a balancing act between an "orthodox" Islam (of whatever shape) and a pragmatic Islam judged politically expedient.

That, of course, is an inter-Muslim issue. The outsider may well enquire whether the primacy of the nation—whatever its implications for Christian citizens and their kinship with Islam—can feasibly square with historic Islam. To make the national the ultimate would seem a form of idolatry. How does it ride with *Allāhu akbar* ("greater is God")? Does not the Qur'ān declare that "religion, with God, is Islam" (Surah 3.19)? It would seem, then, invalid to diversify *Al-Dīn* ("religion") and let the term embrace what is not Islam, unless one translates the term in the common-noun sense of *islām* as "submission" or "God-consciousness," presumably present outside Islam institutionally established.[35] Is not the nub of the whole issue precisely there? Does, or can, Islam legitimize other faiths as sharing society and its guidance, the state and its membership? Can it recognize them in terms other than those of the old *dhimmī* contract, which permitted their communal continuity of creed and liturgy and law but disallowed their role otherwise? On that question hangs the feasibility of shared nationality and statehood and, by means of these, a shared Arabism. It is clear that what Christians have to debate with themselves is essentially also a debate about the definition of Islam.

Christian decisions, therefore, turn crucially on factors outside them. Hence the tension, the timidity, and the jeopardy they involve, aggravated by varying degrees of minority status. Michel 'Aflaq's story may be said to enshrine the hard realities of Christian Arabism. What, in his day, were ordinary members of a Christian minority to do, its percentage of the population numbered in low single figures, its clerical leadership largely monopolized by foreign ecclesiastics, and its spirit smarting under the indignities of French occupation and the frustration of national hopes under Mandate? Would not all these factors of circumstance, in the context of confessional divisions, send ardent minds to the theme of "the nation" as a refuge of hope and a call to escape from religious futility? This is precisely what the young 'Aflaq did, with his Muslim colleague Ṣalāḥ al-Dīn al-Biṭār, in the 1930s and 1940s before and after French withdrawal. They issued pamphlets, organized groups and fired the young, in the praise of their identity and the task of "resurrection." They were joined later by Zakī al-Arsūzī, bringing two movements into one.[36] It is true they were saddled, in the view of some, by their Sorbonne connection, their intellectualism, and their western temper. Eventually officers and political realists took over in the 1950s and 1960s, men with organizational thrust and more schooled in coups and intrigue. ʿAflaq came, inevitably, to represent a passé generation and suffered expulsion from the Baʿth and frustration in exile in Iraq. But his dynamism and his personality served to lift the sights and kindle the hearts of Syrians.

His initiatives, coming from a member of a Christian minority, required high courage, inviting as they did the suspicion of rigorous Muslims and the reproach of *dhimmī*-minded Christians, by whom he was named "Muḥammad ʿAflaq." But what his career signifies in longer perspective is the question of how Christian meanings can engage within the Christian situation. It would probably be wrong to see ʿAflaq's Christian "denominator" (obtaining under Syrian law and custom) as primary in his inspiration. It was as an Arab, readily partnered by Muslims, that he was striving to galvanize nationhood and intellectually charter independence. That political concern explained his readiness to accommodate, even to commend, Islam within Christian terms and for Christian acceptance. Christian loyalty was, in effect, turned into an ideology of inter-Arab compatibility, and of socialist passion. Given the context, the dynamics, and the limitations of the situation, could it be otherwise? There would be no realism in unilateral Christian politics or ideology, still less evangelism, as futures for Syria.

Yet what happens, in that *mise-en-scène,* to the meanings by which Christian faith exists and because of which Christian liturgies proceed? How is Christian "nation-participation" authentic and honest with itself, if its essentials of faith and worship are left only latent, and not articulated, in its cooperative postures? How will its vital dimensions of grace and forgiveness, of suffering and redemption, indeed of "resurrection," (*baʿth*), inform the ideology it agrees to share? It will not suffice to say that ʿAflaq did not pretend to be a theologian—though it may be necessary to deplore that ecclesiastics are not activists. It is not theology by theologians that is here at stake but rather the impact, the critique, and the ministry that distinctive Christian understandings of God and humanity have for the cult of nation and the thrust of politics.

Arabism, for all its participants, may well warrant and properly require, on manifest historical and cultural grounds, the kind of inward realization of its Islamic definition for which ʿAflaq and kindred Christian thinkers pleaded and enjoined upon their people. But the very legitimacy of such response, and its sincerity when made, must surely argue that a Christian sense of participation in the Arab Muḥammad and the Arabic Qur'ān, for the sake of an Arabness shared, has to move into the positive bearings of Christian faith upon that heritage.

The notion implicit here of a non-Muslim sharing or belonging with Muslims would seem, initially at least, to be an uncongenial Islamic proceeding. It implies a motive other than that of outright "submission" and approves a kind of Muslim-Christian duality very different from the contractual *dhimmī* relationship as historically understood—a relationship for which there was no expectation of faith (which could not be other than entire if it was to be "Muslim") and no thought of shared belief or common community. Evidently Muslims who have advocated or implied these, in the name of Arabism, have ventured, wittingly or unwittingly, into a new reading of Islam, no less strenuous for them than the corresponding invitation within Christianity. So much the advocacy of a unitary Arabness would seem to entail, requiring of either party a full encounter between their respective universes of faith if it is to be consistent with the authentic quality of either.

Otherwise, would common Arabness simply be a secular form of the traditional Islamic assumption under which Islam must dominate the body politic and determine society? Could Islam ever be other than its traditional self or be reduced, for some citizens, to a purely notional culture factor? Did contemporaries of 'Aflaq in their Islam, like 'Abd al-Raḥmān al-Bazzāz, appreciate what was involved when they required that Christians should "cherish Islam as their brother Muslims do"?[37] Islam, as they observed, is certainly "a political religion." But did that mean it could admit a "cherishing" that was not also creedal? It is true that original Christianity was "devoid of any active share in political organization" and so could presumably recognize Islam on simply political (i.e., nationalist) grounds. But that argument from Roman/New Testament times did not stay to reckon with the veto the Qur'ān laid on the central themes of the scriptures Christians read and chanted in their daily liturgy and the meanings their faith transacted there. Were these to be held in abeyance or were the vetoes to be lifted? Should the Christian Arabs isolate the citizen in them from the believer? If so, would the Muslim Arabs do the same?

Positive answers to those twin questions pointed the way to complete secularism, with every person's religion a private, sectarian affair. There were Muslim thinkers, such as Saṭi' al-Ḥuṣrī, who wanted it so.[38] But then, what of the sacred *Sharī'ah* and the many problems attending on law, custom, society, and culture, not to say the gathering strength of rigorist Muslim positions strongly resistant to such diminution (as they saw it) of the whole genius of Islam? That problem, too, was double-edged, for it was precisely rigorism and the rigorists, with their divisive zeal, that inspired in others the will to secular escape. Perhaps it was the duty of Christians not to connive with such provocation by holding closely to their doctrinal conviction and communal identity. But, if these were effectively muted or ignored, what–in the end–would the churches have to contribute to the achievement of nationhood? How would Christian faith be liberated to serve in turn the liberation of secularism from its many temptations? Or should the whole guidance of state and society be left unilaterally to the ethics and counsels of a "privatized" Islam? If, given the numerical frailty (e.g., in Syria) of Christian minorities, that were reasonably the case, how might Christian Arabism share that situation?

These exacting issues we remit to chapter 12 and, meanwhile turn back to study the themes of this chapter in the distinctive Christianities of Egypt and Lebanon, where geography and history gave them significantly different quality.

Notes

1. The term needs the definite article *Al,* for it denotes the whole Islamic faithful of every time and place and has been insistently cherished by those who hold a unity beyond and, if need be, against all particular Muslim nations and states.

2. As the very need to describe them, ecclesiastically, by this foreign adjective indicates.

3. Many Muslim writers also found haven in Egypt and became influential there, among them 'Abbās al-'Aqqād and Muḥammad Rashīd Riḍā, editor of *Al-Hilāl,* both of whom had lively relations with Christian journalists as fellow emigrés.

4. One of the most notable contributors was Jurjī Zaydān (1861–1914), prolific author of historical essays and novels that aroused and satisfied a sense of Arab pride in the past. He brought to life Arab antiquities and explored the corporate memory in studies on society and ethics. Father and son, Nāṣīf (1800–1871) and Ibrāhim (1847–1906) al-Yazijī, in their poetry, prose, and hymns, in years of Turkish dominance, brought a new sense of Arabic into Christian communities and a new quality of Arabic expression into currency, which vigorous journalism, especially in Cairo, took in its stride.

5. The most famous of lexicographers was the Lebanese Buṭrus al-Bustānī (1819–1883), a Maronite deeply influenced by American missionaries, who produced *Al-Muḥīṭ* (literally, "the Comprehensive") dictionary of Arabic and a pioneer in the modernizing of style and vocabulary necessary to the development of both literature and education. These ends he served prodigiously in his encyclopedia, *Dā'irat al-Ma'ārif,* and through his many pupils. "Love of the fatherland" (*ḥubb al-waṭan*) was his salient theme, which he used both to counter fanaticism in the tragedy of 1860 and to reconcile religious communities.

6. This partly explains the attraction of mission schools, which made available

Arabic teaching as well as stimulating *ḥubb al-waṭan* in a time of ambiguous tensions in the soul of Arab youth. This missionary factor in Arab nationalism needs to be recalled when westernism and its "orientalism" are so readily and frequently reproached by the educated heirs of those "alien" institutions.

7. Christian Arabs had a certain paradoxical asset in this literary sphere, in that Muslim Arabs were more deeply bound over to Quranic norms and claims in respect of idiom, usage, and vocabulary. Reverence for these could well ride with changes of literary sentiment, but Christians were psychologically freer to initiate them. There had long been also distinctive religious Arabics in the two faiths.

8. M. E. Yapp writes: "Lest his subjects should find inspiration in the murder of foreign rulers, no Ottoman newspaper ever permitted any foreign potentates to depart this life other than by natural causes," in 'Abd al-Ḥamīd's reign (*The Making of the Modern Near East, 1792–1923* [White Plains, N.Y.: Longman, 1987], p. 183).

9. Such pan-Islamism had been the focal point at first of Jamāl al-Dīn al-Afghānī (1839–1897) in his powerful initiatives to galvanize Muslims against the political and intellectual inroads of the West. Though inclusive of other than Muslim Arabs it was a vital factor in Arab revival, since the unique role of the Arab dimension in Islam would become pivotal as and when pan-Islamism became anti, rather than pro, Ottoman.

10. The effect of this Turkification on Arab mentality was sharpened by the contrast with the Balkan provinces of the empire, which enjoyed some cultural autonomy despite the religious divide; Balkan Christians had what Arab Muslims were denied. The quotation is from Z. N. Zeine, *The Emergence of Arab Nationalism* (Delmar, N.Y.: Caravan Books, 1973), p. 81.

11. Consequences included the forfeiture of (old-style) "Syrian" territory (1) to Turkey in the northwest after Versailles and (2) in 1939, more importantly, to the French-created, enlarged dimensions of Lebanon, in which areas in south and north of the "new" Lebanon were added to the old Maronite and Druze enclaves in the medial mountains. See chapter 9.

12. Saṭi' al-Ḥuṣrī (1882–1968), a Syrian theorist of nationalism, born in the Yemen, of Syrian-Turkish parents and educated in Istanbul. He crossed swords with the eminent Egyptian writer Tāhā Ḥusain (1889–1973), who held insistently to the Europeanness of true Egypt, which Al-Ḥuṣrī strongly rejected. Egypt had to be reckoned "Islamic" in a sense that incorporated the pharaonic. On Al-Ḥuṣrī, see Bassām Ṭibi, *Arab Nationalism: A Critical Enquiry,* ed. and trans. M. Farouk-Sluglett and P. Sluglett (New York: St. Martin's Press, 1971).

13. Hence his use of the Quranic phrase denoting Mecca as *Umm al-Qurā*, "the mother of the villages," as the title of his major work, pleading, in a wide-ranging interfaith debate, for an Arab caliphate, at Mecca, to assert against Ottomans the Arab origin of Islam. *Umm al-Qurā* was published in Cairo in 1900.

14. The possession of the two sacred shrines and cities of Islam, Mecca and Medina, was always of great political as well as spiritual significance. It contributed to the prestige of Sharif Ḥusain in instigating the Arab Revolt and in turn to the new Saudī/Wahhābī regime in Arabia, the rigorist character of which—though not

treated here—had sharp repercussions in the thinking of Arab Christians about the likely evolution of their Muslim relationships.

15. "Religion and state" in the rigorist view could only feasibly obtain in their proper partnership within *Al-Ummah,* not in fragmented "patriotism." See, for example, the exchanges at the trial of Sayyid Qutb in Cairo in 1965 in my *The Pen and the Faith: Eight Modern Muslim Writers and the Qur'ān* (Winchester, Mass.: Allen & Unwin, 1985), ch. 4.

16. This was the point of the late Golda Meir's remark, when she was prime minister of Israel: "There are no Palestinians." She was negating not their physical existence but their political existence. Politically they belonged only in Arab states outside Israel.

17. Both excluded the Nile valley from truly Arab character.

18. There was, of course, no Zionist dimension to Turkey's predicament in the early 1920s. Outside Mandates, Turkey's future lay in its own hands in recovery from postwar prostration, enemy inroads, and Greek hostility, under the leadership of Muṣṭafā Kamāl Ataturk.

19. Perhaps the speech was influenced by its venue, the American University at Cairo. See *Arab Nationalism: An Anthology,* ed. Sylvia Haim (Berkeley, Calif.: University of California Press, 1974), p. 160.

20. 'Abd al-'Alayīlī, *Dastūr al-'Arab al-Qawmī* (Beirut, 1941), pp. 87f. In similar vein was Hazīm Zakī Nuseibeh, *The Ideas of Arab Nationalism* (Ithaca, N.Y.: Cornell University Press, 1956), p. 91: "In order to forge a progressive and homogeneous nation, religion must be taken out of politics as was done in the West after the Reformation" [*sic*]. He adds: "this is now realised, at least by the leaders of thought."

21. A Christian Arab's despair about religion and its custodian clergy may be discerned in the career and writing of Fā'iz Ṣāyigh, philosopher and diplomat, himself a pastor's son. See my "The Iron in the Soul," *Muslim World Quarterly* 76, no. 2 (April 1986), 67–79.

22. Constantine Zurayq, *Al-Wa'ī al-Qawmī* (Beirut, 1949), cited in *Arab Nationalism,* ed. Haim, pp. 167–171.

23. George Antonius, *The Arab Awakening* (1938; New York: Capricorn Books, 1965). His critics queried his enthusiasm and the range of society (the literate) that the writing he surveyed actually affected. Some also reacted against the emphasis he gave to Christians even though there was no denying the Christian founding of such notable journals as *Al-Ahrām* and *Al-Muqtaṭaf* nor the lively emergence of Christian Arab consciousness from the insulation of *dhimmī* mentality, via the literary revival and the pride of Arabic.

24. The writer was Hazīm Khaldī, cited from *A Middle East Reader,* ed. I. L. Gendzier (New York, 1969), p. 439.

25. On Anṭūn, see Donald M. Reid, *The Odyssey of Farah Antūn: A Syrian Christian's Quest for Secularism,* Studies in Middle Eastern History 2 (Minneapolis: Bibliotheca Islamica, 1975).

26. See Elie Kedourie, "Religion and Politics: The Diaries of Khalīl Sakākīnī," *St. Antony's Papers,* no.4 (New York: Frederick A. Praeger, 1958). Kedourie adopts a skeptical tone in his presentation, casting doubt on the ability of Christians to

surmount *dhimmī* mentality and think themselves partners in an Arab nation. In any event, he adds, cynically, Islam would be well able to put them in their place when the time came—a rather warped judgment.

27. Yūsuf al-Qardāwī, *Ghair al-Muslimīn fi-l-Mujtamī'-l-Islāmī* (The Non-Muslim in Islamic Society) (Alexandria, 1977). The passage Al-Qardāwī cites is Surah 3.85, excluding from community—indeed from eternal bliss—any who do not "desire Islam as religion."

28. *Arab Nationalism,* ed. Haim, pp. 168f.

29. Qubrūsī's work was published in Cairo, 1931; quoted from *Arab Nationalism,* ed. Haim, pp. 59–61.

30. The links are analyzed in Tibi, *Arab Nationalism: A Critical Enquiry.* One may recall the earlier Zionist work by Moses Hess, *Rome and Jerusalem*—"Rome" being not the Vatican but the capital city of Italian nationalism.

31. Franz Fanon was a West Indian writer who espoused the Algerian cause with his doctrine of "violence" as not only a means to dislodge empire but itself a positive school of self-assertion, of militant identity, necessary to the decolonializing of the mind.

32. Quoted by Eric Rouleau in *A Middle East Reader,* ed. Gendzier, p. 161.

33. Michel 'Aflaq, *Fī Sabīl al-Ba'th* (Beirut, 1959), cited in *Arab Nationalism,* ed. Haim, pp. 29–30.

34. After a brief episode in control in Iraq, as a philosopher 'Aflaq always fell foul of pragmatic and ambitious soldiery, who nevertheless found his fervor and appeal useful. He died a discarded figure, a visionary broken by the men of power, in the late spring of 1989.

35. There is much point in the distinction between Islam and *islām.* Arabic has no capitals. Study, nevertheless, must distinguish between "surrender to God" and the final "institution" of doctrine, ritual, and law, in which such surrender is made, called for by, and called Islam.

36. Patrick Seale writes: "'Aflaq's Ba'th was a debating society, a seedbed of ideas at a time of Arab intellectual poverty: this was its great appeal to students, schoolteachers and aspiring *petits fonctionnaires* in the early years and for decades afterwards evoked nostalgia among those whose lives it had touched. 'Aflaq preached a message of Arab pride which fired young people with the vision that their backward and colonised countries could take their place in the modern world" (*Asad of Syria: The Struggle for the Middle East* [Berkeley, Calif.: University of California Press, 1988], p. 98).

37. 'Abd al-Raḥmān al-Bazzāz, *Min Ruh al-Islām* (Baghdad), p. 153; quoted from *Arab Nationalism,* ed. Haim, p. 57. Here as elsewhere in Muslim Arab writing, the "days of ignorance" (*Al-Jāhiliyyah*) before Islam posed a certain problem for too ready an identification of Arabism with Islam. For was not vital "Arabism" exemplified in the Meccans of those days and was it not traditional to regard them as uncouth, wild, and despicable? Bazzāz's solution was to query those traditions and, in effect, to rehabilitate the pre-Islamic Arabs as much maligned worthies of whom Muslims need not be ashamed.

38. See n. 12 above.

CHAPTER

8

Perspectives of Egypt

I

IN MAY 1911, at an Egyptian congress convened in Heliopolis, Aḥmad Luṭfī al-Sayyid, an outstanding Muslim writer of that quarter century, read as follows from the Congress Report:

> That a state should have more than one religion is perfectly unthinkable and it would be absurd to admit that religious minorities can exist animated by political ambitions towards the exercising of public rights other than those of an essentially religious nature that are guaranteed by freedom of worship. The religion of the Egyptian people is Islam. For Islam is both the religion of the government and of the majority.[1]

In all the vicissitudes that have flowed over the Coptic minority in Egypt for thirteen centuries since the arrival of Islam the Congress of 1911 merits no more than passing notice. But it serves us well in its context as an introduction to the story of that minority since it became one in the arabicization we earlier studied through the first two or three of those thirteen centuries. The statement asserts afresh the age-old notion of *dhimmī* status as the proper destiny of all but Muslims. It does so despite the fact that Ottoman measures in the previous century had modified that notion juridically.[2] It does not pause to reflect that whereas Islam claims to relate to the whole of life—and government especially—other faiths must be excluded from all but their own pieties and so must subsist without those elements which Islam finds inseparable from religion.[3]

That "the religion of the Egyptian people is Islam" disputed—no doubt rhetorically—the fact that there were Copts numbering (according to the vagaries of census taking) one in every six, or every ten, of the population and belonging to the ethnic identity of the Nile Valley from the time of the pharaohs. Whether retroactively the Muslim invasion in 640 submerged the pharaonic and Coptic past so that the human exemptions from islamicization became negligible has—as we must see—been a constant issue in the perspectives of Egypt. The Egyptian dimension, which was so powerful a factor in the doctrinal tensions with Byzantium, has played an equally vigorous part in the modern nationalist debate, setting "Egyptianism" over against "Arabism," the former an ally of Coptic consciousness only approved and championed by Muslims at times of will to unity and otherwise seen by them as part of a conspiracy of separatism invoking overtaken history. Who really owns the pharaohs?[4]

But the declaration of 1911 had a context. It was convened as a calculated response to a Coptic congress held in Asyūt the previous spring. It was a time of heightened feeling such as punctuates the periods of relative calm between the communities. In 1908 the Coptic Reform Society, founded by Akhnūkh Fānūs, a wealthy Coptic landowner, himself a Presbyterian Copt, had taken up Coptic grievances—discrimination in employment and promotion, and religious disabilities. He had voiced them in a vigorous press campaign and elicited the familiar charge of *istikbār,* or "arrogance," from alarmed or aggressive Muslim quarters. Confrontation was sharpened by the assassination, in November 1910, of Buṭrus Ghālī, a Copt who had been prime minister for two years. The assassin, Wardānī, was a Muslim. Moderate Muslims took the murder for a political act occasioned by real or alleged charges against Ghālī's leadership, but partisan Muslims, backed by a virulent press campaign, celebrated their riddance of one they saw as properly eliminated. Wardānī was feted by these as a national hero.[5]

The Coptic Congress was the community's response of alarm, protest, and condemnation. It deplored how short-lived had been the "tolerance" that admitted of a Coptic premiership. It sought redress of grievances in civil service and other appointments, petitioned for Sunday as a holiday, and requested Christian instruction in state schools. The Coptic newspapers energetically supported the meeting and its findings, though there were leading Copts who demurred, feeling that the congress was liable to worsen their position. Circumspection has been ingrained in the Coptic temperament for centuries by dint of minority experience.

Such reservations were vindicated by the counteracting Heliopolis assembly, which condemned the Asyūt meeting as provocative, tending to communal animosity and exhibiting Coptic "insubordination." But there was a third party, the British presence, and the Ottoman representative, the khedive, was the fourth dimension. Muslim–Coptic relations have always been entangled in the web of intrigue or influence from "the Residency" or "the Palace" or their equivalent. This feature we have to note at least from the time of the Mamlūks, Napoleon in Egypt, Muḥammad 'Alī, and, from 1881 for seven decades, the British Resident. Did the khedive encourage the Copts to convene in order to embarrass the British? Or, as the contemporary nationalist leader Muḥammad Farīḍ thought, were both congresses a British ploy to divide Egyptians? Coptic grievances were always, in the eyes of nationalists, a means to do so. Copts were often minded to see hope and support in the British factor, yet at other times were loathe to use or count on it, for fear of straining relations with Islam. Was even modest belligerence advisable on the part of Copts? Or did their best hope lie in docility and traditional introspection? Or, again, should they engage whole-heartedly in nationalist Egyptianism against the British presence, trusting as they did so the dependability of those elements in Islam and Muslim society which seemed, or could be argued to seem, reassuring?

Certainly a Coptic premiership had proved desolating when an assassin could be, for many, a patriot to salute. Would aspiration and communal vigor only spell disillusion and give vent to intercommunal antagonisms fanned by sectarian newspapers? The sharp crisis of 1908–1912 passed, soon to be overtaken by the exigencies of the First World War, but it provides here a sort of prologue by episode to the quality of Coptic survival and the dilemmas we have to explore. Then, and recurrently before and after, the internal quandaries in which it placed the Coptic church were made more vexing by the strains within, between clergy and laity, between the hierarchy and the *Majlis Millī*, or Coptic Church Council. The Coptic patriarch of 1911, then totally incapacitated by age, officially disapproved of the Asyūt meeting at government persuasion. Some Coptic notables disavowed it for personal reasons, seeing their careers disserved by it. Some Orthodox Copts were also deterred by the fact that evangelical Copts were prominently involved. Divided counsels dogged the quest for a common front and confused the diagnosis of what, tactically and totally, it required.

II

Episodes as a means to overview avail if used with caution. Incidents that recede into obscurity nevertheless suggest the clues essential to the story as a whole. Egypt has often been likened to a palimpsest, a parchment on which the old survives beneath the new, as scribes in sequence write upon a fading past. Coptic Christianity is the text that persists below the Arabic and the Arabism of Islam and is itself a superscription on pharaonic Egypt through the Greco-Roman heritage.

Alexander's Alexandria is the crowning symbol of the fusion, with its celebrated library in classic times and its commanding position in the geography of both the Mediterranean and the Nile. The city of Clement and Pantaenus, of Origen, Cyril, and Athanasius, it outdid both the western and the eastern Rome in the quality of its learning and its liturgy, despite the political assets that those other capitals enjoyed. Egypt, as custodian through those first Christian centuries of its own characteristic Christianity—ardent, monastic, versatile—perpetuated its identity as legatee alike of the pharaohs and the fathers. In Greek characters the hieroglyphics of ancient Thebes and Memphis yield themselves into the Coptic language.[6]

That undertext of Coptic Christianity has to be read within the different document that Egypt became in the seventh century and following, with the advent of Islam. The new script of Islam was superimposed commandingly. Debate has continued ever since as to whether it should be seen as an alien identity disrupting a living tradition or, rather, a claimant—albeit from without—to the authentic custody of an Egypt surviving beyond the Egypt it displaced. Copts themselves, though confident of their inward answer, have long been tactfully ambivalent about an outward one. Muslims, for their part, see themselves as properly masters of the Nile Valley in *Dār al-Islām.* Invasions, multiple in history everywhere, are rewritten in retrospect into proper destinies. As for the events of 640 and the Muslim occupation, had not Muḥammad—according to tradition—adjured his forces: "When you conquer Egypt, be kind to the Copts . . . for they are your kith and kin."[7] Historians have differed about how "kind" the conquest was, according to their point of view.[8] But the intention, implicit in the tradition, to differentiate "Egypt" from "the Copts" has ever since been in dispute.

When, as we have seen in chapter 7, the concept of nationality developed—either within Ottomanism or against it—even Muslims in Egypt were liable to set Egypt over against Islam. The invading Arabs, on that view, were simply enemies who, like Turks, Kurds, Mamlūks, French, and British after them, had been outwardly resisted and inwardly rejected as spoilers of the real Egypt.[9] Ṭāhā Ḥusain, the most celebrated of Islamic scholars in the first decades of the twentieth century in Egypt, treated the Islamic conquest of his country as an episode in a national history which native genius had surmounted. The assimilative power of the Nile Valley (*al-ḥayyawwiyah al-miṣriyyah*) had been able to absorb and master it. Egyptian personality, as the dramatist Tawfīq al-Ḥakīm saw it, had imprinted itself on Egyptian Islam to the point where it would be absurd to consider Egypt Arab.[10] It was an ironic comment on the Prophet's "kith-and-kin" reminder when Marqus Simaika as a Copt could tell his hearers: "All of you are Copts: some of you are Muslim Copts, others are Christian Copts but all of you are descended from the ancient Egyptians."[11]

Such egyptianizing of each and all no doubt owed much to the politics of this century, but history could equally well be read in the contrary sense. Were there not those ancient Egyptians, the Hyksos, who, like Muslims, had been "raiders from the desert"? Could not both instances be seen not as "invasion" but as the reciprocal migration of Semitic people? In that event one could claim that

> Modern Egypt is Semitic because it is Arabic and its modern people, even though not of purely Semitic blood, are nevertheless Semites by virtue of their conviction, their situation, their interest . . . and their destiny. . . . We feel no shame that the Semitic Muslim Arabs conquered Egypt by force and Arabized it and spread in it their religion and accepted it as a trust for the preservation of their legacy.[12]

Such conflicting views as to how the pharaohs, with the Copts, were to be discerned beneath their supersession by Islam, though intriguing and politically contrived, remain academic. The conquest under Amr ibn al-ʿĀṣ was catastrophic enough in the fifth decade of the seventh century, hard on the heels of the surrenders of Damascus and Jerusalem. It is customary to regard the Copts as having in fact welcomed the Muslim army with lively, or perhaps only sullen, emotion as a liberation from the tyranny of Byzantium.[13] But the evidence is not conclusive. While it is true that deep resentments persisted from the time of the Chalcedonian issues, the sense of calamity rather than of exuberance seems to have been the dominant emotion—and, with calamity, the pondering of the judgment of God upon the emperor Heraclius. That burden about providence in the strange and sudden demise of the furniture of the world as symbolized by empire dogged the minds of intelligent Copts for at least two centuries,[14] despite the diverse factors of estrangement that existed between the Christianities of the Nile and the Bosphorus.

It was for them a mystery compounded by the supine behavior of the Orthodox (non-Coptic) patriarch Cyrus and the futility of Byzantine resistance, which ended after one forlorn naval attempt at redress with the evacuation of Alexandria and a farewell to Egypt as plaintive as that which, reportedly, Heraclius had said to the Syria he loved. The Copts, at once bereft of the solace—for all its contradictions—of eastern Christendom, puzzled long over the strange fate that had overtaken Christian sovereignty and left them prey to the exigencies of *Dār al-Islām.* Coptic would hold out for several centuries against the siege of Arabic. Copts remained for long the larger element in the population. Muslim Arabs were not saturation colonizers but slow assimilators to themselves of native people by dint of the inferiorizing implicit in *dhimmī* status and the economic and other attractions of accession to the dominant faith and the ascendant society.

The gradual process of the islamicization of Copts was conditioned by the necessities of their recruitment, as elsewhere, for the business of administration and for areas of economic life where their skills and familiarity were requisite. But, weighing always in the religious scales, was the perplexity of conquest itself and—given the gathering sense of its finality—the orphanhood to which it led. If there was satisfaction initially at the discomfiture of the Byzantines, it gave way steadily to the realization that, with the end of conflict with Byzantium, something of Coptic reality itself had been forfeited.

III

Coptic history then presents a paradox. On the one hand, as noted earlier, Coptic theology, even in its post-Chalcedon conflict with Byzantium, was thoroughly Greek in its terms and concerns over Christology. Even in controversy, its Christology spoke Greek conceptually. So doing, it stood, an observer might say, for a European Egypt. Yet, on the other hand, that distinctive Christology had become the symbol of its own identity as Egyptian. Its distinctions over the "person" and the "nature(s)" of Christ had their energy more from national than metaphysical constraints. They might have been readily reconciled, had minds and tempers been free to ponder them in detachment from the rival wills to persecute and to resist. Coptic Christianity in the subsequent experience with Islam was rugged in its faith about Jesus as its core of creedal identity, but it was so as still participant in a Greek world of discourse and concept. The entail of this paradox is present throughout the Coptic story and will emerge for us again in the final chapter.

But if, vocabulary-wise and intellectually, the doctrine of the Copts belonged to the ethos of the Mediterranean, its truly native genius belonged squarely with the ethos of the Nile and the desert. Here, in Egyptian Christian monasticism, there was no paradox but only what perhaps we may call the geography of genius. From the time of Antony in the third century the monk and the desert have been the special mark of the Coptic church, which, it is fair to say, taught the rest of Christendom the role of hermit and hermitage. It had its roots in the tradition of martyrdom that began as early as its first patriarch and patron saint, Mark the evangelist, nephew of Barnabas, who was reportedly put to death in Alexandria in A.D. 68. The aura of martyrdom was grimly renewed in the reign of the emperor Diocletian, the archpersecutor, the opening year of which, A.D. 284, marks the beginning of the Old Egyptian calendar as "the year of the martyrs." Origen, one of the greatest names of the catechetical school of Alexandria, barely escaped martyrdom, with his father, in his youth and died at seventy as a result of his ordeal during imprisonment and persecution. The ravages of the Diocletian years (284–305) coincided with the prime of the long-lived Antony, who pioneered the habit of withdrawal into desert solitude, ascetic prayer, and meditation. His example generated both a pattern and a legend of private sanctity, as emulators sought him out and coveted the wisdom which so impressed his client devotees and which Athanasius later gathered into his *Life of Antony*, a work that greatly served to disseminate the monastic ideals and patterns he had pioneered. Their influence has been traced as far west as the church in Ireland and left its mark on the *Rule* of Benedict and the Latin monasticism he nurtured.

A Copt who knew no Greek and was indeed barely literate, Antony was motivated from his youth by the Gospel precept of simplicity and dispossession. His will to isolation was copied by hermits who first sought his proximity and were later encouraged by Pachomius (d. 346), a major successor to Antony, to gather in communal houses, or *cenobia*, under vows but active in good works. Thus came into being the great houses of monastic liturgy and study from which the leadership of the Coptic church has ever since been recruited, among them Dayr Abū Saifain, Dayr al Surainī and Al-Barāmus. Both the Red Sea mountains and the western desert, Nitria and Pentapolis, were dotted with abodes of monks at prayer and meditation, educated and educating in the life aptly mirrored in the *Sayings of the Fathers*, a manual of spiritual counsel, their main legacy and their *vade mecum* in the world.

The *Sayings* enshrine a kind of moralism that is not merely expository of the virtues and temptations but is replete with a ready immediacy of effect, as pithy and incisive as the best of proverbs, with what the Hebrew prophet called "the word in season" (Isa. 50:4), that comes from "the tongue of the learned," skilled as any Buddhist to guide the inner self. Among its themes is *hēsychia*, or inner tranquillity, the possession of inward peace, as the antidote to that listlessness or *accidie* to which the monk is most exposed, whenever prayer is faint and dry.

It would be fair to say that there is something quite un-Arab about Coptic monasticism. To this day a strong instinct persists in Islam to see Coptic piety as an odd anachronism.[15] The Qur'ān, to be sure, pays a tribute to the tender purity of monks whom it finds awed and reverent before God's revelations (Surah 5.82–83), but monasticism in general the Qur'ān reprobates as "an invention" for which Christians had no divine directive (57.27). It accuses them of acknowledging their monks as "lords" (9.31), displacing the fealty due to God alone. Nevertheless, there is something in Coptic *hēsychia* akin to the *Iṭmi'nān* of the Qur'ān, that quality of "contentment in God" into which the Prophet knew himself invited in the loved words of Surah 89.27–28: "Soul at rest, return to your Lord, welcome in His welcoming." There was, further, in the discipline of the monk the dimension of *Jihād,* to which–in the inner sense of its meaning, "in the way of God"–Islamic fidelity also called the faithful. As Antony had it: "Without temptations, no one can be saved." As Islam rooted itself in Egyptian history in its early centuries, it is hard to know how it reacted to the evidences on every hand of Coptic spirituality as it pondered the ambiguity of its own scripture with reference to "men withdrawn from the outer world dwelling in houses God had permitted to be raised" innocent of merchandise and gain (Surah 24.36f.).

There was one accent in the devotion of the disciples of Antony and Pachomius and their heirs that might be attuned to the feel of the Qur'ān. It had to do with what John Bunyan–in his different tradition–called "much conflict with the devil."[16] Antony and his successors, after the pattern of the Gospels, knew the desert as the place of temptation. They saw its wildness as the setting, if not the haunt, of the demonic, where they must endure their Lord's battles. In that quality of their vision there are echoes of the *Shaiṭān al-Rajīm* ("Accursed Satan") of Quranic conflict with "evil whisperings," notably in Surahs 113 and 114 but also frequently in the experience of the prophetic word, into which the accursed Satan might cast unwanted intrusions. The body, for the Coptic monk, was the locale of many of those insinuated thoughts. However, by and large, it was not the perverted shame of being in the body at all–as in some Asian as well as Greek ideas–but rather the excesses into which a wayward physicality could beguile the self. Centuries later the great Cairene poet-mystic Ibn al-Fāriḍ (1182–1235) would give eloquent voice to that *Jihād* of the soul in his *The Poem of the Way:* "In poverty I sought her (the divine wisdom) yet was rich in having poverty my attribute."[17]

Another feature of Coptic Christianity, and of its monastic piety, which incoming Muslims would have been less minded to esteem, lay in its history of entirely verbal mission. Copts spread their Christian faith into eastern Libya (the area they called Pentapolis) and were its planters in Nubia, the Sudan, and Ethiopia. The lively churches that once proliferated in the Sudan,[18] and the christianizing of Ethiopia, were alike the fruit of their endeavor between the fourth and fifth centuries. Earlier Pantaenus himself was sent by his patriarch to the Yemen and to India. Persia, Gaul, and Britain came within their circle of action. Insofar as imperial power belonged with evangelism, it lay with Byzantium and the Melchites. By criteria of the great Tunisian Muslim historian Ibn Khaldūn (1332–1406), who in his final years adorned the Cairo scene, Christianity was, and is, not a truly "missionary religion" because it does not opt for statehood and the political arm, without which, in his view, a realistic intention to propagate a faith is impossible.[19] Coptic Christianity has been an abiding witness to the contrary. On the theory of *Dār al-Islām* true faith expansion takes place both out of an *imperium* and with a view to establishing one.

IV

Such were some of the points at stake, or in common, which Islam was to find in becoming Egyptian and Copts were to experience in coming under Islam. The narrative of the conquest and its sequel has little room to chronicle these larger issues. The immediacies of misfortune and the drastic rupture of the past have center stage. They had to do with shock and the uncertain quest for survival. At least the double, often contending, patriarchates were ended. Cyrus, the Byzantine, ignominiously departed, and his Melchite church became a remnant. Benjamin, the Monophysite, was approved in office by the Muslims, and increasingly his community came to be virtually synonymous with Egypt's Christianity.

But if the burden of the Byzantine nexus was lifted, the new and untried burden of the Islamic presence had to be shouldered with its implications only slowly disclosed as the decades passed and then the centuries. Damascus and then Baghdad replaced Constantinople as the citadels of power, while the Mediterranean—always so significant in the fortunes of Egypt—became battle territory between the new lords of the Copts and their former coreligionaries. Their islamicization was a slow, painful, and fitful process, as Arabic subtly displaced Coptic as the language in control and the latter retreated to its sanctuary in liturgy and family. An inferiority complex inevitably settled upon the Coptic soul with the prohibition of faith commendation, of the building of new churches, or, at times, of the repair of old ones. Identity had to recede into a sort of spiritual hibernation and faith resolve itself into a community of birth and private nurture to which none would belong on other grounds and those who did belong were steadily a prey to economic, social, and psychological pressures to abandon it. So began a long process of introversion, which deepened as lapsing years made plain the inexorable logic of being under *Dār al-Islām.* It was a logic painfully confirmed by the vagaries through which Islamic hegemony passed and the weary sense that, whatever the name of the ruler, his philosophy—indeed his theology—of power was unyielding in its will to subordinate and frequently to despise. Coptic Christianity through the Muslim centuries was condemned to be preoccupied with survival—a condition that any faith finds crippling. For when survival becomes an end in itself it forfeits the liveliness that is free from such anxiety. To become a community of the once-born is to forsake the entire quality of the New Testament faith as a theme that can no longer anticipate recruits. To be destined to do so, under another faith which preaches the indispensability of power and exclusively wields it, is to be doubly deprived, burdened alike by the fact and the theory.

This destiny of Coptic Christianity has persisted, variously, into this twentieth century. Yet survive it has—through what surviving takes and exacts, and in the very doggedness there are compensations. The interiority required of Copts by the exigencies of Islamic rule has given their identity a quality of mind expressed in family allegiance, a practice of piety despite recurrent tensions between clergy and laity, and a cherishing of art and tradition. Divorce and prostitution, it has often been noted, are rare among Copts, even though the ease of divorce in Islam has tempted some to islamize in the context of domestic strife. That fact in itself is witness to community values, seeing that values and community, if abandoned, are abandoned together. Through all vicissitudes, it has been the life of liturgy and lection, in the abiding Coptic speech, that has been the bond within the identity. With a fully human share of frailty, perversity, sluggishness, and contention, Copts have nevertheless endured, their imprint on the palimpsest of Egypt legible and decipherable through all that Islam has subsequently and concurrently inscribed there.

The story of Islam in Egypt belongs with a long sequence of regimes, which concern us only for their bearing on the Arab Christian field of study. For the first Islamic century the Umayyads ruled a single caliphate from beyond the Caspian Sea to the Pyrenees. Syria had primacy, and Egypt was regarded as a granary and a profitably taxable territory—a province for Damascus. The Muslim dimension increased mainly through the entry of tribal elements brought by Arab governors. Coptic Christianity remained predominant in the countryside and the old city centers. Initially, incoming military and their retainers were forbidden to acquire land lest their martial role should be lost to the onward movement of Umayyad conquest, but as the prohibition was relaxed so the economic pressure on the natives increased.

Around the middle of their century in Egypt, the Umayyads terminated the use of Greek in the administration—a step that began to detach the Copts from their long mental fascination with the Greek ethos, to which their scholarship and theology had been wedded from the days of Mark. It would be two centuries, via Ṭulūnids and Fāṭimids, before the Greek aura of Alexandria, as the intellectual symbol of an Egyptian millennium dating back to Alexander the Great, would give way to the Islamic prestige of Cairo. But the change would be as symbolic as that by which the Greek factor had reoriented pharaonic Egypt.

The displacement of the Umayyad caliphate by the ʿAbbāsids in 750 removed the seat of empire eastward to Baghdad. Islamic power in Egypt passed to a territory from which the Nile Valley had long experienced conquest and control, the last desperate occasion being two decades prior to the advent of Amr ibn al-ʿĀṣ. The ʿAbbāsids relied on Arab and Turk governors, and islamicization quickened, particularly during the reign of Al-Mutawakkil (847–861) with increasing burdens of taxation and discrimination on the Copts. The degree of persianization of Islam under the ʿAbbāsids made for a more despotic mentality, which in turn stimulated rebellious potential in its satraps remote from the caliphal center. Ibn Ṭulūn in 868 was able to establish an Egyptian state that lasted until 905. The Ṭulūnids briefly controlled an area embracing Syria, Palestine, and Libya and with their building energies set in train the emergence of Cairo as symbol of the growing equation between Egypt and Islam.

With them also began the pattern of history that delivered Egypt serially into the hands of dynasties from outside, able to establish themselves from within the ranks of slave soldiery, on whom governors had to rely and by whom they could be overthrown. The fortunes of the population—and most precariously of the Copts within it—were at the mercy of military adventurers on whose quality, or otherwise, the vagaries of government, for good or ill, depended. The pattern continued into the nineteenth century and contributed to that stolid realism about the expectations to be had of governments so characteristic of the Egyptian peasantry with their innate capacity for sheer endurance.

Thus the Ṭulūnids were followed by the Ikhshids (935–969), when a Turkish soldier, Muḥammad ibn Tughī, set up a brief and unstable succession, until the Fāṭimid power, already established in North Africa reversed the direction of early Islamic conquest and took over Egypt. Under the Fāṭimids the land had two centuries of sustained authority, before adventurers returned, though the loyalty of their armies was always the critical factor in their regime (969–1171). With the Fāṭimids, Cairo came finally into its own. Already splendid with the architecture of their predecessors, it was made the base of government. A new Cairo was developed, and Al-Azhar mosque-university inaugurated, destined to become the world center of Islamic lore and learning.

With their Ismāʿīlī Shīʿah version of Islam, the Fāṭimids repudiated ʿAbbāsid, Sunnī authority; white replaced black on their banners. Though Nubian Christianity to the south still succeeded in holding off Muslim expansion, the Copts within Egypt entered a new chapter of mixed fortune and oppression. The new Al-Azhar's masonry and pillars were permanently borrowed from their churches.[20] After two rulers of able quality, Copts were caught in perhaps the most devastating chapter in their tribulations, when the third Fāṭimid, Al-Ḥākim (996–1021) came to power. This archpersecutor had a (Melchite) Christian mother, but it was after her death that he conceived the belief that he was himself a divine incarnation in some sense, and with it a sharp animosity against the Copts and against Christians elsewhere within his power. The Holy Sepulchre in Jerusalem was ravaged and its patriarch, Jeremiah, brought to Cairo and beheaded, though he was also Al-Ḥākim's uncle, for whom his mother had secured appointment.

What psychic tensions lay behind the madness of Al-Ḥākim must be left to conjecture, as must the origins of the Druze faith, to which his personality gave rise. In the Coptic scene the twenty years of his oppression exacted a heavy price from its victims both physical and venal. The persecution that may purify can also degrade and corrupt. The period was rife with the bribery, intrigue, simony, and brutality to which minorities are liable in the stress of insecurity. Distinctive marks on clothing, the carrying of heavy crosses on the person, the destruction of churches and their use for the Islamic *adhān*, or call to prayer, and other humiliations belonged grievously to this period. But ruling madness was also inimical to Muslims and, a year after terminating the persecution, Al-Ḥākim was murdered by Muslim hands. In the long reign of his successor, Al-Mustanṣir (1056–1094) the wheel of circumstance turned, save for a disastrous earthquake and the incidence of famine. The patriarch Christodoulos (1047–1077) moved his seat from Alexandria to Cairo, and some churches were rebuilt, notably in Damanhūr. His successor, the canonist Cyril II, developed close association with incoming Armenians and conceded the importance of Arabic by undertaking its study.

The turn of the eleventh and twelfth centuries saw the establishment of the crusaders in Jerusalem and the decline of the Fāṭimids through the treacherous ambitions of their slave soldiery and their own incompetence. Instability was aggravated by the crusading incursions into Egypt and the crusaders' brief tenure of Damietta, where they set up a titular Latin patriarchate for Alexandria. The Fāṭimid era was finally terminated by the rise to power of Ṣalāḥ al-Dīn al-Ayyūbī, known to the West as Saladin, a Kurdish soldier and master architect of the demise of the Latin kingdom of Jerusalem through the skillful consolidation of Islamic power that he was able to achieve in Syria, Palestine, and Egypt. The Ayyūbids ruled Egypt from 1170 until 1250. As champions of Islam against the western Christians, they brought new vitality to Sunnī Islam in the Egyptian context by their emphasis on Muslim learning, the establishment of collegiate mosques, and the aura of Islamic prestige that they enjoyed. Nubian Christians to the south caused them some political anxiety, but the Copts at least found a degree of economic prosperity, not least through commercial openings with Venetians.

V

To summarize history as a bare catalogue of dynasties is not to register what it meant to the Copts that these dynasties were all, in their sequence and diversity, Islamic. Historians may assign the centuries to narrative, but they are lived in days and years of biography. The times before Muḥammad receded below the average horizon, and the Coptic condition lapsed into a proven irreversibility by the sheer passage of Islamic time. Subjection and stolidity defined each other in the Coptic psyche, accentuated by outward changes under which, until the nineteenth century, nothing changed. Ṣalāḥ al-Dīn might raise the mighty—and symbolic—Citadel of Cairo, characteristically rugged and resolute, but the Ayyūbids could not long sustain the regime adventure had contrived and new adventurers removed.

These were the so-called Mamlūks, who in various guises reigned in Egypt from 1250 until the arrival in 1517 of Salīm I, the Ottoman sultan. Administration was thoroughly militarized with mercenary (literally, "slave") soldiery granted land tenure for martial control. It was a system that bred endless adventurism on the part of ambitious or ruthless barons and a contempt for legitimacy and authority. The titular 'Abbāsid caliph might be installed in Cairo after the sack of Baghdad by the Mongols in 1258, but that nominal status was at the mercy of *realpolitik,* its aura captive to its masters. Egypt was in effect a land bound over to a garrison, which might, from time to time, construct an empire stretching far beyond Egypt's borders east into Arabia and west into Libya and Tunis and contrive to preserve Egyptians from Mongols and crusaders alike.

The military structure of government depressed the condition of the peasantry. The Egyptian population suffered a long infiltration of alien elements, Kurds, Turks, Circassians, and others, following the massive incursions of distant Asia into western Asia during the later medieval centuries. On both counts the Copts suffered acutely and their condition further declined. Islam in dominance might be racially diversified, but politically its rigors were in no way mitigated by its power struggles, while some of the Mamlūks, striving to emulate the legend of Ṣalāḥ al-Dīn, made themselves active patrons and champions of a resolute Islam, founding mosques and endowments and schools of law.

Historians divide the Mamlūks into Baḥrī and Burjī, from 1250 to 1382 and from 1382 to 1517 respectively, the one Turkish, the other mainly Circassian. In the fourteenth century the former became hereditary, but, in the main, opportunism not heredity determined the sequence. Palace revolution became an Egyptian way of life. Brigandage succeeded to the pharaohs: luxury and high culture alternated with near anarchy. Some of the Mamlūks exercised a wide patronage in the arts and in the building of public works, as well as in the protection of Islam. Copts might be preferred by them in administration either for their greater aptitude or their greater dependence. The increase of commerce across the Mediterranean held some advantage for them, and there were efforts in the fifteenth century around the time of the Council of Florence to renew formal relations with the western church.[21] But such overtures, abortive then, never held for Copts the fascination they had for the Maronites of Lebanon, and latent within them was the dubiety of European connection.

The greatest of the pre-Ottoman Mamlūks[22] was among the earliest, namely, Baybars (1260–1277), victor over the Mongols, spoiler of the crusaders, and a ruler who became a legend in Egypt. But tenacious as the later Baḥrī and Burjī Mamlūks were in their military prowess, keeping Tamerlane at bay and holding their Syrian territories, their internal conflicts and political instability became endemic. Rivalries and economic disasters, heightened by plague and famine and aggravated by brutal taxation, led finally to their supersession by the Ottomans, who in 1517 added Egypt to their already vast domains in Anatolia, the Levant, Persia, and the Balkans. Their rule in Egypt, effectively or nominally, lasted into the twentieth century.

Even in its victorious heyday under Salīm I and his successor Sulaymān the Magnificent (1520–1566), the Ottoman Empire ruled in Egypt only by "imperial proxy," through beys, or officers, on whom it had to rely for the fiscal yield to the central treasury and for recruitment to the imperial forces. Its major preoccupation was with the external defense of its vast territories and its oscillating borders in the Balkans and beyond. Affairs internal to Egypt were in the control of local leaders, tax farmers, and notables in a pattern that virtually perpetuated the times of the Baḥrī and Burjī Mamlūks. The sultan was unable to dispense with their role internally and only once, in 1775, did an expedition from Istanbul attempt to exert direct intervention. Egypt was basically a taxable entity necessarily farmed out to an officialdom that was often rapacious, a ruling caste remote from the local population with whom they dealt only through a minor bureaucracy. For almost three centuries between Salīm I and the rise of Muḥammad 'Alī after Napoleon's brief intrusion, Egyptians, as subjects of a distant caliph-sultan, were victims of the agents of his absenteeism. It was a strange version of *Dār al-Islām,* which gave rise to the Arab dilemma of Ottomanism, examined in the previous chapter.

It was a situation that had a deep impact on the Coptic population. Occasionally their notables might rise to positions of prominence in administration and capitalize on commercial opportunity, but the gulf between officialdom and the people at large, both citizens and peasants, tended to intensify sharply the role of religious leadership among both Muslims and Copts. The best of the Mamlūks had presided over a vigorous institutionalizing of Egyptian Islam in academies, schools, and pious foundations in theology, law, and historiography. The Ottoman assumption of the caliphate from the last of the 'Abbāsids added symbolic weight, however lightly the citizens may have regarded it.[23] The very shape of Ottoman authority via surrogates remote in their vested interests from those they ruled–and taxed–threw an onus for community cohesion, not to say support and solace, on the religious leadership. In the case of Islam, the prestige of *Sharī'ah* judges and mosque *'ulamā'* became increasingly important as the only persons able, if at all, to restrain the bureaucracy.

Copts, of course, had no such recourse, but the more the principle of religious Islam–if we may so speak–became significant the more the Coptic community also had to look in increasing isolation to its own religious mentors. This necessity underlined what had been and was long to remain an urgent issue for Copts, namely, the tension between clergy and laity, due in part to the monastic tradition of the hierarchy and in part to the aspirations of those Copts who were able to prosper materially. The issue is better studied in the nineteenth century, when it was accentuated by western influences sometimes attractive to laity but anathema to suspicious clerics. Its elements, however, were implicit much earlier.

The degree to which the Turkish sultans, with the customary brevity of their tenures, fell victim to local pashas as *Shuyūkh al-Balad*, "masters of the place," increased in the late seventeenth and in the eighteenth centuries, as the decline of Ottoman power began to be evident–a decline that stemmed from overextension of military resources in Europe and chronic fiscal oppression. A pattern akin to that of the pre-Ottoman Mamlūks returned, with Egypt at the mercy of unscrupulous chiefs, plagued by infighting and local conflict. A state of near civil war existed between Cairo and Upper Egypt in the mid-eighteenth century. Briefly, between 1769 and 1773 'Alī Bey al-Kabīr, the best of the rulers of that century, succeeded in throwing off Ottoman allegiance altogether. In a fleeting independence he was able to make incursions into Syria and Arabia, reviving Egyptian dreams and setting a precedent for the more durable Muḥammad 'Alī in the next century. His abortive ventures beyond the Nile Valley posed the issue–always latent–between an Egypt laboring under Ottoman connection and an Egypt asserting a national identity against a provincial identity. Given that the Ottomans were the caliphs of Islam, that issue concealed the deeper question concerning Egypt and Islam and, for the Copts, the dilemma of being Egyptian in their non-Islam.

The opening of the nineteenth century contrived persistent forms both of the issue and of the dilemma, with Napoleon's short-lived incursion into

Egypt in 1798 and the regime of Muḥammad ʿAlī that followed it. The arrival of the French in Napoleonic ardor spelled subtle changes in the fortunes and the temptations of the Copts. It brought the Mediterranean back into Egyptian reckoning after the lapse of centuries since the Greeks and the Byzantines. The Mediterranean thus renewed the mediation of Europe to Egypt and the fascination of intellectual Egypt with Europe. The papacy had been cajoling and enticing the Copts intermittently for almost two centuries.[24] But Napoleon's intervention came with a different *imperium.* He presented himself as champion of Islam, and the French savants, engineers, and pundits whom he brought with him had a longer impact than his armies, cut off and frustrated by British naval power. Caught in the toils of a European rivalry, Egypt found itself counter-coveting the techniques and arts possessed by those competing for possession of its terrain. Some at least of the Muslim population registered the first impulses to modernity. These in turn were to affect profoundly the fortunes and mentality of the Coptic community, only partially awakened to new perspectives on religious faith and practice.

The brief presence of the French forces in such dramatic form at once aroused the ambiguity of Coptic emotions and the Muslim suspicion of them. Would the self-styled Islamic guardian exploit, beguile, or embroil the interests of Christian Egyptians? Under the last of the Ottoman Mamlūks, Coptic notables such as Muʿallim Rizq and Muʿallim Yaʿqūb (General) Ḥannā, with the brothers Jirjus and Ibrāhīm Jawharī,[25] had emerged to great prominence through their competence in finance and public affairs, to become benefactors of their church through the wealth they amassed. It was natural that those who survived to the coming of the French should have remained indispensable in the new day. Jirjus Jawharī called upon Napoleon, on the basis of the principles of the Revolution, to make all Egyptians equal and terminate the inferior status of the Copts in general.

The brevity of the French tenure robbed the request of any long significance, but Yaʿqūb Ḥanna, for his part, was tempted into a total commitment to the French, in the conviction that with them lay good hope of final deliverance from the miseries of the past. He fought with the French in Upper Egypt and in the closing months of their tenure organized and trained a Coptic legion with himself as general. His confidence in this route to Coptic equality, balancing the unilaterally Muslim militarism of the Ottomans and the beys, ended—though not ignominiously—in his withdrawal by sea on a British vessel to find an untimely grave on French soil.[26] Fate has never, before or since, looked kindly on Coptic initiatives for an independent Egypt. The Coptic role in independence can only obtain in tow to the Islamic.[27]

A quick nemesis overtook the Copts until, in 1805, the regime of the Albanian adventurer Muḥammad ʿAlī began. He emerged in the manner of the Mamlūks before him, by dint of military ambition, astutely served by resolute authority and, at times, ruthless cunning. He had arrived in Egypt in 1801 with a contingent of fellow Albanians to help expedite the French defeat. He rapidly became the leading force in Egyptian affairs, was recognized in 1807 by the Turks as governor of Egypt, eliminated the last Mamlūks, and began a twin process of reorganization within, and military expansion beyond, its borders. Egypt was divided into provinces and, for the first time—perhaps taking a hint from "General" Ḥannā—Muḥammad ʿAlī recruited local Arabic-speaking Egyptian Muslims into military service, while still maintaining the long tradition of an alien militia. Egyptians deeply resented their forced inclusion into his armed forces, the more so as it did nothing to alter the pattern of Turco-Circassian, foreign dominance within the land.

Muḥammad ʿAlī was a firm believer in the emulation of Europe in army discipline and modern techniques, serviced by education and science. Teachers were imported and an elite of students sent abroad, mainly to France. There were rapid developments in the economy and the structure of government. Muḥammad ʿAlī was useful to the Ottomans in curbing Wahhābī revolt in Arabia, but his ambitions, with those of his son, Ibrāhīm, grew to threaten the sultan himself, when they brought the whole of the Levant into their control and penetrated into Anatolia. So doing, Muḥammad ʿAlī overreached himself by alarming European powers, who were ill at ease also about his conquests in Greece and Crete, to the point of contriving his expulsion from Syria, leaving him with only the governorship of Egypt until his death in 1849.

Although Muḥammad ʿAlī thus impressively employed Egypt as a base and dramatically stimulated its modern development, there is little sign that he thought in terms of an Egyptian nationalism requiring a Muslim/Copt solution to its meaning. Though his energies and abilities were phenomenal, they belonged with the Ottoman-Mamlūk world of sultan and pasha. They left to the future the emergence of Arabism from Ottomanism and, with it, the Coptic Christian part in such emergence. Nevertheless, the European dimension of his instincts and their vigorous pursuit did much to shape, and complicate, that emergence when it came.

The Copts, in the near half century of Muḥammad ʿAlī's regime, suffered initially from their flirtation with the French. Muʿallim Malāṭī, head of Napoleon's legal commission, was beheaded after their withdrawal and angry mobs sacked the Coptic areas of Cairo. *Dhimmī* status was reestablished with its restrictions on movement and dress, and the *jizyah* (until 1855) continued to be levied. Copts suffered with other Egyptians in the rigors of the ruler's exactions, confiscations, and corvées.[28] But, as earlier, the regime had to depend in part on the acumen of Coptic officials whose skills—or non-Muslim aura of vulnerability—made them suitable. Mu'allim Ghālī, later murdered, became Muḥammad 'Alī's chief treasurer. Copts did not benefit from educational forays to Europe, and the growing involvement of Europe's politics, personnel, and—we must add—priests in Egypt's story had repercussions for Coptic hopes and circumspection. A European coalition finally rescuing the Ottomans from Muḥammad 'Alī's pretensions to empire could only be an embarrassing factor for Coptic relationships.

VI

Patriarch Peter VII (1809–1852) presided over his church as durably as Muḥammad 'Alī over the state. Though he was able to establish a Coptic bishopric in the Sudan, he had to be circumspect about holding off the blandishments of European powers (e.g., Russia and Austria) and churches pressing their doubtful patronage and protection upon him. It was, however, under his successor for a mere seven years, Cyril IV (1854–1861), that significant renewal of the Coptic church ensued. To have his work in focus it is well to note that the previous two centuries had seen a partial revival of non-Coptic Christian elements within Egypt stimulated by the constant exposure of Egypt to alien infiltration under the Mamlūks and by the extension of Egypt-based power, under 'Alī Bey al-Kabīr and Muḥammad 'Alī, into the Levant. Syrians in particular came to play an increasing role in the Arabic idiom within Egypt and to stimulate Orthodoxy of the Greek Chalcedonian variety. The parallel patriarchate of (Greek) Alexandria, for long so tenuous after Cyrus's ignominious exodus in 641, assumed new significance. It will be remembered, for example, that the reformer Cyril Lucar had been patriarch of Alexandria from 1602 to 1621 before he became patriarch of Constantinople. His grim fate later at the hands of the sultan may have atoned for his dismissive verdict against the Copts of his day.[29] But by Cyril the Coptic Reformer's time,[30] two and a half centuries on, the sundry influences external to the church had stirred new alertness among the Copts.

Through these factors—the stimulus of Muḥammad 'Alī's regime and the sense of a new rivalry, whether benign or sinister, from the Greek Orthodox presence—came a challenge to the Coptic leadership and a sense of an incubus to be cast off and inertia to be overcome. There was also the fact of the urge to Coptic Uniatism coming from Rome and often abetted, as diplomats and Jesuit clergy knew well to do, by political offers of aid and comfort. Though a Coptic Catholic patriarchate did not come into being until 1895 and their personal status courts not until 1908, there had been

Coptic Catholic clergy from the seventeenth century, despite the fact that Mamlūk and Ottoman rulers looked upon such suspect foreign entanglements of their Christian subjects as a clear threat to the *dhimmī* system. Some patriarchs sensed the attraction of the education, the languages, and the connections that Rome's emissaries could offer, as did some Coptic laity, especially in the nineteenth century. In general, however, the traditional loyalty of the hierarchy and the community kept either intact.

It was near the end of Muḥammad 'Alī's rule that the Coptic mind had also to reckon with evangelical Christian overtures from England and, after his demise, from the United States. The American Presbyterian Mission achieved the formation later in the century of the Coptic Evangelical Church, whose leading members, in the Coptic Congress of 1911, exerted strong influence among Copts at large. But the early Anglican ventures, led by Henry Tattam and James Lieder, with their informed concern for Coptic theological education, had a direct, if discreet, impact on the patriarch Cyril in the 1830s prior to his elevation to the patriarchal throne.[31] Unlike the uniatizing Jesuits, the English-speaking evangelicals were not interested in jurisdictions, but in an ongoing Coptic church instilled with their vision.

But, if these various factors obtained, it must be to the initiative and quality of Cyril IV himself that history must credit the changes over which he briefly presided. Educated in part through evangelicals and in part in the Monastery of St. Antony and groomed by a commission in Ethiopia, he owed his election to popular support against the reluctance of the hierarchy. His election was accomplished in two stages, via a proxy patriarchal tenure as metropolitan of Babylon, followed in 1854 by full office. He energetically set about enlivening the temper and the teaching of the clergy, setting up the Coptic Orthodox College with education in Arabic, Turkish, and three main European languages as well as Coptic. He acquired a printing press and saluted its ventures with great acclaim, while bracing church discipline and kindling new attention to the quality of liturgy, ritual, and instruction. He pioneered female education and supervised the repair and founding of church buildings, including the Basilica of St. Mark in Ezbekiyyah. His vision extended to fraternity with the Greek, the Russian, and the Anglican traditions, and he strengthened the Coptic presence in Jerusalem with provision for pilgrimage from Egypt.

The precarious nature of such initiatives, in the Muslim context, was evident in the sudden death of Cyril, by poisoning, after a visit to the khedive—as the successors, descendants of Muḥammad 'Alī, came to be described after his death in 1849. By the time of Cyril's successor at one remove, Cyril V (1875–1927), the khedive Ismā'īl, grandnephew of

Muḥammad ʻAlī, was entering on that profligacy in grandiose expenditure which, coupled with the crisis in cotton after the close of the American Civil War, was to land Egypt in the financial straits that precipitated the British occupation of 1881. Meanwhile the opening of the Suez Canal in 1869 and other features of modernity aggravated the stresses of Coptic Christianity and made at once more urgent and more complex the hopes and hazards that Cyril IV's tenure had disclosed.

His educational influence lived on and helped to engender a more lively and critical laity, impressed by European standards of theological nurture and depressed, if not at times scandalized, by their own Coptic clericalism. Cyril V's long patriarchate synchronized with massive developments in the shaping of contemporary Egypt in which he was in every way unfitted to provide discerning or adequate spiritual leadership. Nurtured in monastic discipline and with a scribe's set of mind, Cyril V was both ill-disposed and ill-equipped to work with the *Majlis Millī,* or community council of twenty-four elected representatives, which had been instituted just prior to his accession to cooperate with him in the management of church property. Initial collaboration soon turned to conflict and patriarchal obduracy. Progressive laity responded by establishing a variety of societies to support schools and causes outside the clerical dominance of *awqāf,* or endowment resources. But they could do little about clerical retaliation in matters of ecclesiastical law, marriage, and inheritance.

The tension inevitably involved appeals to the khedive and to the British, and the patriarch was briefly banished to a monastery by the former. Some sympathy for him was engendered, and on his return to Cairo he was somewhat passively reconciled to the role and the hopes of the *Majlis Millī.* Educational projects proceeded more readily, but the inner tragedy of these long conflicts lay in their coinciding with the strong emergence of an Egyptian nationalism fueled by the British presence and within it the rise of the theme of an Egyptian identity "de-Ottomanized" and independent. The new nationalists saw little point in a nationalism whose success, if attained, would only perpetuate the non-Egyptian control to which, for long centuries, Egypt had been victim. Though led by Muslims, such nationalists were calling in question the whole caliphal structure of Islam and so raising, in acute form, the question of the place of Copts, as Egyptians, in their endeavor.

VII

The first spasm of this "Egypt for Egyptians"—however uncertainly meant—was evident in the revolt of Aḥmad ʻUrābī (1841–1911) in 1881/82, which began as a reaction of Arabic-speaking army officers resentful of

Turco-Circassian dominance in the army and developed into a popular uprising against both the khedive and the British. It was quelled by the latter at the rout of Tell al-Kabīr and the exiling of ʿUrābī. At the time it merely heralded the regime of the British "Residence," but it posed for the decades through which that regime endured the basic issue of Egyptian identity and its intercommunal expression. It did so within the triangular situation of the khedive, the British, and the nationalists, with all its potential for reciprocal intrigue, suspicion, and maneuver, and with the Copts uneasily set as pawns between all three.

Lord Cromer, Britain's Consul-General in Egypt from 1883 to 1906, professed to see Copts and Muslims as indifferently Egyptians.[32] Secured by the British garrison in the control of the diminished Egyptian army, he contrived successfully to manipulate the khedive and the legislative council and to contain recalcitrant tendencies, generally preferring non-Coptic Christians (Syrian and Armenian) to Copts in his dealings with the minorities. He distrusted Copts for what he saw as their opportunism, but the changes ensuing during his time in the Egyptian economy, administration, and population stimulated Egyptian consciousness, despite the stultifying effects of his policy. When, in 1910, the nationalist theme erupted with Mustafā Kāmil it had a much more Islamic flavor. Its leader wanted to comprehend all Copts and other non-Muslim elements as somehow "Muslims," if only culturally, so that pan-Islamic solidarity might not be compromised by extraneous scruples. All "sons of the pharaohs" were now, by long sanction, Islamic; all were orientals against Europe. Such concepts owed themselves, in part, to the arousal of Islamic thought by such leaders as Jamāl al-Dīn al-Afghānī (1839–1897) and Muḥammad ʿAbduh (1849–1905) and a lively press activity around the Muslim–Copt issue. A sense of Europe as the adversary had, at least for the time being, displaced the Ottomans in Egyptian feeling. Hence the difficulties with which we began around the rival congresses of 1911. Copts, by and large, as the genuine "Egyptians," preferred the British alternative.[33]

The long future, however, was not with them in that sentiment. With the post–World War situation in the 1920s came a new Egyptian constitutionalism and the demise of the Ottomans themselves. Coptic emotion had then less reason for unease about pan-Islam. The British became the sole target of nationalist aims, and Copts could recognize that their best interests lay not in Coptic separatism but in opting for inclusivism. This meant trusting Islam (defined in the 1923 constitution as the state religion) and participating in a broadly common front in the name of an Egypt committed to the British departure.

Through the tortuous vicissitudes marking the stages of that exodus, 1936, 1954, 1957, this was broadly the Coptic position. Though it meant renouncing the force of an identity from a pre-Islamic past, with vital stake in the mood and mercy of a non-Christian religion, it also meant the final end of *dhimmī* status. British imperialism, which had begun almost unwittingly in Egypt in 1882, had ensured that Egyptian nationalism would leave Egyptian Copts with no option but an Islamic future. The decision was at once painful, risky, and ineluctable. It committed Coptic destiny to the open question of Muslim self-definition within the new context of liability for a highly self-conscious community, no longer "*dhimmī*-ized," but still precariously hostage to Islamic will.

Remitting further analysis to chapter 12, it suffices to illustrate rather than narrate the course of Coptic affairs between the World Wars, the *Wafd*, the 1952 Revolution, the confrontation with Israel, the Sadāt years and beyond. Two interacting factors are central, namely, the secular dimension—to which we will return, and which played its part in reconciling Coptic thought to a national Egypt under Islam—and the course of Islamic rigorism determined to rewrite the *modus vivendi* on strict *dhimmī* lines.[34] In the first Egyptian parliament, more Copts were in fact elected than the special status provision, originally proposed by the British (with respect to *some* Coptic concern), would have yielded. Confidence among Copts oscillated with misgiving. The grievances of minority disadvantage in politics, the professions, education, and the armed forces have persisted. Successive regimes, by and large, have aimed to sustain a basic continuity of majority/minority relationship. At the time of the Revolution heralding the 'Abd al-Nāṣir period, the slogan "We are all Egyptians" was prominent and the leader attended the inauguration of the new Basilica of St. Mark. Tensions internal to the Coptic community might arouse a certain contempt for it in ruling quarters, while the nationalization of education deprived Copts of the direct control of their schools.

But it was the activities of the rigorous Muslims, of the *Ikhwān al-Muslimūn* and still more radical groups, that both dismayed Coptic minds and required firm government response, notably in the 1960s under 'Abd al-Nāṣir and in the 1970s under Sadāt.[35] Insofar as the dismay inspired communal belligerence on the part of extremist Copts, Sadāt felt obliged, in curbing the Islamic dissidents, also to exile the patriarch Shenouda.[36] When, despite that evenhandedness, he paid with his life at the hands of Muslim assassins the Coptic bishop Samuel died with him on the reviewing stand.[37]

The threat of the rigorists in Islam and of their clandestine propaganda against the state especially in artisan and student circles required not only alert but also repressive vigilance. This evoked in limited quarters an intellectual attention to the liberal, spiritual obligations of Islam in a secular climate. It also required a governmental accent on Muslim *pietas* and identity in a conscious effort to align a "true Islam" away from the rigorists and toward a pattern more reassuring to minorities. Copts, musing on such efforts, especially in the time of Sadāt, were torn between apprehension about the necessity of them and misgivings about their success.

The situation, either way, was and is liable to be bedeviled by fanatics trading in absolutes. The old slogans of "crusaders" and "Zionists" prove a ready stock-in-trade, given the sequence of Egypt's policies in relation to Israel, with which to implicate the Copts. One such dissident preacher in the 1980s was the blind shaikh 'Abd al-Ḥamīd Kishk. Though preachers in official mosques are firmly controlled, *Al-Wā'iẓ* ("the preacher"), as he came to be known, had a large following at a small private mosque and his cassettes were widely available.[38] Such preachers castigate "official" Islam as apostate, deplore the moral state of the nation, decry the establishment *'ulamā'*, and demand an Egypt exclusively Islamic by their own definition of Islam. Resentful Copts have been tempted into vociferous reaction, especially in areas such as the Asyūt province, in which they are most numerous. The fears they had of the pan-Arabism of 'Abd al-Nāṣir's adventurism may have passed, only to be deepened by the would-be pan-Islamic zeal of a version of Islam that fundamentally repudiates the un-Islamic invalidity (as it sees it) of the entire state and nation of Egypt as conceived and constituted since 1919. Fully a third of Copts still bear pharaonic names. If they conceded the trust of Egypt to Islam, it was in the hope of an Islam in genuine trust with Egypt.

VIII

It may be useful, in this context, to consider how the Coptic mind responds to the secular issue implicit in that open question. As we note in the next chapter, biography—whether of persons or institutions—is often a convenient context in which to sense and savor things too large for detailed survey. One such autobiography is that of a lively, vocal Copt, Salāmah Mūsā (1887–1958), whose journalism and personality offer an intriguing index into how minority status might alleviate itself by appeal to modern factors calculated to neutralize religious differences in a secular confidence in common citizenship. Obduracy, to be sure, only breeds obduracy, but more sober, devout Coptic minds have ample reason to distrust such expectations at least in reckoning with Islam.

Salāmah Mūsā's story he called *Tarbiyat Salāmah Mūsā* (The Education of Salāmah Mūsā).[39] A voracious reader with an eclectic mind, he opined and wrote energetically about the political and intellectual affairs through which his seventy years were spent, before, during, between, and after the World Wars. Europe, it seemed to him, taught one to sit loosely by religious dogma. With means to travel and a refreshing curiosity, he relished a willing initiation into the mind of modern Europe in Paris, London, and elsewhere. Rousseau, H. G. Wells, and Bernard Shaw became the stock-in-trade of his mind. He grew enamored of evolutionary science and developed a philosophy of "Egyptianism" grounded in social theory and liberated from the shackles of theological tradition. On a chance encounter with Bernard Shaw he mistook the latter's query about Monophysitism for vegetarianism.[40] James Frazer's ideas in *The Golden Bough* of the social origin and role of religion led Mūsā to accommodate his Coptic heritage to a visionary image of "the land of the pharaohs," the very ancestors of the world, to whom Greece and the West owed their wisdom. From his youth he had been impatient with Coptic doctrine: he found his church negligent of social tasks and fossilized. He preferred a Tolstoyan Jesus. In middle life, however, he grew a little more conscious of how Coptic identity at least symbolized the long-suffering of his people.[41]

This romantic sense of Egypt seemed to ignore the virility, even the possible virulence, of Islam, unless he hoped that it would be susceptible to participation in the essential unity of all religions. But his ideas involved implications, hardly feasible, about the role of Arabic as Egypt's language. Wanting, as it were, to hear the pharaohs in pulpits,[42] he sought to colloquialize Arabic and make its inflection Egyptian, in order to arrest the unwelcome assimilation to the Arabs which the classical Arabic entailed.[43] Here he touched on a sensitive problem. For Arabic, by virtue of the Holy Qur'ān as its supreme form and the Prophet Muḥammad as its heaven-mandated user, associates its users with Islam even when they want dissociation. Indeed, there are and have long been moods among Muslims to deny Christian Arabs the use of the language or at least to prohibit a Christian Arab use of religiously sensitive vocabulary in the language.[44]

Salāmah Mūsā had a point but no solution. Arabic can hardly be "declassicized" for the sake of Egypt and, as we saw in chapter 7, Christian Arabs have been in the forefront of its modern literary revival. The issue persists. Mūsā did not favor any Coptic emulation of the Zionist revival of Hebrew, as if the old tongue, though pharaonic in source, could serve the Egypt he envisaged. He recognized the appeal of Coptic studies but did so too late, as he believed, to be serious about them himself.

For all his verve and ventures of mind, how feasible was Salāmah Mūsā's prescript for a Coptic presence in Egypt? How viable could it be, as a unilateral adventure into Europeanism? Any such enamorment with the West spelled suspicion within Muslim minds, some of whom deliberately fostered the idea that God willed them to cultivate Coptic friendships in order to keep Copts from western directions of mind. How practicable, then, could be such a heady embrace of secular, or agnostic, ideas whatever their source? How durable would be a Coptic identity itself staked in such evacuation of its own inner faith and history, such aloofness from its inner soul? Could the admitted clergy-laity strains within it, as a traditionally monastic, highly liturgical entity, survive such worldly mindedness?

Mūsā was significant as much for the *non sequiturs* of his case, as for the slant of his ideas, but he represented a mood of the times and had his disciples. One such was a Greek Orthodox Egyptian, Ibrāhīm al-Miṣrī, who shared his desire to free Egyptian literature from the faults, as he saw them, of the Arabic language—an inadequate instrument for modern thought. Like Mūsā, he believed in the solidity of the peasantry as the real core of the Egyptian identity.

Such views in the 1920s look different near century end. But one significant sequel to Salāmah Mūsā's expression of Egypt is his influence on the early authorship of Najīb Maḥfūẓ, winner of the Nobel Prize and the most celebrated of Muslim Egyptian men of letters this half century. Maḥfūẓ's trilogy of historical novels about ancient Egyptians owed something to encouragement from Mūsā, who published a beginner's story in *Al-Majallat al-Jadīdah* ("The New Magazine"), which he controlled. Maḥfūẓ's mature response to life's bewilderments and enigmas, however, in its radical sense of futility and the absurd, moved far beyond the naïveté and Wellsianism of his Coptic mentor and the association is worth noting for that very reason.[45] The relation of his Islam and of Muslims at large to the travail in the soul of the West, which his novels reflect, we must remit to chapter 12.

Coptic theology, like any other faith, needs to reckon with the counsel Salāmah Mūsā had for his community and with its sources in the wider world, but his stance was more a temptation than a living option. If followed, it would attenuate Coptic Christianity and undermine its existence, for its ultimate vocation lies in its quality of Christian thought and society. That fact returns us to the prime condition of its existence, namely, the temper of the dominant Islam.

IX

There is an intriguing parable of this situation in the tradition common in the Egyptian story—mostly in the village setting—whereby Copts may find a protecting "ally" in some Muslim family. It happens in the context of the blood feud. Copts have no right of retaliation against Muslims, as we saw at the outset of this chapter in the strange protest against the execution of the assassin of Buṭrus Ghālī, when *Sharī'ah* lawyers contested the death sentence of the state court. This non-right endangers Copts, by ensuring that molesters will escape retaliation. Hence the device whereby a friendly Muslim family, known locally to be primed with this retaliatory task, gives such security as threat of retaliation may afford to the Coptic "ally" otherwise in jeopardy. (When Copts kill Copts, no blood feud generally results.) But what if the protecting family deserts or is itself minded to attack its protégés?

There is something of this necessary dependence in the minority situation, for it belongs with the very fabric of Islam itself, bequeathed from the *dhimmī* system. That system, juridically, is at an end in modern society, but perpetual minority status and survival at majority behest persist. The Egyptian delegate to the United Nations had reassuring words in 1952 in a comment on the U.N. Charter:

> Islamic Law rejects all kinds of religious persecution. By participating in the elaboration of this text [the Charter] Egypt wishes fully to safeguard religious liberty. Article 12 of the last Egyptian Constitution, which sanctions the liberty of religion, does not merely mean that every individual can embrace any religion, but that he can freely pass from one religion to another.[46]

But such "passing freely" has little point or incidence in practice, given the long classical tradition of Islam on the status of non-Muslims in the midst.

And what when "passing freely" in the Muslim direction happens—at the expense of the Coptic community—in cases of marital conflict where "passing" to Islam offers a ready means of divorce difficult or impossible within Coptic tradition? The abolition in 1955 of the religious courts opened that door further to exit from Christian regulations. It was enough, at that point, to send the Holy Synod into a state of mourning and partly to abolish Christmas.[47]

Yet the plea made around that time by a cabinet minister, Farīḍ Anṭūn, for constitutional principles reached and recognized without reference to religion, was attacked by ʿAbd al-Qādir ʿAwḍah as requiring a constitution "devoid of religion."[48] Even less aggressive Muslims, at least in the Arab context,[49] find it well-nigh impossible to distinguish between "secular law" and "secularized society," between legal, civil status indifferent to creed and a society denying worship, moral will, and "due fear of God."[50]

Those vexed issues apart, a cynic might conclude that Copts have the best occasions at times of national crisis when their loyalty has higher immediate value. It happened in 1919 in the post-Ottoman crisis. An interfaith "Unity Rally" was held in Suez on October 3, 1956, as the Canal crisis intensified. Coptic priests preached sermons in three of Alexandria's mosques, and the minister of *Awqāf* reciprocated in Cairo *Injīlī* Church. It may be added that in crises Muslim elements within ʿAbd al-Nāṣir's power had a similar tactic of compliance. But were Copts then gaining some bargain ground? Were they merely avoiding trouble, or simply reassuring authority that they were well in hand? Or were any effective obligations transacted the other way? Not projecting their continuing anxieties gives no promise that they have any real or abiding bargaining power. They are merely reminded of how maneuverable and manipulable they are.

In the routine of the ordinary times, latent issues may disconcertingly erupt when communal apprehensions are kindled. A maverick Copt, for example, Nazmī Lūkā wrote a book entitled *Muḥammad, Al-Rasūl wa-l-Risālah* (Muḥammad, the Messenger and the Message), in which he discredited both Judaism and Christianity and called on his fellow Copts to acknowledge the finality and perfection of Islam. The (Muslim) Minister of Education lavishly praised the book and ordered it to be used in schools. It achieved a high circulation.[51] Copts were bitter, resentful, and alarmed. Was the writer sincere or only a sycophant? They protested. The book was retained on the official list but not required for exams.

No doubt in any mixed society such incidents are to be expected, but some societies are better than others at ignoring or absorbing them. Egypt is Middle Eastern. In a strange way there is a sense in which Copts, for all their exposure to power not their own, are seen as a threat to the dominant community—an imagined threat, to be sure, yet significant nevertheless. From the time of the Qur'ān itself is the query as to the obduracy—as it must be seen—of nonaccession to the final faith and the ultimate Prophet. Who are these who persist in the disavowal implicit in their separatism? And what of their Arabism? Outside Islam must it not be phoney? Yet it exists. Why should it? It constitutes a kind of caveat about Islam itself, about the legitimacy of the equation between being Muslim and being Arab. So it offends an *amour propre* and troubles an equanimity that its absence would confirm. Some aspects of these intangibles we must defer to the final chapter. Oddly they obtain within a remarkable interpenetration of Muslim and Coptic folk religion—a theme we have not touched on. In the finitude of human hope and fear, holy *barakah* (sacred protection) may be interchanged, with Muslims finding solace, or magic, or protection in Coptic sanctities of place, or person, or ritual, or time.[52] But in official and intellectual circles such humanness in common does not avail to alleviate the sense of separation as annoyance to Muslims and apprehension to Copts.

It is true also that through many centuries the wealth and prosperity of a few Copts—thanks to their role in administration and finance—have drawn upon the whole community a kind of envious suspicion and reproach. They are suspected or accused of possessing hidden resources, of exercising a power beyond their numbers or their deserts, of conspiratorial capacities that offend the pride of those who should properly exercise their functions and reap their rewards. This situation bears some resemblance to that of Jews in Europe. The Copt village or local community, both like and unlike the Jewish ghetto, can be made the scapegoat of ills that pride resents and anger must identify for source and reason. Such emotions are often undefined and latent but no less menacing for their unproven or their conjectural nature. And often, as in Jewish experience, the will on the minority's part to be public-spirited, assimilable, self-effacing, or apologetic only serves to fuel the animosity. To that is added, in the Muslim context of the Copts, the age-old offense which, since the Qur'ān, Muslims find in the foundation convictions of Christianity about "God in Christ," incarnate and crucified.

Those convictions, further, are enshrined and cherished among Copts in patterns of liturgy, art, and architecture and housed in a theology that is sadly opaque and uncongenial even to thoughtful Muslims. Some aspects of that situation will be treated in chapter 11. We reach them, however, only through the trauma of Lebanon and the long conflict between Palestine and Zion. Both tragedies have written their pain and perplexity into the soul of Coptic Christianity. No minority status anywhere in the Arab world enjoys exemption from the crises it separately undergoes and can only separately resolve. The tragedy in Lebanon was that status itself was in festering, then chronic, contention. Egypt and her Copts escaped that bitter impasse. Lebanon may suggest to Copts a wry gratitude that the fact of their being a minority was never, through all the Islamic centuries, pretentiously in dispute.

Notes

1. *Minutes of the Proceedings of the First Egyptian Conference,* Heliopolis, April 1911 (Alexandria), p. 6.

2. Though the *Dhimmah* (or *Millah*) system remained until the end of the Ottoman Empire, in fact and theory, it was somewhat mitigated by the liberal reforms of the nineteenth century in pursuit of a universal Ottomanism. The *jizyah* tax was abolished in 1855 (and military service substituted). There were better safeguards for patriarchal tenure and economic initiative and official inferiorization was discouraged.

3. The irony implicit here in "rights of an essentially religious nature" ensured by law for *all* communities who argue a purely secular basis for the state. To confine the essentially religious to freedom of worship is of course contrary to the basic claim of Islam that religion embraces everything and is atrophied (at least in Islamic terms) if limited to acts of devotion and ritual.

4. The question has added point if we note the cry of Khālid al-Islāmbūlī, leader

of the assassins of President Sadāt on October 6, 1981: "I have killed Pharaoh!" See Gilles Kepel, *The Prophet and the Pharaoh: Muslim Extremism in Contemporary Egypt,* trans. Jon Rothschild (London: Al Saqi Books, 1985), p. 213.

5. Wardānī was, in fact, convicted and executed, but it is significant that the Grand Mufti resisted the death sentence on the ground that the murder weapon, a revolver, is not mentioned in the *Sharī'ah* and that Buṭrus Ghālī's next of kin had not participated in the prosecution (i.e., they were not in the business of blood revenge). Moreover, a Muslim slaying "a pagan" did not render himself liable to the death penalty.

6. Richard Pococke, the English orientalist, wrote in 1743: "The ancient Coptic language is without doubt the Egyptian, though much corrupted especially by the Greek language" (*Description of the East* 1:245). Modern opinion concurs and dates the emergence of Coptic from the close of the first century A.D. It took over the Greek alphabet with seven letters from Egyptian script. Much of its religious vocabulary is also from Greek, but a large number of Coptic names like Shenouda and Akhnukh, derive from pharaonic times. Such continuity has relevance to the modern consciousness of "being Egyptian."

7. See Shaikh Damanhūrī, *Shaykh Damanhūrī on the Churches of Cairo,* ed. M. Perlmann (Berkeley, Calif.: University of California Press, 1975), p. 4. Mary the Copt was one of Muḥammad's later wives.

8. Alfred Joshua Butler denies there is any good evidence for the popular view that Copts welcomed the Arabs and believes that Coptic enmity to Byzantium and therefore alleged delight in its defeat are exaggerated (*The Arab Conquest of Egypt and the Last Thirty Years of Roman Dominion,* 2nd ed., 2 vols., ed. P. M. Fraser [New York: Oxford University Press, 1978]). It is difficult to know how far disparity in faith between conquered and conquerors weighed with the former in the initial years.

9. So wrote 'Abbās al-'Aqqād (1889–1964), a well-known figure in Egyptian letters in his *Sa'd Zaghlūl* (Cairo, 1936), pp. 18–27. 'Aqqād had migrated to Egypt in his youth from Syria and was of partly Kurdish descent.

10. On the Egyptianism of Al-Ḥakīm (1898–1987), see M. M. Badawi, "Literary Profile," in *Third World Quarterly,* ed. A. Gauhar, 10, no. 2 (April 1988), 949–960. In particular, see his novel *'Awdat al-Rūḥ* (The Return of the Spirit) (1933), celebrating the abiding identity of Egypt—a novel said to have deeply affected President 'Abd al-Nāṣir and to have helped inspire the 1952 revolution.

11. Quoted from *Al-Ahram,* Feb. 3, 1926, in B. L. Carter, *The Copts in Egyptian Politics* (Dover, N.H.: Croom Helm, 1986), p. 97.

12. In *Rūz al-Yūsuf,* July 17, 1967, taking Muḥammad al-'Azab Mūsā to task for describing the Hyksos as "raiders from the desert" and not an integral factor in the life of Egypt. Salāmah Mūsā, a prolific Coptic writer, had similar views on the egyptianization of Islam. See below.

13. The idea of deliberate connivance with the Muslims misses the point of the perplexity concerning divine judgment. Thus William Hugh Clifford Frend writes: "By accepting the 'Ishmaelites' as instruments of God wherewith to punish the Chalcedonians the Monophysites purchased not their liberty but their grave" (*The*

Rise of the Monophysite Movement: Chapters in the History of the Church in the 5th and 6th Centuries [New York: Cambridge University Press, 1972], p. 359). While it is true that no Muslim ruler required particular versions of Christian doctrine of their Christian *dhimmīs*, and were in that sense "tolerant," neither liberty nor the grave was the Coptic option in the advent of Islam.

14. Thus the Bishop of Nikiu was writing of the conquest, some sixty years on, as a calamity and a judgment. In his retrospect of Byzantine oppression in the years of dual patriarchates in Alexandria, he does not ignore the emperors who showed sympathy with Monophysitism. See R. H. Charles, *The Chronicle of John, Bishop of Nikiu* (London, 1916), p. cxv.9.

15. Thus, for example, 'Abd al-Nāṣir regarded his Coptic "man" and Minister of Supply, Kamāl Ramzȳ Stino, as a mere stooge, a man to send on errands. He was dismissive even of Patriarch Ma'ūshī of Lebanon. He had been acquainted with wealthy Copts in his native village of Benī Mor, near Asyūt—but then 'Abd al-Nāṣir seems to have had little respect for the Christianity he encountered on foreign visits.

16. John Bunyan, *Grace Abounding*, para. 180, his comment on "an ancient Christian" whom he consulted in deep crisis and found uncomprehending.

17. *The Poem of the Way*, trans. A. J. Arberry (London, 1952), lines 560–561.

18. See John Spencer Trimingham, *Islam in the Sudan* (New York: Oxford University Press, 1949), p. 79; and Charles Pelham Groves, *The Planting of Christianity in Africa* (London: Lutterworth Press, 1948), 1:34–54, 106–109. The Christian faith, in the region of Nubia between the first and third Nile cataracts endured from the sixth century to the fourteenth.

19. Ibn Khaldūn, *Al-Muqaddimah*, trans. F. Rosenthal (New York, 1958), 1:187f., 256, 322, 416.

20. So Montague Fowler, *Christian Egypt, Past, Present and Future* (London, 1901), p. 80. He notes, however, that the caliph gave authority for the reconstruction of St. Mercurius's Church at Asyūt, ordering his soldiers to protect the builders from Muslim attackers.

21. See chapter 5 above, p. 124. The patriarch John XI sent an abbot to the council in 1439.

22. So described in view of the resumption of the same pattern under the Ottoman sultans after their conquest of Egypt in 1517.

23. See T. W. Arnold, *The Caliphate* (Oxford, 1924), chs. 11, 14.

24. See below and chapter 5 above.

25. Mu'allim Rizq had been 'Alī Bey's chief of the mint. Ya'qūb Ḥannā had served the Mamlūks to good effect as a soldier against the Turks before his exploits for Napoleon. Ibrāhīm Jawharī died just before the advent of the French, and his brother Jirjus survived to become finance secretary to Muḥammad 'Alī. The brothers were extremely wealthy but were lavish benefactors of their church, securing a firman for its basilica, endowing studies and promoting Coptic awareness of history and liturgy. His reputation in fiscal matters was unsullied and widely esteemed. Coptic wealth, however, in such officials did arouse envy and suspicion among non-Copts.

26. He died at sea but not before urging on the captain of the battleship a plea to the British to sponsor Egyptian independence. See Aziz S. Atiya, *A History of Eastern Christianity* (Millwood, N.Y.: Kraus Reprint & Periodicals, 1980), pp. 102–103.

27. Despite Napoleon's proclamation of adherence to Islam, it is clear that popular resistance to him, doubtless stirred by Ottoman denunciation of his pseudo-Muslim posture, cohered around the *'ulamā'* of Al-Azhar and gave a new relevance to their role in Egyptian consciousness. The Cairo uprising against the French had its center in Al-Azhar, and Muslim notables suffered at their hands. It was they who were undeceived, but the Islam that enabled them to reject Napoleon's Muslim postures was still tied to Ottoman strings.

28. M. E. Yapp notes: "It has been estimated that at one time in rent and taxes Muḥammad 'Alī secured over 80% of the agricultural production of Egypt and that one third of the entire Egyptian labour force was employed, mainly unwillingly, on public works or in the army" (*The Making of the Modern Near East, 1792–1923* [White Plains, N.Y.: Longman, 1987], p. 152).

29. He wrote disparagingly about them not only for their Monophysitism but for their secretiveness (as it seemed to him). "He [the Coptic patriarch on several visits] never showed me any part of his face except his eyes" (J. M. Neale, *The Holy Eastern Church* [London, 1850], 2:376).

30. "Reformer," that is, in the different idiom appropriate to a loyal Copt and in a different century.

31. Cyril had studied during contact with Church Missionary Society personnel. Lieder had gone to Egypt in 1830, and Tattam edited an edition of the Four Gospels in Arabic and Coptic and was an ardent student of Coptic liturgy and monastic manuscripts. C.M.S. activity lapsed in 1840 and was not resumed until 1884.

32. His bland comment was: "A Copt is an Egyptian who worships in a church and a Muslim one who worships in a mosque" (Cromer, *Modern Egypt* [London, 1908], 2:206).

33. The Coptic Reform Society was set up at this juncture by the (evangelical) Copt Akhnūkh Fānūs to counter the dismissal, by nationalists, of communal interests and to insist on a Coptic separatism. One advocate of full cooperation by Copts with the nationalist cause, Wāṣif Wisā', was dubbed Judas Iscariot by the Coptic journal *Al-Waṭan.* It was a very different story in 1919 and after when Sa'd Zaghlūl and the *Wafd* held religious differences irrelevant to the nationalist struggle. Two of the *Wafd* leaders exiled to the Seychelles in 1921 were Copts. According to Otto Meinardus, Abūnā Sergius, a Coptic priest, preached from the *minbar* of Al-Azhar mosque at that time (*Christian Egypt: Ancient and Modern,* 2nd ed. [Cairo: American University in Cairo Press, 1977], p. 41).

34. "Islamic rigorism" is a preferred term here. "Extremism" is vague, "puritanism" unfair to a different entity, while the popular usage "fundamentalism"—unknown as it is to Arabic—conveys meaning to westerners but ignores the fact that in a real sense *all* Islam is "fundamentalist" by virtue of the doctrine of the infallible Qur'ān in verbal form. Among the groups even more "rigorist" than the *Ikhwān* are *Al-Takfīr wa-l-Hijrah* and *Tanẓīm al-Jihād* ("Organ of *Jihād*"). The

Ikhwān made some effort to accommodate in the light of Sadāt's appeal to Islamic values (a stance that made Copts apprehensive) but the ultra-aggressive groups dismissed the president's "Islam" as a mere empty tactic. They were also vitriolic in attacks on *'ulamā'* who welcomed it.

35. The conspiratorial stance of the *Ikhwān* against 'Abd al-Nāṣir was due in part to their disillusion with the Army officers who had initially borrowed some of their ideas and admired their organizational potential. They were embittered by the statism of the Revolution as it developed and saw its Arab nationalism as inimical to a true Islam. Sadāt, in different terms, incurred their enmity by virtue of his open westernism and his policy over Israel.

36. Anti-Coptic riots in 1980/81 prompted Sadāt, a month before his assassination, to arrest 1,500 Muslim agitators and some 150 Coptic clergy, and to exile the patriarch to a monastery, suspended from his office. The riots in Al-Zāwiyah al-Ḥamrā in Cairo occurred when a land dispute incited a Coptic attack on Muslims in the disputed area. It was inflamed by Muslim allegations of plots against Islam. Imām Ḥāfiẓ Salāmah, a fiery orator and foe of Sadāt, alleged that Copts had a sinister intention to set up an independent state around Asyūt, backed by the Vatican. A Muslim conference demanded the dismissal of Shenouda, a veto on church building, and a boycott of Christian shops and businesses. Those soon to be Sadāt's assassins were among the instigators of attacks on Copts.

37. Bishop Samuel was the patriarch's chief advisor on ecumenical affairs. He represented the Coptic hierarchy in the absence, through monastic exile, of Shenouda himself.

38. The number of such private, or *ahlī,* mosques doubled from twenty to forty thousand between 1970 and 1981. As social foundations they came under the Ministry of Social Affairs and so escaped the control on preachers at the mosques of Imāms approved by the Ministry of *Awqāf,* of which in 1981 there were only six thousand out of forty-six thousand mosques in all. Islāmbūlī, Sadāt's murderer, made his plans in a local *ahlī* mosque.

39. Salāma Mūsā, *The Education of Salāma Mūsā,* trans. L. O. Schuman (Leiden: E. J. Brill, 1961). The title was culled from the nineteenth-century American work *The Education of Henry Adams,* a study in the nurture of one's own mind.

40. The conversation is intriguing: "When he knew that I was a Copt, he said: 'Are you Monophysite?' (the word transliterated from the English). The question puzzled me. It occurred to me that the word had to do with vegetarian food. For Bernard Shaw was associated in my mind with vegetarian diet and I had been toying with the thought that I would restrict myself to vegetables also and I had desisted from meat for some months. I supposed that what he said was meant for us in general, since 'you' in English may be both singular and plural, and that he assumed we were like the Hindus in their vegetarianism. I replied: 'No. We eat meat in Egypt.' He burst out laughing and asked me to look up the word 'Monophysite' in the dictionary. That very evening I looked it out and found it had to do with Christian mysteries and that Copts believe that the human nature of Christ assimilated into his divine nature, so that he had one nature, thus 'Monophysite.' I found further that this is the essential point between us and the Catholics who

believe that the nature of Christ while he was on earth was human and that his divine nature began with his being raised to heaven after crucifixion" (Arabic edition, p. 81). It is clear that the author was ill-versed in theology.

41. He wrote: "I returned to her [the Coptic church] with affection, finding in her our tormented and broken history" (Arabic edition, p. 213).

42. "I found the voice of the Pharaohs sounding loudly from her pulpits" (ibid.).

43. He wrote in the magazine *Al-Hilāl,* no. 34 (July 1926), 1075: "Literary Arabic assimilates our Egyptian nationalism to the Arabs and makes it part of Arab nationalism. He who adopts literary Arabic absorbs the Arab spirit. He marvels at the heroes of Baghdad instead of absorbing the Egyptian spirit." Had he in mind *The Arabian Nights* or the age-old rivalry between the twin rivers of Assyria and the Nile? Either way the equation between Egypt and Arabic seems irreversible with little prospect for what he called *tamṣīr al-lughah* ("egyptianizing of the language"). He castigated Arabic for its habit of empty rhetoric and as "a language of primitiveness." There is evidence that some Muslim Egyptian nationalists shared his view of language, especially when nationalism was no longer within Ottomanism.

Others, however, turned the argument the other way around insisting that Arabic was already "egyptianized." Aḥmad Ḥusain denied that using it necessitated being or feeling "Arab." He went on to say, roundly: "The fact is that religion and language are precisely the proof that everything in Egypt cannot be other than Egyptian" (*Al-Muqaṭṭam,* Sept. 6, 1930, p. 7).

44. Copts have been discouraged from entering the Arabic Department at Cairo University on the ground that "real knowledge of Arabic comes only from knowledge of the Qur'ān." There is resentment in some Muslim quarters that words properly current in Christian, as well as in Islamic, Arabic (such as *Allāh, Injīl, Rasūl, īmān, kitāb* ("God," "Gospel," "apostle," "faith," "Book") are not made exclusive to Islam.

45. There is a growing body of writing on Najīb Maḥfūẓ (b. 1912) and translations of his stories. See, e.g., Ismat Mahdi, *Modern Arabic Literature, 1900–1967* (Hyderabad, 1983), pp. 244–254; and Sasson Somekh, *The Changing Rhythm: A Study of Najīb Mahfūz's Novels* (Leiden: E. J. Brill, 1973). My *The Pen and the Faith* (Winchester, Mass.: Allen & Unwin, 1985), has a short introduction to him on pp. 145–164.

46. The delegate was Dr. Maḥmūd 'Azmī; quoted from O. F. A. Meinardus, *Christian Egypt: Faith and Life* (Cairo: American University in Cairo Press, 1970), p. 47.

47. There were to be no Christmas visits, celebrations, or traditional observance. Latins joined in the effort to influence 'Abd al-Nāṣir's regime. The ban was finally called off when a minister met a Coptic delegation and made promises about the prevention of divorce-prompted conversions. These were ineffectual.

48. 'Awḍah was one of the six Muslim Brothers executed for plotting against 'Abd al-Nāṣir.

49. It is different, for example, in India, where Muslims themselves are a minority community, and there are some Muslim thinkers readily distinguishing between a secular state and secularization of society.

50. One route to such a distinction for Muslims might be a distinction between "Meccan" and "Medinan" in the Qur'ān—Muḥammad as "preacher of faith" being the essential core at Mecca, and Muḥammad as "armed and political" at Medina. This distinction would be an ad hoc necessity of *that* situation and *not* an abiding or definitive element in Islam. But such depoliticizing, though propounded by a few at great risk, finds little favor and would appear to deny the unity of the Qur'ān.

51. Cairo, 1958. Kamāl al-Dīn Ḥusain was the Minister of Education.

52. A recent study explores with lively illustrative material the folk religion within Islam; see Bill A. Musk, *The Unseen Face of Islam* (London, 1989).

CHAPTER

9

The Tragedy of Lebanon

I

> I have been quietly dining in a monastery when shouts have been heard and shots have been fired against the stout bulwarks of the outer walls . . . which had but little effect in altering the monotonous cadence in which one of the brotherhood read a homily of St. Chrysostom from the pulpit . . . in the refectory.[1]

ROBERT CURZON WAS WRITING in 1849, visiting monasteries in the Levant in search of manuscripts for museums and gleanings for his pen. He reported a world of monks and guns, of high walls and ancient liturgies. Faiths could be traditional because bulwarks were intact. The years around his travels, and 1860 most notorious of all, were beset with turbulence and communal strife in a Lebanon already caught in the toils of Ottoman decline and the conflicting wiles of western powers. Chrysostom of golden tongue, of Antioch and the fourth century, exhorted his listeners of the nineteenth behind ramparts of continuity surviving the attentions of Persians and Byzantines, Arabs and Turks, crusaders and Latins through more than a thousand years. Curzon found custodians retentive of their manuscripts but capable of yielding them to a curator from the West, who did not pause to note the theme of the homily.

He was an exuberant traveler and considered himself brave. Did he register the pathos in the episode or read the future in it—a future in which the bulwarks would no longer hold, in which the bastions of faith and community would disintegrate and homilies surrender to hate? Intent on what he wanted from the hospitality, he could regard the incident as trivial. But in that very quality the episode captures what imagination must now entail in the story of Lebanon—religions indulged and entrenched, immunities prized and threatened, liturgies and weapons, traditions and encounters, partisans and aliens, devotions and shouts, walls under siege.

The sober reader begins to suspect excess of sentiment, ill-suited to proper history. But no. What is proper to history is realism and right measure. The Lebanon of the final quarter of this century is a scene of infinite tragedy, a desperate indictment of religions and their role in the bankruptcy of politics and the strangling of hope. Beyond the historian's task of bare analysis, the rehearsal of factors, the puzzle of clues, is the measure of what might have been. The tragedy lies not only in what has eventuated but in what has been forfeited, or the one in the perspective of the other, the anatomy of despair at the autopsy of hope.

II

Precarious, no doubt, the promise always was and, as some would say, ill-founded, fragile, and even dishonest. Yet, given time, given exemption from the strains of Palestinianism and, within these, the malevolence of Israel, the Lebanese venture of Christian–Muslim and Maronite–Sunnī "Concordat" of autonomy might have survived and solidified. We must explore the issues at length; the 1940s must be assessed from the 1970s. They are shattered in the 1980s, but the miscarriage of what might have been born to thrive belongs in the history.

Lebanon has sometimes been imagined as the Switzerland of the Middle East. Mountainous, special, exempt from surrounding tensions, a haven with a hinterland, cantonized perhaps but containing its tensions in a will to one identity, alert to adjacent worlds but wary of their conflicts, secured by commerce—a symbolic nation. The symbol—Lebanese-style—would be a Muslim–Christian amity holding promise of happy contagion in other Arab states with their slender, tenuous, and exposed minorities of Christians, a land in which freedom of religious converse of thought and publication could provide a foothold of sanity and patience in the strife of faiths.

It was not to be, and, by the same token, its negation where it might most readily have eventuated denies its hope elsewhere. Switzerland has no maritime shore, no Mediterranean to distract, no Islam to integrate with a chronically divided Christianity. Nor, as some might add, is it Phoenician in its temper, nor Arab in its rhetoric. There are endless imponderables in any such equation, but the point is the prospect of the parallel adjusted to the vagaries of a different historical and religious context.

How might it have obtained? In the 1940s Lebanon reached at least a form of independence. The French were finally dislodged politically in the wake of the Second World War. They had related to Lebanon from times before the Crusades, and they left behind a culture among many Maronites more Francophile than Arab. It was a legacy liable to threaten the politics they bequeathed in a nation at least nominally independent. The nation's boundaries had been enlarged at French initiative by the addition of mainly Shī'ah areas in the far south by Tyre, and Sunnī and other Muslim elements in the north. These changes were at the expense of political Syria, helpless under Mandate to do other than demur. They ensured that Syria would always claim a stake, if not a dominance, in Lebanese affairs, and they gave emotional occasion to the notions of "greater Syria" as a menace to the viability of an independent Lebanon.

The situation in the late 1940s has to be assessed in the light of those deep tensions between Arabism and Islam, between nationhood and erstwhile *dhimmī* status, which have been discussed in chapter 7. By its very nature, fragmented but more evenly balanced, as well as territorially ambiguous, Lebanon was uniquely beset by those vexations. Christians were ostensibly the majority, though no census after 1946 would be allowed to resolve by how much, if at all. Sunnī Muslims predominated within Islam, and the Shī'ah were disadvantaged economically and socially. Christians other than Maronite were small minorities—Orthodox, Monophysite, Uniate, Latin, and Protestant, with a non-Arab dimension in Armenian refugees and citizens. The third dimension was the Druze community with its long tenure in the Lebanese mountains and a history of mingled enmity and co-existence with the Maronites.

In the flush of independent aspiration and the sobering retrospect of strife, aware of the surrender of old instincts for "protected" status—for some a reluctant surrender—the major parties resolved on the National Concordat, an agreement of mutual accommodation based on a confessional order of power. While the president would always be Maronite, the prime minister Sunnī, the speaker of Parliament from the Shī'ah, Parliament would consist of representation according to fixed ratios. This structure had to live with the feudal loyalties that cut across confessional lines, but it was hoped that it would curb if not tame them. Sanctioned by old commercial instincts, this new Phoenicia might ride out its centuries of fragmentation, of communal distrust, of Mamlūk, Ottoman, and European misadventure.

There was an initial confidence. The architects and first mentors of the agreement, the Maronite president, Bishāra al-Khoury, and the Sunnī prime minister, Ri'āḍ al-Ṣolḥ, augured well despite a last fling of French intransigence. Able Christians such as Charles Malik could give rein to their romanticism and hail the historic destiny of Lebanon mediating between East and West.[2] Left alone, the elements might have coalesced at least sufficiently to give stability and to keep the incipient factions quiescent.

It is true that the underlying fragility of a confessional structure had to be faced but was readily ignored. Purists could say that all was archaic, a surrender to convenience, a false pragmatism, but was the secular option ever really viable in the given complexity of Lebanese tradition, its chronic complexity of tribe, sect, and cult? Might it not be argued that tacit solutions, avoiding the precipitation of crisis and contention, would best serve the hope of more permanent decisions requiring stronger nerve and a more confidently mutual identity? Neither the political instincts of Islam nor the age-old defensiveness of Christians was ready for the radical secularity of the modern state–and only the possible is politic.

Whether the confessional structure could ever have been effectively redrawn must be left to vain conjecture. Formidable as were the vetoes on such change within Lebanon itself, the most crucial factors were outside the country's control–in the politics of Syria, the claims of the Palestinians, the postures of Israel and, through all these, the stakes of the major powers. Within three decades of the hopes and devices of 1946 came conflict and disaster. It is important for the study of Arab Christianity to read those decades aright in the broad perspective that a tortuous story must be made to yield. Only so can we pass to the more intimate study of its Christian ingredients. Why could Beirut not make good its bid to be a sort of Geneva-cum-Zurich of the Middle East and Lebanon its context?

The central issue is the fact of the Arabness of Lebanon, its range and the proper liabilities. There could be no doubting Lebanon's location, its language, its Islam, or its experience. These all confirmed it as belonging in the Arab world, but with what degree of indulgence for its particularity? Lebanese Christians, and Maronites especially, were concerned for the country's particularity, to the partial compromise of their membership in the Arab world, if need be. How might such "need be" arise and, if it did, how far could the claims of a Lebanese special identity be conceded? The questions were always latent within the general issue we have earlier studied as to the relation of Arabness to nationhood and of both to Islam. On every count Lebanon was the territory where it was most acute. What made it incorrigibly more so was the political, emotional, and military fallout from the fact of Israel.

The *modus vivendi* of mutual balance of interest and influence came under severe strain in the late 1950s in the heyday of ʻAbd al-Nāṣir's pan-Arabism. Ephemeral though it proved, it loomed large at the time, fanned by Anglo-French-Israeli turpitude at the Suez crisis. The government of Maronite president Chamoun, with the Orthodox Charles Malik as his Foreign Minister, sought to take Lebanese policy too far in the pro-western direction, in their apprehension aiming to offset the menace to their view of Lebanon. So doing, they drew down on themselves the suspicion of treachery to Arabism—the more so when, if only briefly, armed U.S. intervention occurred to support them. Happily the tensions of 1957/58 were for the time being soothed by the tact and common "trustability" of General Shihāb, bearer of a magic name in Lebanese history and still able to hold both government and army in some sort of two-sidedness.

In the 1970s it was different, and there was no feasible Shihāb to hold the ring and unbreed suspicion. The issues were sharper and more intractable, and to grasp them requires a review of the Palestinian story. In the immediate aftermath of exile in 1948, the world saw Palestinians as refugees set on repatriation—an aim that made them also nationalists, for, in their identity, they still cherished a *patria.* The steady perpetuation of their refugeedom as years passed was cruelly interpreted by some as a wicked device to perpetuate accusation of Israel. Dispersal, it was said, was their obvious future. They were obtuse and their mentors callous in not conceding it to be so, though dispersal in a precarious world was precisely what Zionism, for its part, was set to disavow.

But dispersed, effectively, they were and so remained. Lebanon—Jordan apart—had the largest share of them, and they were hospitably, if pitiably, received. They waited patiently—and, for long, in vain—for the world community to realize their nationality. They waited, still more in vain, for salvation through their Arab kin in Arab states. Indeed, those states ineptly aggravated the tragic condition of the Palestinians, and intensified the futility in their dispersion. In the wake of 1967–the nadir of such futility as of Arab ebullience—they began to repudiate their long passivity as refugees and concert their own salvation. The P.L.O. emerged.[3]

Guerrilla violence, or the suspicion of it, against Israel only kindled the vengeful vigilance always near the surface of Israeli minds imbued with the long retrospect of the world's—and the Arabs'—enmity. The Zionist state has an instinct of inveterate suspicion, a determination never to be taken with impunity. How grim, how resolute, and how cruel, Palestinians were soon to discover. After 1967 their resistance to Israel hinged on Arab territory. The first and best option was obviously Jordan, where Palestinians were one in every two of the population, thanks to the double exodus of 1948 and 1967. But Palestinian military operations from Jordanian territory incurred Israeli retaliation against Jordan, while Palestinian training camps, demanding unfettered freedom of action, called in question Jordanian sovereignty. The issue of a state within the state became acute. King Ḥusain had the resolve and the competence to end it by the costly expulsion of the Palestinian militants in Black September, 1970.[4]

There followed the export of the identical issue to Lebanon, where, cynically escorted through Syria,[5] the P.L.O. withdrew. Merged in the existing Palestinianism in Lebanon, the militants, embittered and more fervid, were set to embroil the Lebanese in their unrelenting cause—and in the venom of Israeli self-defense. Given all that was already fragile and febrile in the Lebanese condition, this new dimension of stress and tribulation plunged the country into the disintegration of civil war from 1974.

The reasons are tragically plain. Here in the P.L.O.'s need of facility against Israel was the most urgent and strident claim of a pan-Arab task. Were not the Palestinians fellow-Arabs? Was not Israel the common enemy? Had not Jordan betrayed its honor? Should Lebanon follow suit? Christians in Lebanon, however, mainly but not only Maronite, saw in the most menacing form the old spectre of forfeited identity, of Arab-Muslim dominance, and themselves a crippled, broken minority in a state no longer their own. A Palestinian state within the state must not be allowed to become the Trojan horse to seize the city. Torn as it was by this fundamental stake and plagued by feudal loyalties and regional quarrels, Lebanon was in no shape to emulate Ḥusain. The Black Septembers of Lebanon would bloody their own calendar as recurring months of conflict, massacre, and outrage—a cycle of P.L.O. action, barren of result, and of surgical and deadly Israeli retaliation. In all the given factors of the Arab scene, the tragedy of Lebanon is the neighborhood of Israel.

The narrative is tortuous and its detail bewildering, as factions and causes shifted and changed. Sunnīs, the Shī'ah, Maronites, and Druzes conflicted, bargained, dallied, aligned, and realigned with fickle tactics or brutal cynicism. Assassinations took their steady toll both of leadership and hope. The old confessional structure of the state crumbled into the strife of impasse to which, realists would say, it had always been liable. Palestinianism ensured its utter collapse and created circumstances in which no viable alternative could be debated, still less concerted and achieved. The former sanctions of trading prowess with its assumption of tolerable peace, as well as human counsels of reason sharpened by common adversity, were overborne by passion and dogma.

Israeli policy, set to perpetuate Palestinian dispersion by refusing Palestinian repatriation, was necessarily engaged within the Lebanese scene. Some of its interests could well be served by Lebanese clients, just as the interests of Syria predominantly and of other Arab states generally could be transacted by Lebanese proxies. Such entanglements only deepened suspicions and compounded hatreds. Among the worst instances of Israeli connivance with Christian Lebanese was the breakaway "army" of Colonel Haddad, an Orthodox Christian, on the southern border. His militia, armed by Israel, not only impugned Lebanon's sovereignty but compromised the integrity of the national army and seemed to proclaim that Lebanon was unable to defend its own on its own. The Shī'ah in the south were bitterly resentful in their greater exposure.

But incriminating connivance with Israel, as "true Arab" patriots saw it, was even more sinister in politics at the heart than from insubordinates at the border. Might diehard Christian Lebanese be susceptible to the temptation of an independent cliency to Israel? There could be logic in the thought. Was not Israel itself a sort of paradigm? In a sea of irreducible Arabism the right course lay in creating a vigorous, defensible, separate enclave of common identity, such as Israel was, beleaguered no doubt but redoubtable. Might not a Maronite Lebanon emulate Zion? Israel's need for such a client to the north argued for its creation if Maronites were resolute and united enough to seize on the idea. By the same token, the slightest suspicion of any such intention spelled a base treachery, and protested repudiation of it only tended to sound less convincing, or convincing only as deception.

There is no doubt that such calculations in Israel played their part in Sharon's invasion of Lebanon in 1982. "Peace in Galilee" was the code name: war on Lebanon was the reality—to do for Lebanon what it could not, or would not, do for itself, namely, Maronitize itself with Israeli prompting. The twenty-five-mile zone needed for "peace in Galilee" was quickly overpassed. Indeed, there had been peace in Galilee *de facto* since 1978. The speeches of Menachem Begin recalled the bunkers of Berlin in 1945 and the grim end of Hitler in clear anticipation of a parallel "final solution" for Lebanon by the eviction of the Palestinians. The element of grim triumphalism in the Israeli psyche was unmistakable. Reckoning in Lebanon would be vicarious vengeance for the Holocaust. By such legacies was the tragedy of a divided war-torn Lebanon compounded. The Palestinian presence which was, differently, the bane of both would be expelled to satisfy both Jewish mood and Lebanese Maronite dream.

In retrospect, despite the temporary withdrawal of the P.L.O., the mood and the dream—only controversially indulged as they were—were alike frustrated. But the sanguinary bid for success that Israel had made against the wiser counsels of her peace-seeking minority only further intensified the Lebanese imbroglio. The dark shadow of Zionism lay more somberly still on the politics of Lebanon.

The effective partition of the country continued despite the six-year presidency of Amir Gemayel, begun in the autumn of 1982, with its semblance of the form of the confessional state. By the time it drew to its mandatory conclusion in the summer of 1988, even that facade of constitutionality became well-nigh defunct. Illegal ports for the import of arms, serial assassinations of key figures, such as the moderate Sunnī premier, Rashid Karameh, and the Druze leader Kamāl Jumblātt, indiscriminate shellings and bombardments, through patched and broken truces—some two hundred of them in fifteen years—fed an agonizing cycle of enmity, futility, and despair, in which ordinary folk had forlornly to retrieve what remnants they could of personal existence. There is no point here in rehearsing the grim toll of those bitter vicissitudes in which Lebanon experienced the agony of its own divided Arabism and the criminal ineptness of Arabism at large, with external paymasters and patrons serving their own ends in shifting confusion and discordancy.

Even the constitutional form of Lebanon became symbolically the victim of attrition. Death and intimidation diminished the legal Parliament, which alone could choose a successor president. The National Army was confessionally compromised beyond possibility of effective action and, despite the Syrian presence, separatist militias sundered and plundered the population. A national agreement cobbled together in late 1985 was quickly repudiated with intractable Maronite resistance to any alteration of the confessional structure that would concede greater power to Muslim and Druze. Embroilment only served to intensify division within the conflicting parties themselves, and Maronite intransigence hardened despite the pleas of the Maronite patriarch, Nasrallah Sfeir, for a will to moderation. Only late in 1988, when the speaker's term of office ended with no parliamentary quorum to replace him, was a surviving muster of deputies persuaded or cajoled at a conference under Saudi auspices to agree to a formula modifying the Maronite place in constitutional confessionalism and attempting to resolve the tangle of rival cabinets and competing militias. When Rene Moawad was finally elected president in line with this "solution" he was murdered within days. His successor, Elias Hrawi, has happily survived but for another eighteen months was frustrated by the resistance of General Aoun, in his "presidential" bastion, to the "legitimate" forces of the presidency and of the national commander Samir Geagea. When General Aoun finally capitulated in October 1990, after sanguinary exchanges with Syrian forces, he found ambiguous sanctuary in the French Embassy—an irony true to the long story of Christian ambivalence—where legitimate Lebanon claims him for "crimes against the state" and France holds him a legitimate refugee.

In the wake of his surrender, the militias agreed to leave Beirut, but the shape of the further future is obscure. How will Syria interpret its long-standing interest in the Lebanese scene? How will the precarious constitutionalism, still confessional in shape if concessionary to Muslim and Druze, survive the aftermath of years of anguish and the retrospect of death and despair? The Christian presence is desperately attenuated by emigration, slaughter, forfeiture of leadership, and internecine distrust—the old feudal tradition of Lebanese history. There is also deeply ingrained a sense of betrayal by a tarnished and implausible Arabism and even more by the seeming indifference or cynical aloofness of the international community. Lebanon emerges, if it does, as the tragic, self-wounded, self-pitying, and self-distraught victim of a wretched trauma, and there is the guilt as well as the cost of their treatment of the Palestinians.

Contemporary history writing is notoriously hazardous, that of the Middle East more than most. It is enough to ponder the enmities and their antecedents through the long years, in particular that dark Palestinian factor and the Israeli connection behind it.

The Phalange and the National Party of Maronite lineage were increasingly implacable in their hatred of Palestinians as the chronic destroyers of their country. Fierce massacres at Tell al-Zaater, Chatila, and Sabra vented this anger on the helpless camp inmates and intensified the Palestinian fighters in their desperate will to retain and exploit the only terrain from which they could respond to Israel. That they grossly abused Lebanese hospitality in their insistent demand for freedom of action few would deny, but they claimed, almost in the mood of Zionism, the right of indisputable legitimacy. No Lebanese curbs—especially as Lebanese were not unanimous about them—should be heeded. There was Palestinian retaliation, as at Damour, against the enemies of their presence, the more desperately because the militant Palestinians knew that most of their people otherwise were hapless hostages of the situation, as they were to Israeli vengeance on the militants.

The only way in which Lebanon's appalling cycle of disaster and its descent into chaos could have been halted and perhaps painfully reversed would have been the repatriation to Palestine of the Palestinians. But that policy, never remotely practicable from the outset of their exile—given the Israeli logic of Zion—was abysmally the more anathema in the wake of the events of 1982. Israel could only concede its departure from Lebanon in terms of the still further removal of the Palestinians into political limbo and physical diaspora. The deep conscience of the peace-lovers in Israel[6] could be given rein only when the ultimate issue of the war policy led to a weary readiness to withdraw. Israel was then frustrated by the return of the Palestinian fighters, the shelving of the idea of a client state, and a return to the pattern of attrition and reprisal.

In the meantime, however, factors long endemic in Lebanon and native to its soil, for which Israel was not responsible, had been fatally aggravated. Syria had maneuvered throughout in terms of how the labyrinthine situation might be manipulated to its own satisfaction in line with its long claim to the decisive voice in every Lebanese eventuality. Syria sided alternatively with Palestinian and Maronite elements in calculated concern to outwit others, to ensure that shifting political factors were engineered to Syria's ends and to repay the stake of military risk invested by its forces.[7] The will, on Syria's part, to impose peace was never free from subtle calculation to frustrate any emerging result that was not to Syria's advantage, with the fear of Israel always in view. Inter-Arab rivalries elsewhere took devious form in the conflicts of the Lebanese and by their presence contributed to the descending spiral of cynicism and desperation.

The Shīʿah Muslims in the south and increasingly in Beirut sharpened their communal image. Long denied due place in the economic stakes, growing rapidly in population and maximum victims of the state's incapacity to defend its people, they found a new militancy and with it a more factious character. The Druzes with tactical advantages of terrain sharpened both their ancient feud with the Maronites[8] and the passion always latent in their identity. All groups and alignments were plagued with inner stresses of local, tribal, or economic origin, made the more virulent by atrocity, hatred, and mutual defiance. Truces innumerable were quickly shattered by utter distrust of the parties, using them both for political maneuver and military guile. Hope of any internal authority, governmental or otherwise, capable of imposing order or meriting trust was steadily extinguished. It was—and is—as if the very concept of "Lebanon" had been surrendered in a welter of ungovernable and irreconcilable division, for which *de facto* partition was the only, and the bitter, fate. But how it might be accomplished *de jure* simply eluded the passions the very notion aroused. For it was a notion that destroyed the image of an identity that could be had only by being shared—an identity which each element might wish to control but which none could unilaterally possess. Staying together was mandatory on every realistic count of geography, the mandated frontiers, the political constraints, the Phoenician tradition, and the commercial realities. Yet all of these were hostage to the crucial inter-Arab, interreligious, and intersectarian issue of where such a single Lebanon belonged in the definition of destiny which the challenge of Israel had made at once so imperative and so divisive.

III

There was deep romance in the psyche of Lebanon, yet unrelenting realism in the denial that contemporary history gave it. Saʿīd ʿAql wrote in 1947:

> On the doorstep of Asia . . . a homeland for the truth . . . Six thousand years of patience, thought, contempt for the material, self-denial, aspiration and careful scrutiny of detail have led us to a unique mission which qualifies us to libanize the world.[9]

That idealism needs to be critically understood by realists minded to see in "libanization" the disintegration more usually exemplified in the Balkans. But, given the Maronite dimension, how could it survive in the setting of the insistence of which Yassir ʿArafat made himself the strident spokesman?

> The battle we are fighting in Lebanon is for the preservation of the country's Arab character. I declare in the name of the Palestinian revolution and the Lebanese and nationalist and progressive movement that every inch of Arab land will remain Arab and Lebanon will remain Arab.[10]

Bashir Gemayel gave a cryptic response: "Liban—il y a un peuple de trop" ("Lebanon has one people too many"). This captured the anguish and the paradox of what could only survive in the pluralism and the compromise of which Lebanon was proving inherently incapable.[11]

To grapple with the Christian liability in that impasse requires a long retrospect over the Maronite church—the most assertive form of Arab Christianity in "national" terms and the most significant organ of western, Christian and Latin relation to the Arab world. There is a certain irony in the likelihood that the Maronites originated from Arabia shortly before the rise of Islam. Among the many south Arabian tribes who emigrated to northern Syria, history first encounters them in the valley of the Orontes in north Syria. Long before their migration to Lebanon and the movement of their settlements within it, they reportedly held the Monothelite doctrine about Christ.[12] It is not clear whether they arrived in the far north as Christians already. But, whatever its origins, their Christianity became as rugged a communal identity as the faith of those Shīʿah Muslims and of the Druzes who shared their place of origin in the far south. Their tradition likes to date their tenure in Lebanon from the earliest times in the Islamic calendar, but it is more likely to have been in the ninth century A.D., at which time there is continuing evidence of their presence in the Aleppo region.

From the outset of their Syrian locale their identity had the strong tribal quality that has always characterized them, whatever their sectarian differences from the Orthodox and the Monophysite groupings around them. It may have been resistance to the former that inspired their move into Lebanon, if this occurred in the wake of the advance made by Byzantine forces into their territory when Nicephorus Phocas recovered much of it from the Muslims, if only briefly. Once they were ensconced in Lebanon, the mountainous terrain somehow married with their clan tenacity to make the strong fusion of place and people history knows, a tenacity destined, despite odd vicissitudes, to define itself in sharp distinction from Muslim and Druze and from other Christians.[13]

The First Crusade occasioned the initial contact with the Latins, their papacy, their liturgy, and the image they brought of a power-proud faith with its pilgrimage stake in the East. There was no consistent pattern in their relations with the crusaders in the two centuries of their presence in the Maronite world. On some occasions they won the admiration of western warriors for their aid and qualities. On other occasions Maronite marauding and intrigue gave pause to the crusaders' amity. But something of the legacy of the crusading image, its kingdom in the East, and its battling symbols seems to have passed into Maronite mythology to be disastrously revived in the psyche of the Phalange. An ingrained belligerence and a sense of a western church tied into the emotions and the power equations of the East took root in the Maronite soul.[14] That western church had repudiated the Monophysites; it was rival to Byzantium, "orthodox" in its own idiom of papal power; and it had stakes that suggested a will for clients in the East. On all those counts it had appeal.

If history can rightly be guessed proleptically in the light of sequels, those were the hidden imponderables of the crusading centuries. In the fourth decade of the twelfth century Maronite patriarch Gregory and a papal legate discussed the idea of a link with Rome. The papacy had attraction, not least for the Maronite hierarchy, as an exponent of the kind of authority that could discipline communities liable, as rank-and-file Maronites were, to follow their own devices. This refractoriness was fully proved when, around 1180, several higher ecclesiastics made formal espousal of Roman allegiance.

The papacy encouraged the "unionists" when adversaries voiced opposition. Pope Innocent III invited Patriarch Jeremiah to the Lateran Council held in Rome in 1215. Armed with the prestige gained, he returned to Lebanon with a papal bull that, in effect, treated the Maronite accession as already made by absolving the nonunionists of their "disobedience to the Mother Church," save for those of them who had committed violence or murder against the clergy. However, those opposed to Rome were not quelled, and schism within the church followed late in the century and the issue was overtaken by the end of the crusading presence and the arrival of Mamlūk rule—a factor that tended to make the western, papal association even more desirable than in the days of mixed intrigue with the crusaders. Commercial interests between Venetians and the Mamlūks helped to foster relationships and to bring other western Christian elements into the region, notably the Franciscans, through whom further contacts between Maronites and Rome could be concerted.

However, the papacy did not perceive—or at least develop—the full significance of the Maronite potential as a Christian bastion in the East until after the failure of the Council of Florence in the 1440s when hope of mending the schism with Byzantium was ended and the Ottoman capture of Constantinople in 1453 changed the whole complexion of ecclesial affairs. Earlier relations with the Maronites had not entailed formal recognition of their orders or their orthodoxy. At that time a resident advisor from Rome was posted with the Maronite patriarch, now partially recognized—in default of the Orthodox—as "Patriarch of Antioch." Maronites began to travel to Rome for study under Franciscan or, later, Jesuit auspices. A century later this initiative ripened into the establishment of the Maronite College in Rome by Gregory XIII in 1584.

This institution proved a crucial element in the Latin nurture of the Maronites and, in turn, of their European orientation. Looking to the Catholic West, they were able to indulge a degree of defiance of the Ottomans (as of the Mamlūks earlier) at least in neither seeking nor receiving investiture of patriarchs at their hands. Their scholars in, or from, Rome wrote their early history as never heretical but as the true orthodoxy of the saintly John Mārūn, a Syrian villager in the fifth century, from whom they took their name. On this score they had no Arab origin, despite the fact that their spoken tongue seems always to have been Arabic and their Syriac liturgy in Arabic characters.[15]

But the role of the Maronite College, and of earlier Lebanese students in Rome, was much more than image making in popular history. It produced some eminent scholars whose repute and influence not only enriched the Maronite soul but contributed notably to western learning. Jibrā'īl al-Sahyūnī (1577–1648) became Professor of Semitic Languages in Paris. Ibrāhīm al-Ḥaqilānī (1600–1664) edited the Polyglot Bible, while Yūsuf Sima'an al-Simi'ānī (1687–1768) became librarian at the Vatican.[16] Their latinized names—Sionita, Ecchelensis, and Assemani, respectively—became symbolic in the West of the lore of the land of their birth. The currency of Latin, French, and Italian in Maronite Lebanon brought a lively sense of Europe, and the transit of scholars to and fro, together with the Latin missionaries who played so large a part in the exchanges, fortified the spiritual autonomy vis-à-vis both Ottoman Islam and non-Latin Christianity, by which the Maronite identity was nourished, though it did not preclude the forming of Uniates from within the Orthodox and Monophysite communities. Rome's cultivation of the Maronites was never an exclusive policy. For their part, the Maronites were to find in their Latin ecclesial ties an increasing escape from the insecurities of *dhimmī* status, which was to stand them in good stead as Ottoman power declined, while still leaving ample scope for their local and internal rivalries.

The latinization became complete in liturgy and dogma, thanks to thorough supervision by papal legates sent by Rome, and given facility by the Maronite hierarchy to inspect their documents and practices and ensure that *nihil obstat* was met and all lingering traces of Monophysitism expunged.[17] In 1649 the Maronites were placed under the protection of Louis XIV of France and his consuls were active in promoting the Roman allegiance, even recruiting leading lay Maronites for the office. Finally, in 1736, with Sima'an al-Simi'ānī as legate and chairman, the Council at the Monastery of Louiza confirmed the Latin rite and usages. The absolute supremacy of the pope was acknowledged, Maronite "patriarchs" became "bishops of Rome," and the hierarchy pledged allegiance first to the Supreme Pontiff and only then to their "patriarch." There was some internal resistance, but its only success was a continuation for another century of the custom of mixed monasteries of which Rome disapproved. Pope Benedict XIV in 1741 confirmed the council's decisions, and formal adherence was sealed.

The final replacement of the ancient, Syriac focus of Antioch by the Latin authority of Rome had abiding consequences for the mentality and ethos of the Maronite church. It estranged them from their own Syriac roots and from the rest of eastern Christendom and gave them a western orientation at odds with the logic both of geography and politics. It made them suspect as "Europeans" in Ottoman domain. Under the Druze emirs in whose hands the Ottomans were content to leave local rule, notably Fakhr al-Dīn II (1590–1634), the Maronites prospered commercially and politically and moved their communities more firmly into middle Lebanon. Fakhr al-Dīn (known as Al-Ma'nī) favored their advancing fortunes and intensified their ambitions and their pretensions to the right of possession of Lebanon. These were further enlarged when Emir 'Alī al-Shihābī, a Druze, converted to Maronite Christianity, thus bringing an important clan into its story and into its feudal rivalries. His principality within the Ottoman system came to be increasingly dominated by Maronites and they, thereby, with Lebanon *per se.* Even when Muḥammad 'Alī and his son Ibrāhīm established their power in Syria, from Egypt, in the first four decades of the nineteenth century, another Shihābī, Bashīr II, was able to hold his own, consolidating Maronite influence at the expense of the Druzes—and indeed of all others—only being forced to abdicate at the end of the Egyptian hegemony.

There followed two decades of increasing antagonism, with a sequence of massacres, culminating in 1860. Maronite peasantry provoked their Druze landlords and an enflamed communalism, religiously encouraged, brought on a situation verging on civil war in which Druzes vented accumulated wrath on a Maronite population whose will apparently was to arrogate Lebanon to themselves. The tragedy of 1860 sharpened the involvement of European powers. Intervention with the Ottoman sultan resulted in a new administrative pattern, which, under *mutaṣarrifs,* or governors, from outside the country, allowed a degree of communal tolerance—with continual maneuvering—until the First World War brought on direct Ottoman control. Prewar and postwar Arabism and its struggle for decision within Ottomanism we have traced in chapter 7. Precisely because of its distinctive character, Lebanon had a crucial role and stake in that history.

The actual political shape it took in the French Mandate over Syria and Lebanon—with the frontier changes we have noted—served to fulfill the instincts of the Maronites in that they now had their traditional French protector in governmental charge of their destiny and a potential statehood closely identified with themselves. But the political self-interest of the French was too circumspect to admit of an unbalanced *penchant* toward the Maronites, who would be their clients anyway. The redrawing of the frontiers indicated as much. For, while resisting (mainly) Muslim ideas of "greater Syria," the French in creating "greater Lebanon," with its added non-Maronite areas, clearly complicated the equation Lebanese equals Maronite. Nevertheless, the French period, with its confessional constitution promulgated in 1926 and implemented in 1946, gave ample occasion in education, culture, and society for a further Maronite marriage into "the French connection," while postponing—and thereby aggravating—the essential decision as to Lebanese identity and the discipline of communities within it.

IV

Basic decisions deferred tend to intensify the issues they concern. So it was in the decades between 1920 and the civil war of the 1970s, leading up to the collapse into chaos already summarized. The lesson of a retrospect beyond it simply underlines the heavy liability of Christianity—in Maronite form—for the bitter tragedy of a Lebanon impaled on sectarian strife. It encouraged—or at least it quite failed to dissuade—other communities, Sunnīs, Shī'ahs, and Druzes, in their will to emulate its drift to final incompatibility. No doubt intransigence elsewhere "justified" the Maronites. Yet had they not also merited a reciprocal intransigence? It was clear from long history that Muslims would always be prone to political solutions determined by themselves and that Lebanese Muslims would therefore need to be patiently wooed away from these by a bold and honest will to mutuality such as Maronite Christianity quite failed, with rare exceptions, either to conceive or to afford. How signally they failed may be briefly told below. The tragedy of Lebanon is the tragedy of the Maronites writ large.

It is time to ask concerning the other Christianities in Lebanon, which means, primarily the Orthodox in the Greek tradition. All other groups are relatively small, and none has either the weight or the image, with respect to Lebanon, which the Maronites possess.[18] The Greek Catholics and the Latins, with their French and Italian connections, are more open to ecumenical and communal perspectives that elude the Maronites and are more alert in their scholarship and education.[19] The Protestants whose educational stimulus to Arabism we studied in chapter 7, are least numerous of all. But the impact of the education brought by their mentors from the West—more diffused than that of French and Jesuit educators[20] has profoundly influenced, even molded, generations of Lebanese of all communities through a century and a half. Indeed, it is illuminating to set the tragedy of Lebanon within the framework of the American University of Beirut (A.U.B.). As a pivotal institution, American in inspiration and Lebanese by locale, at once academic and cultural, two worlds in one, it ministered to the romantic vision of Lebanon and plumbed the depth of its tragedy. Its own institutional history serves eloquently to state both the dimensions and the elements of that tragedy.

They have their epitome in the career of Charles Malik (1906–1987), one of its most distinguished Christian alumni and professors, Greek Orthodox by conviction, a philosopher by vocation, a diplomat and a politician by adoption. Personal biography is often the most telling form of larger history. It allows perspective to be seen in both clarity and pathos. Charles Malik embodied an ideal Lebanon of his dreams—Christian in "the mystery and freedom of Being," mediating between East and West, in "the dimension of transcendence one with Islam," and requiring to "be and feel secure in her existence."[21] By the last he meant, in effect, American guarantees. After a brilliant period in philosophic tuition of Arab youth,[22] he became Lebanon's first Ambassador to the United States and the United Nations, following independence in 1946. In that capacity his personality, in the Chair of the General Assembly, became familiar to Americans and helped somewhat to counterbalance U.S. sponsorship of Israel by a sympathy with an articulate, Harvard-trained leader able to evoke and reassure American sentiment toward "sensible Arabs," with Lebanon as the paradigm and the A.U.B. the beneficiary. His image helped to soften anti-Arab prejudice and to remind America of the fact of Arab Christianity.

For his part, saluted—indeed lionized—with honorary degrees as a kind of Abba Eban of the Arabs, Malik became enamored of the American dimension as the hope of his native land. His philosophic mind believed such a vista to be viable with Muslims and—no less important—amenable with Maronites. Consequently, when he returned to Lebanon and, in the late 1950s, became Foreign Minister in the government of Camille Chamoun, he sustained the president in attempting to align Lebanon too far to the West, provoking the 1958 crisis and war between the communities. It was the first postwar violation of the national pact and, though the Shihāb regime rescued the situation, it generated communal distrust.[23]

Maronite propensities were the more aroused when other pressures aimed to redress and then reverse the balance in the pan-Arab direction. Later came the more intransigent Maronitism of Sulayman Frangieh reinforced by internecine feuds in the saddest Maronite tradition.

Malik's political orientation could plead, of course, the menace to his Lebanese vision of 'Abd al-Nāṣir's championship of pan-Arab emotions. He could also plead the moderation of the then patriarch of the Maronites, Būlus Ma'ūshī (1955–1975). Unlike his predecessor, Antun Arīḍa (1932–1955), who had interfered constantly in politics and sought to decry and impede the national concordat,[24] Patriarch Ma'ūshī sought Muslim–Christian amity, visited Muslim mosques, and gave ample evidence of a desire for a Lebanon, secure in its character but cautiously cooperative with Arab states and Muslim interests. He was not supported by many of his clergy, nor by prominent laymen, including Chamoun himself. Despite his prestige and tenacity, he represented a minority position that appeared suspect to the rooted confessionalism of the monks of his church and the scheming sectionalism of most of its politicians. Though president and patriarch were on opposite sides in 1958, Malik may have thought that the degree of western reliance he sought could be reconciled with both Maronite and Muslim views. If so, he was disappointed and in the events that followed increasingly disillusioned when in his old age the land of his dreams headed into near anarchy. He had written in 1965 of his beloved Orthodoxy that "a certain degree of anarchy is . . . apparent. . . ."[25] But he was then thinking of things imprecise in faith not calamitous in experience. A splendid representative of Lebanese Christianity, its quality and promise, he was defeated by the intractable facts of his heritage and betrayed by his confidence in faithful reason.

The American University of Beirut, founded in 1866 as "the Syrian Protestant College," may be said to have exemplified in institutional form the same paradox and irony that belonged biographically with Charles Malik. The university certainly has its crucial place in the modern story of Arab Christianity. Its matrix was the missionary impulse of American Protestantism, which, as early as 1823, had brought an Arab printing press from Malta and which played a vital part, as noted in chapter 7, in the growth of nineteenth-century Arab consciousness, journalism, and literature. More incisive and prestigious than the numerous agencies of Christian evangelism and philanthropy that came to Lebanon in the wake of the massacres of 1860,[26] it came to occupy a unique place in the annals of Lebanese education, together with its younger offshoots, International College and the Beirut College for Women. It was the intellectual nursery through more than a century of much of the political and professional leadership of the Arab world from Aleppo to Khartoum. It antedated the

Lebanese National University by more than eighty years. Its French-speaking counterpart, Université St. Joseph, had a more confined French and theological orientation.

But, for all its massive service to the Arab world, the American University of Beirut labored under two crippling constraints. It is part of the tragedy we are studying in this chapter that it was probably so fated—like all authentic tragedy—by the elements of the situation. The one was the Christian motive in Lebanese pluralism; the other was the American connection.

As the progeny of mission, the Syrian Protestant College intended Christian nurture in a context of intellectual freedom and enquiry.[27] It was, *ipso facto*, offering a highly coveted commodity—English-speaking education—with a Christian concern whose theological and spiritual criteria were neither Muslim, nor Druze, nor Maronite, nor Greek Orthodox nor Latin in their ethos and whose impact, however irenic, circumspect, and considerate, would inevitably be read as questioning if not threatening the presuppositions and authority of all those other organs and houses of belief and conduct. Here was the perennial quandary of "mission" in every context. The increasing sophistication of education itself and the national Arab consciousness it did so much to foster only sharpened the issue. In the post–First World War presidency of Bayard Dodge (1922–1948) the policy of his predecessor, Howard S. Bliss (1902–1920), of emphasizing moral and civic virtue while muting at least partially and officially specifically Christian nurture was further applied. It would be fair to say that the crux of interreligious coexistence was never really tackled nor yet the critique of religions—especially in the Lebanese context—in terms of their sharing the guidance of a deconfessionalized society.

Perhaps that more fundamental addressing of the religious problem would have been impossible at the time. "Dialogue" had not then become the code word, often hiding, as it still does, the realities in which it is involved. Certainly a benign and enlightened ethicism was the easier option in the context, avoiding explicit "christianizing" and assigning religious faith to the private—or, more likely, the communal—sector, while science, literature, and learning had their urgent opportunity in the stream of youth. Yet urgent problems do not always pass because they are not addressed, nor do deep issues yield to intelligent neglect. The A.U.B., it might be said, only experienced the abiding dilemma of Christian motivation in the plural world and did so in the peculiarly vexing setting of a Lebanon that so urgently needed the will and the wit to face the strife of its religions and discover how to tame them into fruitful coexistence. In avoiding being theological, the A.U.B. (the Near East School of Theology was mission-based and concerned with the nurture of pastors and clergy) coincided with Lebanon's religious diversity rather than with its religious dilemma. Yet could the university *in situ* have done otherwise?

That question leads into the second crippling constraint—the American factor. It could be said that America's earliest missionary commitment served it best in terms of personal quality. Its personnel came with a genuine love, which fulfilled itself in long service and inner rapport, paternalistic perhaps but in the best tradition of American warmth, vigor, and integrity.[28] Their literary, medical, and historical contributions to the Arab world had the quality of magnanimity and zeal. There could be little legitimate cavil about an "Americanism" of that caliber and temper. Charles Malik's faith in the American dimension even by the 1940s had eloquent warrant.

Yet in the post–Second World War period, especially under the presidencies of Paul Leonard (1957–1961) and of Norman Burns (1961–1965) there came an increasing reliance on U.S. government funds (as distinct from direct philanthropy). One notices the brief tenure of men who had government connections and came not as career teachers but as administrators close to U.S. interests. Leonard described his presidency as "a challenge to keep the Arab world free and a friend of the U.S.A.," and Burns came as a former head of U.S. operations and mission in Jordan. Staff members also became short-termers spending a few years in an interesting locale; they were not deep lovers of Lebanon's soil and soul. There was an unwillingness to have an Arab as president despite the marked stature of Constantine Zurayq as acting president for the three years preceding Paul Leonard.

The times, of course, were changing and hardening. The campus became embroiled in political tensions in spite of sturdy efforts to keep the seething world outside at bay. Student groups began to reflect the passions of the Palestinian and Lebanese factions. The university came to be seen—at least by accusation—as a nesting place for C.I.A. agents, a foothold for U.S. governmental ends, or simply a luxury enjoyed by an Arab elite, false or indifferent in their privilege to the genuine grievances of the Arab poor. The university could argue that its increasing dependence on governmental resources was entailed by its massive extension program in response to urgent educational demands outrunning private funding. But such growth, questioned by some on technical grounds as ill-considered, found no acceptance with the likes of Laila Khālid, a student in 1962 and later a highjacker,[29] nor with George Ḥabash before her, a Greek Orthodox of the P.F.L.P. (Popular Front for the Liberation of Palestine).[30] The tribulations of a much-battered, much-maligned, and much-harassed institution found their ultimate symbol in the assassination in 1984 of President Malcolm Kerr in College Hall, the first of Daniel Bliss's buildings.[31] The son of parents who had served in halcyon days, he represented all that was finest in the old tradition, the order that registered its own desolation in his tragic end. College Hall had stood, in the 1860s as a beacon of hope on the *Rās* of Beirut, far out from the confines of the city near the harbor. It had been surrounded and engulfed by the sprawl of an overgrown capital comprising more than half a nation. Those changes have dwarfed, but not quite extinguished, the meaning of its presence in the skyline. The shape of human intercourse has inevitably to concede the sufferings entailed in the strife of politics and the enmity of religions as these afflict the making and unmaking of nations. As a foreign entity in origin and ethos, the American University of Beirut has lived by the goodwill of a Lebanese authority that has itself disintegrated. Its auspices and its constraints have always made its ministries ambiguous.

As one of its eminent alumni observed in a Founders' Day assembly in 1971, there had been two Americas:

> . . . the foster-carer for academic freedom, the liberal nurse of the arts, and the American with power-interests and political exploitation. . . . Our criticisms stem from the common heritage, the innate sense of justice and historical devotion to the fundamental rights of man. . . .[32]

It was an ambivalence inseparable, in the Lebanese context, from that encounter of West and East which Charles Malik read as a destiny Lebanon, with American aid, could resolve into unity. Now the A.U.B. campus stands in the Muslim sector of a sundered city and a self-partitioning nation. On every count of achievement and immolation its own tragedy stands within the tragedy of Lebanon. That is its place in Arab Christianity.

V

If the A.U.B. nurtured many politicians, it also helped to educate church leaders.[33] It is time to turn from the self-limiting stance of A.U.B. Christianity to the role of the churches in general. We have sufficiently outlined the Maronite dimension and noted the exceptional role of Patriarch Ma'ūshī in striving for a temperate attitude within it. Greek Orthodoxy for long felt the uncertainties of intent and result within the Protestant presence of which initially the A.U.B. was a powerful symbol. Its pupils, such as Muslims and Druzes, sought its educational assets while reserving their spiritual and confessional privacies, though influenced by teachers of their own, or other, allegiance, such as the Orthodox Charles Malik and Constantine Zurayq and the Quaker Roger Soltau. Inevitably their inward loyalties were tempered by factors that would not otherwise have affected their lives or churches, but those leavening factors were always subject to the reservations implicit in cherished identities caring for an image and a heritage.

Ecumenical cooperation developed when in 1974 the Near East Council of Churches, which in origin had been a missionary initiative, was enlarged by the entry of the Orthodox church and, in salute, renamed itself the Middle East Council of Churches. Embracing many countries, it had its headquarters in Beirut—or alternatively in Cyprus—and pursued the kind of interchurch action of which Lebanon, by its very character, had long been the symbol and haven. Its energetic, long-serving general secretary, Gabriel Ḥabīb, struggled valiantly with the burdens and agonies of a deteriorating situation in which the council's association with the World Council of Churches in Geneva helped to sustain its will to courage and sanity. Prior to its 1985 assembly in Cyprus, the Orthodox patriarch of Antioch, Ignatius IV, one of its presidents, invited the heads of all the Middle East Christian churches to a meeting at which to prepare a pastoral message to all their communities in unison. Patriarch Ignatius leads a church that, in the long anguish of Lebanon, has always avoided and repudiated violence. He has called for a will on the part of all to return to a pre-Chalcedonian (i.e., Nicean) formula of faith, leaving patient resolution of the issues which Chalcedon made divisive to future intent, in an effort to bring communities out of their instinctive habit of separation.[34]

The Youth Movement of the Orthodox in Lebanon, founded in 1942 by (now Bishop) George Khoḍr, has brought new vitality and vision into the church through deepened awareness of its spiritual meaning, through social action, and by fostering an alert laity and a clergy close to the people. It has also sought to aid the Maronites to interrogate their partisan tradition and wrestle more fundamentally with the guilt and issue of the Lebanese tragedy and how heart searching might find the springs of hope. How do Latins and Uniates see their bond with Rome in relation to the life and liturgies deriving from the undivided centuries? Can the urgency of common distress bring all into a "common pastorate" in which the actualities of the local churches draw them into a true oneness able at length to resolve ancient formulas and diversity of jurisdictions? For its part the Middle East Council of Churches struggles to retrieve from the political calamity of Lebanon the enabling vision of Christian renewal, "cast down but not destroyed."

It will be well to defer to chapter 12 some study of what the Lebanese tragedy entails upon the Christian churches with respect to relations with Islam. It is inevitable that the strife of communities has desperately impeded and desolated both the hopes and the efforts of intercommunal faith relationships—in the very context where they had most expectation of fruitfulness before the agonies supervened. Precisely where Arabness might have found more evenhandedness with its religious dimensions, through factors unique to Lebanon, it has most bitterly prejudiced them, with repercussions everywhere else in the Arab world.

But the fact that presses—and oppresses—here and is inseparable from all interfaith intellectual and spiritual relation is the indictment of religion in the behavior of religions. It may be claimed that the elements of the strife in Lebanon were such that no church or tradition, no order of doctrine and liturgy of worship, could avail to discipline or control or resolve. To agree might be some measure of absolution but only as also a measure of futility. The plea of incapacity to have history otherwise, apart from evacuating religious faith of positive healing relevance, cannot hide or excuse its ample capacities in contributing to the situation as a whole. There is no exoneration either way.

So it is that Lebanon belongs darkly in recent history as a symbol of religions as the malady rather than the remedy in their societies. Obscurantism and bigotry on the part of any tend to provoke the like in others. Belligerence is reproduced where it is waged. Lebanon has become progressively the victim of its discordant faiths. Where their enmities could be laid at the door of economic disadvantage, personal cupidity, or human passion, as distinct from sectarian allegiance, the alibi—even if it holds—is still a part of the condemnation. Innocence in the situation could not be pleaded without thereby conceding guilt—the guilt of failure to subdue the circumstantial to the claims of the Spirit.

Sociology has often pondered the distinction between a church and a sect. The difference is often clouded by the fact that the former behaves like the latter. Presumably a sect has the instinct to tighten, to foreclose questions, to let fear override generosity, to intensify allegiance in exclusivism, whereas a true church has dimensions of patience, charity, compassion, and hospitality. May it be that the long feudal, tribal, and martial instincts of the Maronites—"church" though they undoubtedly are—have made them essentially sectarian despite the papal connection? Orthodoxy in its Greek ancestry, for all its tensions, comes closer to the dimensions that distinguish church from sect. Yet how, in turn, does a veritable "churchness" cope with the wider ecumenical destiny that other faiths require of it—prone as all other faiths are to the "sectarian" disease?

Lebanon this century (because of long strains in all its centuries) has become the arena of this unresolved issue. Asked about his *modus operandi* in 1925, Chaim Weizmann of the Zionist Executive wrote: "If I want to take a decision, I stand in front of a mirror and hold a conference with my reflection and that is how the organization is run."[35] The mirror into which the Maronites all too often looked gave back in reflection not the features of the wounded Christ, as in some Turin shroud, but the lineaments of communal willfulness and passion. There was a harshness about their response to western influences outside the Latin aegis. As early as 1825 the Maronite patriarch required his people, on pain of excommunication, to have no dealings whatever with American missionaries and not to handle their publications or attend schools or meetings.[36] Their church tended to bear down heavily not only on outside Christian associations but also on Maronites showing enthusiasm for Ottomanism as a dimension of the self-awareness of thoughtful Arabs in the nineteenth century.

The career of Fāris al-Shidyāq (1804–1887) is a case in point. His brother, As'ad, had consorted with the American mission and was sent to prison by the patriarch, where he died. In indignation, Fāris emigrated to Egypt and fled later to Malta. He became a Protestant and wrote extensively on Arab and religious themes. But his "conversion" within Christianity, in the context of his ex-Maronite distresses, brought him no final inner peace. Nor, in perspective, could it resolve the problem it only aggravated, namely, that of the true destiny of the loyal Arab. His ultimate decision led him to embrace Islam and to champion the Ottoman option, within loyalty to the caliphate, as the only viable course for the Arab spirit. The bitter virulence of his autobiography against Maronite intransigence and his personal sense of the tensions within Arab Christian existence were a measure of the anguish that was to come in the land he forsook to become, finally, a pensioner of the sultan.[37]

Emigration, of course, was seen as salvation by many Christian Lebanese, though the story of the *Hijrah* cannot detain us here, except as an index to the unease of unresolved dilemmas. Some notable Lebanese exiles, like Khalīl Jibrān (1883–1912) and Mikhā'il Nu'aymah (1889–1975) took refuge not only in foreign lands but in a kind of spiritual monism which aimed to repudiate and transcend the dogma of ecclesiastics and the turmoil of politics.[38] Escaping thereby the burden of these, they absented themselves from its bearing.

Perhaps theirs was the true wisdom. Exile at least was surely preferable to the excesses of the Maronites. When Pierre Gemayel founded the Phalange in the late 1930s, he was inspired in part by a visit in 1936 to Nazi Germany, where he was impressed by uniforms and paramilitary zeal. His vision–though sometimes moderated in his later years–was a Maronite view of Lebanon, "Fatherland and family," in the fascist terms of Vichy France, flourishing crusading symbols and idealizing "the one Catholic nation in Asia." "The Knights of the Virgin" and "the Wood of the Cross" were hardly slogans of peace in the stresses of–supposedly–a national concordat.

Camille Chamoun had a more suave and politic image but earned no less justly the taunt of Kamāl Jumblātt, the Druze leader, calling Maronites "that minority obsessed with their sense of being a minority."[39] Chamoun defied his own patriarch, Būlus Ma'ūshī, and resisted more moderate Maronite politicians, like Raymond Edde, who recognized the danger of their community becoming a hated ghetto. Chamoun openly hated 'Abd al-Nāṣir and deplored the failure of the Suez venture. As seen by Odd Bull of the U.N.O. peace force, he had "the impertinence [in 1958] to call in American armed forces to protect his personal interests."[40]

Sulaymān Frangieh, a successor as president, who aimed to Maronitize the army, was corrupt and incompetent, a vowed foe of ideas of concordat and given to clan warfare in his stronghold at Zghorta. Three hundred Muslims were massacred in one day in the Matn region in revenge for four Maronites found slain. Bashīr Gemayel, in a speech on the morning of his assassination, days after his inauguration in 1982, avowed: "We must today conquer all Lebanon, all its 10,452 square kilometres," despite his earlier hints of an awareness that intercommunal cooperation was indispensable for all, and for Maronites most of all.

Such was the church, self-crucified on its own intransigence, which—perhaps more than any other factor—polarized Lebanon into tragic anarchy. The despair at the spectacle has to be a despair about religion, about the ultimate consultation with the mirror. This was the community that, as early as 1799 had sent a delegation to meet Napoleon in Palestine and was said to have received from him the greeting: "I recognize that you have been French from time immemorial."[41] Perhaps the most ironical index of the Maronite will to separatism and the latent desperation of it, in the light of the Arabism studied in chapters 7 and 10, is to be found in the evidence of Archbishop Ignace Mubārak of Beirut to the United Nations Commission on Palestine in 1947. He denied that Palestine was Arab: it was Jewish homeland from which Jews had been driven. There were two religions—Judaism and Christianity. Palestine and Lebanon were the Jewish home of the one and the Christian home of the other, in mutual support. As "a Christian sanctuary," Lebanon must be "out of the clutches of surrounding nations. . . . That is the opinion of the Lebanese whom I represent."[42] Thirty-five years later that reading of the autonomy of the one enclave became victim to outright invasion by the other. History has a way of identifying folly, but at what cost!

The best minds in the Orthodox church in Lebanon have sought to respond to compounded tragedy by interpreting the Christian role as that of an intercommunal ecumenism seeking to offer a Christian version of Arab identity that would avail to merit and to elicit from Arab Islam (at least in Lebanon) the quality of partnership, which could ensure a patient, constructive transition into an understanding of religion free from the sanction of state power. The hope of doing so entails an intra-Christian freedom from the sect mentality, in pursuit of a will to churchness that reconciles its historical diversities and their passions by a common dedication to the paramount task set by Islam as the ultimate factor in their Arabness.

They realize how pluralism is inescapable, that a purely Christian "nationalism" is invalid on every score and that Christian resistance to the marginalizing they traditionally experience, under the Islamic *dhimmī* theory of contracted sufferance, must try positively to develop those aspects of Islam which might sustain equal citizenship within a state understood as being itself "under God." Orthodoxy of the Byzantine tradition must be aware of "the wounded historical consciousness" of non-Byzantine churches. Christians must learn to overcome the psychological separatisms that are even more persistent than the doctrinal ones. Relinquishing the illusion of being "privileged partners of the West," they must be ready for that recognition of others which means feeling "vulnerable to their being different." Arabism, which in the nineteenth century renewed itself as a strategy to deal with Ottoman polity, must now find, out of the trauma of Lebanon, the way to be at once plural and free.[43]

Brave sentiments in the grim actualities Lebanon presents. We have to remit to chapter 11 the interior resources that belong with the soul of Arab Christianity there and elsewhere in its liturgies, its poetry, and its art—resources from which, if at all, must spring their fulfillment. Hope belongs where politics—for all its damning and dismaying reach—cannot bring a final veto and where even the political can be rescued from tragedy. It will fall to chapter 12 to take further such Christian future with Islam.

Notes

1. Robert Curzon, *Visits to Monasteries in the Levant* (1849; London, 1983), pp. 25–26.

2. See n. 21 below. For example, Malik insisted that Lebanon's "basic idea was not political" ("The Near East: The Search for Truth," *Foreign Affairs* 50, no. 2 [Jan. 1952], p. 239). Rather, Lebanon carried "the burden of mediation between East and West." Internally, it was precisely in being so intensely "political" in confessional terms, that Lebanon succumbed under the burden of "non-mediation"—effectively—between the "east" and "west" within it. Yet his romanticism was part of the equation, as love is in divorce. Malik could be deceived in his judgments, as when he wrote in the same article concerning Faiṣal II of Iraq: "Nothing seems to be more firmly established in Iraq than this house [i.e., Faiṣal's] and the love of the people for their boy-monarch" (p. 237). Six years later, Faiṣal and his "house" lay brutally murdered.

3. The Palestine Liberation Organization dates, effectively, from the trauma of 1967, which disclosed how deceptive were hopes centering on the Arab states. It

had, however, been in embryonic existence some two years earlier. The long years of Palestinian refugee-status quiescence are often forgotten. See Jonathan Dimbleby, *The Palestinians* (Boston: Charles River Books, 1979).

4. It was a very sanguinary expulsion after pitched battles between Palestinian *fidā'īyūn* and the, mainly bedouin, army of Jordan. Hence the "Beds/Feds" usage to describe the encounter.

5. Syria had received the fewest refugees from 1948 of the three neighboring countries and had always kept a tight rein on the militants, mainly *Al-Sā'iqah,* which it allowed to operate.

6. Israel has never lacked persons of conscience both inside and outside the army (always significantly called Israeli Defense Forces, there being no aggressive army), as, for example Oz va Shalom and Soldiers for Peace. But while they have helped the image of Israel, they have not availed politically except in the withdrawal from Lebanon, when political factors of exhaustion and frustration played the major part.

7. Those risks were, of course, significant, not least because of the Israeli factor in every Syrian calculation. Syrian policy went through a variety of changes both before and after the so-called Cairo Agreement of 1976, relating to the operations of Palestinians on Lebanese soil. Syria's tactic was to try to obviate any Arab influence other than its own within Lebanon. Syria's (major) share in the Arab Peace-keeping Force and its (later) single-handed policing served, to a degree, to "hold the ring," but not to resolve the strife. The intrigues of the factions were aggravated within Lebanese politics and in the Lebanese Army by the conflict of wider interests both regional and global. There was throughout a cynical hypocrisy in requiring Lebanon to bear the burden—and be the battleground—of the challenge of Israel, via the Palestinians, to Arabism as a whole. Lebanon was the one Arab country least qualified to sustain it yet forced to do so by the devious patterns of action and inaction.

8. Despite the impact of the massacres of 1860 on the mind of the West, Maronite suffering—in perspective—was by no means one-sided. Maronite movement into fresh territory, the tensions within peasant economy, Maronite arrogance, and, from time to time, belligerence at Druze cost helped to provoke the widespread Druze retaliation and vengeance. The Druze identity had its long tradition of militancy, and the aura of its secretive beliefs served to foster an image of the sinister. But through long decades the communities had given proof of viable relations of coexistence, if not amity.

9. Sa'īd 'Aql, *Qadmus,* 2nd ed. (Beirut, 1947), p. 22. In this verse tragedy the poet-author sees Lebanon as enshrining a threefold heritage—Phoenician, Hellenistic, and Roman. Phoenicia first gave the East—and the world—an alphabet.

10. So 'Arafāt is reported to have said on Nov. 30, 1975, in a speech to the Administrative Council of the Palestinian Student Association (*Ṣauṭ Falastīn,* Dec. 1, 1975; *Jerusalem Post,* Dec. 3). By contrast there were Lebanese who denied that either Palestine or Lebanon was "Arab," totally disowning Palestinianism in order to possess Lebanon as "non-Arab." See, e.g., n. 43.

11. Bashīr Gemayel in *Le Nouvel Observateur* (Paris), June 19, 1982, p. 62.

12. Monothelitism was the doctrine that tried to obviate the conflict within

Christology as to the unity of the divine and human "natures" by relocating the issue in "the will." Some historians have thought that if the Maronites originated from Arabia their "heretical" strain might bear out the old image of Arabia as *ferax haeresis*, "fertile ground of heresy." But the Monothelite doctrine belongs with the post-Chalcedon tensions in the Orient. Maronite writers deny that their church ever held it; see Matti Moosa, *The Maronites in History* (Syracuse, N.Y.: Syracuse University Press, 1986).

13. One may say odd in that, for example, the redoubtable Druze Fakhr al-Dīn al-Ma'nī at the end of the sixteenth century positively favored the Maronites and encouraged them to come into territory he controlled as an appointee of the Ottoman sultan. Further, the adoption of Christianity by the Druze Shihābis paved the way for the long dominance of Emīr Bashīr al-Dīn II, the princely Lord of Bait al-Dīn (1788–1840), who, sitting lightly to his religion, was able to survive elegantly, if also cunningly, the stresses of Maronite/Druze feudal politics, Ottoman dominion, European interests, and the Syrian adventures of Muḥammad 'Alī in Egypt, through five decades before final exile to Istanbul. Almost legendary in popular Lebanese history, it was nevertheless his regime that excited in delayed reaction the Druze massacres of Christians, which culminated in 1860.

14. The double sense of protégé-status and emulation characterizes militant Maronitism in its relation to Rome and to France. It spells for some an identity "because of . . . and on behalf of," which sees the *raison d'être* of Lebanon as western not Arab, seaward not landward. Beirut, as a grossly overgrown coast city, divided by the hinterland it shares, may be read as a symbol of that issue.

15. John Mārūn, from whom Maronites take their name, as tradition has it, was their original founder. A monk of the fifth century, friend of John Chrysostom, saint of the monastery that bears his name, he spent his days, perhaps somewhat in the tradition of St. Simon Stylites in the Orontes valley area of northern Syria. See Moosa, *Maronites*, pp. 16–38.

16. In 1583 Vatican presses printed the first Arabic Bible. Ecclesiastical connections westward encouraged the Maronites to venture political overtures, as when, for example, the Maronite patriarch in 1527 wrote to Emperor Charles V pledging entire support if he would come to Syria. Francis I of France was also solicited, and in the next century the princes of Italy. Such links gave promise of a way of escape from the *dhimmī* pattern of the Ottoman system and an alternative way of "security." Unlike other Christians, the Maronites long contrived to avoid accepting investitute of their patriarchs by the sultan.

17. It is noteworthy that the legate, Giovanni Eliano, had earlier failed in a similar mission to the Copts of Egypt. His success as an "inspector" of the Maronites was completed by the next emissary, Jerome Dandini.

18. The breaking away of the Uniate Greek Catholic diminished the Orthodox. Though there were Maronite elements scattered outside Lebanon, it was the strength of their concentration there that made them dominant locally. Also in the nineteenth century there was a considerable migration of Orthodox from Syria into Egypt.

19. One of the most famous of scholars from the Université St. Joseph earlier this

century was Henri Lammens, whose interpretation of Syro-Lebanese history did much to influence the Maronite "image" of the Christian "nation" at the time of "mandating" to the French. His academic strictures on Islam may be part of the same thesis.

20. These tended to foster the sympathies congenial to the Maronites in their French context and the lines of their historical research and spiritual orientation. Their journal, however, *Al-Mashriq*, has a deservedly honored place in Arabic letters and theology.

21. See Charles Malik, "The Orthodox Church," in *Religion in the Middle East*, ed. A. J. Arberry (Ann Arbor, Mich.: Books on Demand, 1969), 1:297–346; cf. *Al-'Amal*, Nov. 22, 1955: Lebanon "understands the holy of holies of the West, with love, patience and profundity, in a manner the East cannot grasp and in the best way by which the West can communicate its story. . . . It understands the holy of holies of the East, with love, patience and profundity in a manner the West cannot grasp and knows best how to have the East disclose its own secrets."

22. The writer recalls vividly the impact of Charles Malik on a generation of philosophy students in his weekly "Sophomore" lecture, using his mentor of Harvard, W. E. Hocking's *Types of Philosophy*. He brought to life the thrill of study and the pursuit of meaning. He made even his hyperbole (cf. n. 21) convincing by the man he was.

23. See the comment in 1977 of Bashīr Gemayel on the events of 1958: "If the year 1958 was the beginning of the infection of the formula of the National Pact with cancer, 1975 should be considered the date of its real sickness" (cited from Moosa, *Maronites*, p. 291).

24. Patriarch Antun Arīḍā was a staunch champion of a radical Maronite reading of Lebanon, crossing swords even with the French High Commission and his own Maronite lay leaders from time to time. See n. 43 for the lengths to which his suspicions of Arabism could go, Bishop Mubārak there being his personal emissary to the U.N. Commission.

25. See Malik, "Orthodox Church," p. 310.

26. Among them, notably, the Blind School of the British Syrian Mission.

27. There was never proselytism, but in the Dedicatory Statement, Daniel Bliss, the first president, wrote: "It will be impossible for anyone to continue with us long without knowing what we believe to be the truth and our reasons for that belief." See S. B. Penrose, Jr., *That They May Have Life: The Story of the American University of Beirut 1866–1941* (Princeton, N.J.: Princeton University Press, 1941), p. 46.

28. See, e.g., Penrose, *That They May Have Life;* Fred J. Bliss, *Reminiscences of Daniel Bliss* (New York, 1920); and H. H. Jessup, *Fifty-Three Years in Syria*, 2 vols. (New York, 1910).

29. She describes her year on campus in her autobiography, *My People Shall Live* (1969; Arabic ed. Beirut, 1973). She saw the university as a nest of C.I.A. spies.

30. George Ḥabash, a Greek Orthodox student, was president of *Al-'Urwā al-Wuthqā*, a radical society, in 1950 and subsequently a leader of Palestinian resistance.

31. His assailants were Iranian-linked militants using brutal murder to repudiate

the long associations of culture and service for which the university stood and doing so in its first towered and symbolic edifice of 1866.

32. Tueni is a Greek Orthodox layman, newspaper editor (*Al-Nahār*), and diplomat, both student and critic of Charles Malik, and Minister of Education, and of Labor and Social Affairs.

33. Notably, for example, Ignatius Hazīm, philosophy student in the mid-1940s, who became Patriarch Ignatius IV.

34. From an address (given in French) to the Catholic Institute of Paris, June 2, 1983.

35. See *The Essential Chaim Weizmann: The Man, the Statesman, the Scientist,* ed. Barnet Litvinoff (New York: Holmes & Meier, 1983), p. 211.

36. Quoted in Maroun 'Abboud, *Ṣaqar Lubnān* (Beirut, 1950), p. 38.

37. Fāris al-Shidyāq, *Kitāb al-Sāq 'alā-l-Sāq fī mā huwa al-Fārīyāq* (Paris, 1855; Cairo ed. 1919). The high-sounding title might be read as a play on his names with the implication of a restless energy in the pursuit of being Fari . . . yaq, an autobiographical medley on the move.

38. Mikhā'il Nu'aymah's autobiography was published in 3 vols. (Beirut, 1959–60), under the title *Saba'ūn: Ḥikāyat 'Umrī* (Seventy: The Story of My Age).

39. Kamāl Jumblātt, *I Speak for Lebanon,* trans. M. Pallis (London, 1982), p. 39.

40. Odd Bull, *War and Peace in the Middle East: The Experiences of a U.N. Observer* (London: Seeley Service & Cooper, 1976), p. 20.

41. In E. S. Stevens, *Cedars, Saints and Sinners in Syria* (London, n.d.), p. 257.

42. In a letter of Aug. 5, 1947, to the Commission of Enquiry, in U.N.S.C.O.P (United Nations Special Committee on Palestine) Official Records (New York, 1947), pp. 57–59.

43. Quoted and summarized from a talk by Metropolitan George Khoḍr, as bishop of Mount Lebanon, at U.N.E.S.C.O., Paris, Dec. 21, 1983.

CHAPTER

10

Arab Christianity and Israel

I

IT IS REPORTED that on the evening of the day when the Allied Forces entered Damascus in November 1917, the muezzin, calling to prayer over the rooftops, "dropped his voice two tones almost to speaking level and softly added [to the liturgical words]: 'and He [God] is very good to us this day, O people of Damascus!'"[1] Perhaps apocryphal, the story in hindsight has a tragic irony, but it echoes the exuberant hopes that attended the entry into Damascus as the symbol and climax of the Arab Revolt against the Ottoman Turks. The capture of the ancient city, capital of the Umayyad caliphate in the first great heyday of Islam, was thought to have inaugurated the era of Arab sovereignty understood to have been solemnly pledged by those victorious Allies. Jerusalem was already in their hands and Baghdad would shortly be. The elimination of Ottoman power from the Arab provinces of the defeated empire was assumed to be the prelude to an independent Arab sovereignty giving permanent form to the aspirations in which, as we have seen in chapter 7, Arab Christians had fully shared. Implicit in the revolt of Arab Muslims against an Islamic caliphate was the principle of nation-state Arabism, whether in unified or fragmented form. That principle involved the concept of common citizenship. The end of Ottomanism meant the end of *dhimmī* status for Christians and their engagement, in yet untried ways, with a nationally oriented Islam. In theory at least, "God had been very good" to more than the people of the muezzin.

"The goodness of God" had been differently, but no less expectantly, hailed on an adjacent day late in 1917 by an exuberant Zionism, when the British Government issued the famous Balfour Declaration. That document gave political sanction for the first time, by a (then) world power, to the campaign for a Zionist repossession of Palestine. The British Government "viewed with favour the establishment of a national home for the Jewish people in Palestine. . . ." That commitment was the diplomatic achievement of Chaim Weizmann, rewarding his resolute but not always consistent advocacy of the British option as the surest path to the realization of the dream of Jewish statehood. The Declaration was music to the ear and in the heart of Zionists. For it marked a turning point in a protracted story.

It is true that statehood was not explicitly promised and that "the civil and religious rights of the existing population" were to be safeguarded. Oddly, it named "Palestine" but not "Palestinians." They were an actual, but awkward, nonidentity. The shape of the Declaration was, at that stage, entirely satisfactory to most Zionists, and its ambiguity was tactically useful. "A home in," to be sure, was not "a state of," but by Zionist logic there could not be the one without the other. Sequence could be evolutionary.[2] As for civil and religious rights for inhabitants, these, it could be assumed, would not need safeguarding if political rights existed. The caveat could be read as a mandate for an exclusively Jewish state.

This ultimate, if partially hidden, agenda is an important factor to appreciate. Zion, as visualized by dreamers and diplomats alike, could not feasibly be binational or federal. The whole concept of Zion was based on a final rejection of what Zionists called "host-nation" privation in Europe or elsewhere—that condition of things which, on their view, did not allow Jews to live authentically, which constrained them all the while by the censuring jury of the Gentile world and spelled a perpetual existence on sufferance, either in ghetto jeopardy or—no less lethal—the menace of "assimilation." Advocates of Zion were in no way proposing to escape host-nation status in Europe for host-nation condition in the Arab world. They were campaigning to end host-nation existence once and for all, at least for those Jews prepared to read their diaspora condition in those terms. They were terms that in the early decades of this century most Jews were not ready to concede, intending rather to sustain their authentic Jewishness by forthright identification with their states of residence in the confidence that the spiritual resources of their Judaism were the only proper and adequate counter to assimilation. As yet unbeknown to either viewpoint, Hitler's European tyranny would appallingly vindicate the Zionist logic in the Holocaust. That lay in the future, but already multiple experience in Russia, Germany, Poland, and France had disposed Zionists to allow no critical risks with Arab polity whatever shape it might assume in the unfolding of events beyond both Balfour and the Arab Revolt in the post-Ottoman structure of the Middle East. There were many Zionists who felt that they could ignore Arab political ambitions altogether on the basis of their will for and cult of a total innocence.

Thus, November 1917 set two ambitions on collision course, the one or the other doomed, as far as Palestine was concerned, to frustration. There is no need here to rehearse again how the inherent ambiguity ripened into triumph and tragedy or to review the familiar story of the League of Nations Mandate to Britain to implement the Declaration, the chronic impasse which issued into the United Nations partition of Palestine and the stages in the defense, enlargement, and inner crisis of the State of Israel. Nor is it necessary to assess how, Palestine apart, the expectations of Arabism have been only partially and tediously fulfilled in deferred or divided statehoods. The attainment of Israel proceeded through the trauma of the 1930s and 1940s to its siege existence and bitter consolidation in the decades since. Our concern is with the burdens and tensions for Arab Christianity in that story through what is now a long century of Zionist vision, venture, and victory.

Within that Arab Christianity the most tense issue is that of Palestine. The task is to comprehend the ground of Palestinianism, its case, its conscience, its adversity, and its misery. We need to grasp the mystique by which it is opposed, the divine mandate which—in the eyes of many in the West and in Christian quarters—its adversary commands and wields. The sense of what Palestinians are up against in the massive yet elusive sanction Israel enjoys is no small part of their travail. How it may be demystified, how spiritually counterbalanced by more prosaic meanings of justice and peace, is a profound problem for the Palestinian soul—a problem that leads back into vexed areas of biblical interpretation and theology.

These, in turn, are beset, if not bedeviled, by prejudice and obduracy in the West over issues that deserve better of Christian integrity than they frequently receive. Arab Christians, reckoning with them, are adversely affected by their minority status, their ambivalent relations with the West, and the sheer complexity of the interreligious situation. Confronting them is the expertise of Israeli propaganda and image projection. The fact that it all transpires around "the holy land" only makes an honest objectivity more difficult to reach and daunting to sustain. Sharp moral issues are easily submerged by outsiders in archaeology or tourism, while the local Christianity is relegated to sentiment and the museum.

Any effort to do the situation justice had better first occupy itself with the competitive legitimation of identities—the Israeli and the Palestinian. That these are mutually exclusive within the geography of one country and within the prescripts of independent state authority that each invokes is obvious. Nor is either logic obliged to yield to the other, for they are identical.[3] The Palestine National Charter is identical with the case for

Zionism, namely, that territorial sovereignty is a *sine qua non* of security and of identity. Each is grounded in the same nexus of people, land, and power. Either might tolerate the other as minority so long as power is not shared or jeopardized.

It follows that the familiar Israeli claim that "there are no Palestinians" is in the same key as the long Palestinian repudiation of Israel as a state.[4] The sea into which the P.L.O. would allegedly drive Israel is not the Mediterranean but depoliticization, which—in Zionist reckoning—would indeed be drowning in the waters of insecurity. Palestinians realize that an unyielding Israel means the like fate for them. Neither nationalism can be rightly accused of being merely imitative of the other. Their stories are different, but the rationale is one. For both parties the distinction of who denies what is in survival terms purely academic. Stateless landlessness is the same as the sea.

But if, in political terms—and effectively there are no other—each essentially delegitimizes the other's perceived identity, the actual equation is very unequally posed. Israel has "the chosen people" aura, and the Palestinians are today's Philistines, who not only lack such status but, by accident of geography, are the impediment to its due fulfillment. Their resistance cannot be exonerated on any normal grounds of right or justice or humanity because it is resistance against God in divine commitment to "His people."

How should Christians respond to this situation? What are the final criteria by which to judge? Are they ethical or dogmatic, spiritual or merely textual, and, if textual, in what terms? And what of those Christians who have not come to the point of asking any questions at all? The emotions that accompany these issues are as painful and as stressful as the questions themselves.

Surely the paramount Christian fact that must govern all else is the principle of undifferentiating grace. Whatever the mystery of Israel, biblically and since, whatever the warrant of Zion, they do not and cannot constitute for the Christian mind any deviation from equal divine justice and inclusive divine compassion. Specialness in Jewry has been historically, and gratefully, justified for us in the Jewish apostolic discovery from within it of an open New Testament peoplehood under God in which there are "no more strangers" (Eph. 2:19). The category of "mere Gentiles" is at an end. To be sure, rabbinic and contemporary Jewry does not see it so. Their ongoing faith in an exceptionality never fulfilled in openness commands and deserves Christian respect. Indeed all faith, in its own inner recognizances, deserves a genuine tolerance and a discerning right-to-be from those outside it. But such positive awareness does not override the criteria integrity is bound to bring to the situations any faith entails on others in its historical effects. Jewry and Judaism have needed and have invoked that safeguard more than any others in their own long tragedy of misreading and injustice. The overriding criteria of Christian perception have to be those of equal grace and common justice. From these there can be no proper exemption, however alleged or presumed. Chosenness cannot properly be either an ethnic exclusivism or a political facility.

In a strange and paradoxical way the actual history of political Zionism confirms a nonexceptionality about Israel. Though the mythic exceptionality powerfully continues and powerfully avails, it does so within a pattern of events and policies that immerse Israel in a common human quality. On its own showing Zionism wants to be like other nations—and contrives to be. Israel is caught like any other state in the pleas, the ploys, and the crimes of "normal" power behavior. It had its Stern Gang; it has its Mossad and its Beth Shin, as notorious as any. The mystique of faith does not exempt these from the shrug of cynicism or the reproach of regret they would merit anywhere. One cannot unilaterally sacralize statehood in this human world. Experience should perhaps have persuaded Zionists that the mystique cannot ride with the reality.

Yet it vigorously persists. In some realist quarters it does so rather on pragmatic grounds, as it has numerous advantages in respect of "image" and of active partisanship from much Christian approval of its claims. The secular mind of David Ben-Gurion was well apprised of the value of what was to him the biblical legend.[5] Others, however, hold the divine mandate tenaciously and ignore or disavow how compromising is the context of political means and ends in which it is fulfilled.

II

But the actual history of the mystique of Israel in the shape of political Zionism is only a corroboration of the deeper Christian need to disallow Israeli exceptionality in view of its human consequences in the Palestinian situation. To sustain that need as Christian takes us into vexed and tangled questions of biblical authority and exegesis. How should we interpret now the ancient conviction of covenanted election? How should we read now the ardent prophecies about "the land" and return from exile? In particular, how should Arab Christians do so in the painful ambiguity of "blessing the Lord God of Israel" when the Israel is that of Menachem Begin, Moshe Sharon, Rabbi Kahane and the Anṣār internment camps—not the Israel of Zechariah the priest or of Luke the Christian in their Benedictus?

For some, at their distance from this pain, the absolute answer is: It is so; God chose the Jews; the land is theirs by divine gift. These dicta cannot be questioned or resisted. They are final. Such verdicts come infallibly from Christian biblicists for whom Israel can do no wrong—thus fortified. But can such positivism, this unquestioning finality, be compatible with the integrity of the prophets themselves? It certainly cannot square with the open peoplehood under God which is the crux of New Testament faith. Nor can it well be reconciled with the ethical demands central to law and election alike.

It is fair to believe that the Judaic faith in unique destiny has educated us into a perspective that honors it only in gratefully transcending it. This is so because the triad of identity on which it stood—and stands—belongs alike to all human experience in time and place. There is a basic human sense, universally known but separably compelling, of ancestry, territory, and memory. Who and where and whence—the tribe, the land, the story—belong in all corporate consciousness. Jewry had every right to such awareness of destiny in being, occupying, residing, and perpetuating. So doing, they witnessed to their distinctive faith in divine gift, divine warrant, and divine debt. Their faith in the God of Israel was their faith about themselves. It was these deep denominators of community that inspired the chroniclers of patriarchs and the historians of kings. But we must recognize the tribal enmities and the ethnic and territorial tensions that found form and sanction in those narratives about Ishmael and Esau, Agag and the Philistines. We cannot and should not install these as perpetual warrant for contemporary politics nor approve Joshua today because he was once a tribal warrior hero. The great prophets forbid such legitimation of tenancy and tradition in neglect of the weightier matters of compassion, equality, and righteousness. There is no divine mandate to override divine meanings once these have been perceived as universal. A faith's assurance must stand in direct relation to a faith's accountability.

There are happily many in Israel who allow it is so. One of the ironies is that "biblical" Christians in the West, and especially in the U.S.A., embarrass at least some Israeli consciences by the crudity of their sponsorship of Israeli right and their unconcern with Palestinian tragedy. That whole perspective is awry. The sense of history and the sense of identity that together properly relate Jewry with the land of Israel have to be seen in terms which rightly comprehend the nature of biblical revelation, as cumulative, dynamic, and ultimate only in being moral.

The category of "revelation" itself, to which all dogmatists appeal, cannot by its very nature be arbitrary. Its writ turns on its acceptance as such. There are no agreed criteria external to it by which such recognition of it can be evaluated or warranted. It stands only in its own recognizances. Whatever else these may be thought liable to involve, they must surely undertake an honesty with all that its inner assurance entails of outward consequences for others. Palestinians—whatever may have obtained under

Joshua—must be seen now as a test case for the doctrine of Jewish "election." It would be a tragic betrayal of the prophets of that revelation to underwrite injustice, exploitation, or insensitivity to these, by an arbitrary interpretation of what the prophets could have meant. Exoneration of their hearers was the last thing those prophets intended.

That ruling principle of exegesis apart, there is also the question of frames of reference and interpretation. Prophetic ministry was always to an immediate audience. It might well have future implications, but these were always within a present relevance, rather than predictive. Least of all could the predictive element be credibly so in senses that—on the view of some pro-Zionists in the West—only come into calendar fulfillment after two millennia. Where calendar predictions occur in the comfort of exiles, they are likely to be symbolic rather than statistical. The principle of hope is translated into anticipations of times. Hope always has times just as mariners have horizons, but these are never stretched to scores of centuries. Horizons are never invisibly distant.

It seems fair to conclude that promises of return to the land are the form duly taken by the sense of divine fidelity and the durability of vocation. They speak a tenacity in adversity, and they affirm the mutual nonrelinquishment of God and His people, of which tenancy in the land is the sign and exile the seeming—but only seeming—denial. The experience between exile and return is the proving ground of that relationship. The several pledges and visions of renewed occupancy of the land in the prophets of the exile had their measure of historical fulfillment in the biblical story and in the history between the Testaments. Rome in the first and second Christian centuries renewed the exile in seemingly permanent diaspora, after the partial and intermittent renewals of Hasmonean, Maccabean, and Herodian times.

When and as Rome did so, the emerging Christian faith was already detaching itself from the old centrality of land and people, fulfilling itself in openness to all humanity. Being "in Christ" was the essential location of community within "the temple of his body." This emancipated Christians from any necessary preoccupation with other holy territory. Their continuing interest in Jerusalem was with its need of human compassion and interchurch aid or with the sacrament of geography in the memory of redemption.

On its own other premises, it was and is entirely valid for the Judaic mind to draw hope and vigor from prophetic promises and to claim now in Israeli prowess and achievement a fulfillment of their tenor. But it would be wrong to read those promises after the lapse of more than two millennia as adumbrating—still less as mechanically underwriting—what Israeli determination has now accomplished, as if there were thereby a divine order of the day setting aside all moral, human, and spiritual considerations. If we are to join Jeremiah with Weizmann, Ezekiel with Abba Eban, or Micah with Yitzhak Shamir across a score and five centuries we must do so with a livelier imagination of how incommensurate they are. Verbal proof texts will not serve us, but only the urgent righteousness of the prophets we invoke.

To hold that this states a right biblical loyalty may be accused of bringing its own presuppositions, but there is no exegesis that lacks these. All textual interpretation stands in the instincts and sympathies of each interpreter. The intention of scripture is all too easily victim to the intentions of the reader, never more so than when emotions run deep. The arbitrary citation of texts does not escape. Only honest perspective can preserve the text from serving as pretext. Only in a compassionate will to such honesty can the tangled issues of biblical meanings in the current scene be resolved. The plea made here will not deny to Zionism the readings it cherishes but it will subject them to the ultimate themes of the sources they inherit. It will certainly deny to Christians any pro-Zionism alien alike to the prophets and the apostles. Is there not implicit in all faiths a desire to be acknowledged, conceded from outside themselves? Otherwise, why would some of them be missionary? Such desire to be acknowledged, because of "chosen peoplehood," is more crucial to Jewish self-awareness than to any other, but the quest for such acknowledgment must derive from the highest within it and not—as is the case with much western sympathy—from the crudest.

III

All these burdens of mind and spirit devolve most acutely of all on Arab Christians. It is urgent for outsiders to reckon perceptively with the contradiction between spiritual ancestor and political enemy under which Christians suffer in the Middle East. For Israel is both. The very name is double-edged. So is the query so often addressed to Palestinians: Why not peace with Israel? Which Israel? Territorially there are several: that of United Nations' partition of 1947, that of 1948–1949, that of post-Suez invasion 1956, that of 1967, with their different acreages of mandated Palestine.[6] Spiritually the dimensions are no less indeterminate. In what terms, given its sharp internal divisions, does it and will it exist? Zionism has often utilized ambiguity. Its intentions and measures to fulfill them have been deliberately shrewd and flexible. Purposes were kept in reserve for future occasion on the way to the next *fait accompli.* At the outset they could even accommodate dreams of Arab benefit, even Arab acquiescence and profit. There is no such illusory benediction now, whether for Arabs in juridical

Israel or for those on the West Bank in its indeterminate status as neither annexed nor negotiable. Tragedies have run too deep and too far.

Thus Israel presents itself to Arab Palestinian experience as inveterate enemy, with a vested interest in the political nonexistence of Palestinians. Warning in 1969 against the very "concept of Palestine" Menachem Begin wrote: "If this is Palestine and not the land of Israel then you are conquerors and not tillers of the land. You are invaders. If this is Palestine then it belongs to a people who lived here before you."[7] Yet it was explicitly to a "Palestine" that the Balfour Declaration referred, to be greeted as such as the very springboard of political Zionism. A territorial expression which in 1947 was partitionable with enthusiasm and in 1967 arguably negotiable for peace is now an indivisible whole from which there can be never amputation. The existing population embarrasses the dispositions of the map.

The Christian elements of that existing population, however, belong with another Israel of biblical psalmody and prophethood, with something perennially shared and celebrated. It needs more than many western Christians have been prepared to bring to register the tensions here. The Old Testament is read in churches, but "Philistia" figures there as the enemy, the thorn in the flesh, the butt of irony and hatred. Psalm 60, for example ("Philistia, be thou glad of me"), is a satirical hymn of triumph celebrating Philistia's defeat. Psalm 108 repeats the tune. In both psalms Moab is a bowl for Jewish washerwomen. Throughout the histories too and many of the prophets runs the same theme of antipathy and scorn. Christians in the West can have the exploits of Samson, Samuel, Saul, David, and Jehu and the rest, in lectionary and psalm as ancient sagas happening to strange "heathen" far away. Arab Christians have to accommodate them—if at all—in the immediacy of their own dispossession and exile. The biblical victims are their own people, their predecessors in the land. These parts and tones of the Bible have a strange ring in the context of what, for some in Israel, is the worthy emulation of the old triumphs. Given the armed settlements, the military occupation, the internment camps, and the bulldozed villages, there is no refuge in the kind of allegorization that may facilitate biblical loyalties uneasily elsewhere. It would help the imagination if we were to visualize English or American progenitors and places as the villains and victims of the scriptures from which they have their forms of faith: "over Yorkshire will I cast my shoe" or "the Lord will be at war with Californians from generation to generation."

Biblically it is always Philistines (i.e., Palestinians) who are the obstacles to God's own people. How do we—how do they—make good the universal grace in which all belong, against this bias of the old covenant, which casts them in an adversarial role? The question is urgent inasmuch as that role is still widely alleged in contemporary terms.[8] Palestinian Arabs are portrayed as aiming to finish off what Hitler began. Jewish implacability against them and their aspirations is sustained by imagining it to be so. Palestinianism is grimly held within that built-in suspicion of or distrust in the rest of humanity so characteristic of Jewish anxiety, but it is there in more desperate and anguished terms than any other by sheer accident of place. One can hear the overtones of Old Testament literature in the contemporary pen of Amos Oz, foremost among Israeli writers:

> In the distance were more and more strange mountains and strange villages stretching to the end of the world, minarets of mosques, Shu'afat, Nabī Samwil, the wail of a muezzin borne on the wind in the evening twilight, dark women, deadly sly, guttural youths. And a slight hint of brooding evil, distant, infinitely patient, forever observing you unobserved.[9]

Even the patience is sinister, and the sense of being perpetually watched by "unseen" assessors echoes the perennial trauma of the Jewish mind. Yet patience has a point. For it was not in fact until after 1967 that Palestinianism, a score of years in refugeedom, became activist and militant, abandoning the earlier quiescence that awaited the outer world's cognizance of their nationhood and an Arab world's realism in aiding it.[10] Those two nonviolent decades are often forgotten, while facile commentary overlooks the strain for Arab Christians of this daily conflict between tragic circumstance and spiritual meaning entailed by the paradox of "Israel."

How, then, should they respond to this contradiction at the very core of Christian existence? There is no operative point in the ingenious academic thesis that the promised land of biblical history is, after all, in western Arabia and that the Jordan crossed was in fact a *wādī* in the escarpment of the Hijāz.[11] Whatever the merits of that exhaustive study of place-names, it is powerless to alter the politics of belief. There is no salvation in archaeology.

But if studies in topography will not rewrite the traditional understanding of the ancient literature, Arab Christianity has somehow to detach itself from the more menacing parts of its Old Testament heritage. This must be so both in its theological focus and its liturgical usages. Such detachment does not mean repudiation but rather discernment and a perceptive concern to sift the abiding and universal dimensions of biblical heritage from the exclusive, tribal accents that modern political Zionism has emphasized anew in its anti-Arabism.

The task is difficult and painful, but it may be helped by the wider consideration that elsewhere also there are increasing questions about the monopoly of biblical sources in the lectionaries of Christian worship.[12] Interfaith studies suggest the need to rethink the confinement of lections at worship to the biblical Canon. Are there not more antecedents of grace, it is asked, than those explicit from Genesis to Malachi and arguably more inspiring than Leviticus or Chronicles?

But the specifically Arab case for such enlargement of perspective is more exacting and stressful because of the emotionally charged situation and the bitterness of daily experience. A response to the tension, for Arabs, between Israel-in-Scripture and Israel-in-Zionism can come only from within the conscience and wisdom of the local churches, not from external or patronizing advice. It may be helped, however, by a realization that in some degree other Christian churches are faced with urgent problems arising from the biblical tradition and its due place in liturgy. This is the more so because of the stridency in some quarters of the view that any biblically argued misgivings about political Zionism are no more than a crude and crafty anti-Semitism.

Therefore, one paramount duty of Arab Christianity, which has been patiently shouldered, is to insist that antipathy to Israel belongs within a "Semitism" that Arabs share and is in no sense anti-Semitic. Jewish hostility, to be sure, makes this insistence a painstaking task. It is Israeli Jewry itself, as we have seen, that forbids an abstract, ideal relation toward it on the part of Arab Christians. This is so because of the inevitable politicization of all relationships that Zionism imposes. Nevertheless, it is both right and urgent to distinguish between opposition to the state and attitudes toward a people and their faith. The common Abrahamic heritage of both Jews and Arabs could more readily come into its own were it not well-nigh canceled by the tyranny of the political confrontation.

Side by side with a steady repudiation of anti-Semitism goes a positive emphasis on the universal dimensions of psalmody and the prophets. Thankfully, passages such as Psalms 67 and 100 have their joyful currency in Arabic even though Psalms 60 and 108 and their like are topically impossible in Arab Christian worship. This is not some selective censorship of scripture but simply the exigencies of truth as demanded by the New Testament and induced by the daily situation. Admittedly, it is a vexing exercise. Some of the finest passages in the Hebrew scriptures—prophet, psalm, and history—are almost inextricably tied into triumphalist or vindictive sentiment impossible of Arab Christian currency in the present, or any, situation. External critics minded to reproach this position must, by the same token, have failed to understand what necessitates it.

IV

Apart from the issue of Arab Christian use of Hebrew scriptures, what of efforts on their part to relate to the spiritual heart of Judaism in Israel?

Should not the will to reconciliation and mutual conversation be paramount? Is it not the prime duty "to seek peace and ensue it"? Is not the peace movement in Israel the surest hope of all Arabs? Is it not vital to encourage and maximize the elements within Israeli society concerned for justice and alert to the Palestinian case? Strategy apart, are not peace and forgiveness the obligatory posture of any and every Christian?

Indeed so, despite the almost insuperable conditions of military control and political resistance. But for many in the Palestinian situation there is a near despair about the viability and the relevance of the religious factor. As we saw in Lebanon, the secular option seems the only feasible way, given that religions themselves have so far and so grimly contributed to the tragedy and given also their seeming futility as agents of peace. Palestinians have some cause to be skeptical of the efficacy of peace advocacy within Israel, useful perhaps in helping an image for the outside world but unlikely to be operative in the corridors of decision. If such conclusions are a guilty cynicism, at least they exist, and the realism they represent is certainly a heavy burden, which those who resist them must continually carry.

Where Arab Christian and Israeli Jewish dialogue has been undertaken, inexorably the constraints of the situation take over and things political nullify things spiritual. A will to dialogue on the part of Palestinian Christians can be used as proof that all is well. It can be cited as welcome evidence of actual, or potential, "normalcy," contentedness with the status quo. The other party may desire and pursue it for just those reasons. The genuine sincerity of peace-seeking Israelis may be approved by the cynical precisely for its merit in presenting the situation as other than it truly is. Many in Arab Christianity have, therefore, felt that they must forgo, or at least defer, any will to dialogue in the Spirit until the claim for justice in the land has first been satisfied. They sense a hypocrisy in doing otherwise, arguing that such priority of the political is forced upon them by the very nature of political Zionism. Since the political logic of Zionism was required of and by Jews from their European experience, it suggests no reason for the Arab mind to suppose otherwise in response to experience of Jewry.

Arab Christian vocation in Israel is thus the prisoner of Zionist prerequisites, which are "submission." Positive spiritual rapport has either to concede this or to imply it. Either way it cannot be authentic. To behave in neighborly terms is to imply that neighborhood exists. The implication is denied by the daily toll of oppression and bitterness. To forgive would then be to condone, until the scene of the forgiveness is ready for amends. Thus, dialogue from the Israeli side remains suspect and ambiguous unless and until it incorporates a will to political solution. The outsider may see ways of escaping from this impasse, but only by the detachment outsiders enjoy. Participants have this inescapable sense of compromise as long as parties, appearing to meet as equals, in fact exist as the occupied and the occupiers, the powerless and the powered.

Furthermore, the very topics of potential religious dialogue are issues of political contention, whether the mutual significance of Jerusalem, the nature of land sanctity, or the interpretation of biblical and immediate history. There is a sense in which the law, rather than theology, has hope of actual relevance *in situ.* Lawyers have successfully fought cases in the courts on behalf of Arabs dispossessed, fined, exiled, or imprisoned under repressive measures by the state or the army. They know that a new law or *diktat* will override the legal verdict and reinstate the punishment or fill the loophole. But the pyrrhic legal victory, however short-lived, at least witnesses to the actual suffering and the official ambivalence around the rule of law. This is not something which religious conversation can achieve—or not so squarely.[13] There is a precision about cases in court. As long as legal ideals obtain and courts can sustain a rugged independence of the state, then rulings—if not redress—bear their witness. Such concreteness is seldom within the reach of dialogue about faith. For those, on either side, engaged in the latter may well be quite unable to implement what they agree. The exercise is then close to futility and may become an indulgence in wishfulness.

To fear so, it might be said, is a counsel of despair. Reconciliation must proceed despite its pitfalls. Yet hard experience sobers hope. Christian minority status, in any event, means that the major religious factor must be Islamic. That returns us to the problematics of religious motivations and divisions. When the Palestinian cause was strongly islamicized in the 1930s and 1940s during the ascendancy of the then Grand Muftī, Ḥajj Amīn al-Ḥusainī, leadership ended in total failure. Subsequently, the P.L.O. has been largely secular in its orientation. That may be changing now, given how barren of results that pattern has been. Yet it did hold promise on the view that if Zionist Israel has to be deromanticized and its mythicization countered, then a secular logic must be invoked.

A still more compelling factor for some has been the acute disillusion, in sensitive minds, about the role of religion throughout the Arab story. Palestinian Christianity, in its several modes, has had to respond to this mood of near despair. A notable exponent of the betrayal by religion was Fā'iz Sāyigh (1922–1980), a son of the Presbyterian pastor serving finally in Tiberias, though originating from Syria. With degrees in Philosophy from the American University of Beirut Fā'iz Sāyigh held political appointments at the United Nations and in the Arab Office in New York. He used them skillfully to further the Palestinian cause but with no illusory hopes. Indeed, his penchant for the Danish philosopher Søren Kierkegaard bred in him a kindred despair. He was acutely critical of what he saw as the religious factors in the disarray of Arabism. Early in his diplomatic career he wrote:

> How and of what ought I to think? What may and must I hope for? In what ought I to believe and in what faith ought I to live, now that the basic concepts of the traditional religions have shrunk into hollow catchwords and religious fellowships have degenerated into fossilised groupings, generating blind fanaticism but not edifying communion, stimulating self-seeking attachments but not self-giving loyalties, and serving particular political purposes, disruptive of national unity, instead of promoting inward, loving, joyful, creative, spiritual experience? Whither ought I to turn for guidance? Where am I to find fellowship?[14]

Depressed by the frustration of his youthful enthusiasm for Arab unity and by the culpable futility over Palestine of the major Arab states, he deplored the failure of the clerics of both religions to transcend communal self-interest and to lift their people to a spiritual interpretation of their tragedy. He regretted Islam's claim to displace all else, by virtue of postdating others, as a betrayal of the principle of integration vital to Arab unity. He saw Christian minorities as too prudent, too self-preoccupied, and too introverted for any genuine spirituality.

Some aspects of such existential despair will concern us in the two final chapters. Fā'iz Sāyigh was an Arab thinker of rare quality of mind—a man of deep spirituality moving, nevertheless, in the realist world of international politics and penetrating beyond the vulgarities of propaganda. He sensed the sharp Christian dilemma within Palestinianism and took the measure of the tragedy with which Zionism confronted it. Other mentors, of different cast of mind, have seen secularity as the political option without appreciating that secular solutions cannot avail merely by marginalizing religion. For the more religions disclaim politically, the more urgent become their spiritual maturity and vision.

The specifically Christian role within the Palestinian reckoning with Israel is thus resolved into two comparably exacting aspects, namely, its part in a secular pattern and/or its situation within a response denominated by Islam. The Palestine National Covenant proposed to accommodate pre-1948 Jews in a secular "Palestine."[15] Though irrelevant in practical terms, that stance reflects the desire—surely corroborated by the tragedy of Lebanon—to align Muslim and Christian identities together in a national cause. In the story of the P.L.O. since 1967, there has been a steady concert between them avoiding invidious discrimination. Christians, proportionate to their number in the whole, have played an equal, if not at times greater, part in the political, literary, and activist struggle. Despite the association of Christians with western interests and with biblical "problematics," there has been no marked tendency to equate Palestinian with Islamic. Whether that situation and the policy of the secular image will continue to hold is unclear. Islamic militants have reason to argue that the secular option has failed, except in achieving a transition for Palestinianism from being perceived as "refugeedom" to being acknowledged as a nationhood. But image recognition is a frustrating success if it cannot be translated into political reality.

The Christian vocation would, of course, be harder still in the setting of a Palestinian move into Islamic militancy. Such a development may arise not only from frustration over secular policy but in response to the increasing element of religious fanaticism within Israel. Like breeds like. Perhaps the mystique of Israel, it might be argued, is best confronted by a rival invocation of God in the tradition of *Allāhu akbar*. Islam, after all, has a long experience of the militant legitimation of identity. It is perhaps remarkable that, given the nature of Zionism, Palestinian secular counsels have persisted so long.

Moreover, there is much in the drift of events to conspire against moderation. Palestinian Christians have their share in the trauma of creeping annexation, deportation, and distress. Polarization intensifies for all as the local population wearies under privation and in despair of change and Israeli attitudes harden in the toils of an intractable destiny of confrontation. New Jewish settlements, financially encouraged by official policy, spell a provocation often rewarded with confiscations and the bulldozing of homes. There are grievous constraints on Arab agriculture: new vines and olives may not be planted, nor wells sunk, without official permit, which is hard, or impossible, to obtain, but wells for Jewish settlers are drilled by army engineers.

The fact that these oppressive measures and the asperity they embody are the subject of deep internal dispute within Israel is tribute to the conscience of some Israelis and to the surviving, if embattled, ideals of original Zionism. But the anxiety complex and the momentum of suspicion and enmity mean that advocates of restraint and fair dealing are roundly disowned. The post-1967 case for territorial concession in the interests of Jewish homogeneity is now scarcely heard. Homogeneity, coveted as it is, may be secured in other ways, and meanwhile maximum territory is seen as the vital condition of the Zionist future. The strength of diehard views is so great that any Israeli government that might suggest serious negotiation with Palestinian demands, even if ever electable, would have its policy overturned by popular resistance or coup d'état. The much-vaunted democracy of Israel would not itself be safe from erosion or subversion in the trauma of that scenario.

That calculus of realism by which, in effect, it is *politically* impossible for Israel to make peace, by reason of the dire consequences of doing so for its own unity, has been bitterly confirmed by the events of the late summer of 1990. The Iraqi invasion and brief annexation of Kuwait have intensified Israeli apprehension of Arab—or at least Iraqi—intentions and strengthened the case for total intransigence. Israeli abstention from retaliation against Iraq during the repeated Scud missile attacks, though eminently sensible in itself, earned arguable assets in U.S. esteem, to be cashed later against expected pressures to peace conferences and concessions. Peace negotiation on the part of Israel can be urged by the plea that if the occupancy of Kuwait demanded to be reversed, so also did that of Palestine. That case, however, is readily countered by the obvious disparity in the antecedent circumstances. Linkage between U.N. Resolutions 242 and 660 did, and did not, exist. Meanwhile, Palestinian alignment with Saddam Ḥusain, though emotionally comprehensible, seriously prejudiced the hope of American sponsorship over Resolution 242, as well as bitterly exposing them to retaliation on the part of the restored Kuwaitis. The whole trauma of 1990–1991 has grievously accentuated the Palestinians' tragedy, immersing them in chronic distress, cutting off their grants in aid and leaving their ultimate goal to the mercy of vague and pious western sentiment about a "peace process" made the more forlorn by Israeli unyieldingness.

V

In weighing these and other pressures of circumstance on the Palestinian Christian minority, it is important also to remember how far it has been attenuated by emigration. Whether in Israel proper (post-1948) or in the West Bank and Gaza, Palestinians have been hostages of this impasse in the clash of the Zionist dream with the facts of Arab demography. In the slow but sure judaization of their homeland and the dismaying prospect of their future, it is no surprise that there has been a wide dispersion, both elsewhere into the Middle East and to the Americas and Canada. That quest for a geographical salvation Jews themselves know well, but it only deepens the forlornness of the residue that remains, withdrawing the personnel and the initiatives that might have cheered and served it. Jews also know the sense of departure as betrayal and the yearning through absence to repair it. In some cases emigration has been goaded or forced by Israeli pressures. Those who remain know that much Israeli sentiment regards their presence as a frustration, casts reproachful eyes upon the birthrate, and waits for a land rid of them. In that atmosphere—at best ambiguous, at worst menacing—it is hard to anticipate genuine, feasible efforts at conciliation or to arrest, on Christian grounds, the gravitation to extremism implicit in all such confrontation.

It has often been remarked that the future of Palestinians lies in the hands of American Jews. The crucial dependence of Israeli militarism and the Israeli economy on U.S. grants, loans, and loan cancellation is such that U.S. policy has, arguably, the leverage (were Jewish American lobbies to allow) to require policies in Israel conformable to Arab aspirations. That very fact—aside from the large question of its eventuation—could arouse a diehardness in Zion that only intensifies Palestinian suffering. Israel is no client state—except financially. The autonomy of Israel, passionately cherished, would not be amenable to economic or political duress, but the very suggestion of it, in a showdown situation, would excite all the deep phobias in Zionism to the further despair of the Palestinians. Thus the politics of realism prove also to be the politics of peril. Every shape of hope conjures up prospects for the worse. There would seem to be now no substance in the western direction of Arab Christian appeal. The final crux can only be in Israel itself, where the crucial factors lie and where few hopeful ones survive.

Another daunting feature of the situation for the Christian mind, Arab or western, is its chronic captivity to lobbies. Everything at stake between Zionism and the Arab world is victim to partisanship and propaganda. The business of lobbies is to anesthetize the mind, to resist all reasoned case making, and to imprison all issues in obduracy. Truth may sometimes be reached in courts of law by this habit of aggressive case making with insistent shutting out of contrary evidence by either party, but courts have authority to reach a verdict. There is no parallel to that judicial arbiter in the welter of propaganda by which Palestinian themes are overborne. Trial by lobby is instant condemnation.

The political and religious scene in the United States is chronically liable to such mind-sealing confrontation, where things Israeli are at issue. Elections, to be sure, take place to formulate and then effectuate the democratic will, but executive and congressional careers can be intimidated, if not untimely terminated, by the pressures and the wiles of Jewish interests operating in Israeli causes.[16] Initiatives that might well effectuate a wiser future for Israel itself are daunted or deterred by the closed mind of partisans, whose verdicts exclude all considerations but their own. Arab elements are, to be sure, numerous and vocal in the American context, but even if they could command the expertise and influence of Israel's lobbyists the evil of sheer partisanship would only be intensified. Politics may well seem to the bemused observer to be an untidy and an ugly means to necessary ends, but where its devices are recruited and suborned to passionate prejudice its deep vocation is compromised and betrayed. It is then deprived of the open mind, the honest will, and the genuine debate without which it cannot register its proper ends. Prejudice becomes the despair of truth.

With the exception of Suez and 1956, the years have chronicled a variety of themes around the politics of Zion in Washington in which this partisan mind has shaped or otherwise frustrated policy and—perhaps more seriously—obscured the due criteria of ethics and wisdom. There has been a constant ambivalence about the issue of "settlements" in occupied territory and their bearing on U.S. grants and Israeli obligations. The status of Jerusalem and the location of embassies, the conditions of arms utilization, the military measures overriding normal civilian rights, the exiling of dissidents, the practice of detention without trial, the treatment of peace activists—all these have figured in the instant and constant vigilance of the lobbyists, urging or discounting as the case required. It has been a vigilance which, more than all else, needed—yet instinctively shunned—a compassionate, ethical, and spiritual reckoning with its own assumptions and with the vision of original Zion with "watchmen on the walls." The lobbyists, by and large, do not consort well with the prophets.

These are, no doubt, issues for the American conscience, but they weigh heavily on Christian Arabs, thanks to the ties and sympathies that relate them to the West and to the wide dispersion there of Arab emigration.

The developments in Palestinian policy in 1988 have fallen foul of this same lobby mentality or are only painfully and slowly reprieved from it. Recognition of the State of Israel has always been a hard quandary for the P.L.O. To recognize was problematic because "Israel" was an indeterminate entity both on the map and in international law. Was its juridical extent—that of the 1947 U.N.O. vote—being accepted, or the various *de facto* extents of 1956, 1967, and since? Recognition meant something conclusive in advance, or in default, of something unnegotiated. It meant, furthermore, a reconciling to the final failure of a long-cherished loyalty to "justice," an implied confession that a costly fidelity to land and identity had, indeed, been intransigence as viewed by the realists of this world. It meant a verdict against oneself in the sharpest terms, a concession of long-term defeat as the price of a limited, precarious, and perhaps nonviable hope. It meant being cast upon the goodwill, the wisdom, the peace-will of one's own despoilers, one's old and still-enigmatic adversaries.

Palestinian Christians have had some notable part in the initiation of that still unmapped and unfrontiered recognition, but to have it saluted with skeptical distrust, dismissed as a mere ploy, a subterfuge, or an evident conspiracy is painful to all its mentors. These, of course, are not the whole of Palestinians, and the new situation is dangerously poised on the restraint of other elements implacably opposed to the recognition. Nonrestraint may well jeopardize the whole initiative and play into the hands of those in Israel who dismiss it out of hand. A proper caution need not foreclose a due exploration of its promise, for, if Palestinianism has risked the disowning of its intransigence, so also must Israel.

Through the long years of Palestinian obduracy about recovery of the whole territory, idle as that vision has long been, Israeli opportunism has had a free hand. The advocates of a smaller, homogeneous Israel, trading land for true Zion, had no clinching occasion after 1967 since no Palestinian overtures responded. Creeping annexation by settlements has proceeded in the decades since 1967 unhindered by any "settlement" of peace. Palestinian policy has merely facilitated Israeli options offered by the lack of it. This feature of the situation, so advantageous to Israelis, so inhibiting to Palestinians, is now ended, at least insofar as Palestinian will to recognition of Israel holds and is not torpedoed by hostile elements.

Its ending, if sustained, puts the onus squarely and unavoidably—as it has not hitherto been—on the Israelis. Given how sharply divided the population of Israel is with respect to policy toward the Palestinians, it is natural that Israel should regret the post-1988 Palestinian position, inasmuch as it forecloses the option that existed beforehand. Yet it is one which international opinion—not to say a discerning Israeli perception of the future—requires to be acknowledged and undertaken. For Israel is now more directly and less escapably confronted with the necessity of coming to political and psychological terms with Palestinianism.

Yet precisely for that reason the instinct to continue to evade it is strong. Hence the twofold stance, the one side of which is to continue discounting the genuineness of the recognition, the other the insistence on responding only in the context of "the Arab states." Israel, it is said, will gladly negotiate directly with its Arab neighbors, but that deliberately excludes the Palestine equation. To arabize the matter is to calculate on its perpetual avoidance. It is to repudiate a Palestinian nationality as party to negotiation which, by Palestinian definition, is to repudiate it altogether. Not since the 1960s have Palestinians been looking to other Arabs for their salvation. Within the realities of inter-Arab politics they have become as insistently self-reliant as Zionists themselves. For neither in the confrontation are there saviors by proxy.

VI

In the balance of realism, Israeli policy seems set to prefer the obduracy of denying negotiability to the P.L.O. to the domestic political and religious upheaval any negotiated accommodation with Palestinians would entail. But that preference, so evident to date, could at length be still more inimical to the future of Israel, given the growing international will to see negotiation concluded and the ever-deteriorating compromise of Zionism for lack of it. If there was a logic, between 1948 and 1967, in the Israeli mind, of waiting for Palestinianism to acquiesce in the irretrievable loss of 80 percent of the land, there could be a similar logic in awaiting, interminably, since 1967 an acquiescence in the loss of 100 percent. It worked in the former score of years. For the 20-percent West Bank, so called, is what is now at stake. Why cannot it be expected to work again, while riding out meanwhile the clamor of outsiders and the postures, of any and every kind, of the Palestinians? But history is more than logic, and there is another and different logic, thought to belong with Zionism itself, whereby cynical disavowal of a mutual humanity finally destroys one's own.

In this chronic tangle of history, what of Christian Palestinians insofar as they can influence events? We noted earlier their case for refraining from spiritual dialogue prior to any overall solution, since relationships can be distorted to prove that normalcy exists without one. Nevertheless, it remains a Christian principle that the measure we would receive is the measure we must give. What we would like to generate in the other we must be ready to anticipate within ourselves. Only trust has the power to evoke what it awaits. In a context so vexed and so prolonged, skepticism is the easiest of options and, by the same token, the one likeliest to vex and prolong it further.

Two ventures of hope on the part of Palestinians within juridical Israel proper (i.e., the 1947–1948 borders) may be instanced here. The one is the joint Jewish/Palestinian enterprise, Neve Shalom; the other, the writings of Father Elias Chacour and Canon Na'im Ateek. Neve Shalom, known in Arabic as *Wāḥat al-Salām*, or Oasis of Peace, is located, symbolically, on the frontier of Israel with the West Bank. Its site is leased from the monks of the Trappist Monastery at Latrun and commands a splendid vista westward across the *Shephelah* and coastal plain. But its logic is directed into the Judean hills and Jerusalem, from which visually the escarpment cuts it off. It receives no grant-in-aid from the Israeli government though it may be sometimes cited as a proof of tolerance. It embodies a vision of a future in which Jew and Arab would harmonize but it cannot of itself fill out the vision with the hard factors of political solution. Those factors might be said to be withdrawn as far as the silent monks who are its landlords. Along the highway close at hand are the preserved items of military hardware left by the Israeli Haganah courageously defending the line to Jerusalem from the coast in 1948.

Neve Shalom was founded in 1972 by Father Bruno, a Dominican and by birth a Jew. The joint Jew/Christian community numbers less than a hundred. All are Israeli citizens. Membership is a difficult surrender of alienation, a will to equal participation in which identity is mutually honored. The members are not isolated from their respective worlds but maintain family and other visits outside and aim to bring their leaven there and to engage their vision with the facts they carry back. They live with the pain of how marginal they are and with the realism of observers who dismiss them as dreamers subsisting on foreign gifts or as "liberals" responding to feelings of guilt. They believe, nevertheless, that theirs is a gesture of silence in the midst of stridency and of mutuality in the face of stereotyping enmity.

Father Elias Chacour is a priest of the Melchite church, born in the village of Biram in Galilee and serving in Ibillīn in the same region of Israel proper. His village was destroyed in 1948 by the Israeli army, and he has lived through a long sequence of embittering events—confiscation, deportation of friends, bulldozing of homes, and military exactions against his community. These he has undertaken in his priestly, pastoral ministry among his people and has narrated in a reflective autobiography, *Blood Brothers.* The title refers to the relations that should exist between Jews and Arabs as fellow Semites.[17]

What makes his book remarkable is his ability, despite adversity via Zionism, to register with sympathy the Jewish reasons for Israel. During studies in France Chacour took a journey into Germany. An Arab armed with an Israeli passport with the enormity of the Holocaust still close in time, he mused on his predicament—an Israeli entering into Holocaust territory, external to its history, caught in its sequel, and traveling by its leave. He discovered the desperate logic of Zionism and wanted to approve. He explored its pre-Holocaust incentives, as Europe taught him what they had been. He contrasted those pure motives, that urgent logic, with the actualities of brutal oppression which he, as Palestinian, had witnessed and suffered. Inevitably he wondered why and how such beginnings in legitimacy had arrived at such illegitimate developments, such betrayal of themselves. His story is a telling example of an Arab Christian venture into painful comprehension of the Israeli soul, painful because both unable to exonerate and yet anxious to understand.

The pain is only sharpened by the fact that all too often Israeli sentiment, in requiring to be only justified, is unable to accept the sympathy. For to do so has implications that offend against its self-esteem. There is about us all a self-love that shuns the kind of honesty that presents its reproach of us in genuine empathy. We prefer a total animosity that we can dismiss as prejudice of mind and perversion of fact. The security of our intransigence is breached if we sense what, albeit against us, does not confront us with its own.

Thus a reviewer of *Blood Brothers* concedes that it is a rare and moving document but goes on to dismiss its effort to comprehend. The writer is not "a historian," lacks "a complete and accurate picture of historical reality," misses "most of the political nuances, diversities, and complexities of Zionism," and fails "to comprehend the motivation for establishing the Jewish state and the mentality of its Jewish citizens."[18] An initiative meant to identify seeds of hope sees them sown on apparently barren ground.

Prejudice against Palestinians may urge similar reservations about Na'im Ateek's *Justice and Only Justice: A Palestinian Theology of Liberation,*[19] in which an exposition of the Palestinian struggle incorporates a strenuous effort to appreciate the emotion, and the logic, within the Zionist dream. He shares with Chacour a will to comprehend the human travail of the Holocaust within the Jewish soul. But his lucid survey of the history of Zionism in his motherland, shot through with personal recollection, pleads the injustice of building Jewish vindication on the tragedy of another people. Should Palestinians be immolated for the sins of Hitler? He sees the "benediction of the peace-makers" as belonging only with an honest acknowledgment of the brutal facts of history *and* a perceptive reading of the import of scriptural promises and demands. The book communicates with telling authority the experience out of which mutual initiatives must arise. Palestinians must know themselves possessed of the Christian clues by which tragedy has to be interpreted. "Those who suffer can forgive," but forgiveness is not transacted unless there is an end, in the other party, to the illusion of innocence. The "liberation" for which Ateek bravely pleads is from the hardness of heart that excludes the others' humanity and from the enmity that abandons hope. In political terms it means the divisibility of the land and the equal right of both parties to the perceived requisite of statehood as the shape of self-fulfillment. *Justice and Only Justice* goes beyond the proviso in its own title. But it is those other dimensions, beyond justice, dimensions of mutual compassion, of love and mercy, that are so far to seek, making justice also no less distant, no less elusive.

Nowhere is this impasse more tragically symbolized than in the status of Jerusalem agreed by all to be the ultimate index to the issue on which there is never agreement. Early and sanguine expositions of the ideal of Zion could concede its internationalization as the capital of an arguable federal or binational state. Not so any longer. Jerusalem, annexed and enlarged in 1967, categorically exempt from any feasible dispositions of the West Bank, and inalienably Judaic, cannot be shared unless politically monopolized. There where all emotions meet, exceptionality and distinction are insistently signified. Yet it is by name "the possession of peace" denied and denying "the peace of possession."[20] The core of all we can say of Palestinian Christianity is that it shares, for reasons both Arab and

Christian, in the despair of that paradox. What may be to others regretful and remote is to those who belong there intimate and tragic.

Notes

1. Quoted in T. E. Lawrence, *The Seven Pillars of Wisdom* (Garden City, N.Y.: Doubleday, Doran & Co., 1935), p. 674.

2. The term *Heimstatte* ("national home") was coined by Max Nordau, with a view to disarming suspicion about any larger intentions for statehood. Writing to fellow Zionists who needed persuading, he described it as "a circumlocution that would express all that we meant, but would say it in a way that would avoid provoking the Turkish rulers of the coveted land. . . . I suggested it," he went on, "as a synonym for 'State.' This is the history of the much commented expression. It was equivocal, but we all understood what it meant. To us it signified *Judenstaat* then and it signifies the same now." See Christopher Sykes, *Two Studies in Virtues* (New York: Alfred A. Knopf, 1953), p. 100.

3. Unless one says that Palestinians have their homeland elsewhere. But to do so denies them their own self-awareness, proved at great cost. A nation is best defined as a people believing themselves to be one.

4. Though in her famous remark denying the existence of any Palestinians, Golda Meir was not always consistent. In *My Life* (London: George Weidenfeld & Nicholson, 1975), p. 39 she wrote: "The first Palestinians I ever encountered were . . . ." There follow the names of Ben-Zvi, Israel's second president, David Ben-Gurion, and Ya'akov Zerubavel, a well-known writer. "I listened spellbound to the Palestinians," she continued, but restricted the denominator to Jewish immigrants.

5. David Ben-Gurion wrote: "The message of the Chosen People makes sense in secular, nationalist and historical terms. . . . The Jews can be considered a self-chosen people. . . . Though I reject theology, the single most important book in my life is the Bible" (*Recollections,* ed. Thomas R. Bransten [London: MacDonald & Co., 1970], pp. 120–125).

6. The partition vote of 1947 awarded 52 percent of mandated Palestine to the Zionists and 48 percent to the Palestinians. After the battles and armistices of 1948–1949 the percentages were 80 and 20. While Sinai was held in 1956 and post-1967 along with the Golan Heights, the total equalled around 300 percent. Sinai was returned to Egypt in negotiations in the 1970s. Juridically Israel to date is 52 percent, enlarged by annexation to 80 percent and by occupancy to 100 percent.

7. Menachem Begin in *Yediot Aharanot,*Oct. 17, 1969; quoted from Arie Bober, ed., *The Other Israel: The Radical Case Against Zionism* (Garden City, N.Y.: Doubleday & Co., Anchor Books, 1972), p. 77.

8. A recent example is Joan Peters, *From Time Immemorial: The Origins of the Arab-Jewish Conflict over Palestine* (Salem, N.H.: Michael Joseph, 1985).

9. Amos Oz, *The Hill of Evil Counsel: Three Stories,* trans. Nicholas De Lange (London: Chatto & Windus, 1978). See also the novels of Moshe Shamir, e.g., *Beneath the Sun* (Jerusalem, 1950), with its stress on the "blood, sand and sun" of

the Sabra possession of the holy soil and the mood of vigilant physical virility set against all human impediments.

10. The P.L.O. dates, in military terms, from around 1965. It was the 1967 defeat of the Arab armies and the further exile that effectively launched it.

11. This is the thesis of Kamāl S. Salībī. His case "rests mainly on a linguistic analysis of Biblical place-names . . . consistently mistranslated" and, on his view, persuasively identifiable in western Arabia (*The Bible Came from Arabia* [London, 1985]).

12. The confining of lectionary readings in Christian worship to the biblical Canon belongs with the western Reformation. The Eastern churches from the times of Origen and Jerome have used other writings and lives of the saints, as is clear from listings, for example, in the *Shepherd of Hermas* and the *First Letter of Clement.* In any event the device of set lectionaries was meant (a) to ensure orthodox teaching, and (b) to discriminate by selection between what was well suited, in clarity and content, for public listening and what was not. Both these ancient principles could sustain intelligent and temperate selection both from within and from outside the biblical Canon on the part of Arab Christians in their present adversities and the pains of scriptural ambiguity.

13. As, for example, in a lecture given by the Palestinian lawyer Jonathan Kuttāb at the Tantur Institute for Higher Theological Studies, Jerusalem. See, further, Rajah Shehadeh and Jonathan Kuttāb, *The West Bank and the Rule of Law* (Geneva: International Commission of Jurists and Law in the Service of Man, 1980).

14. Fā'iz Sāyigh, in *The Muslim World Quarterly* 43 (1952), p. 251.

15. See my *This Year in Jerusalem: Israel in Experience* (Greenwood, S.C.: Attic Press, n.d.), pp. 138f.

16. A conspicuous example is that of Senator Charles Percy of Illinois, whose political career was effectively destroyed by Zionist lobby avenging his readiness for Palestinian logic, guarded and balanced as it was. Other representatives took due note of their vulnerability.

17. Elias Chacour and David Hazard, *Blood Brothers* (Old Tappan, N.J.: Fleming H. Revell Co., 1984).

18. Don Peretz, in *International Review of Middle East Studies* (New York) 19 (1987), pp. 247–251.

19. Na'im Stifan Ateek, *Justice and Only Justice: A Palestinian Theology of Liberation* (New York: Orbis Books, 1990). See, further, the conclusion to chapter 11.

20. Through the long and notable mayoralty of Teddy Kollek, from 1967, Jerusalem may be said to have been predominantly "possessed of peace," in terms of civic amenities. It sustained a tourism competently administered and a vigorous, if also controversial, development. The resolve of post-1967 never to let the city be divided again has been physically achieved, but humanly it remains forever divided—by a unilateral success. See Teddy Kollek, *For Jerusalem: A Life* (New York: Random House, 1978); also Teddy Kollek and M. Perlmann, *Jerusalem,* 5th ed. (London, 1985).

CHAPTER

11

The Arab Christian Soul in Poetry, Art, and Liturgy

I

THERE IS A LEGEND in the tradition of Muḥammad in which a tree trunk, as he reclined beside it, began to yield music. The Muslim Palestinian poet Maḥmūd Darwish (b. 1942) takes the story into one of his verses and "the tree" becomes the cross of Jesus.[1] Music has not been central to Islam, except as it passes into Quranic chant or figures as reed and flute in the devotion of the Sufis, while the cross must be denied as neither actual, nor fitting, nor suited to save. Poetry, however, and the symbol of the suffering Jesus in it have found new expression in the life of the Arab world this century. The pain and perplexity of the politics we have traced in the preceding chapters have found voice in the search of poets for identity and meaning. No study of Arab Christianity would be complete if it failed to grasp the soul in poetry.

Art also is an index to the soul. It was the icon rather than the tome which John of Damascus commended to any inquirer about the faith of the church. The Greek factor, as we have seen, may have been ecclesiastically a burden hard to be endured by day-to-day Arab Christians. But the wealth of Christian art that came into their lives by the Greek connection, despite the puzzlement entailed in the Islamic context, contributed long and far to their vitality and their survival.

Christian liturgies in the Arab East sustained the continuity of pre-Islamic centuries in their quality as the final haven of mother tongues resistant to the entire dominance elsewhere of the first language of Islam. Even when Arabic made its way alongside Syriac, Aramaic, or Coptic into the Christian sanctuary, those grammars helped to christianize the shape it found. Liturgies thus had their crucial role in preserving the distinctiveness of Christian faith even while conceding the reign of Arabic in other spheres. It was in worship that Christians knew themselves for who they were. Other aspects of their being might be forfeit in minority condition, but not identity itself as long as there existed—to borrow the Qur'ān's own description of them—"houses God has permitted to be erected in which His Name is remembered and where, morning and evening, there are men chanting His praise whom neither trading nor merchandising distract from the remembrance of God." The sanctuary lamp of such houses in the eastern *ecclesia* serves as an analogy for "the likeness of the light of God," though without the sacramental themes of bread and wine the light discloses in its Christian setting (Surah 24.35–37).[2]

Poetry, art, and liturgy, then, must be our windows into the soul of Arab Christianity. As this chapter follows hard on the harsh politics of recent decades, it will be well to begin with the poets of the same period, with their sharp register of the pains of current history and their freedom from the long conventions of rhyme and meter and the romantic themes traditional in Arabic poesy down the centuries. There were, to be sure, estimable Christian poets at the courts of the Ghassānids and the Lakhmids in the times before Islam, though it is not always possible to be sure of their allegiance in the time of their poetry. The Ḥamāsah of Ibrāhīm ibn Kunaif al-Nabhānī could well represent the vigor of such other poets as Zuhair and Labīd, Al-Nābighah and Al-Aʿshā, whose poems ruminate on life and death and courage in a Christian strain. Al-Nabhānī belonged to the Ṭayy tribal grouping in the north of Najd, which appears to have migrated from origins in Najran and to have been in contact with the Ghassānids farther north. Their territory was on the eastern flank of the pilgrim route to Mecca. The fortitude which the New Testament called *hypomonē* is heard in an Arab key in these lines:

Be patient: for freeborn men to bear is the fairest thing,
Refuge from time's wrong or help from time's hurt is none.
If it availed man ought to bow him to fluttering fear,
Or if he could ward off hurt by humbling himself to ill,
To bear with a valiant front the full brunt of every stroke
And onset of fate were still the fairest and best of things.

But how much the more, when none outruns by a span his doom,
And refuge from God's decree nor was nor ever will be.
And if the changing days have wrought us, as is their wonted way,
A lot mixed of weal and woe, yet one thing they could not do.
They have not made soft or weak the stock of our sturdy spear:
They have not abased our hearts to doing deeds of shame.
To bear their weight we offer a handful of noble souls:

Though laden beyond all might of man, they uplift the load.
So shield we with patience fair our souls from the stroke of shame:
Our honours are whole and sound, though others be lean enow.[3]

Adversity is very much the theme of contemporary Arabic verse, both Muslim and Christian, but a certain despair, rather than conscious resilience, contrasts it with those precursors of the sixth century who coincided with the rise of Islam. Despite the tribal conflicts and the reverberations of Byzantine–Persian rivalry echoing both north and south, Mecca was then in growing commercial prosperity. But the twentieth century has brought a poetic mood of misgiving and distress. For poetry always lies deeper than politics and brings to the finite the measures of infinity. Does not the word *dīwān,* used so readily by poets for their volumes of verse, mean "a register"?

What is registered today arises, it would seem, from three sources, all of which have occupied us in preceding chapters. The first is a general unease and frustration about the politics and patterns of the Arab world since the 1920s—the blighted hopes, the lip service to unity, the actualities of division and strife. The second is a will to read the first by the tuition of western literature with its sense of a human malaise, an oppression of the spirit arising from the perplexities and ironies of the contemporary scene. Writers like T. S. Eliot with his *Waste Land,* Gide, Proust, Kafka, Camus, Brecht, and Yeats—the first-named most deeply of all—have stimulated a native Arab emulation of their disenchantment and their irony. The third is the degree to which the ultimate Arab frustration of Israel and Zionism has seemed, to some, to call not merely for resistance but for a search for meaning that could comprehend the tragic and could also fortify the soul in the face of Zionism not merely as a physical invader with immense resources but as an entity holding and wielding a sanction allegedly divine, a warrant from on high. Zionism, in a paradoxical way, forces the sensitive Arab soul to wonder about divine invocation, to seek for the mystery by which one's own legitimacy can be received and fulfilled.

It is on all three counts that contemporary Arabic poetry has sought out biblical metaphor and religious clues and, most of all, has invoked the figure of Jesus and the fact of the crucifixion. Thus, for example, Yūsuf al-Khāl, a Lebanese Christian poet (1917–), writes in *Al-Ḥiwār al-Azalī:*

Thirsty? Take the rock and strike it.
In the deep darkness? Roll it away from the tomb.
Is it hunger that has seized you? Look, here is the manna
And the quails. Are you brought to nakedness?
Take fig leaves for a garment to cover
Iniquity and hide it from men.

> In the great temptation have the patience
> Of Job and do not despair of blatant evil:
> The Cross of God is reared on the hill of endless time.[4]

The allusions are various, but the final line boldly states the central reality of Christian faith—the wounds of Jesus as key to the divine sovereignty.

Before exploring further the poetic voice in this key it will be wise to note that in many instances it takes its place among Greco-Syrian myths of Tammuz and rebirth, which are far removed from the Christian history of Gethsemane and Easter. Is it that the poets have failed to appreciate that faith in the crucified and risen Christ cannot ride with the myth of an annually dying god, Tammuz, whose blood fertilized the ground and whose return fulfilled the hope of spring? Perhaps. But if so, should the unhappy mingling of allusions deter us from the recognition of the inner yearning? It must rightly preclude a too-facile adoption of the poets into the ranks of theologians or orthodox believers. But such alertness and precaution need not discourage our sense of their significance. Imprecision, not least in poetic guise, may simply be the proof of yearning. Logicians, not poets, are required to be consistent.

The pagan myths in their verses had two sources. They were obviously eloquent in the models of western writers, T. S. Eliot in particular, with his allusions to Tiresias, the womb, the sea, and the seasons.[5] There could be no doubting, nevertheless, the Christian commitment out of which Eliot wrote and lived. Mentors yield both imagery and meaning to their emulators, the two being inseparable from their influence.

But that influence belonged within the second source of Arab poetic ardor for Tammuz and symbols of "resurrection." Was not *ba'th* the name of the Syrian National Socialist Party? There is evidence that Anṭūn Sa'ādah argued for the duty of poetry to "syrianize" itself in service to the nation and the party. He believed it should cherish Canaanite legends, salute how Syria taught Greece the alphabet, and help create a unity of Syrian imagination. Later his own assassination, in the month of July (Arabic *Tammūz*), was poetically linked by 'Alī Aḥmad Sa'īd, who adopted the pen name Adonis, with the sacrifice that renews, the bloodshedding that must fertilize the nation.[6]

If poetry, taking sides so consciously, offends against the true canons of art—as some would hold—the intensity of the emotion involved is more evident. It signaled its concerns by its adoption of *shi'r manthūr,* or *verse libre,* forsaking the rule of rhyme and meter in deliberate repudiation of the language worship of the traditional forms of Arabic poesy. It relied instead on imagery and feeling in the belief that inner poetry must dispense with the tyranny of forms. So doing, it also gave vent to its will to emancipation from dry formalism in the spirit, the desire to break free from conventional faith and barren dogma.[7] The true cultural self of the Arab had to be retrieved from the emptiness of lethargy and old tradition.

An early pioneer of innovation, though competent also in the classical *qaṣā'id,* was Khalīl Muṭrān (1872–1949), known as *Shā'ir al-Qatrain,* "poet of the two spheres"—Syria of his birth and Egypt of his sojourn. He was a pupil of the celebrated Ibrāhīm al-Yazijī (1847–1906), and his four-volume *Dīwān* opened new perspectives both of social criticism and literary range. But his generation predated the measures of malaise in the Arab spirit which belong with the rise of Israel. The school of Yūsuf al-Khāl wrote out of a profounder unease, caught between a painful past and a puzzling future.[8] In *Al-Judhūr* he played on the title theme: "In the roots there lies our past: in the roots there lies our future," reminiscent of another poet's plea: "Give my roots rain." One of his "Syrian" images was the contrast between sea and sand. The latter stood for the adjacent desert of Arabia, and the sea symbolized Lebanon it bounded on the west. It was a risky metaphor for Christian Arabism to use with its implied regretting of the invading sands of Islam/Arabia, but that issue could not be excluded from the search for authentic identity that was the quest of his poetry. On the coast of Lebanon he stands and cries, "a tourist without identity," chewing *qāṭ* for a thousand years, his body "a forsaken crutch," and seeing no sails on the horizon. The paradox of *The Last Supper* is that "eating and drinking," the Teacher is no longer present, and "when the cock crows there are few to witness to the Lord of the earth." Conjecture and illusion wrestle in his verses with invocation and yearning. He is entombed but not yet dead and awaiting the new life that will give the lie to fears and futilities which, meanwhile, call up a variety of strange images to speak their lines. "Lord, give us the sign" is his prayer.[9]

Do the old signs hold? Fu'ād Rifqā, associate with Yūsuf al-Khāl in the *Shi'r* journal of their literary circle tells how:

> At the rituals I carried
> An incense burner whose heaven was Jesus.
> All at once the smoke changed its course
> And moved away from the Christmas bell,
> And did not return
> As the host for the stones of the church.[10]

In no poet, however, is the Christian wistfulness more intense than in Tawfīq Sāyigh (1923–1971), Syrian by origin and Palestinian by adoption, the son of a Presbyterian minister in Tiberias. Following studies at the American University of Beirut, where he was a member of St. Justin's House, Sāyigh had a notable, if sadly abridged, career in Arabic letters. He taught in the West, founded and edited the journal *Al-Ḥiwār* in the 1960s, and was among the earliest pioneers of free verse. T. S. Eliot, whose *Four Quartets* he translated, was his early inspiration. He saw in the loss of Palestine the symptom of a wider human exile from which, "travelling never to arrive," he found no refuge. He took up Franz Kafka's enigmatic "K" to signify forlorn quest.[11] Lacking the vital passport, one forfeits entry; one is deprived of identity. The embassy to supply it is no more. For "there are no embassies on the sea." Questing love is the synonym for desolation. He borrows the story of Jeremiah in the mire of the deep well (Jer. 38:1–13) with his arms too weak and the rescuing rope too short. "From the depths I cried to you, O death." In *Ayḍan wa Ayḍan*, among his last poems, he wrote:

> My land is a wasteland,
> Its cities are silent:
> Even the vultures have abandoned it.
> Its trees have been uprooted,
> Its earth is mud and excrement.
> This land is not mine, I never saw it in the past.
> My heart is far away and my feet hasten to
>   follow it . . .
> That to which I returned yesterday
> Is a handful of earth which I lost.

Earlier, in his travels, he had carried a handful of the soil he loved to bind him to his home, but on coming back east he scatters it like winnowed chaff into the air. His joy in return is quickly enveloped in disillusion, and he renews his travels, never to return. Neither love nor patriotism avails. Can faith? Do repentants count their beads to no salvation? The answer is enigmatic, belief struggling to help unbelief as stated, most eloquently of all, in Tawfīq Sāyigh's poem *The Sermon on the Mount.* The English translation is his own:

> I too followed him,
> Married my frailty to his virtue
> And helped him reveal himself.
>
> On the lisping hill, long waited for
> By the dull arms of drowsy Kinnereth
> (Like a couple of tears the cheeks expect
> That cling to feeble eyes) I shared the meal
> Of the thick-necked multitude. Well fed
> They hailed him Lord and rolled down after him.
> Alone I lay upon the hill, watched him

Accept the silent homage of water
Amid the crow-like shrieks of his elect.
Alone I lay, waiting for his return.

I knew he would return . . .
. . . water turned to wine
Tasted water to my lips. The mud
That cleared Bartimaeus' eyes of mud made mine
Unsatisfied with what they feasted on.
The call that once restored to life the lad
Of Nain, left my mother in black . . .
I too was tempted in no wilderness.

And he came . . . I thought he talked
Only to me. He called me not, and I came forth.
He broke no loaves and touched no jars:
Baskets were full again. The wedding guests
Unconscious, conscious sipped the bitter wine.[12]

The irony is Kafkaesque, but why does the poem will to set it in the Galilean context unless the paradox of hope is there? Sāyigh writes out of a Christian nurture that strives within him to interpret how it faces the contradictions of the world. There is no more wistful voice of Christian Arabism.

Some of his associates, less desolated because less universal in their vision, could be more assured, if still enigmatic, for example, Jabrā Ibrāhīm Jabrā (b. 1926), a Christian Palestinian from Bethlehem who was a literary critic and teacher in Baghdad with a generous literary output. His poem in *Al-Madār al-Mughlaq* (The Closed Circle) entitled "A Stranger at the Fountain" sings in extravagant imagery of "the Stranger who . . . kissed the crown of thorns," "the cock's crow resounded, pierced the darkness . . . and proclaimed the sovereignty of day." His language has something of the exuberance of Walt Whitman, whom he admired. But the theme is certainly the road to Golgotha and the wood of the cross under the biblical analogy of the smitten rock, whence the waters flowed.[13]

II

In the wealth of Arabic literature, prose and poetry, of the last half century, the foregoing may seem a subjective choice. But, the subject being Christian Arabism, these are windows into its troubled mind. What is remarkable is the degree to which that mind and its literary expression have been shared by Muslim poets also. To implications of this fact we must return in chapter 12. It would seem to belie the comment of Salwā Khadrā Jayyūsī, herself a poetess and critic, that there was a "silent avoidance of any religious interpretation of the political problems."[14] While Palestinianism, by and large, has maintained a secular mentality, below that surface there has been this anguished search for light and hope and a groping toward the key that might belong with the figure of the Christ. "My soul is such," wrote 'Abd al-Rahmān Shukrī (after a period in atheism), "that it can never be satisfied with atheism."[15] But it is one of the credentials of theism that, when the mind returns to it, tragedy has to be faced, and, with tragedy, the accents of Jesus. One Muslim example must suffice, drawn from a contemporary of the Christian writers we have been studying, Badr Shākir al-Sayyāb (1926–1964) of Iraq. He writes of a Christ looking for someone to take off the crown of thorns or lift him down from the cross and asks:

> Who is he who bears the reproach of the cross
> In that long fearful night?
> Who will weep and who will answer the naked hungred?
> Who will bring the crucified down from his placard?
> Who will drive away the preying bird from his wounds?
> And who will lift the darkness from his dawn
> And change the thorns to laurel?[16]

Elsewhere he adopts the survival theme from the Quranic denial (Surah 4.158) of the actual death of Jesus on the cross and draws analogies with the revitalizing myth of the Greeks. Yet the image of the suffering Christ, however perceived, abides within that tension and, in fact, drew sharp protest from orthodox Muslim circles deploring such Christian allusions on the part of Muslim writers.[17]

These anxious and troubled voices of Christian Arabism in the twentieth century were nevertheless heirs to a very different tradition of Christian hymnody in Arabic owed to the impact of western mission, both Catholic and Protestant, in the previous century and even earlier in the case of the Maronites in Lebanon. Those orthodox and assured versifiers of a more serene faith, despite their debt to external influences in form and content, gave an impetus to Arabic poetry that liberated it from conventions of rhetoric and panegyric and furnished it with new patterns of meter, rhythm, and music. Literary critics, to be sure, have accused their Arabic of awkwardness—or worse. But those verdicts are due in part to the very different ethos of Islamic Arabic in reference to which they are generally made. But, as with the Arabic Bible translation (see below) contemporary with the hymnody, there was a considered policy of classical but direct simplicity, which yielded a syntax and diction uncongenial to Quranic norms. The case for an alternative shape of Arabic familiar to Qur'ān readers was strenuously resisted by local Christian communities. Happily, however, demurs from the Muslim side were not entirely unanimous, and some Muslim poets cooperated in the enterprise of Christian hymnology with a ready will. The contrast between the expression of Islamic and Christian spirituality in the Arabic language has never yet been adequately faced, still less overcome.[18]

The long tradition of Greek, Syriac, and Latin hymnody to which the modern pioneers were heir falls more properly in the field of liturgy. Rich and precious as it was, it did not belong in an Arabic mold dominated by Islamic norms. The first Maronite poets of the faith, notably in Aleppo, from the seventeenth century found their inspiration through the contacts with Rome of which the Maronite College there was the symbol. Some of their work, and that in the Uniate churches as they came into being, was translation from Latin and Greek sources and versification of psalms, but there was also new composition using the rhyme and strophe forms of the western pattern. *Shi'r Manthūr* was then unknown and, we may say, undesired, for rhyme and rhythm kindle the expectation and approval of the ear and are therefore well suited to the public celebration of faith which tentative twentieth-century souls hold in doubt and reserve.

It was the Protestant factor via the press in Malta that was most innovative, and the influence of its hymns has been far-reaching in and beyond the Arab churches, thanks to the educational activities—always eager about Arabic—in which American mission was engaged. Leaders in the interchange of faith, music, and poesy which took place between Syrian/Lebanese tutors of Arabic-loving Americans were Nāṣīf al-Yazijī (1800–1871), Buṭrus al-Bustānī (1819–1883), and Yūsuf al-'Asir (1814–1889)—the last-named a Muslim. Fāris al-Shidyāq, whose chequered career we noted in chapter 9, was also an anthologist with lively ideas. Through these writers and their numerous successors editions of hymns and psalmody made their way into schools and churches popularizing in Arabic form a long heritage of western spirituality—Tate and Brady, George Herbert, Isaac Watts, the Wesleys, H. F. Lyte, and J. G. Whittier, with the tunes of Bach, Handel, and many lesser lights. Inasmuch as song avails where dogmas fail, Christian Arabic came to participate in a community of meaning and expression not otherwise attainable. Inevitably there were disparaging and adverse comments from sources tenacious of old Arab and Arabic traditions both of language and convention[19] but *tarānīm ruḥiyyah* or *aghānī ruḥiyyah,* as the hymnbooks were known, in their numerous editions diffused their devotional meanings and gave new heart to faith and new usage to language. It seems that this modern hymnology and the new techniques that translation evoked also stimulated ventures in wider fields, such as Sulaymān al-Bustānī's (1848–1884) Arabic poetic version of *The Iliad* and sundry attempts at Shakespeare. Egypt, thanks to the British occupation and, more, to the presence there of Syrian Christian emigrés, also shared in the impact of new hymnology.[20]

Inasmuch as the new hymnody helped to broaden and enhearten Christian Arab identity, its new range of metaphor and aspiration contributed in turn to new accents in Muslim thinking and authorship. Christians, in their social station, were freer than Muslim writers from the conventions of Ottoman eulogy and literary norms inseparable from the mental habits of *Dār al-Islām.* On the one hand, literature and its themes served to bring together the thoughts of the two faiths: on the other, it tended to sharpen Muslim misgivings and suspicion resistant to the "foreign" ring both of church hymns and *The Iliad.* Christian Arabic has always had to labor under the sense that enterprise in Arabic *may* be construed as a violation of the Qur'ān as the vital determinant of what the language is. Happily, there have been numerous Muslim Arab poets ready to demonstrate in their several *Dīwāns* that a right Quranic loyalty can well engage in a lively inventiveness both of form and content.[21]

III

What, in sum, did this hymning of faith, this celebration of spiritual life, bring into wide diffusion within Christian Arabism? Plainly it repossessed the great notes of the long eastern praise of "God in Christ" to which by earlier translation in the reverse direction, by such writers as J. M. Neale (1818–1866), it was so far in debt. But also it used a language of personal immediacy, of gentle fervor and moral nurture, which were all its own. It sang of salvation and the Savior; it celebrated the generosity of external nature as the handiwork of the sovereign Creator; and it breathed a yearning for guidance through the anxieties of time and the problems of society. It was what might be called an inculcation of identity that was at once irenic and devout, quickening the soul in the grace of life.

To pass to the icons is to enter a different world but one no less aptly described as an inculcation of identity. Despite the censorship, often explicit and always implicit, in the Islamic veto on representational religious art, the churches cherished the visual in worship in the form dear to their soul and congenial to their theology. Had not the evangelist Luke been reputedly a painter, and were not portraits of Jesus and the Virgin, according to the historian Eusebius, in evidence from the earliest days?[22] The iconoclastic controversy, as noted in chapter 4, came and went. Whether consciously or not—who shall say?—the impulse to iconography overrode the option to forgo it in the interests of Muslim scruple and of converse with the other faith. For would not such self-censorship disown the meaning of God's own metaphor in the Incarnation? Would not this, in any event, be the central stumbling block for the Islamic mind and one which iconography, far from disserving, could only positively commend?

Doubtless the skills lavished on the icons were enfeebled within *Dār al-Islām* in its expansion and the diversion of the crafts of gilders and painters to the different demands of Islam. The great cities of northern Syria lying between Antioch and Edessa and below the Taurus range, which were ancient centers of Christian culture and notable in their iconography, were casualties of the Muslim advance in the seventh century and yielded up their architectural and artistic treasures to the exigencies of strife between the retreating and the advancing empires and to the breakup of the trade that had sustained their well-being. The Greek and Russian tradition of iconography, with that of the Nestorians eastward of the Arab orbit, became the main standard-bearers of the art from which precariously, as opportunity allowed, the churches under Islam could renew their vision.

By their place on the iconostasis, or icon screen, between the inner and the outer sanctuaries of all Orthodox churches, the icons stood as guardians of the sacramental mysteries, portals between the inner consecration and the outer celebration of redemption in Christ with its pledge of the "divinization" of humanity through the indwelling Spirit. Apostles and saints symbolized the vocation of all the faithful, rooted in the events of the Gospel from the annunciation of Mary to the resurrection and the enthronement of the Lord. The icons were not only a visual recital of the faith as both history and inward truth; they were also a sacrament of devotion, requiring in their making the same tangible surrender to meaning that calligraphy demanded of the scribes and gilders of Islam. There was the same expenditure of skill and scruple, of exacting and self-conscious excellence, only differing as the theme of the face or the flow of the script. The habit of the iconographer was to fast and meditate in anticipation of his art, to consecrate his wood and colors in a rite of preparation, so that in their handling he took on a priestly task in which purity of heart had to match the exercise of skill.

The finished work might thus express the truth that beauty belongs in the created order only by gift of the Creator and that the gift had been made to turn on its reverent employment in a context of adoration. Iconography, in this way, was an active parable of the meaning of sanctity both in its practice and in its finished works. It invited the beholder into a conformity to the prototype portrayed, but, so doing, it was itself in the making an occasion of grace. Where the English hymn writer sang "Be of sin the double cure," the iconographer's prayer was "Be of grace the double sign"—at once a thing wrought and a meaning at work.

The painting of icons was not pictorial art intending to create a natural likeness against a natural background. Care was taken to have the theme identifiable by clues the eye could read, but the aim was always to witness to the transfigured state of humanity as bearing the image of the divine. There were no separate icons of creatures without humans, for nature was hallowed only in its human bearings. The surface of the panel contrived no illusions of real space or volume. No shadows were cast, nor was light thrown on the subject from this side or that. Light was simply the area around the figure. Icons were almost always full face, or three-quarter face, even where grouping centered on a focal point. Profile meant abstraction and remoteness. The face, so central to biblical tradition from the time of the Aaronic blessing, which echoes through the New Testament, must offer its meaning in open directness, so that beholders also do not profile themselves in sidelong glances, but see face to face.

In this way the emotions within the meaning can be clearly read—the Virgin's trouble of mind at the annunciation, the tender pathos of the Madonna and Child, the yearning of the crucified, the anguish of entombment, and the awed wonderment of disciples at the ascension. In the ascesis, the endurance, the serenity, and the calmness of the faces of the saints, the icons minister the meaning of divine indwelling to the eye and heart. John of Damascus wrote: "The saints were filled with the Holy Spirit even in their lifetime. After their death too the grace of the Holy Spirit dwells in their souls and in their bodies lying in their graves, in their faces and in their holy images."[23] That irradiation of personality with the light of grace is the source of the halo in iconography—a tradition that Islamic art utilized in portrayal of the Prophet and his Companions.

By long habit icons are left unsigned; they are not a personal creation. There were, to be sure, famous iconographers and discernible schools with founders. Forms and trends developed and were reproduced. There were masters and perpetual novices, but none were mere copyists indulging personal repute. It is here that the eastern iconographer differs so markedly from the Michaelangelos and the Botticellis of the Renaissance in the West, with their highly sensual creations and their appetite for pagan classicism and the cult of the exotic in their masterpieces of religious art. From time to time mosaics in the East may have accepted such impulses, but the severe discipline and sustained tradition of the holy icon precluded the indulgence of surrender to the passions and patterns kindled by the patronage of popes and princes. Icons and the Medicis were different worlds.

The lighting of candles before the icons by the faithful united them in intention with the meaning of sainthood as both veneration and aspiration. Likewise the kissing of the icons took the normal sign of a physical affection into the realm of mystical participation in and with the saints. By other criteria both such acts of devotion might be taken for superstition, but so to think would seem to the eastern Christian a view of matter as essentially unclean. Rather, as the whole liturgy proclaimed, matter was the locale of hallowedness, the bearer of that holiness which was the central truth of incarnation and the transforming of the bread and wine which served for Eucharist. Just as art invested beauty and meaning in the stuff of matter by the will to turn potential into being, so holiness likewise–and by the same purpose of will–might enlist line, color, and fabric to its ends. Orthodoxy in the East may have been inconsistent in denying this purpose to the chisel and to stone by its prohibition of statuary, but the two-dimensionality of the icon was its chosen love:

> The domed interior swallows up the day.
> Here, where to light a candle is to pray,
> The candle flame shows up the almond eyes
> Of local saints who view with no surprise
> Their martyrdom depicted on the walls. . .[24]

Veneration, further, reminded the people that they, in turn, were called to be living icons reflecting the divine glory in the meaning of that *theosis* which was the crowning goal of their ecclesial theology. Did not the iconostasis, the icon screen, symbolize the human creature as both the boundary and the uniting link between the two realms of time and eternity, of flesh and spirit? Why not people it, as the Copts did, with the legend of St. Barsumas sharing his cave with a wild beast, of St. Mercurius, antagonist of the pagan king, Julian, and of Sts. Menas, Tadros, and Boktor and the martyrs of A.D. 284?[25]

IV

Beyond the visual world of iconography, eastern Christianity found its soul supremely in the Divine Liturgy. In the celebration of sacred mysteries its ethos, through all the diversity of its territories, was enshrined. The most frequently followed of the four liturgies is that of St. John Chrysostom, the others being those of St. James, St. Gregory, and St. Basil. They might be described as a corporate concert of meaning, a sacramental unison of things earthly and heavenly. They celebrate "God in Christ" in an idiom that differs deeply from the rite of the Latin West. The contrast may be read in the theme of "transformation," rather than "transubstantiation," in the consecration and reception of the bread and wine. The latter, with its Thomist Aristotelian provenance, is too technical and too abstract a concept to suit either the Greek Orthodox mind or the quality of receiving faith. Its categories and their logic do not well belong with sacramental wonder. The *epiclesis,* or invocation of the Spirit, in the *Anaphora* at the climax of the liturgy reads:

> We offer to Thee this spiritual worship without shedding of blood and we pray and beseech and implore Thee Send down Thy Holy Spirit upon us and upon these gifts here set forth. And make this bread the precious body of Thy Christ and what is in this cup the precious blood of Thy Christ, transforming them by Thy Holy Spirit.

The role of the priest differs subtly from that of his counterpart in western Latin ritual. The Office is not powerfully focused in a single dramatic action performed by clergy only. The *epiclesis* belongs within an inclusive movement with the deacons and the laity integral to the whole. It is the latter's "bread" and "wine" which, via the Offertory, supply the sacrament, and unconsecrated portions of the same bread are distributed among them at dispersion.

The people, for the most part, stand throughout, not held by western habits of standing, sitting, kneeling according to the sequences. The space before the iconostasis and, frequently, beneath a crowning dome is felt to be neither for spectacle nor for audition, but for communion. Three doors lead through the screen into the area within—itself "the altar" where stands "the Throne" or "Table." The icons ensure a place of honor to the saints at the banquet, for death only partially changes the fellowship to which all belong. The revelation of the divine love comes from within the screen. Hence the concealment of the priest, so that in the coming forth of the mystery all may know their reincorporation into the body of Christ.

But that climax has its careful preludes, like the movements of a deepening drama, a spiral movement of Christian disclosure. First comes the *Prothesis,* the preparation of gifts, which also symbolizes the hidden, unrecorded years of Jesus prior to his ministry. Then follows the *Synaxis,* the assembly, or "Liturgy of Catechumens," originally meant for trainees and initiates but still relevant to communicants in that it rehearses in readings by the deacons the open teaching and healing ministry of Jesus, perhaps accompanied by a singing of the Beatitudes.

Following the sermon and the intercession comes the Liturgy of the Faithful, with the *Anaphora* after "the Great Entrance." "Let us who in mystery represent the cherubim lay aside all worldly cares and sing to the life-giving Trinity the thrice holy hymn." Here the final events of Jesus' passion and beyond to resurrection, ascension, and the coming of the Spirit crown the worship, which recalls them in *anamnesis,* or "memorial," and receives them in communion. But in that dual participation it is not the theme of sacrifice and propitiation which dominates but that of *theosis,* or participating in the divine nature. The bread is to the body in communion as the container is to the content. With the wine it is figure to the meaning, a form of manifestation, but only in the entire context of the action of God toward humanity, of which Christ is the drama in life, death, and resurrection.

The soul of eastern Orthodoxy, both pro and contra Chalcedon, as epitomized in the liturgy, must be interrogated precisely where it is most distinctive. Does the relative recession of the dimension of sacrifice and atonement suggest a neglect of moral obligation in the worshiper, of Christ's claim on the will within and beyond the wonder? That question, for some outside assessors, turns on the concept of "deification," belonging to *theosis.* Does the believer indeed "become God by grace while remaining creature," as Vladimir Lossky has it?[26] In what sense can the human ever be described as divine if we are to do justice to the entire transcendence of God, to the true creaturehood of humans, and to the incarnate Christ of the New Testament? "The indwelling Spirit," as told in the Epistles, has to do with a yielding of the self into the energies of the Spirit, so that mind, heart, and will are truly informed and motivated. But this, by its very quality and purpose, leaves creaturehood intact and in no way identifies the being of the human with the being of God. At no point is the formulation of Christian faith more open to misunderstanding and to repudiation from within Islam than here in the eastern Christian doctrine of the human "becoming divine." Moreover, to write of "becoming God by grace" violates one of the first rules of theological statement, namely, the need, in saying what one intends to mean, to avoid saying what one cannot mean.[27]

It may be right, at this point, to observe what some have felt to be the lack of the dimension of intellect in eastern Christian worship. We have rightly stressed its sense of soul. There is nothing corresponding to that wrestling with truth and its expression that is characteristic of the best in western preaching, where the will to integrity in the study is vocal in the pulpit and the critical exposition of meaning is reckoned to be, in itself, an act of worship, a "loving of the Lord with all the mind." It is true that some traditions of preaching may turn the sanctuary merely into an auditorium, and worship into lecture. But such aberration does not disqualify a faith that thinks aloud about its mysteries precisely where the soul transacts them. Eastern Orthodoxy, whether Greek or Coptic or other, is content with soul. In the *antidoron* (the unconsecrated bread from which the bread of the *Anaphora* was taken), the faithful as they depart receive the token of their bond with grace even if they have refrained from communion proper. Their identity as believers is confirmed without deliberate exercise of mind to explore it.

In communion proper, the communicants whisper their baptismal name to the deacon, who repeats it to the priest who then inserts it into the words: "The servant of God (name) is made partaker of the holy body and blood of the Lord and God and Savior Jesus Christ, for the remission of his/her sins and unto life everlasting." The prayer for all communicants is also for "those whom each of us hath in mind," incorporating the absent, the sick, the needy, and the departed. That community in faith is powerfully underlined in the announcement of the Gospel and the Creed: "Wisdom, stand and attend. . . . Let us hear the Holy Gospel. . . . the peace of the Lord be with you." The congregation is standing, so the words are not a summons out of chairs or pews, but rather to vigorous engagement with what is heard.

One significant feature of eastern worship is the frequency of "secret prayer" made at the several points of vesting, hand washing, preparation, censing, and other liturgical actions, to ensure that the priest is in a right frame of mind. Such focus of intention may be compared to the *niyyah,* which must prelude each and every act of Islamic devotion, the conscious attentiveness that safeguards worship against "rite by rote." The fourteenth-century liturgist Nicholas Cabasilas wrote: "This intention can be seen in many parts of the prayers."[28] One example is the secret prayer of the priest before the reading of the Gospel:

> Kindle in our hearts, O Lord, lover of men, the pure light of the divine knowledge of Thee. Open the eyes of our mind to the understanding of Thy Gospel. Implant in us the fear of Thy blessed commandments that, trampling down all carnal desires, we may come unto a spiritual citizenship both thinking and doing all things to Thy good pleasure.
> Thou art the light of our souls, O Christ our God, and to Thee we give glory, with Thy eternal Father and Thine all holy, good and life-giving Spirit, now and evermore.

Those intimate devotions lead us back to the hymnology of Greek, Syriac, and Coptic churches, so different in its ethos from the congregational singing of versified doctrine and piety we noted earlier in the Protestant tradition. Such hymns of personal origin may have unwitting liability to ill-balanced sentiment or even heresy. The eastern churches prefer the ejaculatory Alleluias, the cries of the psalmists, and the refrains of the fathers—all chanted in the ancient mode of the Gregorian and other chant, not sung with orchestration or instrumental music. Antiphonal parallelism or responsive meanings, known as early as Ignatius of Antioch in the second century, were heir to the tradition of the Hebrew Psalter. Homilies too might take metrical form and be punctuated with responding affirmation. Liturgical music could become to the person as vocal what the icon was to the person as mortal. Both consecrated the resource of mind and member to the divine praise. The prolific Syriac leader Ephraem, of the fourth century in Edessa, addressed his clergy at ordination:

Purify the harp of thy spirit from contention.
Let it not play to thee of thyself,
For self-deceit is deadly . . .
Because thou art a harp
Thou art animated and eloquent.
There is freedom in thy numbers
And in thy songs . . .
Put then thy soul in tune
And sing harmoniously.[29]

The Coptic liturgy has a hymn to be chanted at the time of the receiving of the holy sacrament:

Hosanna, Son of David
Thou who hast made good to us thy bounty
And granted us the bread of immortality,
Hosanna in the highest.

This is the mystery of mysteries,
This is the pride of the righteous,
This is the joy of the pure in heart,
This is the supreme secret.

This is indeed the bread of heaven,
This the nourishment of the wise,
This is the life of those who understand.
Who receives it will never be distressed.

This is the crown of priesthood,
This is the oblation of the divine,
This is the pledge of the kingdom,
This is the gate of the heights.

This is the surpassing bread,
The body of the one and only Son,
His glorious righteous blood,
Made the very life of the saints.

O sanctified people
Sing the harmonies of joy.
Raise the sound of gladness,
Hosanna in the highest.

Know the worth of wisdom
For this grace give thanks,

Magnify the Son, the Word,
Lord of glory, exalted over all.

O people of the choice
With all awe draw near
That we may receive this most gladsome
of mysteries
Mystery hidden and supreme.

We thank the grace of Christ
And glorify Him with praises
With the voice of Alleluias we cry
Hosanna in the highest.

Thus "the grace of music was added to the truth of doctrine," and, as the great Chrysostom wrote: "Together we make up a single choir in perfect equality of rights and of expression whereby earth imitates heaven. Such is the noble character of the Church where singing blends all voices together."[30] The ancient *Gloria in excelsis* was renewed in *Phōs hilarion,* "O gladsome Light," and the chant at the point of the Great Entrance to accompany Christ on the way to his passion. "Let our mouth be filled with thy praise" precedes the chant at the distribution.

V

In the Arab Christian context, all such liturgical worship must return the soul to the realities painfully studied in chapter 10. How does spirituality relate to contemporary history experienced as injustice, anger, exile, and oppression? The oblation in the sanctuary returns us to the theme of the poets. In the one is celebrated the crux of suffering in the economy of God. What is its meaning in the other? How does the Eucharist translate into anxiety or offer the clue to perplexity? Is there a "liberation theology" in the soul of Arab Christianity, and what might it say?

The Latin American precedent has certainly been alive in Palestinian thinking, but the situations are not parallel. For Brazilians, Peruvians, for Amerindians at large, the issues are economic and so also political, inasmuch as the political order impedes and must be made to serve economic justice. Passion is directed against domestic authority and the exploitation of multinationals and foreign finance. These are no analogy for the sharply racial, political, and emotional issues explicit in Jewish Zionism, experienced as a political imperialism rooted in a mystique of faith concerning land and destiny. There is obvious contrast in the resulting sense of deprivation.

Furthermore, the Bible that furnishes writers such as Gutierrez and Miranda in the Latin American scene with Amos-style protest against poverty is, in the Arab context, the very fount of Joshua-style vindication of possession. Where, in the one case, the Bible effectively incriminates, in the other, as interpreted, it decisively exonerates. To be sure, the passion of Amos against injustice abides and may be invoked, as Amos did, against his own people, but the case can be neatly turned by biblical promises and precedents, which are held to justify all that Israel entails on others. The warrant is beyond the reach of any current Amos disposed to reverse the mandate to the land itself.

Thus any "liberation theology" in the Palestinian situation encounters the built-in veto of a Zionist reading of the Bible as underwriting the unquestioned marriage of Jewish land and Jewish people. Zionism, in that sense, dispossesses Arab Christians of the moral relevance of the Hebrew scriptures to their state of suffering and wrong. Any liberation theology in their setting will only plead the Hebrew prophets to hear them overridden.

There remains the New Testament, but what theology of liberation will it offer? Only the conviction that there is redemption *within* suffering, the possibility of being what Fyodor Dostoevsky in *The Possessed* called "a God-bearing people," whose response to evil lay in the will to transmute it into good. We have seen earlier in this chapter the urge in poetry—Muslim as well as Christian—to identify with suffering, to be on behalf of the people in the voicing of despair, so that evil is not silenced, dismissed, disregarded—which is the way of untruth—but held, pilloried, taken for the evil it is. To that extent it is being borne, carried in the heart, and essentially known. In that sense it is right to liken oppressors to Judas Iscariot and to identify the crown of thorns. Poetry is thus the acceptance of evil, the vocal realization that it has been suffered.

But this is not liberation. Indeed, it may even become a captivity to bitterness or a lapse into enervating hate. It undertakes a "having-suffered," explores its depths and lives its meaning. But is there an acceptance that can go further, an acceptance that, while letting the wrong be the wrong it is and poignantly saying so, nevertheless outlives it in the will to suffer, and suffer toward an end beyond it and because of it?

Such was and is the principle of Jesus' cross. It is not a political solution, draws no maps on territories, negotiates no treaties. But it liberates from the evil imprisoning the future and releases hope from the bondage of the past. After more than a century of political Zionism on the move, after four decades of exile or distraint, it is clear that Arab Palestinians are a martyr people, with Poles, Armenians, and many others. Two generations of refugees in tents and squalor cannot be as if they had known normality.

Final peace tomorrow would not undo their experience or restore what time has forever undone. Solutions ahead must ensue from tragedies they cannot ever retrieve. History, in that sense, compels us to be vicarious in surviving what it inflicts. The final question about wrong and tribulation is not whether it befalls but how we respond. So to realize is the ultimate interrogation of the soul within.

Notes

1. His lines are as follows:

Thus the Cross will become *minbar*
And a piece of wood on which we play our airs,
While the nails will be strings. . . .

(*'Āshiq min Falasṭīn* [One in Longing, from Palestine] [Beirut, 1966]). Without the legend the lines must seem odd and crude, but the writer is linking his faith in human meaning to the crucifixion of Jesus.

2. The verse adds: ". . . and who fulfill the prayer-rite and bring the alms," i.e., duties of the Muslim. But there can be no doubt that the reference is to Christian monastic communities, to which there was no Muslim parallel in Muḥammad's time and very rarely since in a few forms of Sufism. The sanctuary, or cell, light occurs in the metaphors of pre-Islamic poetry as, for example, in a *Mu'allaqah* of Imrū al-Qais:

Nay, was it the lamps of a hermit who dwells alone
And pours o'er the twisted wicks the oil from his slender cruse?

(in C. J. Lyall, *Translations of Ancient Arabian Poetry* [1885; reprint, Westport, Conn.: Hyperion Press, 1987], p. 103).

3. Lyall, *Translations,* p. 24. As Lyall explains, the "spear" reference in line 11 is not the literal weapon but the posture a man adopts in the face of adversity. It has a proverbial force akin to the English "a man's 'mettle.'"

4. In *Al-Bi'r al-Mahjūrah* (The Abandoned Well) (Beirut, 1958), pp. 56–57. Al-Khāl was born in Tripoli and after studies in the American University of Beirut served in the U.N.O. secretariat. Returning to Lebanon he fostered "free verse" poetry as writer, publisher, and critic. 'Alī Aḥmad Sa'īd (b. 1930), with the pen name Adonis, described Al-Khāl's poetry as "the first Christian experience in the purely metaphysical sense in Arabic poetry" (see M. M. Badawi, *A Critical Introduction to Modern Arabic Poetry* [New York: Cambridge University Press, 1975], p. 235).

5. Tiresias is "the spectator" in Eliot's *The Waste Land,* through whose eyes the poem's allusive scenes are witnessed. The profound influence of Eliot on contemporary Arabic literature is one of the fascinating aspects of interfaith–or interdoubt–this century. It gives the lie both to the alleged aridity of Europe and the assumed self-sufficiency of Islam.

6. On Adonis as pen name, see n. 4. The young god, Adonis, in Phoenician mythology, killed in hunting, was believed to return yearly in the spring, his blood

fertilizing the ground. Aphrodite, the goddess in love with him, had her devotees in Cyprus, the island Syrian nationalism included, romantically, in its own sphere and state.

7. The *shi'r manthūr* movement meant to raise the issue, What is poetry? It was not constituted, for them, by the claims of meter, rhyme, and diction, but by the thrust of its passion, its power of imagery, and its protest against complacent tradition.

8. It seems fair to speak of a school, inasmuch as it presented a sharp identity with a journal *Shi'r* around which its ideals gathered. It was Al-Khāl's publishing firm, attached to the Beirut newspaper *Al-Nahār* that issued the *Dīwāns* and translations the movement inspired. See *Journal of Arabic Literature* 10 (1979), pp. 70–94.

9. Al-Khāl, *Al-Judhūr,* in *Al-I'māl al-Shi'riyyah al-Kāmilah, 1938–1968* (Beirut, 1973), pp. 207, 213. "The Last Supper" occurs on pp. 279–280, and "The Long Poem" on pp. 280–292.

10. Quoted by permission from *Modern Poetry in the Arab World,* ed. and trans. 'Abdullāh al-Udhari (New York: Penguin Books, 1986), pp. 84–85.

11. Tawfīq Sāyigh, *Al-Qaṣīdah K.* In *Journal of Arabic Literature* 4 (1973), p. 82. Quoted by permission of E. J. Brill.

12. *Ayḍan wa Ayḍan* in *Ḥiwār* (March/April 1967), pp. 162–170. "The Sermon on the Mount" is in *Critical Perspectives on Modern Arabic Literature,* trans. and ed. I. J. Boullata (Washington, D.C., 1980), p. 299. Quoted by permission.

13. Quoted from *Modern Arabic Poets, 1950–1975* (Beirut, 1964; trans. and ed. I. Boullata, Washington, D.C.: Three Continents Press, 1976), pp. 125–126.

14. In *Studies in Modern Arabic Literature,* ed. R. C. Ostle (Warminster, Wiltshire: Aris & Phillips, 1976), p. 51.

15. 'Abd al-Raḥmān Shukrī, *Dīwān* (Alexandria, 1960), p. 25.

16. Badr Shākir al-Sayyāb, *Unshūdat al-Maṭar* (The Song of the Rain) (Beirut, 1960), pp. 110–111.

17. The journal *Al-Thaqāfah* (Cairo) reports that the Supreme Council of Arts was petitioned to institute direct censorship on verse because of Christian references by Muslims to the cross (70 [Nov. 1964], 13–15; 71, pp. 8–10).

18. One pioneer venture in familiarizing Christians with the vocabulary and feel of Islamic spirituality was that of C. E. Padwick, *Muslim Devotions: A Study of Prayer-Manuals in Common Use* (London: SPCK, 1961), a study of the prayer manuals of the Sufi orders. There is little sustained Muslim study of the elements of Christian spirituality.

19. See, e.g., Muḥammad al-Khālidī and 'Umar Farrūkh, *Al-Tabshīr wa-l-Isti'mār* (Mission and Imperialism) (Beirut, 1953), pp. 212–224. The authors attack what they call the "mutilation" of Arabic by Christian usage, local or missionary.

20. See S. Moreh, *Modern Arabic Poetry, 1800–1970: The Development of Its Forms and Themes Under the Influence of Western Literature* (Leiden: E. J. Brill, 1976), p. 57. Khalīl Muṭrān (1872–1940), born in Baalbec and long resident in Egypt as a poet and journalist, is representative of Christian Arab efforts to free Arabic from archaisms and to make poetry a truly introspective art ready for experimentation and realism. His four-volume *Dīwān* shunned rhetoric and hyperbole and aimed at a lyrical unity of theme and style.

21. Moreh, *Modern Arabic Poetry*, p. 47, 57f.

22. Eusebius, *History of the Christian Church* 7.18 (*PG* 20:680).

23. John of Damascus, *First Discourses on Defence of the Holy Icons* (*PG* 94:1249cd).

24. The candle suggests an image of the trinity of humanity. Tallow sustains wick which carries flame—body, mind, and spirit. The dome, as the arch rotated, holds analogy of the solidity of truth creating the space beneath in which life ensues and to which worship belongs. The lines are John Betjeman's.

25. See C. Mulock and M. T. Langdon, *The Icons of Yūhannā and Ibrahim the Scribe* (London: Nicholson & Watson, 1946).

26. Vladimir Lossky, *Mystical Theology of the Eastern Church*, trans. by members of the Fellowship of St. Alban and St. Sergius (London: James Clarke & Co., 1957), p. 87.

27. To name a human subject and add the predicate "is God" is plainly nonsensical. The meaning that can attach to the words in 2 Pet. 1:4, to which *theosis* appeals ("partakers of the divine nature") is more surely had in the indwelling of the Holy Spirit within human selfhood, sanctifying and fulfilling human surrender to the divine will and grace. (The passage in Ps. 82:6, sometimes invoked here, "You are gods" is ironically used by Jesus in John 10:34 not to "deify" humans but to lift a controversy out of its minutiae into its essentials. *Yahweh,* too, in the Psalm is also ironically telling the judges they "shall be [behave] like men.") It is unfortunate that the all-important theme of divine transcendence should have been compromised by misreading of passages having a very different motif. Nor does it help to conserve that transcendence by differentiating between divine "being" and divine "energies" with the latter—in *theosis*—passing over to believers.

28. Nicholas Cabasilas, *A Commentary on the Divine Liturgy,* trans. J. M. Hussey and P. A. McNulty (London: SPCK, 1960), p. 26.

29. See *Select Metrical Hymns and Homilies of Ephraem Syrus,* trans. from Syriac by Henry Burgess (London, 1853), p. 127. The Syriac language has a very rich hymnology.

30. John Chrysostom, *Homily 5* (*PG* 63:486–487).

CHAPTER

12

A Future with Islam?

I

THE QUESTION MARK can be removed, for there is no future for Arab Christianity except with Islam. Yet the interrogative remains. It is the quality of that future which is in perpetual question. The fifteenth Islamic century is only one decade on, while the twenty-first Christian century is only one decade away. What may the common century hold? Against the long background we have traced of minority condition, western entanglement, communal stresses, and identity crises, how are relationships and fortunes likely to unfold? How will the task of survival decide the quality of what survives?

The most critical factor in the answer is precisely the one least in doubt—namely, the inherently political nature of Islam. Pan-Arabism, in which physically and numerically Christian Arabs play so small a part, is now firmly expressed in the nationality principle, as witnessed by the varied membership of the Arab League. There are many theorists within it, mainly of the radical religious kind, who insist that such separate nationhoods have no legitimate part in a true Arabism, being in evil contradiction to the vital Islamic principle of one inclusive *Ummah.*[1] Yet such an inclusive *Ummah,* or unified household, of Islam would have to transcend Arab populations it vastly outnumbered. That problematic apart, it was in revolt against such an actual, if decaying, caliphate of all Islam, the Ottoman Empire as the *de jure Ummah,* that the twentieth-century nationhoods had their mandates to separatism, as we have seen in chapter 7. Though political map making by western powers had part in the fashion of them, the major Arab Muslim states express long instincts and traditions—historical, geographical and cultural—which sanction their separate political identities and strongly suggest their continuing existence. Indeed, a conspicuous feature of twentieth-century Arab history is the total failure, despite large rhetoric, to effectuate political unity. Nor is there, discernibly, any hope of or realistic will for a renewed caliphate.

It must, therefore, be assumed that the nation-states will continue through whatever vicissitudes and, with them, the familiar dilemmas of their Christian fragmentary elements. That fact, however, does not resolve the Muslim debate within them about the nature and fulfillment of their Islamic destiny. On the contrary, it increases it, precisely because it leaves the responsibility separatist and so, to a degree, competitive. It aligns the perennial debate about a true Islamicity with the tensions of the Arab political diversity within which it proceeds. All this makes for a highly self-conscious Islam, a faith at pains within itself to fulfill itself across a whole spectrum of ideology as to what that self is, expressed perhaps compromisingly for some but currently for all, in the form of nationalisms—Egyptian, Syrian, Saudi, Iraqi, Libyan, Yemeni, and the rest.

There is little or nothing Christian Arab elements, where they exist, can do about that situation except await (if as nonemigrants they do) its uncertain issue. A vital question mark of their well-being is outside their control. In that predicament, as studied earlier in its features hitherto, Christian Arabism has to reckon with the abiding instinct of Islam to conscious superiority and dominance. This is as real in the feel of society as it is manifest in the statistics of numbers. Relationships seem destined to be always unequal, however secure or insecure minority right may be to ritual acts, communal religious nurture, and the legal legacies of the old *dhimmī* status. These, happily, allow of survival but hardly of equal engagement with destiny or partnership in affairs.

There is in the very ethos of Islam an implied, often explicit, antithesis to all that it reads outside its own thesis. The sharp divisions in the Qur'ān between the categories of faith and unfaith, the opposition to non-Islam which is built into the being of Islam, the necessary marriage of *Dīn wa Dawlah,* of religion and power—all preclude the kind of feasible mutuality within citizenship and indeed within conviction, which would emancipate both majority and minority alike for genuine partnership. Current passions and conflicts however diagnosed, however eventuating in the future, seem to negate any realistic hope of a depoliticization of Arab Islam. We will look later at the secular option, which has attracted some intellectuals, more deeply in non-Arab than in Arab Islam, and which certainly needs to be studied, however long-range its emergence into practicality. It is, furthermore, at the heart of the theological issue between the two faiths. But such study must be prospective for a time whose prospect is a distant horizon and, like all horizons, receding elusively. The future has, then, to be on Islam's terms. These seem likely to remain incorrigibly assertive, unequal, sometimes hostile, and rarely other than superior, politically inferiorizing and religiously entrenched, as spiritual finalities whose credentials are not open to or in need of Christian participation.

II

That conclusion suggests a future of continuing domestication of Arab Christianity within itself. Its long vulnerability through the centuries predisposed it to introversion. There are, however, aspects of modernity that enliven the Christian vocation, despite the adverse assessments. Christian faith should never be deterred from living in hope of opportunity even in situations where it cannot readily foresee how it may eventuate. To make hopes actual first requires that they are not forfeited.

Christianity's future with Islam is, therefore, thrown back on the content and quality of its own relevance. The task, we may say, in the present impasse of exterior political and contemporary relationships, stands essentially in theology, in bringing together what Islam means by *Allāhu akbar* and what the New Testament understands by "God in Christ." To see the task this way is not to be evasive of current sharp realities, nor to retreat into the arcane and the remote. On the contrary, it is to be braced for the essential meanings and ministries—the more so because their present prospects are, for the most part, dim.

Islam is a vocal, insistent, assured, and institutionalized theism. Arab Christianity within it shares with wider Christianity a kindred, though contrasted, theism for which the Christology Islam forbids is crucial. The two have often been supposed incompatible and contradictory.[2] That view does justice to neither. Theism, by definition, cannot be plural and competitive. To confess divine unity presupposes a oneness that makes a will to meet within it inseparable from sincerity about it. The Oneness must undertake the issues that divide its differing "theists."

Muslims, by and large, have been unwilling to see this, for it offends their finalities. But sooner or later, at least among those who care for meaning and its integrity, the equation implicit within monotheism must be resolved, allowing as it does no escape into dualism or plurality or non-theism. What must be resolved?

The sense of the One God that informs New Testament faith affirms a divine capacity to yearn and suffer for humanity. Such love is its ultimate clue to how divine transcendence, evident also in creation, law, and prophethood, is finally measured and known. By contrast, Islam affirms a transcendence in which, despite the common dimensions of creation, law, and prophethood, such pathos and such compassion have no place. Islam believes itself commissioned with a mandate of power to institutionalize divine sovereignty on earth via the *Sharīʿah,* the *Ummah,* and the *Dawlah,* sacred law, community, and the state. These leave no place for inward question.

This disparity about divine greatness, about wherein the *akbar* fact of God resides, is central to the Muslim-Christian relation, and uniquely so to Arab Christians. This, as we have seen, is by dint of ethnic and historical factors not shared elsewhere in the West or further Asia. Arab Christians live this disparity within proximity. They have a language, a culture, and a memory that incorporate them within an isolation. They are caught in a paradox of belonging in exemption.

III

Let us illustrate this situation by reference to the Arabic Bible. The inherent problematics of intelligent and intelligible communication between Christians and Muslims in the Arab context are there, disconcertingly, in the very feel of the Christian scriptures in Arabic. It has often been observed from within Arab Islam that these do not read congenially. The reason is not simply the distinctive themes of Christian faith nor the overall shape of the New Testament with its fourfold Gospels and its church "correspondence."[3] It has also to do with the strange quality of the text when registered by readers whose sense of the scriptural in Arabic is made by the Qur'ān. The style, the idiom, the grammar, and the syntax all convey an impression that puzzles, if it does not altogether deter, the Muslim Arab.

This basic reaction—seen here as both symptom and cause of an impasse of mind between Arab and Arab—stems from the Aramaic and Greek in the ancestry of the early Arabic versions and from the western ethos, American and Jesuit, belonging to the nineteenth-century versions. These have worthily established themselves in the affections of Christian Arabs, if not to the degree attained by the seventeenth-century English Bible in the English church. But those affections do not tally with Islamic sympathies. Understanding this liability of Arabic Christian scriptures to depreciation by Arab Muslims involves a brief review of their history. This was deliberately deferred from chapter 11—though clearly part of "the soul"—because it has much to do with what occupies us in this chapter.

The Islamic Qur'ān is so far within the very genius of Arabic as to be the supreme expression of the language. Not so the Arabic Bibles, cherished as they are by generations of Arab Christians. They lack the mystique that the Qur'ān possesses so powerfully for Muslim Arabs—the mystique of a status where meaning and language, fused into one, are music to the ear and home to the mind. That native quality in the native soul no translation could well emulate or convey.

As noted in chapter 3, liturgy in the churches was the last area to yield to arabicization of speech in the wake of Muslim conquest. Worship was the last haven of the old tongues, but as Arabic came to dominate in daily life and society, the liturgical Aramaic, Coptic, Syriac, and Greek needed verbal interpretation for the comprehension of the worshipers. Arabic expositions educated the faithful but left the faith enshrined in its sacred languages. The earliest Christian Arabic emerged in this context,[4] though, in the light of chapter 2, it must be assumed that there was at least a modicum of Christian Arabic through tribe and trade migrations preceding the advent of Islam. But insofar as "scriptuarizing" in Arabic by and for Christians took place in such *targum* form within worship, its terms and themes were of interior Christian vintage and innocent of the Arabness which the Qur'ān had come to dominate and determine.

When the Arabic versions in the Polyglot Bibles of Paris and London and elsewhere in Europe were produced in the sixteenth and seventeenth centuries with the help of Maronite and other scholars, the context, again, was within the *targum* tradition and was domestic to the ancient Christian languages.[5] They did not mediate vocabulary into the mental world of Islam. Their norms of thought remained unrelated to the world of the Qur'ān.[6]

The nineteenth-century enterprises of Bible translation came within a strongly missionary impulse aided by Arab Christian scholars who—if they were not actually converts to the missionary, or to the Uniate, churches—shared their approach. In countering Islam as they saw it, they were not minded to model their Arabic on the Qur'ān's. They were, however, very able practitioners. Eli Smith (1801–1857) and Cornelius Van Dyck (1818–1895) were the American Arabists, and Buṭrus al-Bustānī (1819–1893) and Nāṣīf al-Yazijī (1800–1871) were their Syrian colleagues—figures well known within the renewal of Arabic literature studied in chapter 7. The Beirut Bible they produced holds a prime place, from the 1860s, in the modern development of Arab Christianity.[7] It stimulated the project of the Jesuit Bible, published in the 1870s through the efforts of Augustine Rodst (1826–1906) and Ibrāhīm al-Yazigī (1847–1906) to meet Roman susceptibilities and to seek a more elaborate style. They drew on the Propaganda Bible, which Maronite and Roman scholars had produced, from the Vulgate, in the seventeenth century.[8]

The twentieth century has brought significant revisions of both the Van Dyck and the Jesuit Bibles of a hundred years earlier. These have taken advantage of the steady critical refinement of the Greek and Hebrew texts. They have also facilitated comprehension by paragraphing and introductory guidelines. The new version of the New Testament, published under Jesuit auspices in 1969, draws on the insights of the French *Bible de Jérusalem.* Ecumenical enterprise, meanwhile, concerted resources from the 1950s on, for a complete revision of the Van Dyck Bible. Buṭrus 'Abd al-Malik, with John Thompson, presided over the first ventures with a variety of assessors and reviewers. Their work on the New Testament paved the way for the more ambitious *Today's Arabic Version* (N.T.) published in 1979. It had the Lebanese poet Yūsuf al-Khāl as its main "stylist," and three Egyptians (Bishop Antoine Najīb of the Coptic Catholic Church, Dr. Fahīm 'Azīz of the Coptic Evangelical Church, and Maurice Tawadros) as referees for exegetical questions, with Dr. William Rayburn of the United Bible Societies as translations consultant.

The hope to achieve a common, ecumenical Arabic Bible is still in active pursuit. The New Testament of 1979 has been assessed by a sequence of consultations involving ecclesiastics and scholars within the Middle East Council of Churches. The agreed aim is to attain what Orthodox, Catholic, and Roman alike can unitedly possess and commend. Publication of the Old Testament, translated and exhaustively reviewed, is expected soon. Reporting on their work, the responsible committee explains that the intention has been to find the utmost communication of the original meaning in a modern Arabic "chosen with careful intellectual concern . . . in a clear and free-flowing style" and in hope that phrasing and vocabulary will help in the development of Christian thought itself in the exploration of the divine Word.

There have been other efforts worthy of note alongside this central ecumenical achievement. In the 1970s scholars of the Coptic church issued renderings in Arabic of the Gospels according to Mark and Matthew, printed with patristic commentary and illuminated with iconography. The Maronite Yūsuf 'Awn, in 1978, offered his revision of the New Jesuit version of the four Gospels. Individual initiatives, as in the West, are properly suspect, yet they bear witness to increasing awareness of the fascination of the language dimension—and vocation—in all scriptural faith and of the thoroughness with which all eagerness must be tempered in pursuing it.

But for present purposes the main lesson in the complex story of the Christian scriptures in Arabic is their distance from Islam. In literary shape they enshrine the same otherness that characterizes traditional attitudes on the personal level and in society. There is a deep-seated distinctiveness both in the terms they use and the consciousness they evoke. Phrases in the Qur'ān that might conceivably carry the Christian meaning in Christian texts have been ignored or suspected by translators intent on pure transmission and fortified by convictions relating to revelation, its limits and securities.[9] It is precisely in the most vital areas of meaning and its vocabulary form that this reluctance for mutual terms, this will against any "vacant possession" of terms earmarked as "private," is most insistent. There has been a greater readiness, on the part of some, to colloquialize the language of Arabic translation—despite strong opposition—than to facilitate Muslim understanding by recourse to Islamic terminology.[10] There are limits to how far one can take the risks that ease comprehension by the outsider.

The issues bristle with difficulty. Perhaps, all in all, they are insurmountable. What is not in doubt is that Christian Arabic scriptures speak in one theological dialect and the Qur'ān in another. Christian Arabic, in all versions, reads incongruously to literate Muslims.[11] It is not a text "to the manner born." To Muslim ears it offers from its Greek and Hebrew originals what needs a running *targum* to translate anew what does not alienate the ear or obfuscate the mind. It still has to mediate beyond the tensions of thought in the incidence of vocabulary. It has to do so within a context in which, reciprocally, Muslims will a reservation of Islamic terms from currency elsewhere. Such reciprocal segregation of expression in a single language and a single national Arabness hampers both faiths in the art of language itself and prejudices their role in contemporary life.

A pronounced self-consciousness results from this dual Arabic in things religious. Each remains tenacious of what distinguishes it from the other. It may help, however, in facing this situation to note how, nevertheless, some joint vocabulary avails to enshrine the common theological themes which, we earlier insisted, preexist the disparities. Even here, though, there is a difficulty, in that some Muslim states have legislated against Christian use of common terms, or theologians have deplored them.[12] However, words such as *Allāh* (God), *Rasūl* (apostle), *Raḥmān* (mercy), and *Injil* (Gospel) are possessed by both Arabics. The crucial unequalness of content is at least negotiated within a shared usage. What, then, will it mean to take the Arab-Christian–Arab-Muslim relationship forward from its Arabic language form into their formal theologies?

IV

Attempting a Christian theology of contemporary life with Islam will mean setting aside the long christological debates that occupied us in chapter 4 and, with them, the subtleties belonging then as now to the issues implicit in Islamic faith. These in controversial form only contributed to puzzlement and contention in which their relevance was lost to sight. They registered with Muslims only as apparent tokens of Christian confusion. A right patience with them can now obtain only in their relation to the focal point of both religions, namely, the way we should understand the unity and sovereignty of God and the due stature of the human in surrender.

What such understanding means is well stated in a passage from a Christian author unaware of how close he stands to Islam.

> Life lived in response to God consists of holding many lesser loyalties in subordination to one ultimate and commanding devotion—not in order that the lesser loyalties be spurned but in order to embrace them in a more sustained framework of meaning.
>
> The primacy of the ultimate trust, as conceived in Biblical faith, is consistent with human devotion to lesser causes unless and until such devotion makes the lesser causes into rival absolutes. Man's devotion to God is not diminished by his attempted conquest of nature as long as such conquest is undertaken in recognition of man's final dependence on the Creator. Man's devotion is not diminished by his acceptance of political responsibility unless such political responsibility is embraced as a substitute for God . . . even coercive struggle may be a legitimate means of service unless it becomes a source of devotion to an earthly crusade and admits of no judgement on itself.[13]

Some fellow Christians may demur about the "coercive struggle," but is there a literate Muslim who could miss how aptly it all fits? Everything is there. The cry "Greater is God" (*Allāhu akbar*) means just this disowning of all rival absolutes, and this realization that only God properly subdues them. The acknowledgment of God, in Islam, qualifies all other allegiance, since "only God is God." This unrivaled lordship is the meaning of the divine unity, understood not as of "a unit' mathematically but as the undivided, inalienable sovereignty in God. The lesser causes of nation, state, tribe, science, politics—even faith itself—are legitimate only in their being subordinate. Only the rule of God appropriately ensures their subordination. These are the very fundamentals of Islam.

Such is the whole thrust of the Qur'ān, the scripture in which God is known in "implacable command," religion in the imperative.[14] The imperative relates insistently to the human dominion; without it whence would obedience come? So "the faithful Creator" anticipates the fidelity of humanity in "the ultimate trust," the *amānah* (Surah 33.72), the *khilāfah* of the human who is the *khalīfah* set over God's good earth (Surah 2.30). There is nothing, for Muslims and Christians alike, derogatory to God about the human freedom allowed to preside over the natural order and to which that order is marvelously, copiously, and capriciously responsive as history and technology discover. We have no need to see the greatness of God arguing the irrelevance of humanity, whose relevance is built into the very fabric of creation. It is there in the endless wonder, the summons of the *āyāt*, or "signs," celebrated on almost every page of the Qur'ān evoking human reason and reverence. For Muslim and Christian alike the sense of humanity over nature and of nature for humanity, and both under God, means a sacramental universe.[15]

These uniting truths are prior to all that can divide. They take us further in a unison of conviction. The passage quoted is tuned to the Qur'ān in that it is aware throughout of a crisis in its consciousness of humanity's vocation under God. The vocation is at risk. As that which must be recognized it is that which therefore is liable to be withheld. Loyalties that should be "lesser" demand to be "greater than God" and cry *Naḥnu akbar,* "we are greater." This, when it happens, is the ultimate violation of the divine unity. The human person is no automaton to be maneuvered like a puppet. Nor is the will of God an automatic fact. There is an evident sense in which, mysteriously, He will not have His purposes except as *we* make them our own. To do so is, precisely, our *islām.* But it hinges on our consent, our vigilance, our readiness to identify and disown "sources of devotion which allow no judgment against themselves." It turns on our refusal of substitutes for God, substitutes which, in our minds and motives, usurp the rule of God.

The Qur'ān has a phrase, everywhere recurrent there, for this usurping, namely, attitudes that are *min dūni-Llāhi,* operating "to the exclusion of God." It is not simply that, with the psalmist, "God is not in all their thoughts" (Ps. 10:4). It is that He is deliberately ousted from them. To realize this implicit crisis in the stake God has in humanity is to understand those numerous passages in the Qur'ān—and alike in the Bible—which deplore the obduracy of wayward peoples and register the bitter nemesis overtaking godless tribes. It is to appreciate how the Qur'ān sets ingratitude in the fathering of unbelief and indicts it as the very essence of atheism.

V

It is also to understand the whole role and necessity of prophethood. If creation were not devised for human entrustment or had opted for innocent automata, there would be no necessity for messengers bringing home the divine command, the transcendent claim. These would find a sort of conformity, neither consciously willed nor offered. In the only world we know, the will has to be exhorted and commanded, a world in which prophethood is vital because humanity is charged with duty and with freedom. "Thou shalt" and "thou shalt not" address only the free. God's messengers, as the Bible and the Qur'ān perceive them, are a long succession—hardly necessary if they readily succeeded. They stood in perpetual jeopardy at the hands of those they would convince. The rejection humanity is liable to have for what they demand passes over into enmity to them for faithfully demanding it. The Old Testament witnesses to this tragic situation. It enters grimly into the pre-*Hijrah* experience of Muḥammad. It has to inform the theology we find between us. We must not envisage a faith about God that holds His messengers either superfluous or invulnerable. They are part of what we must recognize to be His travail. They are explicit witness to the risk of creation.

We take these meanings further only when we recognize the mystery at which we have arrived, namely, that the God who intended the world as we have it, who commissions the human race to be His deputy within it and His messengers to educate that dignity, thereby proves to be a risk taker, an expender of Himself, a "friend" who brings us into His ventures as partners free to fail Him. The New Testament has a word for this: *kenōsis,* or "self-expending," a limitation in the interests of an intention, an exercise in hope and patience. Such *kenōsis* is the prerogative of love and belongs with love's nature. The limitation undergone is not external to its will and does not, therefore, compromise its power. It is the measure, not the discredit, of its greatness. Unless we are to deny the God we confess and the humanity we know in ourselves, we have to make room in the sovereignty of God for the reality of the love that suffers.

It is here that the old Christology belongs despite its conflicts over precision of words—a precision scarcely appropriate to the divine self-giving it meant to confess. There can be no doubt that this is the road by which to find its meaning and to set that meaning where it can belong in a logic, from creation and prophethood, accessible to Islam. The question between us is not about *whether* there is God's stake in our humanity but *how far* it might go in what it entails within the divine power and whether what we have in Jesus might or might not be the measure of the answer. Perhaps "the story of Jesus is the heart of His answer . . . to the divine necessities of His children."[16]

Why, it may be asked, should a theology that thinks into Islam be moved to find in the cross of Jesus the symbolic expression of this divine self-giving implicit in creation? Why should it be moved, further, to understand that cross as interpreted from within a life story read as "incarnation"? What can be meant by "the Word made flesh"? How might it be commended where the "sonship" that traditionally describes it is so sadly misconstrued?

May it be that prophethood itself, so cherished in Islam, affords the vital clue? It is clear in the Hebrew Bible and in the Qur'ān that the message cannot be isolated from the messenger. The content of the one is bound up with the status of the other. What is spoken hinges on the credentials of the speaker, and not on inaugurating credentials only but on those that are active in the ongoing, in the quality and travail of what ensues as the hearers or nonhearers react. Clearly this is so in Muḥammad's *Sīrah,* or "career as Prophet." He becomes himself controversial. He is allegedly a mere poet, a nuisance, an upstart, a traitor to "our fathers." In asserting his message he has to account for himself as divinely warranted. The situation develops into "truth through personality," into embodiment within a *Sitz im Leben* which is a *Leben im Sitz.* All is made contextual in a *persona.* So it clearly was in Mecca/Medina as witnessed by *Ḥadīth,* or Tradition. So it was with Hosea, Amos, and Jeremiah in the Hebrew Bible. So it was, manifestly, with Jesus as witnessed by the content of the Gospels and by the apostolic will to write them. In that sense we cannot comprehend Muḥammad aright without understanding—even if not conceding—the logic within Christian conviction about Jesus as "the Word made flesh."

The question our theology would still have to pursue would be whether events in the interaction of the messenger with the time and the place, with the people, could be dire enough and crucial enough to be described as, qualitatively, "the sin of the world." Whether, again, the messenger might read those events as a vocation to suffer their travail—in a word, to "bear them"—in dying on their account. And whether, further again, it could be held divinely meant that he should do so, that we might affirm God to be present there, in that decision, "commending to us His love" by that sign and measure.

These are what Christians do affirm, by an extension of a logic we can discern in all prophethood. For it is clear that prophets are on behalf of God, that what they undergo they undergo for God's sake. In what sense, then, is God in their undergoing? Truly, remotely, or not at all? If the last, is their message, in effect, disowned in the disowning of where it lands them? If we think so, are we still believing in divine greatness, in *Allāhu akbar?*

Our theology, Islam may wish to say, has pursued its logic too far. Prophethood indeed exacts a toll and conveys its heroes into travail, but there is vindication short of the ultimates of tragedy. There is vindication by rescue, by rapture, and by nemesis on enemies. Or the prophet is guided into "right coercion," by which evil is repelled and the good and true enthroned in manifest victory. In what we have called an extension of the logic of prophetic suffering to a perception of "God in Christ," Christian theology has gone too far. The extension is, in fact, a forfeiture of the premise behind all prophethood, namely, the omnipotence of God. The thought of some divine pathos embodied in a suffering Christ is folly and futility, Muslims will say.

VI

Here we reach an impasse or, rather, a parting of the ways. But if a "theology caring with Islam" in the same human scene has to allow what seems irreconcilable in the theme of God, let us take the open issue into the theme of humanity. We have earlier noted all there is in common in the shared faith about *khilāfah,* a sacramental order in nature, and the liability to align our wills with God's in the freedom His revelation addresses. How does this vocation look? How actual, how adequate is the human *islām?*

Perhaps we can best come upon the question by relating to humanity within the pattern of the cross. Since we are plainly divided as to what may be the significance for God of prophetic suffering, perhaps we may clarify the point more readily by reference to humanity and what the Gospel called "the sin of the world." The *Hijrah* of Muḥammad could be our clue.

When force was invoked in the contest with Mecca, the earlier reproach that prophethood had for Meccans was merged into the enmity which hostilities aroused. The due accusation of plural worship continued, but it became entangled in the combative interests of the Muslim army. Those who had formerly been "associators with God" (*mushrikūn*) now became *a'dā'* (enemies). Warfare generated a vested interest in their defeat on behalf of but other than what was spiritually at stake.

By the same token, on the Medinan side there came an exoneration, a kind of alibi for the enmity involved, on the ground that it was involved on God's behalf. We are always in much danger when we think we wield God's sword. Judgment inevitably passes from any inward reckoning because we see ourselves as God's agent against others. Being justified by virtue of that role we hold ourselves immune from self-reproach. Self-questioning, reluctance to engage the foe, and misgivings in the cause are, as the Qur'ān itself insists, impediments to God's will. We come to associate God's will with our innocence; its warrant, being our mandate, is also our exoneration.

Whatever we can or cannot believe about "God in Christ," the way of Jesus' cross escapes these human snares. It gives us no alibi for a false righteousness, no handle to evade our own sinfulness because we are doing God's business. On the contrary, it leaves us in a situation in which it is we who are accused. It saves us by disallowing us the indulgence of forcing others. It tells us that, if we are to be "jealous" on behalf of God, it must first be against ourselves. This sense of things is the heart of any theology caring for the world as it is in Middle East experience today.

For the Middle East is prey to the tyranny of lesser causes made absolute. In taking as ultimate what can only be right as relative those causes repudiate the unity of God. They make idols out of human structures of power and pride and hold themselves accountable only to their own will. So doing they substitute themselves for God, their authority for His sovereignty. The excesses they then commit—Muslim, Christian, Israeli—are the *shirk* that violates the submission due to God alone. Insistently politicized as they are, the confrontations of mosque and church and Zion underline the irony that it is religion itself that is most prone to harden and brutalize the claims of land and tribe and culture and nation. God's Name is then named only in being denied. Invocation and desecration are one and the same. The cause of God is betrayed into being only ours.

Perhaps it is not strange that religions should be, of all structures in society, the most prone to such corruption of themselves, nor remarkable that the monotheisms should offend most tragically. For the greater the cause we serve the greater the temptation to mistake its greatness for our own. For are we not tempted with our own desires?[17] What of these when we are supposedly confessing that "greater is God"? The notion of *Jihād*—an Islamic term but a general phenomenon—is the crucial factor here, for it embodies precisely this idea of being uninhibitedly on behalf of what is God's. It finds *sabīl Allāh,* "the path of God," conferring self-esteem in a motivation God approves. It is, therefore, such as to obviate both doubt and need of penitence. To be ostensibly obeying God overrides all reservations whether about oneself, one's ends, or one's proceeding. When these are harnessed to things political and military, the likelihood of penitent disquiet recedes still further.

It is true that Islamic writers have distinguished between the greater and the lesser *Jihād* and have identified the former with the inner struggle against pride, self-will, and sin, whereas the latter belonged with the outer world of faithful belligerence. How desperately the distinction needs to be recovered. Too often this relation of greater to lesser is reversed. Indeed, the history of *Jihād,* of Crusade, of the *Gush Emunīm* in every faith, suggests a despair about the distinction ever holding, where coercion obtains and strife is the argument. Only a radical humility about themselves can save religions from themselves. Middle East history would seem to say that all other spheres of salvation wait upon humility.

A theology-with-a-mind-for-Islam has to be one of liberation from the pride and perversity of religions themselves. The meaning of Jesus' cross, both the will to suffer uncoercively *and* the evidence within that suffering of how malign the world can be, comes here into its own. For it has to do with the evil of collectives—of state power, religious expediency, and social instinct. It is collectives that override private conscience, structures that demand conformity and deny compassion.[18] Theology, therefore, must reject an overly individualist notion of evil and wrong. The Qur'ān certainly registers the nemesis that overtook whole peoples, like ʿĀd and Thamūd, for their collective wrongdoing and communal resistance to the word of their prophets, Hūd and Ṣāliḥ. But its emphasis in the final judgment is strongly on the individual and the singular world of the self, its deeds and misdeeds. It is the members of the person rather than the annals of society that are heard in the last judgment. Private conscience is indeed vital, and what each and all, severally, have "forwarded" (as the Qur'ān has it) to the last day is properly indicted or approved. But private conscience is often stilled or duped or suborned by powers beyond its reach. It may be the hapless observer or the victim of what it cannot alter or defy. Politicization of religious causes is not seldom the atrophy of religious conscience. Penitence becomes an irrelevance where power decides.

VII

The vital test of any faith, therefore, is its ability to identify and resist the evils that are collective in their origin and their momentum and to do so most of all when the faith itself is their source and sanction. An honest review of the Middle East story may conclude that all such hope is vain. When they most need to be self-critical and in doubt of themselves, where the passion of creed and greed, of tribe and trade, is rampant, they most readily succumb to aid and abet. Lebanon finds itself shattered and devastated by the strife religious absolutes have entrenched. What can it mean to "command the good and prohibit the evil"—in the sense of the Islamic principle: *al-amr bi-l-maʿrūf wa al-nahī ʿan al-munkar*—when the several structures, both creedal and institutional, of the principle itself leave the sovereignty of God sounding in the situation like a hollow mockery? The commanding and the prohibiting may belong theocratically: they do not obtain theocratically. Sabra and Chatila are witness.

How do we relate what is seen and suffered in current history to high-sounding divine monarchism among such human subjects of the sovereignty as we humans are?

> The governance of God, the One and Only Lord and absolute Monarch and the equality of men in the sight of God, identically dependent upon and subject to Divine Law, each being none the less responsible for his actions and taking upon himself the obligations which devolve from this law . . . in an egalitarian theocracy. . . .[19]

The rhetoric reads well, but how can it ignore the helplessness that all too often cripples the individual responsible for his or her actions in a welter of forces he or she cannot control or escape? Will it suffice to take upon ourselves the obligations that devolve from this law when they are nullified by the structures, including religion, within which we are to do so? Do poverty and wealth, power and powerlessness, leave us identically subject as refugees and warlords, to egalitarian theocracy? If that exists, how can it function so unevenly, eventuate so unjustly, prescribe itself so diversely? Do we not need to interrogate again the faiths that guide us and ask whether an ethical transcendence must not somehow be constrained by the realities we confront when we believe in it? Divine monarchy of the good and the right is surely in travail also, ill-served by a custodian theology too arrogant, too facile, and too impatient, with His Name.

Each of the monotheisms in the Middle East, guilty in their different ways of this bias for themselves against a right loyalty to God, has the onus on itself. Only out of the inner resources of these religions can the answer come. If humility avails, perhaps they can assist each other. But, if the analysis is sound, then Arab Christianity must hold on to the central Christian conviction, at the heart of its scripture and its liturgy, of the God whose sovereignty fulfills itself in the love that comes, suffers, and reconciles, in the measures we can identify in Jesus and the cross. Divine law is presupposed in that Gospel, for it is only the claim of the good that identifies the nature of sin. It is of the nature of sin to need the initiatives of grace, and of the initiatives of grace to go for their fulfillment to the length of the love that takes upon itself what sin means and law seeks. Christianity only avails, both as judgment and salvation, by virtue of this faith. Such is its future with Islam.

This means refraining from the romanticism that characterized the founding of the Ba'th and the thinking of Michel 'Aflaq, reviewed in chapter 7. The subsequent history of the Ba'th belied his inspirational theme of a unitary Arabness. The separate nationalisms that 'Aflaq passionately deplored still hold the field. There was point in the protest against a timid, introverted, separatist version of Arab Christians as sectarians aloof from the main thrust of a dynamic Arab will to unity. But the readiness this protest implied to marginalize what was distinctive in Christian faith and, so doing, to concede that Islam was the decisive cultural and spiritual home of all Arabs misread the continuing vocation to retain for Arab self-understanding the perspectives of Christ and the New Testament. Yet, for all their romanticism as a vision of Arabness, 'Aflaq's ideals served to counsel the will to be distinctive against all that is crudely and negatively sectarian.

VIII

Will a Christianity, resolute about its own distinctive witness and identity, ever enjoy from Islam a reciprocal posture of religious humility and due awe of God, given the built-in instincts of Islamic history—instincts very much currently alive and hardening? Will not an outright secularism hold out better hope in the light of what afflicts the Middle East? Certainly the record of the religious past justifies the impatience about dogma and the disquiet about sectarianism, from which the secular idea springs. It has positive principles to commend of honesty and openness, of reverent agnosticism and the will to unity. These contrast commendably with obscurantism and rigorism in the religious mind. It might arguably claim to be the surer way of enjoining the good and forbidding the evil.

What is the Christian contribution to the debate that secularism arouses within and between the faiths? Not, surely, a suppression of the points it is making nor a blind defensiveness. What is merely denunciatory never realizes the truth. That unbelief happens in this world, that humanity is free to doubt, ignore, or discount the claim of God is evident enough both from history and from the register of revelation itself, whether Christian or Muslim. The prophets know well the obduracy of which humans are capable. Nor can it be corrected, reversed, or countered by compulsion of which, according to Surah 2.256, there is "none in religion," or rather, proper to it.[20] If in the very order of creation and the nature of law, under God, humans are responsible for faith or for unfaith, religions in housing the one must allow of the other. *Kufr,* or "irreligion," cannot then be merely damnable. It cannot be rightly dissuaded and defeated if it is only denounced. There is that about true faith which cannot subsist unless it tolerates what calls it into question. So much is evident in the Christian experience of divine grace. It can also be argued from the freedom necessary to a right Islam.

But, if the secular has to be allowed, it must, in the Christian view, be acknowledged for the reductionism it involves by its forfeiture of the sacred, its disavowal of the transcendent, and its loss of the sense of being claimed by divine law and love. Yet, in knowing those dimensions of our human condition for what they are, faith must beware of condemning *all* secular thinking as dismissive of what faith means by them. There *is* a secularity that is wistful and reverent, an agnosticism that wants help with its unbelief. Muslim assurance and *Jihād* have not generally understood this.

If, therefore, faith is to merit acceptance and carry conviction to the uncertain and the insecure, it must know where these are in their honest perplexity. It will not do to write them off as those for whom "the desert sun no longer scorches or dazzles," having affirmed that "truth—like that desert sun—is overwhelmingly self-evident." Such metaphor refutes itself.[21] Neither Islam nor Christianity can—or should want to—claim that doctrine can dictate consent or truth be other than commended in an open world. At the present juncture the lesson may be harder for the Muslim than for others in the way the calendars of experience run.

Against the fact of irreligion the sacred has to be patiently held in trust and the trust wisely undertaken. Does not the sacred presuppose the secular as the sphere of operation, the arena in which it happens in the hallowing, humanly, of "the things of God"? "The things of God" are, as Islam insists, everywhere and unconfined. There is nothing exempt from their range and relevance. To concede the secular is not to think otherwise: it is to know that only the will to let it be so brings anything under God in an actual *islām* to make it so.[22] Order, tradition, habit, and dogma being a setting for such *islām*, it is right for an ordered faith to believe itself custodian of such patterns of surrender, "letting God be God" within the fabric of life and culture. Such ordered faith may rightly hold majority dominance in society, given a tolerance of diversity and a will to coexist. To allow the secular, in that sense, means no abdication of a faith's vocation. Rather it means a pursuit of it more consonant with the rule of God and the freedom proper to humanity. It fulfills the precept concerning "no compulsion in religion."

What follows, in that case, for the age-old Islamic concept of *Sharī'ah?* Its provisions in the sense of religion as devotion and ritual relate by definition only to the Islamic community, other rites being within approved minority status. Its legal and social provisions would obtain either for Muslims alone or for others insofar as they are consistent with due secular liberty and an equality before the law for all citizens. It follows that law of partly secular origin must supplement or displace the *Sharī'ah* if such liberty and equality are to be ensured. This raises the question of the relation of the human-made to the God-given and the contingent question of how reason and revelation interact. Large issues of legislation and its organs, courts and their jurisdiction, are also involved. But need the human-made be necessarily the God-displeasing, given the evident providence of God in both the gift of reason and the fact of human diversity? Islam as the dominant faith could thus undertake the major guidance of society, fulfill its duty within itself, and so be preserved from the violation of the mercy and sovereignty of God of which a theocracy claimed for itself would always be guilty. To understand God, *Sharī'ah,* and society in this way will not be to surrender to godlessness: it will be to serve God-fearingness more patiently.

Only such a readiness to concede the secular dimension does rightly by the nature of religious faith. The Arabism which invites its Christian elements to take Islam to themselves simply as the expression of Arab culture hardly does justice to Islam as it believes itself to be. What Muslim could well be content to have Christians relate to Islam on those grounds?

And what would Christians have done to their faith if they acceded to those pleas? If faiths are to have the allegiance they demand, they cannot be diminished to a cultural appendage. Indeed, it follows that only in allowing a genuine secularity can faiths exercise a genuine authority. Otherwise, their appeal is not essentially religious.

To conclude thus no doubt raises the issue of what qualifies as religious. Islam in claiming the whole of life as under God—a claim that Christian faith equally affirms—has traditionally understood its inclusiveness to be feasible by law, revelation, precept, and state. But this is to fall foul of its own continuous experience of human non-*islām,* where it has to deplore a *jāhiliyyah* of and within Islam itself.[23] Human obduracy frustrates its bringing all things actually under God. The nonsubordination to God exists; hence, the necessity of identifying, of falling back on, an *islām* that is considered true in quality (by whatever criteria) and yet partial in incidence since there are areas of life and society where it does not obtain. The areas where it does obtain will be characterized by devotion, fidelity with ritual and ethics, and disciplined living. It is these which are denoted in the phrase "religion properly understood," which Islam so strongly rejects. To speak, however, in that way of religion as clearly not coterminous with society, is not to write off society as no longer God's domain or to abandon the claim that all is properly to be "under God." It is simply to serve that principle realistically as the ever-unfinished task in a world that possesses—under God—and exerts the option of being secular. If *islām* was automatic, or instinctive, there would be no point in requiring it. The secular in that sense belongs to the same world as prophethood.

The inevitable disparity between what is and what ought not to be, between what ought to be and is not, is implicit in the whole sphere of ethical monotheism and explicit insistently in the contrasts within the Qur'ān. It is a major part of Christian converse with Islam to bring this logic to bear. For neglect of it relieves faith of exacting duties and tempts it into rigorism and violence of spirit.

IX

There is one related feature of this realm of discourse especially exacting for Arab Christianity. So much in the secular equation derives from the western factor. Technology and the mentality it generates spread from the West and preoccupy the East. Outright political imperialism may have retreated, but other economic and diplomatic forms persist. Arabness and Islam alike are caught in an identity crisis in which the West is at once a measure to emulate and an enemy to reject. Technology may be recently western in its history, but it has a long and honored progenitor in the East of the middle centuries. Yet rightly to note this does not suffice to resolve the complex in the psyche.

This displays itself in a form of counterattack on the West, in which Arab Christians have shared equally with Arab and other Muslims. This response, proper in many senses, of identity assertion proceeds by accusing the West of crude stereotype imaging of the East. It upbraids western orientalism as a gross form of western superiority complex, expressed in a literature and a scholarship that imposed its own false portrayal on the East and refused to care sensitively for the East's own evaluations of itself. By distortion it had its own way with its eastern versions and made these the instrument of control and, indeed, of denigration.

Western learning, these critics add, was not immune from this indictment; indeed, it stood in the forefront. Scholarship was suborned to politics, funded by interested parties and made a tool of derogatory interpretation. Western Christianity, which had an active part in these ventures, was held to be implicated in the disservice they perpetrated. Nineteenth- and twentieth-century western orientalism is thus found uniformly culpable, and a conniver with misrepresentation.[24]

What, then, of the Arab Christianity which during those centuries was so much involved in western ties and western sympathies that, on this count, must be read as western enmities? It will not suffice to point to integrity and sincerity, as well as genuine sympathy, in much western Christian relationship. That is necessary in the interests of truth, but how things are perceived, rightly or wrongly, remains a fact of the situation. It may be observed that there was a certain dishonesty in the indictment in that it spoke from within the assumptions of western intellectualism—and often from western academia—yet faulted these when pursued by orientalists. It may also be observed that what orientalists described about the East often echoed what easterners, ardent for renewal, were saying about themselves.[25]

But the point here is not the scholarly one of right or wrong. It is how to achieve imaginative, uninhibited, and uninhibiting sympathy between Arab and western Christians, given the inextricable bonds in which history sets them and given the liability those ties incur in the perceptions of world Islam. The role of the Middle East Council of Churches and its relationships with the World Council of Churches point the way effectively. They, along with the bonds between the papacy and Uniate churches, are caught in the complexities over Israel and the status of Jerusalem.[26] Arab Melchite Orthodoxy is not yet right with a past that tied its Arabness too long into Greek tutelage, but the will to mend or surmount the circumstances that for so long have estranged relationships is not in doubt.

One factor in this context that must concentrate the mind is the pressure of sheer human yearning for meaning beyond misgiving and for peace out of despair. Our concern over the sacred/secular issue is no indulgence in abstraction, a debate within theology. It has to do with more than turbaned heads and exegesis of our scriptures. It belongs with that *hudā*, that guidance, out of bewilderment, which faith is supposed to give. To read Arabic literature today—novelists and poets, rather than pundits and journalists—is to register the malaise, the futility, and the wistfulness that underlie the turmoil of politics and the formulations of interfaith exchanges in doctrine and language. Those who "hold the mirror up to nature . . . to show the very age and body of the time" are not seldom proved the right index for theology. If there is truth in the dictum that "Islam began as a stranger and will be so at the end,"[27] then perhaps our surest concern today must be with the perplexed and the skeptical, rather than with the assertive and the clamorous. If so, the Gospel of Christ will find such openness to the lostness in daily life a welcome meeting ground.

That lostness, portrayed in numerous stories, dramas, and poems, is captured typically in Najīb Maḥfūẓ's *Tharthara fawq al-Nīl* (Chatter on the Nile), in which a group of Cairenes, cooped up (symbolically) on a houseboat, exchange a dreary catalogue of petty boredoms, the inanities of office routine, the social frustrations and the trivialities by which they are plagued. Moored off the streets, the houseboat hints at the extraction of the disillusion from the medley in which it might be blurred for better focus into irony and skepticism.[28] Here, in a different idiom, is *The Waste Land* of T. S. Eliot, who played, as noted earlier, so large a part in the stimulus of twentieth-century Arabic writing. But discovery of "the death that undoes so many" is no mere western import: it is the acute self-awareness of the human in the eastern context. It identifies the sphere, the mood, and the yearning, where—more than anywhere else—the encounter of faiths has to be. For that same reason it is the context in which the Gospel of the love that cares and suffers and retrieves and does so as the truth of the divine Name will most surely find itself.

"Feed me with wishes," wrote an early Muslim poet, "so that I may live by means of them." But, as another poet wrote, "Wishes are the capital of the bankrupt."[29] What, then, where it is most urgent of investment, is our *ra's māl*, the "capital" we have by which to think and act and relate in the world as humanly lived and as divinely interpreted? How does the majority concede the equal humanity of the minority and, so doing, surmount its passion for self-assurance? How does the minority surmount its fear of being, or proving, peripheral, its cult of the introverted mind, its search for discrete security? How ready is either group for a confidence in God Himself that might allow them to risk habitual versions of themselves? Can the supreme Islamic claim of *Tawḥīd*, of the divine unity, be understood and served as nonpolitical so that "religion may be only God's"

(Surah 2.193)? That is the question implicit in the spiritual defiance of God which by its nature cannot be forcibly transformed into a willing worship and a true society. The central conviction of Christian faith and Eucharist concerning the God who reigns in the meaning of the wounds of Jesus is where the divine unity and the human situation come together.

Arabness was present at the very beginning of the church. By the fact of Islam, Arabness in Christian shape has undertaken the continuity of the church through centuries of trial by circumstance and survival by grace, "winnowed with so rough a wind." The share that Arabness had in the origins and in the perpetuation of the faith in Christ leaves no ground for fearing that it has ended. Its vicissitudes have always been hazardous and its destiny beleaguered. What currently it faces, inwardly and outwardly, lives with a retrospect that suffices for its education into the unknown future. If, in all the foregoing, we have had the spiritual vocation of Arab Christianity in mind, it is precisely because all other aspects turn on unpredictables, the passions and politics around and ahead, by which vocation is attended and survival itself always threatened.

Notes

1. Some Muslim observers reacted to inter-Arab ruptures after the Iraqi invasion of Kuwait by saying, in effect, "A plague on all your houses": nation-states have no valid place in the true order of Islam. For a now-classic statement of this view, see the trial of Sayyid Qutb, in Cairo in 1965. It is discussed in my *The Pen and the Faith: Eight Modern Muslim Writers and the Qur*'ān (Winchester, Mass.: Allen & Unwin, 1985), pp. 53f.

2. How such incompatibility might be overcome, in view of Christian belief in the Incarnation and Islamic transcendence, is discussed in *Truth and Dialogue,* ed. John Hick (London, 1974), pp. 126–139.

3. See my *Jesus and the Muslim: An Exploration* (Winchester, Mass.: Allen & Unwin, 1985), ch. 4, "A Muslim Reader and the New Testament."

4. *Targum,* in the Hebraic tradition, meant an Aramaic paraphrase of scripture. The Arabic *tarjumah,* a translation, is akin to this. In the case of Arabic renderings of non-Arabic originals in the aftermath of the arabicization of common speech, the translators or paraphrasers had their Arabic as an acquired language and were not concerned, or able, to relate their renderings to Islamic thought, since they were operating within situations interior to Christian worship and community. Thus the Christian transition into Arabic, outside learned circles, did not engage religiously with Islam.

5. The Arabic in the Paris Polyglot was the work of scholars from the Maronite College in Rome. The Arabic of the London Polyglot owed much to the Semitic scholarship of John Selden (1584–1654), Edward Pococke (1604–1691), Bishop Brian Walton (1600–1661), and a number of learned editors. See the detailed

analysis by John A. Thompson in *The Bible Translator* 6 (1955), 1–12, 51–55, 98–106, 146–150, with extensive bibliography.

6. There is something of a parallel in the role of the great Jewish Arabist Sa'īd ibn Yūsuf al-Fayyūmī (c. 892–942), or Saadia Gaon, whose Arabic Pentateuch is in the Paris Polyglot. His preface to that work explains that he made it to enable Arabic-speaking Jews to understand their Torah. It is noteworthy that he acknowledges the translator's need to paraphrase in order the convey meaning, handle metaphors, and elucidate perplexities. His work is a measure, in the Hebrew context, of the problematics concerning transitions of meaning into popular Arabic usage in the Christian context. The translator's constituency is a significant determinant of what its language can take.

7. Smith and Van Dyck and their collaborators were superb both in their competence and their diligence, and their work has endured. Critical work on the original texts and other considerations relating to Arabic usage have required their supersession by new ventures. But like long-standing versions in other languages the Van Dyck Bible has an irreplacable status and deep loyalty among Arab Christians.

8. The Propaganda Bible was published in Rome in 1671 after the final adherence of the Maronites to Rome and the increasing Latin factor in their life and thought. Based on the Latin Vulgate, it replaced existing versions and took its name from the Sacred Congregation for the Propagation of the Faith. It owed something, however, to the stimulus of Arabic versions of the Pentateuch and the New Testament made by a Dutch Protestant, Thomas Erpenius, between 1616 and 1622.

9. Arab Islam has always been fortified by the fact that the language native to its people was the only proper, requisite and constitutive language of revelation *qua* Qur'ān. The Bible, in its diversity of contents and forms, proceeds on a very different apprehension of revelation. But even via translation many Christians have been anxious to endow its phrasings and vocabulary with the kind of sanctity that excludes their being allowed to mediate into any other realm of discourse, lest what is held to be their biblical import should be endangered or their revelatory status impugned. See below.

10. That only the literary language should be printed has long been instinctive to Arabic writers. Novels and plays have, it is true, come to concede that conversation is unreal if not colloquialized and so allowable in print. Christian evangelism has been eager to produce and circulate colloquial versions of the Gospel against the resistance of the guardians of true Arabic. Print, of course, presupposes literates, but the sense of a need to colloquialize belongs within the larger problem of how language best serves meaning within the mental and religious exigencies of comprehension.

11. Muḥammad al-Sādiq Ḥusain published a translation of the Psalms, *Sifr al-Mazāmīr* (Cairo, 1961), in which he ventured a style more recognizably Islamic in syntax and phrasing.

12. Some of the Malaysian states, for example, have banned the use of the terms "God," "apostle," "mercy," "Gospel," and other Arabic Christian usages on the part of the churches in those states.

13. Edward Le Roy Long, Jr., *The Role of the Self in Conflicts and Struggle* (Philadelphia: Westminster Press, 1963), p. 143.

14. Thus, for example, Fazlūr Raḥmān urges the imperative nature of Islamic revelation as "functional" to obedience, not declarative of mystery (*Major Themes of the Qur'ān* [Chicago: Bibliotheca Islamica, 1980], chs. 1, 5). Similarly Gai Eaton writes of his Islam as "an implacable religion rooted in the transcendent" (*King of the Castle: Choice and Responsibility in the Modern World* [London, 1977], p. 20). He insists that for "true believers, the truth of their religion—the divine Unity and all that it implies—is so overwhelmingly self-evident that to deny it is like denying the desert sun" (p. 15).

15. "Sacramental" is, of course, a Christian term, but it is not inexact when applied to the Qur'ān's doctrine of the role of humanity in nature and of the "signs" of God. See, further, the case for this view in my *The Mind of the Qur'ān: Chapters in Reflection* (London: George Allen & Unwin, 1973), ch. 9.

16. The phrase is George MacDonald's; see his *Creation in Christ,* ed. R. Hein (Wheaton, Ill.: Harold Shaw Pubs., 1976), p. 213.

17. T. S. Eliot, *Murder in the Cathedral* (London: Faber & Faber, 1968), p. 42.

18. Muḥammad Kāmil Husayn made this theme of the sanctity—and oppression—of individual conscience the major emphasis of his study of Jesus' crucifixion: *Qaryah Ẓālimah* (Cairo, 1942); Eng. trans. *City of Wrong: A Friday in Jerusalem,* trans. Kenneth Cragg (Amsterdam: Djambatan, 1959).

19. Jean-Louis Michon, "Religious Institutions," in *The Islamic City,* ed. R. B. Sergeant (Paris, 1980), p. 67. He writes that *'asabiyyah,* or "solidarity," "extends to the entirety of men who hold to the message of the Qur'ān," but he does not indicate to what such holding extends.

20. The crucial sentence in 2.256 uses what grammarians call "absolute negation": *lā ikrāha* "there is not compulsion . . . ." The words *fī-l-Dīn,* "in religion," imply that there may be force right elsewhere. Therein is a certain approval of the distinction we are making between what rightly obtains in religion and what may be proper *fī-l-dawlah,* "in the state." But the negation has to be read as imperative, "There should not be . . . ," since compulsion exists where force has any role in the circumstances in which belief happens. Since, as the following words say, "the right has truly been made clear and distinct from the wrong," noncoercive truth stands on its own sufficient ground.

21. Eaton, *King of the Castle,* p. 16. The metaphor of the irresistible sun fits the irresistible truth of God, yet is stretched for a situation in which it no longer has that quality. Thus the claim of God is both undeniable and deniable, absolute everywhere yet anywhere ignored.

22. This use of *islām* as a simple noun is its original significance, i.e., personal surrender or submission to the will and law of God as enjoined by the Prophet and the Qur'ān. "Islam" (distinguished from it in English by the initial capital, which Arabic lacks) is a later concept and one for which there is no warrant in the Qur'ān. Indeed, it may be argued—as extensively by the Canadian Islamicist Wilfred Cantwell Smith—that the institutionalizing of religions, as distinguished from the faith of the religious, is a western invention we do well to abandon. In

our present context our concern is simply to differentiate between *islām* (small *i*) and Islam (capital *I*), between believing and behaving, and between structure and history.

23. A *jāhiliyyah* within Islam is in fact like a contradiction in terms, since *jāhiliyyah* was the "state of wild ignorance" before Muḥammad's message, the unruliness prior to Islam. That the condition of Islam after fourteen centuries should be alleged to deserve this term in its reproach is to imply a most damning paradox. Yet the charge is not infrequent on the part of "pure" Muslims disavowing other Muslims than themselves, whose *islām* they see as a kind of virtual apostasy, a reversion to pre-Islamic paganism. There could not be a more paradoxical indictment.

24. The most erudite and forthright example is Edward Said, *Orientalism* (New York: Random House, 1978). See also Asaf Hussain, Robert Olson, and Jami Qureshi, eds., *Orientalism, Islam and Islamicists* (Brattleboro, Vt.: Amana Books, 1984); *Arab Society*, ed. S. K. Farsoum (London, 1985), esp. pp. 105–122 (Said on "Orientalism Reconsidered"). There is, it would seem, a degree of Palestinian nationalism in Edward Said's approach. He insists that all knowledge turns on power and that there is no western orientalism not funded by political, commercial, or imperialist interests. It would seem, on this count, that only insiders to it can know a culture, seeing that all outsiders bring unsurmountable prejudice. The dishonesty lies in propounding this view from within an eastern insidership, which has so eminently demonstrated a capacity to know the West and its ethos and literature on the part of one, by origin an outsider. It would have been generous to acknowledge similar capacities in reverse on the part of those orientalists, e.g., Hamilton Gibb, whom he mostly castigates. For one example of eastern writers making the same points about the East for which western writers are accused, see Wadād al-Qādī, "East and West in ʻAlī Mubārak's Alamuddin, (1823–1893)," in *Life in the Arab East, 1890–1939*, ed. M. R. Buheiry (Beirut, 1981), pp. 20–37. Mubārak finds a static tradition, a lethargy, in which "the East knows little about itself and nothing outside itself" (p. 29) and needs to renew itself urgently. Emīr Shakīb Arslān wrote similarly in *Limādhā Ta'akhkhara al-Muslimūn?* (Why have Muslims been backward?) (Cairo, 1939).

25. When cultures are in academic exposition of each other the psyche is always involved as well as the intelligence and an element of "the mote in the other eye" occurs. It is not escaped when writers are bicultural. Reproach in either direction betrays in some measure a sharing of what deserves it.

26. See *The Vatican, Islam, and the Middle East*, ed. Kall C. Ellis (Syracuse, 1987), pp. 109–162.

27. It continues "Blessed are the strangers" (*Sunan* of Ibn Mājā [Cairo, 1898] 2:477–478). The tradition would seem to refer to the hostile reception Muḥammad encountered in the initiation of his mission and through the years that culminated in the *Hijrah*, or willed exile from Mecca, in 622. He was accused of alienating Meccans from the traditions of the fathers. In what sense Islam will return a stranger readers must decide.

28. The novel was published in Cairo in 1966. See also Roger Allen, *The Arabic*

Novel: An Historical and Critical Introduction (Syracuse, N.Y.: Syracuse University Press, 1982), pp. 101–107; Kenneth Cragg, *The Pen and the Faith: Eight Modern Muslim Writers and the Qur'ān* (Winchester, Mass.: Allen & Unwin, 1985), pp. 145–164.

29. Quoted from F. Rosenthal, *Sweeter than Hope: Complaint and Hope in Medieval Islam* (Leiden, 1983), p. 127. The poet is Ibn Qunbur.

Bibliography

General and Chapter 1

Arberry, Arthur J., ed. *Religion in the Middle East.* 2 vols. Ann Arbor, Mich.: Books on Demand, 1969.

Atiya, Aziz S. *A History of Eastern Christianity.* Millwood, N.Y.: Kraus Reprint & Periodicals, 1980.

Baker, Derek, ed. *The Orthodox Churches and the West.* Oxford: Basil Blackwell Publishers, 1976.

Barrett, David, ed. *World Christian Encyclopedia: A Comparative Survey of Churches and Religions in the Modern World, A.D. 1900–2000.* New York: Oxford University Press, 1982.

Beckingham, C. F., ed. *Atlas of the Arab World and the Middle East.* New York: St. Martin's Press, 1960.

Betts, Robert B. *Christians in the Arab East.* Rev. ed. Atlanta: John Knox Press, 1978.

Carter, Jimmy C., Jr. *The Blood of Abraham.* Boston: Houghton Mifflin, 1986.

Colby, Saul P. *Christianity in the Holy Land: Past and Present.* Tel Aviv: Arn Hasefer, 1969.

Farsoun, Samih K., ed. *Arab Society: Continuity and Change.* Dover, N.H.: Croom Helm, 1985.

al-Faruqi, Ismail. *On Arabism: 'Urūbah and Religion.* Amsterdam: Djambatan, 1962.

Hajjar, Joseph. *Les Chrétiens Uniates du Proche Orient.* Paris, 1962.

Hill, Henry, ed. *Light from the East: A Symposium.* Toronto: Anglican Diocese of Toronto, 1988.

Hitti, Philip K. *A History of the Arabs.* 10th ed. New York: St. Martin's Press, 1970.

Holt, Peter M., ed. *Studies in the History of the Near East.* London: Frank Cass, 1973.
Horner, Norman H. *A Guide to the Churches of the Middle East: Present-Day Christianity in the Middle East and North Africa.* Ed. Wilbert Shenk et al. Elkhart, Ind.: Mennonite Board of Missions, 1989.
Hourani, Albert H. *Arabic Thought in the Liberal Age, 1798–1939.* New York: Cambridge University Press, 1983.
——. *A History of the Arab Peoples.* London: Faber & Faber, 1991.
——. *Minorities in the Arab World.* New York: AMS Press, 1947.
Hussey, J. M. *The Orthodox Church in the Byzantine Empire.* New York: Oxford University Press, 1990.
Ilwas, Mar Ignatius Z. *The Syrian Orthodox Church.* Aleppo, 1983.
Joseph, John. *The Nestorians and Their Muslim Neighbors: A Study of Western Influence on Their Relations.* Princeton, N.J.: Princeton University Press, 1961.
Leroy, Jules. *Monks and Monasteries of the Middle East.* Trans. Peter Collin. London: George G. Harrap & Co., 1963.
Lewis, Bernard. *The Arabs in History.* New York: Harper & Row, 1966.
Mansfield, Peter J. *The Arabs.* Rev. ed. New York: Penguin Books, 1985.
Mubarak, Youakim. *Les Chrétiens et le Monde Arabe.* Beirut, 1973.
Rondet, Pierre. *Les Chrétiens d'Orient.* Paris, 1955.
al-Shabi, A. *The Arab World.* Danbury, 1973.

Chapter 2

Andrae, Tor. *Les Origines de l'Islam et le Christianisme.* Paris: Adrien-Maisonneuve, 1955.
Bell, Richard. *The Origin of Islam in its Christian Environment: The Gunning Lectures.* Reprint of 1925 edition. London: Cass, 1968.
Cheikho, Louis. *Le Christianisme et la Littérature Chrétienne en Arabie.* Beirut, 1912, 1919.
Cragg, Kenneth. *The Event of the Qur'an: Islam in Its Scripture.* London: George Allen & Unwin, 1971.
Hammond, Peter C. *The Nabateans: Their History, Culture and Archaeology.* Gothenburg, 1973.
Lyall, Charles J. *Translations of Ancient Arabian Poetry.* Reprint of 1885 ed. Westport, Conn.: Hyperion Press, 1987.
McCullough, W. S. *A Short History of Syriac Christianity to the Rise of Islam.* Atlanta: Scholars Press, 1982.
Shahid, Irfan. *Byzantium and the Arabs in the Fifth Century.* Washington: Dumbarton Oaks, 1990.

——. *Byzantium and the Arabs in the Fourth Century.* Washington: Dumbarton Oaks, 1984.

——. *The Martyrs of Najran.* Brussels: Bollandist Press, 1971.

——. *Rome and the Arabs in the Third Century.* Washington: Dumbarton Oaks, 1980.

Trimingham, John S. *Christianity among the Arabs in Pre-Islamic Times.* New York: Longman, 1979.

Wilkinson, John, ed. and trans. *Egeria's Travels.* London: SPCK, 1971.

Chapter 3

Arnold, T. W. *The Preaching of Islam.* Chicago: Kazi Publications, n.d.

——, and Alfred Guillaume, eds. *The Legacy of Islam.* New York: Gordon Press, 1976.

Donner, Fred McGraw. *The Early Islamic Conquests.* Princeton, N.J.: Princeton University Press, 1981.

Hill, D. R. *The Termination of Hostilities in the Early Arab Conquests.* London: Luzac & Co., 1971.

Juynboll, G. H. A., ed. *Studies on the First Century of Islamic Society.* Carbondale, Ill.: Southern Illinois University Press, 1982.

Tritton, A. S. *The Caliphs and their Non-Muslim Subjects: Critical Study of the Covenant of the Umar.* Reprint of 1930 ed. Lanham, Md.: Biblio Distribution Center, 1970.

Ye'or, Bat. *The Dhimmi: Jews and Christians under Islam.* Trans. David Maisel et al. Cranbury, N.J.: Fairleigh Dickinson University Press, 1985.

Chapter 4

Haddad, Robert. *Syrian Christians in Muslim Society: An Interpretation.* Reprint of 1970 ed. Westport, Conn.: Greenwood Publishing Group, Inc., 1981.

Khoury, Adel Theodore. *Les Théologiens Byzantins et l'Islam.* Paris, 1969.

Meyendorff, John. *Christ in Eastern Christian Thought.* Crestwood, N.Y.: St. Vladimir's Seminary Press, 1975.

——. *L'Eglise Orthodoxe: Hier et aujourd'hui.* Paris: Editions du Seuil, 1960.

Rustum, Asad J. *The Church of the City of God, Great Antioch.* 3 vols. Beirut, 1963. Arabic.

Sahas, Daniel. *John of Damascus on Islam.* Leiden: E. J. Brill, 1972.

Sweetman, J. Windrow. *Islam and Christian Theology: A Study of the Interpretations of Theological Ideas in the Two Religions.* 3 vols. New York: Gordon Press, 1980.

Walzer, Richard. *Greek into Arabic: Essays on Islamic Philosophy.* Cambridge, Mass., 1962.

Watt, W. Montgomery. *Islamic Philosophy and Theology.* 2nd ed. New York: Columbia University Press, 1988.

——. *Muslim Intellectual: A Study of Al-Ghazali.* Edinburgh: University Press, 1963.

Chapter 5

Atiya, A. S. *Crusade in the Later Middle Ages.* London: Methuen, 1938.

Daniel, Norman. *The Arabs and Mediaeval Europe.* 2nd ed. New York: Longman, 1979.

Gabrieli, Francesco, ed. and trans. *Arab Historians of the Crusades.* Berkeley, Calif.: University of California Press, 1978.

Hill, Rosalind, ed. and trans. *The Deeds of the Franks and Other Pilgrims to Jerusalem.* New York: Thomas Nelson & Sons, 1962.

Holt, Peter M., ed. *The Eastern Mediterranean Lands in the Period of the Crusades.* Warminster, Wiltshire: Aris & Phillips, 1977.

Kedar, Benjamin Z. *Crusade and Mission: European Approaches toward the Muslims.* Princeton, N.J.: Princeton University Press, 1984.

Lane-Poole, Stanley. *Saladin and the Fall of the Kingdom of Jerusalem.* Reprint of 1898 ed. Beirut: Khayats, 1964.

Maalouf, Amin. *The Crusades through Arab Eyes.* Trans. Jon Rothschild. New York: Schocken Books, 1985.

Mayer, Hans Eberhard. *The Crusades.* Trans. J. Gillingham. Oxford: Oxford University Press, 1988.

Muldoon, James. *Popes, Lawyers and Infidels: The Church and the Non-Christian World, 1250–1550.* Philadelphia: University of Pennsylvania Press, 1979.

Prawer, Joshua. *The World of the Crusades.* New York: Quadrangle Books, 1973.

Riley-Smith, Jonathan. *What were the Crusades?* Totowa, N.J.: Rowman & Littlefield, 1977.

——, with Louise Riley-Smith. *The Crusades, Idea and Reality, 1095–1274.* London: E. Arnold, 1981.

Runciman, Steven. *The Eastern Schism: A Study of the Papacy and the Eastern Churches during the XIth and XIIth Centuries.* Reprint of 1956 ed. New York: AMS Press, n.d.

——. *A History of the Crusades.* 3 vols. Reprint of 1954 ed. New York: Cambridge University Press, 1987.

Sivan, Emmanuel. *Modern Arab Historiography of the Crusades.* Tel-Aviv, 1973.

Southern, R. W. *Western Society and the Church in the Middle Ages.* New York: Penguin Books, 1970.
Vasiliev, Alexander A. *History of the Byzantine Empire.* Madison, Wis.: University of Wisconsin Press, 1952.

Chapter 6

Braude, Benjamin, and Bernard Lewis, eds. *Christians and Jews in Ottoman Empire: The Functioning of a Plural Society.* 2 vols. New York: Holmes & Meier, 1982.
Fortescue, Adrian. *The Uniate Eastern Churches.* Ed. G. D. Smith. London: Burns, Oates & Washbourne, 1923.
Hourani, Albert. *The Ottoman Background of the Modern Middle East.* London: Longman, 1970.
Inalcik, Halil. *The Ottoman Empire: The Classical Age, 1300–1600.* Trans. N. Itzkowitz and C. Imber. London: Weidenfeld & Nicolson; Washington, D.C.: Praeger, 1973.
Mansfield, Peter J. *The Ottoman Empire and Its Successors.* New York: St. Martin's Press, 1973.
Ma'oz, Moshe, ed. *Studies on Palestine during the Ottoman Period.* Winona Lake, Ind.: Eisenbrauns, n.d.
Maundrell, Henry. *A Journey from Aleppo to Jerusalem.* 3rd ed. Oxford, 1714. Reprint. Beirut: Khayak, n.d.
Runciman, Steven. *The Great Church in Captivity.* New York: Cambridge University Press, 1986.
Tibawi, Abdul L. *American Interests in Syria, 1800–1901: A Study of Educational, Literary and Religious Work.* Oxford: Clarendon Press, 1966.
——. *British Interests in Palestine, 1800–1901: A Study of Religious and Educational Enterprise.* London: Oxford University Press, 1961.
Vaughan, Dorothy M. *Europe and the Turk: A Pattern of Alliances, 1350–1700.* Reprint of 1954 ed. New York: AMS Press, 1976.

Chapter 7

Ajami, Fouad. *The Arab Predicament: Arab Political Thought and Practice since 1967.* New York: Cambridge University Press, 1982.
Antonius, George. *The Arab Awakening.* Reprint of 2nd ed. New York: Capricorn Books, 1965.
Berkes, Niyazi. *The Development of Secularism in Turkey.* Montreal: McGill University Press, 1964.
Berque, Jacques. *Cultural Expression in Arab Society Today.* Trans. R. W. Stookey. Austin, Tex.: University of Texas Press, 1978.

Buheiry, Marwan R. *The Formation and Perception of the Modern Arab World.* Ed. Lawrence I. Conrad et al. Princeton, N.J.: Darwin Press, 1989.

——, ed. *Intellectual Life in the Arab East, 1890–1939.* Syracuse, N.Y.: Syracuse University Press, 1981.

Dawn, C. Ernest. *From Ottomanism to Arabism: Essays on the Origins of Arab Nationalism.* Ann Arbor, Mich.: Books on Demand, n.d.

Devlin, John F. *The Ba'th Party: A History from Its Origins to 1966.* Stanford, Calif.: Hoover Institution Press, 1976.

Haim, Sylvia G., ed. *Arab Nationalism: An Anthology.* Berkeley, Calif.: University of California Press, 1974.

Kirk, George E. *Contemporary Arab Politics: A Concise History.* New York: F. A. Praeger, 1961.

Lewis, Bernard. *The Middle East and the West.* Bloomington, Ind.: Indiana University Press, 1964.

Mortimer, Edward. *Faith and Power: The Politics of Islam.* New York: Random House, 1982.

Nuseibeh, Hazem Z. *The Ideas of Arab Nationalism.* Ithaca, N.Y.: Cornell University Press, 1956.

Porath, Yehoshua. *In Search of Arab Unity: 1930–1945.* Totowa, N.J.: Cass, 1986.

Richter, Julius. *A History of Protestant Missions in the Near East.* Reprint of 1910 ed. New York: AMS Press, n.d.

Saab, Hassan. *Arab Federalists of the Ottoman Empire.* New York: Gregory Lounz, 1958.

Sharabi, Hisham. *Arab Intellectuals and the West: The Formative Years, 1875–1914.* Ann Arbor, Mich.: Books on Demand, n.d.

Thompson, Jack H., and Robert D. Reischauer, eds. *Modernization of the Arab World.* Princeton, N.J.: D. Van Nostrand Co., 1966.

Tibawi, Abdul L. *A Modern History of Syria, Including Lebanon and Palestine.* New York: St. Martin's Press, 1969.

Tibi, Bassam. *Arab Nationalism: A Critical Enquiry.* Reprint of 1971 ed. Ed. and trans. Marion Farouk-Sluglett and Peter Sluglett. New York: St. Martin's Press, 1971.

Yapp, M. E. *The Making of the Modern Near East, 1792–1923.* White Plains, N.Y.: Longman, Inc., 1987.

Zeine, Z. N. *The Emergence of Arab Nationalism.* 3rd ed. Delmar, N.Y.: Caravan Books, 1973.

Chapter 8

Ahmed, Jamal M. *The Intellectual Origins of Egyptian Nationalism.* Oxford: Oxford University Press, 1960.

Atiya, A. S., Y. Abd al-Masih, and O. H. E. Burmaster, eds. *History of the Patriarchs of the Egyptian Church,* Part 1 to A.D. 849 in *Patrologia Orientalis,* I, xix; Part 2 849–1102 (Cairo, 1942–59).

Badawi, Muhammad Mustafa. *Modern Arabic Literature and the West.* London: Ithaca Press, 1985.

Badawi, Muhammad Zaki. *The Reformers of Egypt.* London: Croom Helm, 1978.

Baer, Gabriel. *Studies in the Social History of Modern Egypt.* Ed. William R. Polk. Chicago: University of Chicago Press, 1969.

Brugman, J. *An Introduction to the History of Modern Arabic Literature in Egypt.* Leiden: E. J. Brill, 1984.

Carter, Barbara Lynn. *The Copts in Egyptian Politics.* Dover, N.H.: Croom Helm, 1986.

Crabbe, J. A., Jr. *The Writing of History in 19th Century Egypt, A Study in National Transformation.* Cairo, 1984.

al-Damanhūri, Ahmad ibn ʿAbd al-Munʿim. *Shaykh Damanhūri on the Churches of Cairo, 1739.* Ed. and trans. Moshe Perlmann. Berkeley, Calif.: University of California Press, 1975.

Erlich, Haggai. *Students and University in 20th Century Egyptian Politics.* Lanham, Md.: Biblio Distribution Center, 1989.

Fowler, M. *Christian Egypt: Past, Present and Future.* London: Church Newspaper Co., 1962.

Gershoni, Israel, and James P. Jankowski. *Egypt, Islam and the Arabs: The Search for Egyptian Nationhood, 1900–1930.* New York: Oxford University Press, 1987.

Hardy, Edward R. *Christian Egypt: Church and People. Christianity and Nationalism in the Patriarchate of Alexandria.* Oxford: Oxford University Press, 1952.

Harris, Christina P. *Nationalism and Revolution in Egypt: The Role of the Muslim Brotherhood.* Reprint of 1964 ed. Westport, Conn.: Hyperion Press, 1987.

Hartmann, Martin. *The Arabic Press of Egypt.* London: Luzac & Co., 1899.

Heyworth-Dunne, James. *Religious and Political Trends in Modern Egypt.* Washington: Brentano's, 1950.

Holt, Peter M. *Egypt and the Fertile Crescent, 1516–1922.* Ithaca, N.Y.: Cornell University Press, 1966.

Hopwood, Derek. *Egypt, Politics and Society, 1945–1981.* 2nd ed. Cambridge, Mass.: Unwin Hyman, 1985.

Khouri, Mounah. *Poetry and the Making of Modern Egypt 1882–1922.* Leiden: E. J. Brill, 1971.

Mansfield, Peter J. *The British in Egypt.* New York: Holt, Rinehart & Winston, 1971.

Meinardus, Otto Frederick A. *Christian Egypt, Ancient and Modern.* 2nd ed. Cairo: American University in Cairo Press, 1977.
——. *Christian Egypt, Faith and Life.* Cairo: American University in Cairo Press, 1970.
——. *Monks and Monasteries of the Egyptian Deserts.* Rev. ed. New York: Columbia University Press, 1989.
North, Richard. *Fools for God.* London: Collins, 1987.
O'Leary, De Lacy. *The Saints of Egypt.* New York: Church History Society, 1937.
Safran, Nadav. *Egypt in Search of Political Community: An Analysis of the Intellectual and Political Evolution of Egypt, 1804–1952.* Cambridge, Mass.: Harvard University Press, 1961.
Salama, Adib V. *A History of the Evangelical Church in Egypt, 1854–1980.* Cairo. Arabic.
al-Sayyid Marsot, Afaf Lutfi. *Egypt's Liberal Experiment, 1922–1936.* Berkeley, Calif.: University of California Press, 1977.
Vatikiotis, Panayiotis J. *A History of Egypt from Muhammad Ali to Sadat.* 2nd ed. Baltimore: Johns Hopkins University Press, 1980.
——. *The Modern History of Egypt.* London: Weidenfeld & Nicolson, 1969.
Wakin, Edward. *A Lonely Minority: The Modern Story of Egypt's Copts.* New York: Wm. Morrow & Co., 1963.
Watterson, Barbara. *Coptic Egypt.* Brookfield, Vt.: Gower Publishing Co., 1989.
Wendell, Charles. *The Evolution of the Egyptian National Image: From Its Origins to Ahmad Lufti al-Sayyid.* Berkeley, Calif.: University of California Press, 1973.

Chapter 9

Ajami, Fouad. *The Vanished Imam: Musa al-Sadr and the Shia of Lebanon.* Ithaca, N.Y.: Cornell University Press, 1986.
Cobban, Helena. *The Making of Modern Lebanon.* Boulder, Colo.: Westview Press, 1985.
Churchill, Charles H. *The Druzes and the Maronites under Turkish Rule, 1840–1860.* Reprint of 1862 ed. Salem, N.H.: Ayer Co., n.d.
Deeb, Marius. *The Lebanese Civil War.* Westport, Conn.: Greenwood Publishing Group, 1980.
Fisk, Robert. *Pity the Nation: Lebanon at War.* New York: Macmillan, 1989.
Gilmour, David. *Lebanon, the Fractured Country.* New York: St. Martin's Press, 1983.

Gordon, David C. *The Republic of Lebanon: A Nation in Jeopardy.* Boulder, Colo.: Westview Press, 1983.
Goria, Wade R. *Sovereignty and Leadership in Lebanon, 1943–1976.* North Hollywood, Calif.: Evergreen Book Distributors, 1985.
Harik, Ilya. *Politics and Change in a Traditional Society: Lebanon, 1711–1845.* Princeton, N.J.: Princeton University Press, 1968.
Hitti, Philip. *Lebanon in History from the Earliest Times to the Present.* 2nd ed. New York: St. Martin's Press, 1962.
Khalidi, Walid. *Conflict and Violence in Lebanon, Confrontation in the Middle East.* Cambridge, Mass.: Center for International Affairs, Harvard University, 1979.
McDowall, David. *Lebanon, a Conflict of Minorities.* London: Minority Rights Group, 1983.
Mousa, Matti. *The Maronites in History.* Syracuse: Syracuse University Press, 1986.
Owen, Roger, ed. *Essays on the Crisis in Lebanon.* London: Ithaca Press, 1976.
Penrose, Stephen B., Jr. *That They May Have Life: The Story of the American University of Beirut, 1866–1941.* Princeton, N.J.: Princeton University Press, 1941.
Petran, Tabitha. *The Struggle over Lebanon.* New York: Monthly Review Press, 1987.
Salībī, Kamal. *Crossroads to Civil War: Lebanon, 1958–1976.* Delmar, N.Y.: Caravan Books, 1988.
——. *A House of Many Mansions: The History of Lebanon Reconsidered.* Berkeley, Calif.: University of California Press, 1989.
——. *The Modern History of Lebanon.* Reprint of 1965 ed. Westport, Conn.: Greenwood Publishing Group, 1976.
Shehadi, Nadim, and D. H. Mills, eds. *Lebanon: A History of Conflict and Consensus.* London, 1988.
Ziadeh, Nicola A. *Syria and Lebanon.* Troy, Mich.: International Book Center, 1968.

Chapter 10

Abu-Lughud, Ibrahim, ed. *The Arab-Israeli Confrontation of June 1967: An Arab Perspective.* Ann Arbor, Mich.: Books on Demand, n.d.
al-Asmar, Fouzi. *To Be an Arab in Israel.* Trans. I. F. Stone. London: F. Pinter, 1975.
Ateek, Naim S. *Justice, and Only Justice: A Palestinian Theology of Liberation.* Maryknoll, N.Y.: Orbis Books, 1989.

Barbour, Nevill. *Nisi Dominus: A Survey of the Palestine Controversy.* Reprint of 1946 ed. Washington, D.C.: Institute for Palestine Studies, 1969.

Bernadotte, Folke G. *To Jerusalem.* Reprint of 1951 ed. Westport, Conn.: Hyperion Press, 1975.

British Council of Churches. *Towards Understanding the Arab-Israeli Conflict.* London, 1982.

Cattan, Henry. *Palestine, the Arabs and Israel: The Search for Justice.* London: Longmans, 1969.

Chacour, Elias, and David Hazard. *Blood Brothers.* Old Tappan, N.J.: Fleming H. Revell Co., 1984.

Chai, Ang Swee. *From Beirut to Jerusalem: A Woman Surgeon with the Palestinians.* London: Grafton Books, 1989.

Chomsky, Noam. *The Fateful Triangle: The United States, Israel and the Palestinians.* Boston: South End Press, 1983.

Cragg, Kenneth. *This Year in Jerusalem: Israel in Experience.* London: Darton, Longman & Todd, 1982.

Davies, William D. *The Gospel and the Land: Early Christianity and Jewish Territorial Doctrines.* Berkeley, Calif.: University of California Press, 1974.

Davis, Uri. *Israel: An Apartheid State.* Atlantic Highlands, N.J.: Humanities Press International, 1987.

Dimbleby, Jonathan. *The Palestinians.* Boston: Charles River Books, n.d.

Ekin, Larry. *Enduring Witness: The Churches and the Palestinians.* Vol. 2. Geneva: World Council of Churches, 1985.

Epp, Frank H. *The Palestinians: Portrait of a People in Conflict.* Scottdale, Penn.: Herald Press, 1976.

Friedman, Robert I. *The False Prophet: Rabbi Meir Kahane—from FBI Informant to Knesset Member.* Chicago: Chicago Review Press, 1990.

Gilmour, David. *Dispossessed: The Ordeal of the Palestinians, 1917–1980.* London: Sidgwick & Jackson, 1980.

Gresh, Alain. *The P.L.O.—The Struggle Within: Towards an Independent Palestinian State.* Rev. ed. London: Zed Books, 1988.

Hadawi, Sami. *Palestine in Focus.* Beirut: Palestine Research Center, 1968.

Harkabi, Y. *Arab Attitudes towards Israel.* Lanham, Md.: Biblio Distribution Center, 1972.

———. *The Palestinian Covenant and Its Meaning.* Lanham, Md.: Biblio Distribution Center, 1979.

Hertzberg, Arthur, ed. *The Zionist Idea: A Historical Analysis and Reader.* Reprint of 1959 ed. Westport, Conn.: Greenwood Publishing Group, 1971.

Kahane, Meir. *They Must Go.* New York: Grosset & Dunlap, 1981.
Kaniuk, Yoram. *Confessions of a Good Arab: A Novel.* Trans. Dalya Bilu. London: Peter Halban Publishers, 1987.
Khalidi, Walid. *Before Their Diaspora: A Photographic History of the Palestinians, 1876–1948.* Washington, D.C.: Institute for Palestine Studies, 1984.
King, Michael C., ed. *The Palestinians and the Churches, 1947–1956.* Vol. 1. Geneva: WCC Publications, 1981.
Kuroda, Alice K., and Yusamusa Kuroda. *Palestinians Without Palestine.* Washington, D.C.: University Press of America, 1978.
Laqueur, Walter, and Barry Rubin, eds. *The Israeli-Arab Reader: A Documentary History of the Middle East Conflict.* 4th ed. New York: Penguin Books, 1984.
Lustick, Ian. *Arabs in the Jewish State: Israel's Control of a National Minority.* Austin, Tex.: University of Texas Press, 1980.
Muslih, M. Y. *The Origins of Palestinian Nationalism.* New York: Columbia University Press, 1988.
O'Brien, Conor C. *The Siege: The Saga of Israel and Zionism.* New York: Touchstone Books, Simon & Schuster, 1987.
Palumbo, Michael. *The Palestinian Catastrophe: The 1948 Expulsion of a People from Their Homeland.* London: Faber & Faber, 1987.
Peretz, Don. *Israel and the Palestine Arabs.* Washington, D.C.: Middle East Institute, 1958.
Reddaway, A. F. John. *Right and Wrong in the Pursuit of Peace in Palestine.* Dublin: Eurabia, 1980.
Rodinson, Maxime. *Israel and the Arabs.* Trans. Michael Perl and B. Pearce. New York: Pantheon Books, 1968.
Sabri, Jiryis. *The Arabs in Israel, 1948–1966.* Trans. Inea Bushnaq. 2d ed. New York: Monthly Review Press, 1976.
Said, Edward W. *After the Last Sky: Palestinian Lives.* New York: Pantheon Books, Random House, 1986.
——. *The Question of Palestine.* New York: Random House, 1980.
Sayigh, Rosemary. *Palestinians: From Peasants to Revolutionaries.* London: Zed Press, 1979.
Shahadeh, Raja. *Occupier's Law: Israel and the West Bank.* Washington, D.C.: Institute for Palestine Studies, 1985.
——. *The Third Way: A Journal of Life in the West Bank.* New York: Quartet Books, 1982.
Sykes, Christopher. *Crossroads to Israel: Balfour to Bevin.* Bloomington, Ind.: Indiana University Press, 1965.
Tannous, Izzat. *The Palestinians: Eye-Witness History of Palestine under British Mandate.* New York: I. G. T. Co., 1982.

Taylor, Alan R. *Prelude to Israel: An Analysis of Zionist Diplomacy, 1897–1947.* Reprint of 1959 ed. Beirut: Institute for Palestine Studies, 1970.

White, Patrick. *Children of Bethlehem: Witnessing the Intifada.* Leominster, U.K.: Gracewing Press, 1989.

Wilson, Evan M. *Jerusalem, Key to Peace.* Washington, D.C.: Middle East Institute, 1970.

Zureik, Elie T. *The Palestinians in Israel: A Study in Internal Colonialism.* London: Routledge & Kegan Paul, 1979.

Chapter 11

Badawi, Muhammad Mustafa. *A Critical Introduction to Modern Arabic Poetry.* New York: Cambridge University Press, 1975.

Barkaba, M. H. *Arabic Culture through Its Language and Literature.* London, 1984.

Boullata, Issa J., trans. and ed. *Modern Arab Poets, 1950–1975.* Washington, D.C.: Three Continents Press, 1976.

——, ed. *Critical Perspectives on Modern Arabic Literature.* Washington, D.C.: Three Continents Press, 1980.

Chrysostom, John. *Divine Liturgy.* Greek and English. London: Faith Press, 1930.

Darwish, Mahmud, et al. *Victims of a Map.* Trans. Abdullah al-Udhari. London: Al Saqi Books, 1984.

Graf, Georg. *Geschichte der christlichen arabischen Literatur.* 4 Vols. Vatican City: Biblioteca Vaticana, 1944–53.

McGinn, Bernard, and John Meyendorff, eds. *Christian Spirituality: Origins to the Twelfth Century.* New York: Crossroad, 1985.

Mahfuz, Najib. *Children of Gebalawi.* Trans. Philip Stewart. Washington, D.C.: Three Continents Press, 1988.

Moreh, Shmuel. *Modern Arabic Poetry, 1800–1970: The Development of Its Forms and Themes Under the Influence of Western Literature.* Leiden: E. J. Brill, 1976.

——. *Studies in Modern Arabic Prose and Poetry.* Leiden: E. J. Brill, 1988.

Ostle, R. C., ed. *Studies in Modern Arabic Literature.* Warminster, Wiltshire: Aris & Phillips, 1976.

Suleiman, Khalid A. *Palestine and Modern Arabic Poetry.* London: Zed Books, 1984.

al-Udhari, ʻAdullah, ed. and trans. *Modern Poetry of the Arab World.* New York: Penguin Books, 1986.

Whybrew, Hugh. *The Orthodox Liturgy.* London: Darton, Longman & Todd, 1989.

General Index

Names

Aaron, 268
'Abd al-Alayīlī, 154, 168
'Abd al-Ḥamīd II, 146, 147, 148, 167
'Abd al-Malik, Caliph, 52, 53, 92, 120
'Abd al-Malik, Butrus, 284
'Abd al-Nāṣir, Jamāl, 152, 161, 191, 192, 195, 198, 199, 201, 202, 207, 220, 227
'Abduh, Muhammad, 156, 157, 190
Abrahah, 39, 41, 50
Abraham, 14, 17, 34, 48, 50, 77, 243, 295; Rock of, 53
Abū Bakr, 50, 54, 55
Abū-l-Faraj ibn 'Abdallāh al-Ṭayyib, 47
Abū Qurrā, 80, 92
Abū Safyān, 70
Abū 'Ubaidah, 54
Abū Yūsuf, 69
Acre, 102, 105, 133
Aden, 116
Adonis. *See* Sa'īd, 'Alī Ahmad
Adrianople, 115
Aegean Islands, 104, 139
Aegean Sea, 115
Al-Afghānī, Jamāl al-Dīn, 167, 190
'Aflaq, Michel, 161, 162, 163, 164, 165, 169, 293
Africanus, Julius, 36, 49
Agag, King, 238
Agatho, Pope, 112
Aḥmad (for Muhammad), 91
Al-Akhtal, 72
Aleppo, 23, 125, 144, 159, 220, 265
Alexander, 19, 62, 64, 70, 172, 179
Alexander, Solomon, 133
Alexander II of Russia, 158
Alexandretta, 159
Alexandria, 15, 22, 23, 37, 38, 41, 42, 43, 55, 69, 86, 125, 129, 172, 174, 175, 179, 181, 187, 195, 199; patriarchate of, 96, 124, 125, 129, 139
Algeria, 141, 145
Algiers, 116
Allen, Roger, 302
Anatolia, 17, 55, 56, 63, 71, 103, 114, 115, 119, 137, 183
Ankara, battle of, 115
Al-Anṣār, 90
Antioch, 15, 22, 37, 42, 43, 55, 69, 125, 204, 217, 267; patriarchate of, 15, 43, 96, 112, 117, 124, 224
Antonius, George, 155, 168
Antony, Saint, 41, 175, 177, 188
Anṭūn, Faraḥ, 156, 157, 168
Anṭūn, Farīd, 195
Aoun, General, 211
'Aqabah, Gulf of, 35, 42
Al-'Aqqād 'Abbās Mahmūd, 166, 198
Al-Aqṣā Mosque, 102
Aquinas, Thomas, 112
Arabia, 14, 16, 17, 20, 31–32, 35, 36, 47, 50, 54, 116, 184, 214, 230, 256, 261; eastern, 40, 41; Felix, 35, 38, 39, 40, 41; Roman province of, 35, 36, 42; southern, 14, 38–39
Arabian Gulf. *See* Persian/Arabian Gulf
'Arafat, Yassir, 214, 229
Arberry, A. J., 140, 199, 231
Arīḍā, Patriarch Anṭūn, 220, 231
Aristotle, 63, 64
Armenia, 108, 116
Arnold, Matthew, 136, 140
Arnold, T. W., 69, 70, 138, 199; *The Caliphate,* 138, 199

Al-Arslān, Amīr Shakīb, 152, 302
Al-Arsūzī, Zakī, 164
Asad, President Ḥāfiẓ, 153, 161
Al-A'shā, 258
Al-Ash'arī, 83, 84, 85, 90
Asia, 16, 22, 36, 43, 56, 111, 182, 213, 282; Asia Minor, 99, 104, 115
Al-'Asīr, Yūsuf, 265
Assemani, 216
Asturia, 98
Asyūt, 171, 172, 192, 199, 201
Ataturk, Muṣṭafā Kamāl, 153, 161, 168
Ateek, Na'im, 252, 254, 256
Athanasius, Saint, 41, 173; *Life of Antony,* 176
Atiya, A. S., 200
Augustine, Saint: *City of God,* 17; *Confessions,* 17
'Awḍah, 'Abd al-Qādir, 195, 202
'Awn, Yūsuf, 284
Axum, 38, 39, 41, 44
Al-Azhar, 180, 200
'Azzām, 'Abd al-Raḥmān, 154
'Azīz, Fahīm, 284
'Azūrī, Najīb, 155

Babylon: in Egypt, 55, 188
Bach, J. S., 265
Bacon, Francis, 68, 70
Badawi, M. M., 198, 276
Badr, battle of, 92
Baghdad, 55, 61, 85, 93, 116, 119, 150, 161, 178, 179, 182, 233, 263; Academy at, 64
Bahrain, 40
Bakhit, M. A., 137
Balkans, 99, 115, 117, 120, 122, 131, 141, 148, 167, 183, 213
Barnabas, 175
Barsumas, Saint, 269
Bartholomew, 38
Bashīr al-Dīn II, 230
Basil, Saint, 269
Basrah, 35, 85
Al-Bazzāz, 'Abd al-Raḥmān, 165, 169
Begin, Menachem, 152, 210, 237, 241, 255
Beirut, 133, 144, 145, 160, 207, 211, 213, 223, 227, 230
Bektash Veli, 137
Bell, Richard, 48
Belmont, 102
Benedict XIV, Pope, 126, 216
Ben-Gurion, David, 237, 255
Benjamin, Patriarch of Alexandria, 178
Ben-Zvi, 255
Bergson, Henri, 162
Bernard of Clairvaux, 99, 102
Beryllus, 37
Bethlehem, 104, 263
Beth Shin, 237
Bibliander, Theodorus, 138
Birge, J. K., 137
Al-Bīrūnī, 65, 92
Al-Biṭār, Ṣalāḥ al-Dīn, 163
Black Sea, 115
Bliss, Daniel, 222, 231
Bliss, Howard S., 221
Blyth, Bishop G. F. P., 134, 140
Boktor, Saint, 269
Bosnia, 115
Bosphorus, the, 23, 103, 120, 174
Bostra, 37, 42
Braude, P., 134, 137
Brecht, Bertolt, 259
Britain, 27, 44, 142, 177, 235; and Copts, 112, 177
Bruno, Father, 252, 253
Brusa, 104
Budny, Simon, 131
Bukhara, 140
Bull, Odd, 227, 232
Bunyan, John, 177, 199
Burckhardt, John, 133, 139
Burns, Norman, 222
Burton, John, 89
Al-Bustānī, Buṭrus, 166, 265, 283
Al-Bustānī, Sulaymān, 266
Butler, Alfred Joshua, 198
Byzantium, 22, 38, 39, 40, 41, 43, 51, 55, 56, 63, 69, 77, 82, 96, 97, 99, 100, 120, 171, 174, 175, 177, 215, 228

Cabasilas, Nicolaus, 272, 278
Caesarea, 17; Council of, 57
Cairo, 65, 116, 119, 137, 154, 155, 166, 168, 177, 180, 181, 186, 189, 195, 201; churches of, 198; Citadel of, 182
Callixtus III, Patriarch, 118
Camp David, 152
Camus, Albert, 259
Canterbury, Archbishop of, 97, 140
Carter, B. L., 198
Caspian Sea, 179
Catalonia, 108
Celsus, 92
Chacour, Fr. Elias, 252, 253, 256

Chalcedon, 17, 18, 19, 22, 54, 81
Chamoun, Camille, 207, 219, 220, 226
Charlemagne, Emperor, 22, 97
Charles V, Emperor, 230
Cheikho, Louis, 47, 51
Chidiac, R., 93
Christodoulos, Coptic patriarch, 181
Chrysostom, Saint John, 204, 230, 269, 274, 278; liturgy of, 269
Clement XI, Pope, 124
Clement of Alexandria, 172–173
Clermont, Council of, 101
Clough, A. H., 136
Comnenus, Alexius, 103
Comte, Auguste, 156
Constantine V, Emperor, 80, 81
Constantine VI, Emperor, 82
Constantinople, 16, 18, 22, 52, 55, 63, 96, 99, 100, 104, 110, 115, 124, 129, 178; fall of 1453, 111, 115, 215; Latin patriarchate at, 23, 101; patriarchate of, 15, 117, 129, 130; sack of 1204, 23, 101, 103
Copronymos (Constantine V), 80
Crete, 95, 186
Crimea, 115
Cromer, Lord, 190; and Copts, 190
Curzon, Robert, 204, 228
Cyprus, 18, 100, 108, 116, 136, 159, 224, 277
Cyril, Patriarch of Jerusalem, 43
Cyril II, Coptic Patriarch, 181
Cyril IV, Coptic Patriarch, 187, 188, 189, 200
Cyril V, Coptic Patriarch, 188, 189
Cyril V, Patriarch of Antioch, 124, 125, 126, 138
Cyril VI, Patriarch of Antioch, 126
Cyrus, Patriarch of Alexandria, 174, 178, 187

Damanhūr, 181
Damanhūrī, Shaikh, 198
Damascus, 10, 35, 53, 93, 95, 116, 118, 119, 125, 132, 137, 144, 146, 149, 150, 153, 159, 160, 174, 178, 179; Allied entry to (1917), 233
Damietta, 106, 107, 181
Damour, 212
Daniel, Norman, 113
Darwin, Charles, 135, 136
Darwish, Maḥmūd, 257
David, 49, 241, 173
Dayr Abū Saifain, 176
Dayr al-Barāmus, 176
Dayr Al-Surianī, 176
Dead Sea, 13, 37, 44, 49
Dhū Nuwās (Yūsuf As'ar), 38, 39, 41, 44
Dhū al-Qarnain, 19, 70
Diocletian, Emperor, 35, 175, 176
Disraeli, Benjamin, 136
Dodge, Bayard, 221
Dominic, 107
Dostoevsky, Fyodor, 275

Eaton, Gai, 301
Eban, Abba, 219, 240
Ecchelensis (Ibrāhīm al-Ḥaqilānī), 216
Edde, Raymond, 227
Edessa, 15, 16, 35, 40, 43, 80, 96, 267, 272
Edirne, 115
Egeria, travels of, 50
Egypt, 11, 14, 21, 22, 23, 24, 25, 35, 39, 57, 80, 92, 103, 104, 115, 122, 124, 141, 143, 144, 152, 156, 166, 167, 170–171, 188, 226, 266; and Arabism, 152, 155, 159, 192; British in, 156, 171, 189, 190, 191, 266; Muslim conquest and, 178; Napoleon and, 24, 172, 184, 185; under the Ottomans, 183–184; as a palimpsest, 172, 179
Eliot, George, 87, 93, 136
Eliot, T. S., 259, 260, 262, 276, 298, 301
Elizabeth I of England, 122
Elkasai, 37, 38
Emerson, 136
Enver Pasha, 149
Ephesus: Council of, 43, 57; Seven Sleepers of, 62, 70
Ephraem, Saint, 272, 273, 274, 278
Esau, 238
Ethiopia, 14, 35, 38, 40, 47, 50, 188; Christianity in, 40, 41, 177
Euphrates River, 35
Europe, 10, 12, 18, 23, 95–96, 108, 114, 116, 129, 130, 136, 159, 185, 186, 192, 216, 234, 283; Jews in, 197, 253
Eusebius, historian, 38, 266, 278
Ezekiel, 240

Al-Fāḍil, Qāḍī, 101
Faisal I, of Iraq, 150
Faisal II, of Iraq, 228
Fakhr al-Dīn II, 217, 230
Fanon, Franz, 160, 169
Fānus, Akhnūkh, 171, 200
Al-Fārābī, 63
Farīḍ, Muḥammad, 112, 172
Al-Fārūqī, Ismā'īl, 14, 30
Al-Fayyūmī, Sa'īd ibn Yūsuf, 300

Fertile Crescent, 35, 44, 153, 159
Florence, Council of, 124, 183, 199, 215
Fortescue, Adrian, 138
Fowler, Montague, 199
France, 95, 122, 136, 155, 158, 211, 216, 230, 234, 253; Vichy, 226
Francis I of France, 122, 230
Francis of Assisi, 105, 106, 107, 108
Frangieh, Sulayman, 220, 227
Frazer, James, 193
Frederick II of Hohenstaufen, 101, 104, 105; diplomacy of, 104, 105
Frend, W. H. C., 198
Frumentius, 41

Galilee, 36, 253, 263; Israeli "peace in" charade, 210
Gaon, Saadia, 300
Gaul, 177
Gaza, 35, 36, 42, 90, 137, 248
Geagea, Samir, 211
Gemayel, Amin, 210
Gemayel, Bashir, 214, 227, 229, 231
Gemayel, Pierre, 226
Geneva, 129
Gennadius, Patriarch of Constantinople, 125
Genoa, 104, 110
Germanos, Patriarch of Constantinople, 117, 118
Germanus, Patriarch of Constantinople, 81
Germany, 28, 29, 148, 160, 234, 253; Nazi, 226
Gethsemane, 260
Ghālī, Buṭrus, 171, 172, 198
Ghālī, Mu'allim, 187
Al-Ghazālī, Abū Ḥāmid, 84, 86, 87, 88, 92, 93, 94, 109
Gibbon, Edward, 141
Gibraltar, 140
Gide, André, 259
Gladstone, W. E., 136, 158
Gobat, Bishop Samuel, 133, 134, 140
Goitein, Solomon Dob Fritz, 69
Gökalp, Ziya, 161
Goldziher, Ignáz, 44, 45, 51
Graber, Olaf, 68
Greece, 19, 20, 114, 115, 142, 186, 193, 260
Gregory, Maronite Patriarch, 215
Gregory, Saint, 269
Gregory II, Pope, 97
Gregory VII, Pope, 99
Gregory IX, Pope, 104
Gregory XIII, Pope, 216
Gush Emunīm, 291

Habash, George, 222, 231
Ḥabīb, Gabriel, 224
Haddad, Colonel, 209
Haddad, R. M., 138
Hadramaut, 13, 51, 142
Hadziantonian, G. A., 139
Hagar, 48, 91
Hagia Sophia, 120
Haim, Sylvia, 148
Al-Ḥākim, Caliph, 101, 180, 181
Al-Ḥakīm, Tawfīq, 173, 198
Handel, G. F., 265
Ḥanīfah, tribe of, 40
Ḥannā, Mu'allim Ya'qūb, General, 185, 200
Al-Haqilānī, Ibrāhīm, 216
Ḥārith ibn Jabala, 51
Harran, 51, 80
Hasselquist, Frederick, 132, 133, 139
Hattin, Horns of, 103
Heliopolis, 170, 171
Heraclius, Emperor, 55, 174
Herbert, George, 265
Hess, Moses, 169
Hijāz, 42, 53, 242; railway, 147
Hilarion, 42
Ḥimyarites, 38, 41
Ḥīrā, 35, 39, 40, 45, 64; capture of, 55
Hitler, 28, 210, 234, 242, 254
Hitti, Philip, 14, 29
Hosea, 76, 289
Hrawi, Elias, 211
Hūd, 292
Hungary, 115, 116, 142
Ḥusain, King, 208, 209
Ḥusain, Muḥammad Kāmil, 70, 301
Ḥusain, Muḥammad al-Ṣādiq, 300
Ḥusain, Saddam, 248
Ḥusain, Sharīf, 149, 152, 167
Ḥusain, Ṭāhā, 167
Ḥusain (of Karbalā'), 137
Al-Ḥusainī, Ḥajj Amīn, 245
Al-Ḥuṣrī, Saṭi', 165, 167
Huss, John, 131, 173
Hussites, 109
Hutt, John, 139

Ibn al-'Āṣ, Amr, 55, 174, 180
Ibn al-Fāriḍ, 177
Ibn Ḥunain, Isḥāq, 64
Ibn Kallikan, 113
Ibn Khaldūn, 69, 177, 198
Ibn Kunaif, Ibrāraīm, 258

Ibn Mājā, 302
Ibn al-Muqaffa, Severus, 92
Ibn Rushd, 109, 156
Ibn Saud, King, 137, 150
Ibn Sīnā, 64
Ibn Tughī, 180
Ibn Ṭulūn, 180
Ibn Żayd, 'Adī, 45
Ibn al-Zubayr, 53
Ignatius IV, Patriarch of Antioch, 224, 232
Imrū-al-Qais, 276
India, 38, 92, 177, 202; in Al-Bīrūnī, 65, 92
Indian Ocean, 155
Innocent III, Pope, 99, 100, 103, 215
Innocent IX, Pope, 105
Iraq, 22, 55, 56, 150, 153, 156, 159, 161, 248, 264, 299
Ireland, 176
Irene (mother of Constantine VI), 82
Isaiah, 76
Isḥāq, Adīb, 158
Ishmael, 77, 91, 238
Al-Islāmbūlī, Khālid, 197, 201
Ismā'īl, Khedive, 188, 189
Israel, 11, 27, 28, 151, 153, 162, 168, 191, 205, 207, 235, 241, 251; ancestor and enemy, 240; democracy in, 247, 248; Judaism in, 243–244; oppression in, 247; overtures with Maronites, 210–211, 229; peace movements in, 210, 212, 228, 244; scripture and Zionism in, 243
Istanbul, 55, 110, 115, 116, 118, 124, 141, 149, 167, 183
Italy, 104, 112, 115
Izmir, 23

Jabrā, Ibrāhīm Jabrā, 263
Al-Jāḥiẓ, 80, 92
Jamāl Pasha and oppression in Syria, 149
James, brother of the Lord, 98
Jamnia, 49
Al-Jawālikī, 51, 70
Jawharī, Ibrāhīm, 185, 199
Jawharī, Jirjus, 185, 199
Jayyūsī, Salwā Khadrā, 264
Jazīrat al-'Arab, 13, 34, 43, 44, 46, 48, 60
Jeffery, Arthur, 49, 51, 70, 91
Jehu, 241
Jeremiah, Maronite Patriarch, 215
Jeremiah, Patriarch of Jerusalem, 181
Jeremiah (prophet), 76, 240, 262, 289
Jeremias II, Patriarch of Constantinople, 129
Jericho, 62
Jerusalem, 15, 33, 35, 36, 37, 48, 52, 53, 69, 93, 99, 101, 103, 109, 111, 129, 132, 137, 155, 174, 181, 233, 239, 245, 252, 254, 256; capture of, in 637, 35; capture of, in First Crusade, 101; Copts in, 188; Latin kingdom of, 23, 102, 181; patriarchate of, 69, 96, 104, 124, 129; synods at, 130, 139; walls of, 132
Jesus, 15, 41, 46, 60, 72, 73, 74, 78, 79, 90, 91, 108, 175, 257, 259, 260, 264, 270, 288, 293, 299; apostles of, 19; death of, 90, 257, 264; in Al-Ghazālī, 85, 86, 88, 94; humanity of, 20; re-semiticization of, 50. *See also* Christ, the; Christology
Jessup, H. H., 135
Jibrān, Khalīl, 226
Job, 37, 260
John, exiled Greek emperor, 104
John XI, Coptic Patriarch, 199
John XXII, Pope, 108
John of Damascus, 60, 77–78, 81, 90, 91, 257, 268, 278; and iconoclasm, 80, 82
John of Segovia, 110
John the Baptist, 11
John the evangelist, 91, 93
Jordan, State of, 150, 209, 222, 229; expulsion from, 208; Palestinians in, 208
Jordan River, 43, 44, 242
Joshua, 238, 239, 275
Jubail, 132
Judas Iscariot, 275
Julian the Apostate, 269
Julius II, Pope, 127
Jumblātt, Kamāl, 210, 226, 232

Kabasilas, Samuel, 125
Kafka, Franz, 259, 262
Kahane, Rabbi, 237
Al-Kāmil, al-Malik, 104, 105, 106, 107
Kāmil, Mustafā, 190
Karachi, 21
Karak, 137, 139
Karameh, Rashid, 210
Karbalā', 137
Al-Kawākibī, 'Abd al-Rahmān, 150, 156
Kedourie, Elie, 168
Kepel, Gilles, 198
Kerr, Malcolm, 222
Al-Khāl, Yūsuf, 259, 260, 261, 276, 277
Khaldī, Hazīm, 168
Khālid, Laila, 222
Khālid ibn Walīd, 77
Khartoum, 220

Khoḍr, Bishop George, 224, 232
Al-Khoury, Bishāra, 206
Khurasan, 137
Kierkegaard, Søren, 246
Al-Kindī, 63, 64
Kishk, ʻAbd al-Ḥamīd, Shaikh, 192
Knolles, Richard, 136
Kollek, Teddy, 256
Krenkow, Ivan, 50
Kuttāb, Jonathan, 256
Kuwait, 14, 35, 153, 247; invasion of, 247, 299

Labīd, 49, 258
Lammens, Henri, 231
Langland, William, 127, 138
Latin America, 274
Lawrence, T. E., 13, 17, 29, 30, 149, 255
Lebanon, 11, 21, 25, 26, 112, 121, 124, 126, 135, 143, 144, 150, 166, 197, 219, 221, 225, 227, 229, 231, 244, 261, 292; Arab and Maronite, 207, 214; civil war in, 209, 218; concordat, the, 205, 219, 226, 231; and confessionalism, 205–206; a failed symbol, 205; French in, 11, 149, 150, 155, 159, 160; frontier changes of, 192, 206, 218; tragedy of, 204–205
Leo III, Pope, 79, 80, 81
Leonard, Paul, 222
Lepanto, battle of, 18, 116
Lewis, Bernard, 134, 137
Libya, 141, 145, 177, 180, 182
Lieder, James, 188, 200
Lightfoot, J. B., 49
Lincoln, Abraham, 136
Linnaeus, Johannes, 133, 139
Livingstone, David, 114, 137
Lossky, Vladimir, 271, 278
Louis XIV, King, 216
Lucar, Cyral, Patriarch of Constantinople, 118, 129, 134, 139, 187
Lūkā, Nazmī, 196
Luke the evangelist, 36, 237, 266
Lull, Raymond, 105, 108, 109, 113; and Arabic studies, 108
Luqmān, 70
Luther, Martin, 114, 129, 130, 139; translation of Qur'ān of, 139
Lyall, C. J., 276
Lyons: Union of, 99, 124
Lyte, H. F., 265

Macedonia, 104
Madyān, 42
Maḥfūẓ, Najīb, 54, 194, 202, 298
Majorca, 108
Malāṭī, Muʻallim, 186
Malaysia, 300
Malik, Charles, 112, 206, 207, 219, 220, 223, 228, 231, 232
Mālik Ibn Anas, 69
Malta, 133, 220, 221, 222, 226, 265
Al-Ma'mūn, Caliph, 63, 64, 67
Al-Maʻnī (Fakhr al-Dīn), 217, 230
Manzikert, 101
Maʻrash, 79
Markabta, Synod of, 43
Mark the evangelist, 175, 179; Coptic Basilica of, 188, 191
Marracci, Louis, 138
Mār Sābā, 77, 79
Marseilles, 110
Mārūn, John, 216, 230
Marx, Karl, 135
Mary, 91, 267
Maundrell, Henry, 132, 139
Maʻūshī, Boulus, Maronite Patriarch, 199, 220, 223, 227
Maysum, 72
Mecca, 10, 18, 39, 42, 49, 50, 53, 62, 70, 78, 85, 90, 119, 120, 137, 149, 150, 151, 167, 203, 258, 259, 289, 290, 302; capitulation of, 51; as *Umm al-Qurā,* 150, 167
Medina, 55, 85, 90, 119, 137, 167, 203, 289, 290
Mediterranean Sea, 10, 16, 18, 23, 36, 43, 62, 95, 96, 108, 111, 112, 122, 135, 136, 140, 145, 155, 159, 172, 175, 178, 183, 184, 205, 235
Meinardus, Otto, 200, 202
Meir, Golda, 168, 255
Mekhitar of Sivas, 127
Melanchthon, 129
Melville, Herman, 136
Memphis, 173
Menas, Saint, 269
Mercurius, Saint, 269
Micah (prophet), 240
Michael VIII, Emperor, 99
Miramar, 108, 109
Miranda, Jose P., 275
Al-Miṣrī, Ibrāhīm, 194
Moab, 241
Moawad, Rene, 211
Mohacs, battle of, 116
Morocco, 17

Moses, 35, 42, 49, 91
Mu'āwiyah, Caliph, 53, 70, 72, 77
Mubārak, Archbishop Ignace, 227
Muḥammad, 13, 17, 21, 32, 33, 34, 37, 40, 42, 45, 50, 58, 66, 107, 129, 161, 196, 203, 257, 288; as Arab, 47; birth of, 50; death of, 16, 18, 54; finality of, 91; "night journey of," 53; and prophecy, 77, 78, 80; relation to Christianity, 154; *Sīrah* of, 84, 85, 139, 289; as *Ummī*, 34, 84
Muḥammad II, Ottoman Sultan, 96, 110, 115
Muḥammad 'Alī, 142, 171, 183, 217, 230; regime of, 185–186
Al-Muḥāsibī, 85, 86, 89, 93
Muldoon, James, 113
Mundhir, 39
Murād IV, Sultan, 130
Murād V, Sultan, 146
Mūsā, Salāmah, 135, 156, 192, 193, 194, 198, 201; autobiography of, 192, 193; views of, on Arabic, 193
Musaylamah, 40, 50
Musk, B. A., 203
Al-Mustanṣir, Fāṭimid Caliph, 181
Al-Mutawakkil, 84, 119, 180
Muṭrān, Khalīl, 261, 277
Muṭrān, Nadrah, 158

Al-Nabhānī, ibn Kunaif, 258
Al-Nābighah, 258
Najd, 14, 35, 39, 258
Najīb, Bishop Antoine, 284
Najran, 38, 39, 44, 258
Napoleon, 24, 131, 133, 135, 145, 172, 183, 184, 199, 200, 227
Nazareth, 73, 104, 137
Neale, J. M., 200, 266
Negev, the, 42
Nestorius, 36, 43
Neusner, Adam, 131
Neve Shalom, 252, 253
Newman, J. H., 133, 140
Nicea, Council of (A.D. 325), 42, 44, 104, 224
Nicea, Council of (A.D. 787), 82
Nicholas of Cusa, 109, 110, 111, 113
Nikiu, Bishop of, 199
Nile River, 21, 159, 168, 170, 172–173, 174, 179, 184, 298
Nisibis, 43
Nitrian desert, 41, 176
Nordau, Max, 255
North Africa, 55, 108, 180
Nu'aymah, Mikhā'il, 226, 232
Nubia, 12, 177, 180, 181, 199
Nuseibeh, H. Z., 168

Oman, 40
Oran, 116
Orhan, 115
Origen: in Arabia, 37, 42, 173, 175
Orontes River, 214, 230
Osman, 115, 119
Outremer, 23, 102
Oxford, 130, 139
Oz, Amos, 242, 255

Pachomius, 41, 176, 177
Padua, 129
Palaeologus, Jacob, 131, 139
Palestine, 23, 69, 70, 101, 103, 110, 180, 197, 227
Palmyra, 35
Pantaenus, 38, 173, 177
Paran, 91
Paris, 193, 216
Parmenides, 19
Paul (apostle), 34, 35, 49; journeys of, 18
Peers, E. Allison, 113
Pella, 49
Pellat, Charles, 92
Pentapolis, 31, 42
Persia, 22, 36, 40, 41, 53, 56, 116, 177, 183; Muslim conquest of, 55
Persian/Arabian Gulf, 13
Peter VII, Coptic Patriarch, 187
Peter of Maiuma, 90
Peter the Hermit, 96, 109
Philistia, 241
Phocas, Nicephorus, 112, 214
Phoenicia, 95, 162, 229; romanticism of, 112, 229
Pisa, 110
Pius II, Pope, 96
Plato, 19, 62, 64
Plotinus, 19
Pococke, Edward, 299
Pococke, Richard, 198
Poland, 234
Prague, 139
Proust, Marcel, 259
Pyrenees, the, 179
Pythagoras, 62

Qādisiyyah, battle of, 55
Qait Bey, 115

Al-Qardāwī, Yūsuf, 157, 169
Qataban, 38
Qatar, 40
Qubrūsī, Khalīl Iskander, 158, 159, 169
Qumran, 37, 49
Quraish, 39, 65, 67, 77, 84, 138
Qutb, Sayyid, 168, 299

Al-Rabb, 45, 51
Rabbula, 43
Al-Raḥmān, 40, 50, 51, 69, 285
Rahman, Fazlur, 49, 301
Rasūl, 90, 285
Rayburn, William, 284
Raymond of St. Gilles, 103
Red Sea, 10, 13, 35, 38, 40, 116, 176
Renan, Ernst, 156
Rhodes, island of, 115, 116
Riḍā, Muḥammad Rashīd, 156, 166
Rifqā, Fu'ād, 261
Rizq, Mu'allim, 185, 199
Robert of Ketton, 138
Rodst, Augustine, 283
Romaioi, true, 99, 100
Rome, 16, 18, 22, 24, 53, 69, 96, 99, 104, 110, 124, 126, 131, 139, 187, 215, 224, 230, 239; the two Romes, 96, 97, 110, 113, 120, 173. *See also Al-Rūm*
Rosenthal, Franz, 199, 300
Rousseau, Jean Jacques, 156, 193
Al-Rūm, 16, 35, 96, 113, 115
Runciman, Steven, 137, 139
Russia, 136, 149, 158, 187, 234; the Third Rome, 120

Sa'ādah, Anṭūn, 160, 161, 168, 260
Sabra camp, 212, 292
Sadat, Anwār, 152, 191, 198, 201
Sahas, Daniel, 90, 91
Al-Sahyūnī, Jibrā'īl, 216
Sa'īd, 'Alī Aḥmad [pseud. Adonis], 260, 276
Said, Edward, 302
Sakākīnī, Khalīl, 157; diaries of, 157
Ṣalāḥ al-Dīn, 101, 103, 104, 113, 149, 152, 159, 181, 182
Salībi, K. S., 112, 256
Ṣāliḥ, 292
Salīm I, Ottoman Sultan, 115, 116, 119, 138, 182, 183
Samson, 241
Samuel, 241
Samuel, Coptic Bishop, 191, 201
Sana', 39
"Saracen-minded" (John of Damascus), 77, 81, 90
Satan, the accursed, 177
Saul, King, 241
Ṣāyigh, Fā'iz, 168, 245, 246, 256
Ṣāyigh, Tawfīq, 261, 262, 263, 277
Al-Sayyāb, Badr Shākīr, 264, 277
Al-Sayyid, Ahmad Lutfī, 170
Schimmel, Annemarie, 93
Seale, Patrick, 169
Selden, John, 299
Seir, 91
Sfeir, Nasrallah, Maronite Patriarch, 211
Shaiṭān al-Rajīm, 177
Shakespeare, William, 266
Shamir, Yitzhak, 240
Sharon, Ariel, 210; invasion of Lebanon by, 210
Sharon, Moshe, 238, 255
Shaw, Bernard, 193, 201
Sheba, 38, 50; Queen of, 41
Shehadeh, Rajah, 256
Shenouda, Coptic Patriarch, 191, 201
Al-Shidyāq, Fāris, 135, 226, 232, 265
Shihāb, General, 208, 219
Al-Shihābī, Amīr 'Alī, 217
Al-Shihābī, Bashīr II, 217
Shukrī, 'Abd al-Raḥmān, 264, 277
Shumayyil, Shibli, 155, 156, 157
Shuwair, monks of, 127
Sicily, 18, 38, 104, 110, 112
Sidon, 125
Al-Sijistānī, 63
Simaika, Marqus, 173
Simeon Stylites, 42, 230
Al-Simi'ānī, Yūsuf, 216, 217
Sinai, 35, 41, 42, 49, 91, 152, 159, 255
Sinān, 'Abd al-Mannām, 120, 138
Sionita (Jibrā'īl al-Sahyūnī), 216, 217
Smith, Eli, 283, 300
Smith, Margaret, 92
Smith, Sydney, 133
Smith, Wilfred Cantwell, 301
Socrates, 62
Al-Ṣolḥ, Ri'āḍ, 206
Solomon, King, 41, 50; Temple of, 52
Soltau, Roger, 223
Sophronius, 52
Sorbonne, the, 161, 164
Southern, R. W., 112, 113
Soviet Union, the, 152

Spain, 55, 95, 98, 108, 116, 122, 159; Islam in, 97
Stern Gang, 237
Stino, Kamāl Ramzȳ, 199
Strauss, David, 135, 136
Sudan, 177, 187
Suez, 195, 250; crisis of 1956, 195, 207, 227, 240
Suez Canal, 157, 189
Sulaymān, Ottoman Sultan, 115, 116, 119, 122, 129, 142, 189; "a new Cyrus," 129
Sweetman, J. Windrow, 93, 94
Switzerland, 205
Sylvester, Greek Patriarch, 126, 138
Syria, 11, 22, 41, 56, 70, 79, 103, 110, 115, 116, 118, 142, 144, 149, 150, 151, 152, 153, 159, 174, 179, 180, 181, 184, 208, 229, 230, 267; in Lebanon, 206, 207, 209, 212

Tabor, Mount, 139
Tabūk, 44
Tadros, Saint, 269
Al-Takfīr wa-l-Hijrah, 200
Tala'at Pasha, 149
Tamerlane, 115, 183
Tangier, 55
Tanūkh, 35
Tanẓīm al-Jihād, 200
Tatian, 47; *Diatessaron* of, 47
Tattam, Henry, 188, 200
Tawadros, Maurice, 284
Al-Ṭayyib, Abū-l-Faraj ibn 'Abdallah, 47
Tell al-Kabīr, 190
Tell al-Zaater, 212
Thamūd, 292
Thebes, 173
Theodore of Canterbury, 97
Thompson, John, 284, 300
Thrace, 104, 114; conquest of, 115
Tibawi, A. L., 140
Tiberias, 261
Ṭibi, Bassām, 167
Al-Tirimmah, 62
Tolstoy, Leo, 193
Torrey, C. C., 48
Trebizond, 104
Trimingham, J. S., 49, 50, 199
Tripoli, Lebanon, 102, 156
Tripoli, Libya, 116
Tueni, Ghassān, 232
Ṭulūnids, 179, 180
Tunis, 141, 145, 151, 173, 182
Turkey, 131, 147, 149, 153, 167, 168
Tyre, 41

'Umar I, Umayyad Caliph, 48, 53, 54, 55, 69
'Umar II, Umayyad Caliph, 60, 79
Umm al-Qurā, 150, 167
'Urābī, Aḥmad, 189, 190
Urban II, Pope, 101
Ussishkin, M., 30
'Uthmān, Caliph, 89
Al-'Uzzā, 37, 49

Van Dyck, Cornelius, 283, 300
Vatican, the, 201, 216, 230, 302
Venice, 104, 110, 122, 129, 139
Versailles: Treaty of, 149, 167
Vienna, 116

Walton, Bishop Brian, 299
Wansborough, John, 89
Wardānī (assassin), 171, 172, 198
Washington, D.C., 250
Wisā', Wāṣif, 200
Watt, W. Montgomery, 93
Watts, Isaac, 265
Weizmann, Chaim, 30, 225, 232, 234, 240
Wells, H. G., 193
Wesley, Charles, 265
Wesley, John, 265
Whitman, Walt, 263
Whittier, J. G., 265
Williams, G. H., 139
Wittenberg, 129, 130, 139
Wolff, Joseph, 133, 140

Yamāmah, 51
Yapp, M. E., 167, 200
Yarmuk, battle of, 52
Yazdagird, Persian Emperor, 55
Yazīd I, Umayyad Caliph, 77
Yazīd II, Umayyad Caliph, 80
Al-Yazijī, Ibrāhīm, 166, 261, 283
Al-Yazijī, Nāṣīf, 166, 265, 283
Yemen, 14, 38, 116, 152, 177

Zabad, inscriptions at, 51
Zaghlūl, Sa'd, 198, 200
Zaydān, Jurjī, 166
Zechariah, 11, 237
Zeine, Z. N., 167
Zeus, 95
Zuhair, 49, 258
Zurayq, Constantine, 154, 158, 168, 222, 223

Topics

ʻAbbāsids, 61, 63, 72, 138, 180
ʻabd, 45, 51, 87
absolutes, religious, 290–291
accidie, 176
Acts of the Apostles, the, 34
ʻĀd, tribe of, 292
adhān, 181
adoptionism: and the Qur'ān, 48
adoration, 267
adversity, 29, 49, 259
agnosticism, wistful, 294
ahl al-Kitāb ("people of the Book"), 34
Al-Ahrām, 168
ʻajamī, 70
Allāh, 11, 30, 45, 51, 285
Allāhu akbar: meaning of, 28, 163, 247, 281, 286, 289
almsgiving, 85. *See also Zakāt*
amānah, human, 286
America. *See* United States
American University of Beirut, 140, 160, 219–220, 231, 245, 261, 276
American University of Cairo, 168
anamnesis, 270
anaphora, the, 270, 271
Anglican Church: bishopric in Jerusalem, 133, 140; members of, in Egypt, 188; parishes, formation of, in Palestine, 133
Ansār internment camps, 237
anticlericalism, 156, 157
antidoron, the, 271
anti-Semitism, 243. *See also* Semitism
Arab: definition of, 10, 14, 17
Arab Christianity, 17, 32, 33, 48, 56–57, 72–73, 121, 143, 153–154, 161–162, 223–224; in Arabia 31–32; and the Crusades, 96–97; and evangelicalism, 133, 134, 135; future of, 280–281; and the Great Schism, 97; and iconoclasm, 80–81; influence of, in Muslim theology, 83–84; and Israel, 233–234; and liberation, 274–275; and nationalism, 160–161; and the West, 296, 297
Arab Congress, First, 148, 155
Arab consciousness and Christianity, 32–33, 47, 48, 161, 279–280
Arab Evangelical Episcopal Church, 134
Arabic Bible, the, 32, 230, 264, 281–282
Arabic language: as sacred, 31, 32, 47, 48, 61, 62, 85, 258; Christian role in, 45, 61, 144, 193, 202
Arabic Press, the, 133, 135, 181, 202, 220, 265
arabicization: of the Middle East, 14, 15, 17, 47, 52–53, 61, 63, 64, 299; and theology, 66–67, 299
Arabics, Islamic and Christian, 167, 202, 265, 266, 282–283, 299
Arabic studies in Europe, 109, 132
Arabism, 9, 12, 14, 26, 58, 115, 123, 142, 172, 210, 211, 228, 235, 246; and Lebanon, 207–208; modern dilemma of, 141, 142, 145, 146, 148, 151, 163, 196, 207, 280; and Reformed Christianity, 128–129; and the West's literature, 259–260, 298
Arab League, the, 152
Arab nationalism, 25, 143, 144, 153, 160, 161, 297
Arabness, 9, 21, 23, 159, 227; and the Qur'ān, 31–32, 34, 142
Arab renaissance, 115, 144–145, 155, 166, 168
Arab Revolt, the, 26, 149, 158, 167, 233, 234
Arabs and non-Arabs after the conquest, 54, 55, 59
Aramaic sources of Christianity, 19, 31, 36, 37, 41, 45, 46, 61, 257, 282
Arameans, 19, 35, 41, 50, 76
Arianism, 77
Armada, Spanish, 122
Armenian language, 127, 181
Armenians: Catholicism of, 24, 123, 127; non-Chalcedonian, 117; as a suffering people, 275
art: in Christianity, 257, 268–269; in Coptic Church, 197; in Islam, 81, 268. *See also* Iconoclastic Controversy
Aryan: myth of chosenness, 28
ʻasabiyyah, 301
asbāb al-nuzūl, 84
asceticism, 40, 85, 86, 176
assimilation: by Christians of Islam, 160, 161; and logic of Zionism, 234
associationism, 78, 91, 93
attrition, factors in Christian, 60
authority, biblical, 237; in issues of faith, 130, 136, 155, 296
āyāt: in the Qur'ān, 65, 286
Ayyūbids, 100, 103, 181

Bahrī Mamlūks, 182, 183
Bait al-Hikmah, 64

Balfour Declaration, 30, 233, 234, 241; ambiguity in, 234, 235
Banū Ghassān, 35–36, 43, 51
Banū-l-Ḥārith, 44
Banū ʻIjl, 44
Banū Ṣāliḥ, 44
Banū Taghlīb, 69, 144
Banū ʻUthra, 44
baptism, 15; in Elkasai, 37; as insurance, 140, 141
baptismal name in eastern Eucharist, 271, 272
barakah, 42, 196
baʻth, 260
Baʻth Party, 159, 160, 161, 164, 169, 193
Baybars, 183
Beatitudes, the, 270
being: concept of, 20
Beirut Bible, 281, 282, 283, 284, 300
Beirut College for Women, 220
Bektashi Order of Sufis, 119, 137
Benedict, *Rule* of, 176
Benedictus, the, 237
Bible: Canon of, 243, 256; exegesis of, and Zionism, 235–236, 275–276; Hebrew, 32, 288, 289; Pentateuch, Arabic versions of, 300; Polyglot, 216, 283; Polyglot of Paris, 253, 299, 300; Polyglot of London; 283, 299; Propaganda, 283; Reformed tradition and, 128, 133
Bibles in Arabic, 282–283; Jerusalem, 284; Propaganda, 283, 300; Today's Arabic (N.T.), 284; Van Dyck, or Beirut, 281, 283, 300
biblicism, 238
Black September (1970), 208, 209, 229
Blanquerna (Lull), 109
Blood Brothers (Chacour), 253
Book of Common Prayer, 114, 137
Book of the Gentile and the Three Wise Men (Lull), 109
"Book of God": problems of, 84, 85
Book of the Lover and His Beloved (Lull), 109
bribery: under Ottomans, 118. *See also* venality
British Missions, 133
Burjī Mamlūks, 182, 183

caliphates: ʻAbbāsid, 114, 116, 119, 130, 179, 182, 184; Islamic, 123, 138, 150, 226, 279; moral decline of, 66; Ottoman, 114–115, 119, 140–141, 184, 279; nonrevival of, 150, 156; removal to Istanbul, 116, 184; spiritual, 155; Umayyad, 10, 58–59, 179
calligraphy, 81, 267
Canon, biblical, 243, 256
Canon Law: theory of power, 106
capitulations, 23, 122, 145
castles, crusaders', 101, 102, 103
cenobia, 176
Chaldean Catholics, 24, 123, 127
chivalry, ideals of, 98, 105, 109
Christ, the, 38, 73, 110, 130; "in Christ," 239; the suffering, 33, 107, 225, 271, 289, 290. *See also* Jesus; God
Christendom, 15, 21, 36, 37, 53, 95, 216; papal view of, 99; concept of "the peace of," 122
Christian division, 18; subtlety in, 33. *See also* Uniatism
Christian pro-Zionism, 28, 239–240
Christianity and Arabism, 15, 33–34, 48, 53; and the contemporary situation, 285, 288; Greek dimension in, 15, 16, 175; and Islam, 279–280
Christmas, 195, 202
Christology, 15, 16, 19, 22, 36–37, 39, 49, 53, 73, 85, 87, 136, 281; of action, 20, 73, 75, 76, 175, 215, 230; and iconoclasm, 81, 82
chosenness, Jewish, 27, 236, 255
Chronicles, books of, 243
Church Missionary Society, 200
Church of the Resurrection, 53
Circassians, 182
Civil War, United States', 189
cliency: of Copts to Muslim families, 194, 195; in early Islam, 58, 59, 69; in Israel, 249; of Maronites to Israel, 210, 212; of Maronites to Rome, 215–216; under the Ottomans, 122
code: Ottoman Commercial, 146; Ottoman Penal, 146
coinage: Arabic, 56
colonialism, 134
collectives, evil of, 291, 292
commerce, European, 110, 111, 117, 122
Committee of Union and Progress, 147, 148
compromise, in dialogue, 245
Confessio Fidei (Lucar), 129
confessionalism, 145, 154, 160, 161
conquest, Muslim, 16, 17, 22, 52–53, 71, 174, 178, 199; conditions under, 56–57
conscience, 292
conscientization, 155

constitutions: Egyptian, 195; Ottoman (1876), 146, 147; Syrian, 163
Constitution of Arab Nationalism, 154
contemplation, 86, 92, 109, 110, 135
controversy, Muslim–Christian, 63, 65, 67, 76–77, 86, 94, 289–290
conversion, 44, 58, 72, 109, 120; in Al-Ghazālī, 86
Coptic Catholicism, 24, 123, 124, 126, 187, 188, 284
Coptic Christianity, 11, 143, 170–171, 189, 194, 197; and the British regime, 171, 172, 194, 195; monasteries of, 176; and Muslim relations, 170, 194, 196, 199; tensions between clergy and laity in, 184, 189, 194. *See also* Antony, Saint
Coptic Congresses, 112, 170–171, 188, 190
Coptic Evangelical Church, 171, 188, 195, 284
Coptic language, 173, 178, 193, 198, 257
Coptic liturgy, 272, 273, 274
Coptic Orthodox College, 188
Coptic Reform Society, 171, 200
Coptic schools, 191
Copts, 19, 20, 55, 56, 61, 71, 112, 117, 120, 157, 269; and Napoleon, 185–186; role in administration, 56, 62, 175, 183, 184, 185, 187; theology of, 175
Councils of the church: Caesarea, 57; Chalcedon, 15, 16, 20, 73, 74, 75, 224, Arabs at, 43; Clermont, 101; Ephesus, 43, 57; Florence, 124, 183, 199, 215; Lateran, 215; Nicea (A.D. 325), 42, 44, 104, 224; Nicea (A.D. 787), 82
covenant, concept of, 27, 237, 241; bias in, 241
creation, doctrine of, 46, 72, 82, 91, 135, 267, 281, 286, 288
Cribratio alchorani (Nicholas of Cusa), 110
cross of Jesus, 39, 46, 74, 78, 80, 84, 88, 89, 257, 260, 263, 275, 276, 288, 290, 291, 293; "semblance of" in Islam, 48, 74
Crusades, 23, 95, 98, 99, 106, 109, 110, 112, 113, 181, 206, 291; First, 96, 100, 101, 214; Third, 99; Fourth, 23, 56, 101, 103, 104; Fifth, 106, 107; Sixth, 101, 104, 107; Greek awareness, 100; local churches, 100; motives of, 97–98
crusaders, 204, 215; abiding stigma of, 192; building by, 101, 102; commercial factors with, 110, 111; intermarriage with easterners, 102, 107, 111; and Maronites, 215; mores of, 102, 107. *See also pullani*
Dā'irat al-Ma'ārif (al-Bustānī), 166
Daniel, book of, 53
Dār al-ḥarb, 122
Dār al-Islām, 52–53, 57, 60, 62, 63, 64, 65, 72, 82, 106, 108, 116, 143, 157, 173, 174, 178, 183, 266, 267
Dastūr al-'Arab al-Qawmī, 154, 168
da'wah, Islamic, 60
Dawlah, 150, 280, 281, 301
deconfessionalism, 156, 157. *See also* 'Aflaq, Michel
De Haeresibus (John of Damascus), 77, 78
deification, 91, 271
demography, 14, 144, 248
depoliticization of Islam, 280–281
desert, 175, 177; and the sown, 13, 35, 41
despair, Palestinian, 249
Devsirme: Ottoman practice of, 120
dhikr, 85, 92, 109
dhimmī status of minorities under Islam, 10, 11, 16, 18, 23, 24, 25, 26, 34, 56–57, 71, 79, 106, 117, 118, 121, 143, 146, 147, 163, 165, 168, 170, 174, 186, 191, 195, 197, 199, 216, 228, 233; and capitulations, 122, 123; Ottomans and, 116, 117; in reverse, 106
dialogue, 221, 279–280; compromise in, 244, 245; Palestinian–Israeli, 244–245, 252
Diatessaron (Tatian), 47
Al-Dīn wa-l-Dawlah, 151, 280
Diophysitism, 15, 36, 39. *See also* Christology
diversity, religious and educational, 221–222
divinization in eastern Christianity, 267
Docetism, 48, 74, 75, 90
Dome of the Rock, 52, 53, 56, 69, 103, 104, 120; calligraphy at, 53, 69; and the crusaders, 102
Dominicans, 107, 131, 252. *See also* Uniatism
doubt, modern, 291
dragomans: Christians as, 122–123; role of, 122
Drang nach Osten, 136
Druze, the, 181, 206, 209, 211, 213, 214, 217, 218, 223, 229

Easter, 260
education in mission, 219, 220, 221
Egypt Congress (1910), 112, 170, 171, 172, 190, 197
Egyptianism, 11, 26, 167, 170–171, 186, 189, 190, 191, 193; and Arabism, 171, 173; and Islam, 173–174; and Salāmah Mūsā, 193
election, notion of, 237, 239

Elkasaites, 37–38, 50
emigration, of Christians, 226, 248
epiclesis, the, 270
episcopacy, 42, 43
Epistles in the New Testament, 86
esotericism, 68, 85, 119
ethicism: at the American University of Beirut, 221
Eucharist, the, 15, 17, 82, 269, 274, 299. *See also* liturgies
European factor, the, 16, 18, 21, 95–96, 124–125; commercial dimension of, 103, 125; and Egypt, 175, 187; response of, to Islam, 98–99
evangelical missions, 133, 134, 219, 220, 221
Evangelical Synod of Syria and Lebanon, 134
evangelism and church order, 24, 133; Coptic, 176; Nestorian, 40; western, 188, 226, 300
exclusivism, 225
exile: return from, 237, 238

faith and works, issue of, 66, 67, 83, 84
fanaticism, religious, 247
fasting, 85
Father, the, in theology, 73–74, 86, 87, 112
Fathers of the church, 144
Fātimids, 179, 180, 181
federalism, Arab/Ottoman, 117. *See also* Ottomanism
Ferax haeresis: Arabia as, 37, 230
Filioque clause, 112
folk religion, Muslim and Copt, 196, 203
forgiveness, 164. *See also* cross of Jesus
Fount of Knowledge (John of Damascus), 77
Franciscans, 107, 125, 215, 216
freedom, human, 286, 290, 295
French Mandate, the, 218
friars, 106

Galatians, Epistle to, 34, 35, 49
Ge'ez: Gospels in, 41, 47
Genesis, book of, 243
Gentiles, 35
Germanic element in the West, 97, 98
Ghassānids, 51, 55, 258. *See also* Banū Ghassān
Gnosticism, 38, 42, 50, 68
God: how *akbar?* 281, 282; "in Christ," 18, 19, 39, 73–74, 76, 87, 88, 89, 107, 197, 266, 271, 281, 286, 289, 290, 298; "exclusion of," 286; "of hope," 33; as "Lord God of Israel," 237, 238; as love, 75, 88, 281; mystery of, 135; and secular theory, 161, 279–280; sovereignty of, 88, 91; unity of, 15, 18, 42, 46, 61, 68, 72, 78, 89, 281–282, 291
Golden Bough, The, 193
Gospels, the, 33, 47, 74, 75, 85, 86, 88, 94, 177, 282, 289, 293; in Arabic, 200, 282–283; in Coptic, 200; reading of, 272
grace, 164, 293, 294; occasions of, 267–268; undifferentiating, 236, 237
Great Schism, the, 22, 96, 97, 98, 99, 100, 110, 112, 124
Greek-Arab relations, 21, 117. *See also* Greek factor in Arab Christianity
Greek Catholicism, 24, 123, 126, 218, 230
Greek factor in Arab Christianity, 19, 20, 31, 75, 94, 99, 117–118, 126, 144, 155, 159, 179, 257, 297
Greek hymnody, 265
Greek language, 61, 94
Greek liturgy, 269–270
Greek Orthodox Church, 19, 21, 71, 155, 157, 187, 220, 223, 225; in Lebanon, 218, 219, 227
Greeks, Muslim view of, 63–64
Gregorian Chant, 272
Gulf War, the, 153

Hadīth, 289
Haganah, Israeli, 252
Hagarenes, 79
Hagarism, 48, 90, 91
hanīf (pl. *hunafā*), 39, 50
Haramain, 119, 137, 150
Hasmoneans, 239
hellenization: of Christianity, 19; of Islam, 52–53, 57, 64, 72; via translation, 63, 64
Herodians, 239
hesychia, 176
Hijrah, the, 54, 70, 90, 162, 228, 290, 302; a modern Arab, 226
Al-Hilāl, 166, 201
Hinduism, 65, 92
holiness, 268, 269
Holocaust, the, 28, 29, 210, 234, 253, 254
holy land, 27, 101, 106, 108, 235
Holy Roman Empire, 97
Holy See, 107
Holy Sepulchre, 101, 102, 181
Holy Spirit, the, 91, 112, 268; invocation of, 270; procession of, 97, 112
homogeneity, Israeli search for, 247, 251
honesty in faith, 294
Hospitallers, 101, 102

host nation, concept of, 234. *See also* Zionism
hudā, 298
humanism, an Arab, 161, 279–280
human rights and juridical theory, 106
humility, radical, 291, 293
Hyksos, 174, 198
hymns, Arabic, 166, 264–265
hypocrisy, in dialogue, 244

Iconoclastic Controversy, the, 80, 81, 82, 90, 97, 266
iconography, 62, 266–267
iconostasis, the, 82, 267, 270
icons, 80, 82, 257, 266–267, 270
idolatry, 76, 77, 81, 91, 92, 135, 163; of the false absolute, 286, 291
Idumeans, 34, 36
Ihyā' 'Ulūm al-Dīn (Al-Ghazālī), 88, 89, 92
I'jāz, of the Qur'ān, 70, 84
Ikhshids, 180
Al-Ikhwān al-Muslimūn, 191, 200, 201
Iliad (Homer), 266
Imam, doctrine of the, 22
imperialism, 191
Incarnation, the faith of the, 17, 39, 73, 74, 75, 76, 78, 79, 82, 84, 86, 87, 90, 91, 93, 130, 135, 267, 269, 288, 299; and imagery, 81, 82; and Islam, 20; meaning of "begotten," 73; not "adoption," 48
ingratitude, 287
Injil, 285
intention, 272
interfaith relations, 224, 242
intermarriage, 102, 107, 111
International College (Beirut), 220
intransigence, 251
invocation of saints, 130
'iqlīmiyyah, 143
Iran–Iraq War, 152
irony in Arab poetry, 259–260
Ishmaelites, 79, 90, 198
Islam, 18, 20, 21, 129, 147, 279–280; adaptation of, after conquest, 61–62; Arabness of, 20, 32–33, 157, 158, 159, 161; Christian future with, 11, 279–280; as a Christian "heresy," 77; coexistence with, 10; expansion of, 52–53; and human will, 83, 84; distinction from *islām*, 286, 295, 296, 301; and iconoclasm, 80–81; *mawālī* in, 58, 59; and nationalism, 154–155; and Ottomanism, 146, 147; "privatized"? 161–162, 166; self-sufficiency of, 72; in Spain, 97; and the state, 53, 170; turkification of, 114–115; vis-à-vis Christian faith, 71–72, 160–161, 279–280; universality of, 21, 32
Islamicity, 280–281
Islamic theology and contemporary issues, 286–287
iṭmi'nān, 85, 92, 176

Jacobites, 100, 108, 111, 117, 118
Al-Jāhiliyyah, 62, 169, 296, 302; within Islam, 296, 302
Janissaries, 120, 137, 145
Jesuits, 124, 125, 129, 187, 188, 216, 284
Jesuit Bible, 283
Jewry, 28, 34, 48, 53, 131, 197, 227, 236, 237, 238; and Zionism, 234, 236
Jihād, 33, 57, 85, 106, 114, 115, 177, 291, 294
jizyah, 54, 57, 59, 79, 186, 197
journalism, Arabic, 166, 220
Judaism, 34, 39, 40, 196, 227, 234, 237
Juderstaat, Der, 255
judgment, last, 83
justice, divine and equal, 236–237
justification by faith, 130

ka'bah, the, 78
kenosis, 75, 288
khalīfah, 286
Kharāj tax, 58
Al-Khawārij, 67, 69, 83
khedive, the, 171, 188, 189, 190
khilāfah, 286, 290
Kitāb al-Aghānī, 45, 51
kufr, 294
Kurds, 173, 182

Lakhmids, 35, 40, 49, 55, 258
Lamarkaziyyah Party, 148, 154
land, in theology, 237, 238, 245
language in liturgy, 22. *See also* liturgies
Lateran Council, 215
Latin America, 105
Latin Catholicism, 123; and the Maronites, 214, 216; and monasticism, 176
Latin connection, 124
Latin fathers, 20
Latin hymnody, 265
Latin kingdom of Jerusalem, 23, 102
Latin liturgies, 270
latinophron, 113
Latin West, the, 23
League of Nations, the, 149, 235

Lebanese National University, 221
Lebanon and Maronitism, 24, 121, 205–206, 218; trauma of, 152, 204–205. *See also* Maronites
lectionaries, Christian, 242, 256
Levant Company, the English, 122, 132, 139; chaplains to, 132, 133; charter of, 122
Leviticus, 243
liberation theology, a Palestinian? 274–275
libertinism, charge of, 111
liturgies, 46, 47, 126, 131, 165, 173, 178, 197, 228, 257, 269–270, 283
Logos, the, 74, 78, 99
love: in God, 75, 279–280; to God, 86, 110
Lutherans, 133

Maccabees, 239
Al-Majallat al-Jadīdah, 194
Majlis Milli (Coptic Church Council), 172, 189
Mamlūks, 115, 116, 121, 138, 146, 171, 180, 182, 183, 184, 185, 215, 216; Bahrī and Burjī, 182
Mandatory system, 149, 163, 168, 235
ma'rifah, 85, 93
Maronite Church, 24, 124, 126, 143, 158, 205–206, 214–215, 224, 225, 226, 227, 264; origins of, 214; and Rome, 215. *See also* Uniatism
Maronite College in Rome, 24, 216, 265; and Bible translation, 283, 299, 300; scholars at, 216, 283
Maronites, 100, 108, 111, 126, 182, 209, 220; connivance with Israel, 210–211; and France, 206; and latinization, 216; and Palestinians, 209–210
marriage, inter-, after conquest, 60, 62
martyrdom, 108, 175
Al-Mashriq, 231
Al-Masīḥ, 73
massacres in Lebanon, 212, 217, 220, 229, 230
mawālī, 58, 59
Mejelle, Ottoman, 146
Mekhitarist Order, 127
Melchites, 16, 19, 56, 100, 111, 120, 124, 177, 180, 253
memory, 238
Middle East Council of Churches, role of, 224, 284, 297
millet system, 16, 121, 145, 155, 197; stigma in, 125. *See also dhimmī* status
minorities, European protection of, 121, 122, 123, 162. *See also* capitulations
minority status, 10, 56–57, 106, 154, 158, 191, 192, 195, 235, 246, 280; and intrigue, 118, 181; violations of, 121, 180
missions: Coptic, 177; quandary of, 221; of Reformed tradition, 133, 134, 135, 188, 221
modernity, challenge of, 135, 136, 279–280
monarchism, divine, 292
monasticism, 41, 42, 60, 173, 175, 276; Coptic, 175, 176; and the Qur'ān, 176
Mongols, 105, 115, 116, 182, 183, 199
Monophysitism, 15, 16, 20, 22, 36, 38, 71, 74, 75, 79, 81, 117, 120, 175, 198, 200, 216
Monothelitism, 214, 229, 230
al-mubāhalah, 108
Al-Muḥīṭ, 166
al-mukhālafah, Islamic sense of, 87
Al-Munqidh min al-Ḍalāl (Al-Ghazālī), 88, 93
Al-Muqtaṭaf, 168
Murjites, 67, 83, 85
murū'ah, 33
Muslim brotherhood, 191, 200, 201
Mu'tazilites, 84
mysticism, Islamic, 85, 86, 119
myths, Greco-Syrian, 260, 264. *See also Tammūz*

Nabateans, 34, 35, 62
Al-Naṣārā, 73, 90, 92
nationalism: Arab, 10, 25, 33–34, 114, 115, 117, 142, 147, 148–149, 161, 162, 173, 202, 236, 280; Egyptian, 173, 189, 191; Palestinian, 208–209; and religion, 154–155, 161, 173, 228
nation-state concept, 126, 143, 160, 162, 233, 279, 280, 299; and Islam, 163
National Party, Lebanon, 212
nature(s) of Christ, 15, 20, 73, 74, 81, 82, 175, 230
Nazism, 160
Near East Council of Churches, 224
Near East School of Theology, 221
Nestorians, 16, 22, 40, 55, 56, 71, 79, 96, 100, 108, 267
New Testament, 18, 19, 28, 31, 32, 34, 43, 47, 86, 88, 89, 90, 93, 165, 178, 243, 258, 268, 275, 281, 282, 288; "Arabs" in, 34, 35, 36; prophethood in, 236–237; universality in, 31–32, 238, 243; versions of, 283, 284, 286
Nicene Creed, the, 15, 72, 73
Night Journey, the, 53
niyyah, 92, 272

obedience: human, to God, 286
obscurantism, 156, 294
Old Testament, 241, 243, 284, 288
omnipotence, divine, 289
opportunism, Israeli, 233–234, 251
orientalism, attacks on, 297, 302
Ottoman caliphate, 10, 24, 25, 56, 183; decline of, 25, 123, 127, 136, 141–142, 184, 204; defeat of, 233; rise of, 110, 114
Ottomanism, 10, 25, 116, 131, 134, 142, 146, 147, 148, 153, 183, 197, 202, 218, 226, 233; Arab attitudes to, 114, 186; Commercial Code of, 146; in Egypt, 183–184; and Islam, 120, 121; Penal Code of, 146

pagans and their non-Islam, 63–64
Palestine Liberation Organization, 151, 208, 209, 210, 228, 236, 245, 246, 250, 251, 256; "recognition" of Israel (1988), 151
Palestine National Charter, 235, 236, 246
Palestinian Christianity, 27, 233–234, 245, 252; biblical loyalties of, 27, 239–240
Palestinianism, 11, 26, 151, 152, 205, 208, 212, 229, 235–236, 242, 250, 255, 264; and Balfour Declaration, 234
Palestinian poetry, 11, 257–258
pan-Arabism, 150, 151, 160, 192, 207, 220, 279
pan-Islam, 21, 117, 123, 143, 147, 167, 190, 192, 279
pan-Turkism, 143, 149
papacy, the, 123, 215, 297; theory of, 99, 106; and Uniatism, 24, 128, 216
Paraclete, the, 91
parables, in Islam, 85
paradox: in Israel, 237, 242, 259; in Muslim–Christian relations, 282
patriarchs, 14, 15, 32, 238
peace: and Israeli impasse, 248
penitence, 291, 292
Pentecost, 31, 42
Phalange Party in Lebanon, 212, 215, 226
pharaohs, 144, 171, 173, 174, 182, 190, 193, 198, 202
philanthropy, 128
Philistines, 236, 238, 241
philosophy: Greek, into Islam, 63, 64, 65
Phoenicia, Lebanon as, 206; romanticism of, 11, 205, 213
Phōs hilarion, 274
Piers Plowman (Langland), 138
pilgrimage: Christian, 96, 101, 103, 104, 113, 214; Muslim, 53, 120
pleroma, 93
pluralism, 228
poetry: Christian-Arab, 46, 47, 228, 257–258; Nabatean, 62; pre-Islamic, 49
polytheism, 76
Popular Front for the Liberation of Palestine, 222
poverty, 106, 176, 177, 293
prayer, 85
preaching: in contemporary Christian worship, 271; in early Islam, 59, 69
predestination, 78, 83
Presbyterians: of United States, 133, 135, 188
priesthood, universal, 133
private conscience, 128, 133
propaganda, Israeli, 235
prophethood, 20, 27, 32, 46, 73, 76, 80, 281, 287, 289; as means to scriptures, 34
prophetism, 37, 39
prophets, 15, 32, 76, 237, 238, 239, 240, 242, 243, 250, 296; Greeks as? 63; interpretation now, 237, 238
protection of minorities, 122, 123; sea power in, 125
Protestantism, western, 128–129; and hymnody, 265, 266, 272; in Lebanon, 219, 226
Prothesis, 270
providence, divine, 17, 68; in Muslim conquest, Christian views of, 60–61, 100, 174
psalmody, biblical, bias of, 241, 242, 243
Psalms, 243, 265; Arabic translation of, 300; Latin translation of, 110, 138
pseudo-scientism and the Qur'ān, 65, 70
pullani, 111

Qadarites, 67, 78
Qānūn, Ottoman, 121
qauwmiyyah, 143
Qiblah, the, 53
Qur'ān, 11, 15, 16, 18, 19, 31, 34, 38, 45, 46, 48, 56, 65, 66, 77, 92, 157, 159, 165, 167, 196, 286; Arabic of, 21, 31, 32, 34, 49, 61, 193, 202; on Christians, 73, 265, 266; controversies in, 20; and Elkasai, 37; eternity of, 78, 84, 85; and humanity, 285, 286; imagery in, 33; inimitability of, 62, 70, 84; and Jews, 27; Latin translation of, 110; monasticism in, 176; *saj'* of, 40, 50; translations, 138; vocabulary of, 36, 45, 49, 51, 61, 285, 286; and war, 290

rationality in belief, 65, 66, 76, 80

"recognition" of Israel, Palestinian (1988), 250, 251; reception of, 250–251
reconciliation, puzzles in, 244, 245
Reformed Christianity: influence on Arabs, 128–129
Reformers in Europe, 129
regio/religio principle, 106
religions, as usurpers of God, 291. *See also Allāhu akbar*
religious courts in Egypt, 267, 271
Renaissance, the, 111, 268
repatriation, Palestinian, denied, 209, 212
representation in art, 81, 92
resurrection, the, 267, 271
retaliation, 33; law of, and Copts, 194, 195
revelation: continuity of, 68, 238; occasions of, 84; and reason, 64, 65; words and, 300. *See also asbāb al-nuzūl*
Revolution, the Egyptian (1952), 191, 195, 201
riddah, the, 50, 54, 55, 58
rigorism, Islamic, 191, 192, 200, 294, 296
rivalry, inter-Arab, in Lebanon, 212, 213
romanticism: Coptic, 193; Lebanese, 213, 219, 231
Al-Rudd al-Jamīl (Al-Ghazālī), 86, 87, 88, 89, 93

Sabbath, the, 37
Sabeans, 50
sabīl Allāh, 291
sacramental, the, 46, 65, 82, 267–268, 287, 290, 301
Safavids, 116
St. Justin's House (Beirut), 261
St. Saviour, monks of, 127
saints, in iconography, 268
Salat, 50
Saracens, 43, 104
Sassanids, 54, 55
Sayings of the Fathers, 176
Schism, the Great. *See* Great Schism, the
scholasticism, 86
sciences, in Islam, 64, 65
scriptures: sacred, 34, 72, 130; corruption of, 86; disparity in, 282–283; Israel in, 242, 243; the Qur'ān as criterion of, 282–283
sectarianism, 161, 162, 218, 293, 294; guilt of, 225, 226
sectaries and Islam, 106, 107, 130, 131, 145
secularism, 165, 168, 191, 195, 197, 202, 207, 244, 280, 291, 292, 294; Palestinian, 245, 246, 247, 264
secularity, 135, 153; and Copts, 192–193
secular state, the, 161, 280–281
self, discipline of, 85
Seljūqs, 96, 100, 101, 115
Semites, 29, 243
Semitic theism, 17, 18, 19
Semitism, common Arab/Jewish, 243, 253
separatism: Arab, 142, 146, 167, 293; Maronite, 24, 227, 228
settlements, Israeli, 250, 251
Seven Pillars of Wisdom (Lawrence), 29
shahādah, the, 30, 59, 61, 89
Sharī'ah, the, 66, 118, 120, 121, 143, 150, 165, 184, 194, 198, 281, 295
Shī'ah Islam, 68, 83, 116, 180, 209, 218; in Lebanon, 206–207, 213; in Persia, 22
Shirk, 78, 87, 91, 93, 291
"signs" of God, the, 65, 286. *See also āyāt*
"sin of the world," the, 76, 88, 289, 290
Sīrah, of Muḥammad, 84, 85, 137, 289
Son, the, 73, 77, 78, 84, 112. *See also* Christology
South Arabian Christianity, 38–39
sovereignty, divine, 281, 286, 288
spirituality, Orthodox, 135; and Arabic, 265–266
statehood, Jewish, 234
state sovereignty, 235, 236
"substance" theology, 20, 73, 74. *See also* Christology
suffering and redemption, 275, 289, 291
Sufism, 68, 85, 86, 92, 118, 257; Christian factors in, 85, 86
Sunni Islam, 22, 68, 116, 209, 218; and the Ottomans, 116
Suriani scholars, 111
Synaxis, 270
Syriac Christianity, 22, 36, 48
Syriac hymnody, 265
Syriac language, 61, 257
Syriac translators, 62, 63, 64
Syria, Greater, 151–152, 159, 160, 218
Syrian Catholicism, 123, 127. *See also* Uniatism
Syrian Constitution, 163
Syrianism, 156, 160, 260
Syrian National Socialist Party, 160, 260
Syrian Protestant College, 155, 220, 221
Syrians in Egypt, 187–188

tahrīf, 86
Tammūz, 260
Tanzīl, 85
Tanzīmāt, Ottoman, 25, 145, 146
Targums, 46, 283, 285, 299
Tartars, 108
tawā'if (sects), 121
Tawḥīd, 68, 298. *See also* God, unity of
Ṭayy, tribe of, 258
technology, east and west, 296, 297
Temple Area, the, 102
Templars, 101, 102, 105
temptation, psychology of, 84, 85
theism, issues for, 281–282, 295, 296
theosis, 269, 270, 271
tolerance, Islamic, 56–57, 71. *See also dhimmī* status
tradition, Muslim, 14, 72, 76, 289, 302
transcendence: of God, 74, 76, 84, 271, 293, 299; love as clue to, 281–282; Islam and, 76, 87
translatio, papal theory of, 99
translation, Bible, 282–283, 299, 300
translators, Syriac, 62, 63, 64
transubstantiation, 269
travelogues, western, 131, 132
Treaty of Versailles, 149, 167
tribalism, 44, 51
Trinity, doctrine of the, 53, 78, 79; in praise, 270
truth through personality, 289
Turk as a term, 114, 137
Turkism, 161
Turks, 23, 129, 131, 136, 139, 147, 148, 161, 182, 185, 186, 204

al-ukhdūd, 39
'ulamā', Ottoman, 121, 145, 155, 160, 184; in Egypt, 192, 200, 201
Umayyads, 10, 53, 62, 63, 67, 69, 79, 83, 95, 97, 121, 137, 159, 179
Al-Ummah, 25, 143, 151, 168, 279, 281
ummī, meaning of, 34, 49, 91
uncreatedness, of the Qur'ān, 84, 85
Uniate churches, 23, 24, 118, 123, 124, 224, 230, 283, 297
Uniatism, 100, 123, 127, 128, 130, 140, 155, 216; and schism, 126
United Bible Societies, 284
United Nations, the, 195, 219, 227, 231, 245, 276; Charter of, 195; General Assembly of, 219; Partition of Palestine and, 235, 240; Peace force, 227; Resolutions of, 247, 250
United States, 133, 166, 167, 219, 222, 238, 248; and Central Intelligence Agency, 222; citizens of, in Lebanon, 222; Civil War, 189; intervention of, in Lebanon, 208; Jews in, 249, 256; missions of, 133–134, 166, 167, 188, 226, 265
Université St. Joseph, 221, 230
Uz, tribe of, 49

vacillation, Ottoman, 118
venality, Ottoman, 58, 118, 127
veneration: of images, 78, 80, 268, 269; of Muḥammad, 93
Venetians, 18, 103, 104, 181, 215
vernacular, the, 32
vicarious suffering, 29. *See also* Christ
Vicar of Christ, theory of, 105, 106, 125
vindication of prophets, 289
violation of divine unity, 286. *See also Shirk*
Virgin, the, 266, 268
vocabulary of faith, 283, 284, 285, 300
vows, in Crusades, 111
Vulgate, the, 283, 300
vulnerability, in religion, 12, 26, 27; in God, 75, 76, 281–282

Wafd party, 191, 200
Wahhabism, 116, 142, 186
Waste Land (Eliot), 259, 276, 298
watan, 25, 151, 166, 167
Al-Waṭan, 200
waṭaniyyah, 143
West Bank, the issue of, 241, 248, 252, 254
western factors in faith relations, 296, 297
will, freedom of the, 66, 67; problems of, 83, 84
"the Word made flesh," 81, 88, 89
World Council of Churches, 297
World War I, 11, 26, 29, 30, 147, 148, 151, 172, 190, 217
World War II, 150, 205
worship, 81, 89, 128, 132, 155, 164, 258, 266, 270, 299; secret prayer in, 272; and veneration, 82, 268–269

Youth Movement, Orthodox, 224

Zakāt, 50, 57, 59
Zion, 197, 210
Zionism, 11, 26, 27, 29, 30, 150, 151, 159, 162, 169, 192, 208, 210, 212, 225, 253, 274; Arab States and, 157; and Balfour Declaration, 233, 234; and Bible, 275; Britain and, 30,

Zionism: Britain and (*cont.*), 233, 234; and Christian advocacy, 28, 239–240; and cult of innocence, 235; end of exceptionality in, 237; German option of, 30; hidden agenda of, 234, 240; logic of, 235–236, 252, 253; paradox of, 259–260; policy on Palestinians, 157, 208, 234; revival of Hebrew in, 193; Revisionism in, 150; scriptural exegesis and, 236–237, 240
Zoroastrianism, 22
zuhd, 85

Index of Scripture

Biblical Books

Genesis
2:11 14
10:26 14
16:12 68

Exodus
20:4–5 81

Deuteronomy
18:18 91
32:30 68
33:2 91

Psalms
10:4 287
60 241, 243
67 243
82:6 88, 93, 278
100 243
108 241, 243

Isaiah
21:5–7 90
50:4 176

Jeremiah
38:1–13 262

Zechariah
3:2 68

Matthew
10:16 106
26:39 93

John
1:1 89
1:14 288, 289
1:16 93
10:34 88, 93, 278
14:16 91
15:26 91, 112

Acts
2:11 34, 36
8:26–40 36

Galatians
1:17 34
4:25 35

Ephesians
1:23 93
2:9 236

Philippians
2:1–11 75

Colossians
1:19 93

2 Peter
1:4 278

Qur'ān

Surah
1.6 45
2.30 286
2.193 299
2.256 294, 301
3.19 163
3.28 57
3.52 90
3.85 169
4.85 70
4.157–158 48, 74, 90, 264
5.21 27
5.57 57
5.82–83 92, 176
7.157–158 34
8 92
9.31 176
12.2 49
12.21 67
16.36 63
17.11 47
17.106 92
18.9–26 70
18.83–102 19, 70
19.30–33 91
19.35 48
20.113 49
24.36–37 42, 50, 177, 258
25.2 48
26.198 49
30.1 113
33.72 286
35.42 49
39.4 48
41.3 49
42.7 49
43.3 49
57.27 176
61.6 91
66 92
68 45
85.4–8 39
85.22 46
89.27–28 176
96.1 46, 48
96.4 45
105 39, 50
112 73, 78, 90, 92
113 177
114 177